THE HIDDEN ORDER OF CORRUPTION

Advances in Criminology

Series Editor: David Nelken

Recent titles in the series

The full list of series titles can be found at the back of the book.

The Hidden Order of Corruption
An Institutional Approach

DONATELLA DELLA PORTA
European University Institute, Italy

and

ALBERTO VANNUCCI
University of Pisa, Italy

ASHGATE

Published by
Ashgate Publishing Limited
Wey Court East
Union Road
Farnham
Surrey, GU9 7PT
England

Ashgate Publishing Company
Suite 420
101 Cherry Street
Burlington
VT 05401-4405
USA

www.ashgate.com

British Library Cataloguing in Publication Data
Della Porta, Donatella, 1956–
    The hidden order of corruption: an institutional approach. – (Advances in criminology)
    1. Political corruption. 2. Democracy. I. Title II. Series III. Vannucci, Alberto.
    364.1'323-dc22

Library of Congress Cataloging-in-Publication Data
Della Porta, Donatella, 1956–
    The hidden order of corruption: an institutional approach / by Donatella della Porta and
        Alberto Vannucci.
       p. cm. — (Advances in criminology)
    Includes bibliographical references and index.
    ISBN 978-0-7546-7899-1 (hardback) — ISBN 978-0-7546-9771-8 (ebook)
    1. Political corruption. 2. Corruption. I. Vannucci, Alberto. II. Title.
    JF1081.D454 2011
    364.1'323—dc23

                                                                            2011031226

ISBN: 9780754678991 (hbk)
ISBN: 9780754697718 (ebk)

Printed and bound in Great Britain by the
MPG Books Group, UK

To Herbert. D.d.P.
To Stefania. A.V.

*Corruption is our only hope. As long as there's corruption,
there'll be merciful judges and even the innocent may get off*
Bertolt Brecht, *Mother Courage and Her Children*

*Unfortunately our politicians are either incompetent or corrupt.
Sometimes both on the same day.*
Woody Allen, *Side Effects*

Contents

List of Figures

List of Tables

Acknowledgments

The authors are obliged to all the judges who helped them collect the judicial acts on which much of this research is based. Our special thanks go to Gherardo Colombo, Piercamillo Davigo, Michele del Gaudio, Maurizio De Lucia, Fabio De Pasquale, Claudio Gittardi, Francesco Greco, Filippo Grisolia, Leonardo Guarnotta, Giovanna Ichino, Fausto Izzo, Giovanni Leopardi, Guido Lo Forte, Marco Maria Maiga, Rosario Minna, Piergiorgio Morosini, Fabio Napoleone, Lorenzo Nicastro, Guido Papalia, Vittorio Paraggio, Luca Pistarelli, Michele Prestipino, Ottavio Sferlazza, Francesco Prete, Maurizio Romanelli, and Roberto Rossi. We would also like to thank Gianni Barbacetto, Enrico Calossi, Salvo Palazzolo, Eugenio Pizzimenti, Pierpaolo Romani, Andrea Roncallo, and Salvatore Sberna for their help in the collection of material. Louisa Parks and Andrew Wallace offered precious help in the English editing of the text.

In this book we develop ideas we have been working on over the last decade, and which were first presented in previous versions in the following articles: "Corruption in Policing and Law Enforcement: A Theoretical Scheme for the Analysis of the Italian Case," in *Police Corruption: Paradigms, Models and Concepts—Challenges for Developing Countries*, edited by S. Einstein and M. Amir (Huntsville, Tex.: Office of International Criminal Justice, 2003) 21–52; "The Governance Mechanisms of Corrupt Transactions," in *The New Institutional Economics of Corruption*, edited by J. Lambsdorff, M. Taube, and M. Schramm (London: Routledge, 2005), 152–80; "The Moral (and Immoral) Costs of Corruption," in *Dimensionen politischer Korruption*, edited by U. von Alemann (Wiesbaden: Vs. Verlag, 2005), 109–34; "A Typology of Corrupt Networks," in *Comparing Political Corruption and Clientelism*, edited by J. Kawata (Fahrnam: Ashgate, 2006), 23–44; "The Godfather's Party. Organized Crime and Political Financing in Italy," in *Dangerous Liaisons: Organized Crime and Political Finance in Latin America and Beyond*, edited by K. Casas-Zamora (Washington, D.C.: Brookings Institution Press, 2011) (forthcoming) as well as in *Mani Impunite* (Laterza, 2007). Some results of our research have also been discussed the recent years in several conferences and seminars in Osaka, Göttingen, Bielefeld, Berlin, Lisbon, Salford, Bononia, Rome, Milan, Florence, Washington, and Laxenburg. We are grateful to all colleagues who organized and participated in those occasions—and in other informal meetings—for their stimulating suggestions. Among them, a special mention goes to Alessandro Pizzorno, James Newell, Johann Graf Lambsdorff, Junichi Kawata, Franco Cazzola, Gustavo Piga, Lucio Picci, Luciano Bardi, and Raimondo Cubeddu.

This volume is the product of a long-lasting, fruitful, and friendly collaboration between the two authors. All of the research and the chapters were extensively discussed and finally approved, after uncountable cross revisions. For the record, Donatella della Porta produced the final version of Chapters 3, 4, and 5; Alberto Vannucci, the final version of Chapters 2, 6, 7, 8, and 9. Chapters 1 (introduction) and 10 (conclusions) were written "four-hands."

Chapter 1
The Hidden Order of Corruption:
An Introduction

Karachi, May 8, 2002. A few minutes past 8 a.m.: a car parked on Club Road, between the two largest hotels in Pakistan's capital, explodes, leaving 14 victims, 11 of which were French engineers and technicians working for the DCN (*Direction des constructions navales*), under the direct control of the French Ministry of Defense. The suicide bomber activated the explosive as their bus passed in front of the parked car. With the memory of September 11 still fresh, the investigations targeted the Al-Qaeda network. President Chirac solemnly proclaimed the French government's intention to fight against terrorism, confirming their cooperation with the Pakistani government: the same government that, in the previous 10 years, had bought arms from French firms for a total of €2.1 billion , 3.5 percent of French exports. Arms deliveries were, however, at the center of several corrupt exchanges, including the payment by French enterprises of large bribes to various Pakistani military and political exponents, among them the brother of general Musharraf, who became Prime Minister after the coup d'etat of 1999. Various military leaders were also sentenced for having received US$7 million in bribes for the construction of Agosta 90B submarines (*Le Figaro*, June 25, 2009). Five months after the bombing, the DCN manager Philippe Japiot wrote, in a letter to a French judge investigating the case, "it is because of the submarine contracts that our French colleagues died" (*Libération*, June 25, 2009). Not Al-Qaeda, but the interruption in the payment of bribes to military and political leaders was, in this interpretation, behind the terrorist attack (*Libération*, July 10, 2009). According to the lawyer for the relatives of seven victims of the attack, "It is all linked to Jacques Chirac's refusal, in 1996, to pay the commissions linked to the selling of the submarines." The attack aimed to convince the French partners to continue to pay the expected bribes.[1]

The Karachi tragedy presents various obscure aspects, which the French judges continue to investigate. In the latest, and most reliable, narrative, however, there are several aspects that are relevant for our perspective on corruption. The reality of corruption, in fact, can take very different forms, including a small exchange involving only two actors, in which a tiny kickback is secretively handed to a public administrator in exchange for a modest favor, such as forgetting a fine or speeding up the procedures for delivering a certificate. But, as in the previous example, corruption can also stratify, involving several actors in the most relevant positions in complex relations, and the change of hands of large sums of money.

---

[1]   See http://www.verite-attentat-karachi.org, accessed: January 31, 2011.

A *double* source of uncertainty derives from the illegal nature of (small and large) corrupt exchanges. First, there is the obvious risk of being discovered, denounced, and punished by the investigating authority, and of being stigmatized by various agencies of social control. Second, there is the risk of being cheated by the partners, who may renege on their promises and fail to pay bribes or provide the agreed favors. In the latter case, the partners cannot of course ask a judge to protect their rights regarding exchanged resources. Other instruments of protection then become necessary—as in the extreme case reported above, this may even include terrorist violence. Other forms of retribution are possible, however, depending on the contacts and resources available to the actors involved. As scholars, we can also note that when these tensions explode, this often reveals hidden aspects that allow us to better understand (and tackle) corruption.[2]

Endogenous weakness notwithstanding, corruption succeeds, in some societies, to take root in all the parts of the public administration, in political processes, and in market relationships. In these societies, the expectation of bribes orients public expenditures as well as other public decisions, and the redistribution and reinvestment of illegal profits define political and economic careers. The *do ut des* of corruption becomes the inexorable norm for all those who enter into relations with the state or other contractual partners. The world of corruption is therefore far away from the anomic reality of the Hobbesian state of nature, in which reciprocal mistrust and a lack of predictability make relations precarious and dangerous. On the contrary, a vast range of regulatory mechanisms and governing structures for corrupt exchange are voluntarily created or spontaneously emerge. Through these informal institutional constraints and resources, the actors involved in corruption can reduce uncertainties and the risk of defections or denunciations and increase hopes of impunity as well as their illicit profits.

In this research, we investigate this hidden order of corruption, looking at the codes and mechanisms that govern and stabilize the links between corrupters and corruptees and that increase the resources (of authority, economic, information, relations, etc.) at their disposal, strengthening the "obscure side of power." Corruption renders public power more unaccountable and invisible, since accountability "depends precisely on the greater or lesser extent to which the actions of the supreme power are offered to the public, are visible, knowable, accessible, and therefore controllable" (Bobbio 1980: 186). This is why corruption is particularly dangerous for the quality of democracy, its consolidation

---

[2]   A third source of uncertainty is related to the possibility of a future change in the preferences affecting the individual's choice to accept—or refuse—a corrupt exchange. *Value uncertainty* influences choices that produce long-lasting consequences: an agent refusing bribes, for instance, may consider the possibility of changing his mind later, when his peers socialize him to corruption; vice versa, a corrupt agent may anticipate possible regret for his past illicit actions, due to moral conversion. In both cases, value uncertainty, which reflects a potential change in the *moral costs of corruption* (a variable that will be examined in detail in Chapter 3), tends to be lower the stronger the social circles of recognition that shape individual's preferences (Pizzorno 2007).

and survival. In this research we therefore concentrate mainly (although not exclusively) on corruption in democratic regimes.

The main aim of this volume is to contribute to our understanding of the ways in which networks of corrupt exchanges develop because of their *hidden order*, that is, through an internal governance that encourages actors to accept the risk of illegal deals, trust each other, and build and enforce invisible codes, norms, and reciprocity rules. In this sense, our analysis is inspired by an institutional approach in so far as we look at the roots of those informal institutions that allow corrupt deals to expand and flourish within certain decision-making processes. Rather than trying to explain the evidence of corruption generally or in specific cases, we use empirical materials on corrupt exchanges in Italy and in other countries with the purpose of illustrating the main actors and mechanisms that play a role in the formation, enlarging, consolidation, and (sometimes) crisis of the hidden order of corruption. Although this book does not focus on anticorruption policies, in the final chapter we reflect on the potential relevance of our analysis for practices aimed at corruption control.

What Is Corruption?

In the social sciences, in parallel with the growing interest in the topic of corruption, there has been an animated debate on the very definition of the phenomenon. True, there is a broad consensus conceptualizing (political and bureaucratic) corruption as an abuse by a public agent: "corruption is commonly defined as the misuse of public power for private benefits" (Lambsdorff 2007: 16). However, the problem of singling out the standards against which this violation can be assessed remains open to discussion: formal norms, public interests, and public opinion standards being among these standards. Moreover, the abuse of entrusted power for private gain can assume different forms and contents. Besides corruption in a stricter sense, embezzlement, favoritism, nepotism, clientelism, vote-buying, fraud, extortion, or maladministration are often used as synonymous or corresponding terms to describe corrupt relationships involving public administrators.[3]

In our perspective, however, there is a risk of concept-stretching in the adoption of a similar "almost all-encompassing" definition of corruption.[4] To avoid (or at least reduce) this, we believe it better to differentiate the basic constitutive

---

[3]   See, for instance, Andvig et al. (2000: 14–7), who classify "some basic varieties of corruption" that include very different phenomena, ranging from embezzlement (where no private agent is usually involved) to extortion (where no exchange takes place).

[4]   Following Sartori (1970), concept-stretching occurs when there is an arbitrary extension of the set of empirical entities—in our case, forms of misconduct of public agents—that are included in the same category of "corruption," thereby lessening its intension, i.e., the set of attributes or meanings that define the concept.

components of corruption by adopting a principal-agent scheme.[5] There are different kinds of illicit, dysfunctional, or malfunctioning operations within the political and administrative realm, and corruption is but one of them. As Bryce (1921: 477–8) observes, "'Corruption' may be taken to include those modes of employing money to attain private ends by political means which are criminal or at least illegal, because they induce persons charged with a public duty to transgress that duty and misuse the functions assigned to them."

The so called principal-agent approach offers a clear way to conceptualize the logic of corruption. In formal terms, corruption (see also Figure 1.1) is defined as:

> (i) the *illegal* and therefore *hidden violation* of an explicit or implicit contract
> (ii) that states a delegation of responsibility from a *principal* to an *agent* who has the legal authority, as well as the official and informal obligation, to use his discretionary power, capacity, and information to pursue the principal's interests;
> (iii) the violation occurs when the agent exchanges these resources in a (*corrupt) transaction*
> (iv) with a *client* (the *briber*), for which the agent receives as a reward a quantity of money—the bribe—or other valuable resources.

In political and bureaucratic corruption, moreover:

> (va) the principal is the *state* (in a democracy, the citizens) while the corrupted actor is a *public agent;*

while in private corruption:

(vb) the principal is a *private actor* or *organization*, and the corrupted actor is a *private agent.*

Within any organization there are contractual relations—which can be expressed in more or less formal terms—between agents, delegated to make specific decisions, and the principal, who delegates to the corresponding power. The latter can be a collective actor: in liberal democracies, politicians and bureaucrats are agents to which the state—as a principal, that is, the sovereign people—delegates, through various mechanisms (electoral competition, public competition, lot, etc.) the task of pursuing the public interest in the formation and implementation of public policies. The complexity of the tasks delegated to agents makes a detailed list of clauses in the relations between the principal and the agent impossible. The distinction of roles and functions nevertheless responds to this

5 Cfr. among others Banfield (1975), Rose-Ackerman (1975; 1978), Klitgaard (1988), Pizzorno (1992), Groenendijk (1997), della Porta and Vannucci (1999a), and Lambsdorff (2007).

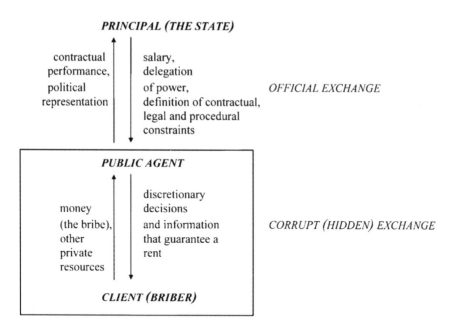

Fig. 1.1   Public corruption within a principal-agent model.

fundamental distinction: public agents do not act on their own account, but are delegated to accomplish those tasks that are expressions of the interests of their collective principal, to whom the exercise of their power has to be—at least to a certain extent—accountable.

Any agent, however, is also a bearer of private interests that may not necessarily coincide with those of its collective principal, from which he can hide information on the characteristics and content of his activities. So, in delegating power and tasks to the agent, the principal lays down rules and procedures that limit his range of discretion, and develops various mechanisms of control and (legal, administrative, social, political) sanctions in case of the misuse of delegation, thereby reducing risks of conflicts of (private and public) interest. Among these rules is the prohibition against accepting illicit payments from other actors for the accomplishment of delegated tasks, as this would increase the risk of the agent disregarding the interest of the principal. Illegality is therefore an essential attribute of corruption. Legal norms, and specifically the norm prohibiting the agent from accepting "bribes" in the exercise of his public duties, define the constraints on the agent's activities in accordance with the principal's interests, as perceived and stated in that particular context. Moreover, the very illegality of corrupt activities increases their transaction costs and expected risks, therefore generating a demand for protection within that murky environment. This implies a substantial difference from the social mechanisms regulating contiguous but legal practices, such as clientelism, favoritism, and so on, which if exposed are eventually sanctioned only by social stigma.

We can speak of corruption when a third actor enters into, and distorts, the relations between agent and principal. The intervention of a client or a briber pushes the agent to sidestep the constraints and controls imposed by norms and procedures. The corrupter, by offering resources such as money or other utilities, succeeds in obtaining favorable decisions, reserved information, or the broader protection of his interests.

In its elementary logic, corruption is therefore a "three-player game," in which an invisible and illegal exchange between an agent and a client/briber distorts the incentives to fulfill the terms of the contract with which the principal delegates responsibilities and discretionary power to the agent, in favor of the private interests of the agent and to the detriment of the interests of the principal.[6] Even though corruption can also emerge in private relations, in this work, we focus on politico-bureaucratic corruption within the state, with a special focus on advanced democratic countries. The exercise of public power in a democratic government can be more realistically conceived as a complex chain of principal-agent relationships between electorate, elected officials, and bureaucrats in their functional and hierarchical attribution of roles and functions. Moreover, the collective nature of the *basic* principal—that is, the sovereign people—makes it even more difficult to define univocally and to state contractually the principal's interests and preferences, the realization of which is delegated to public agents. While bureaucrats are relatively limited in their activity by normative and procedural constraints, politicians can operate with greater discretion in pursuit of some presumed "true" general interests.

In the transaction between the corrupt agent and the client, *property rights* to *rents* created through the political process are exchanged. Corruption is "actually

---

[6]   Advocates of "functional" corruption emphasize the hypothetical possibility that the principal's interests are better served by the violation of formal rules involving bribe payments: for instance, the incentive of "speedy money" makes public bureaucracies work more efficiently; the capacity to pay greater bribes determines the success of more efficient firms in the allocation of public contracts, etc. (Huntington 1968; Lui 1985). As stated by Leff (1964: 11): "if the government has erred in its decisions, the course made possible by corruption may well be the better one." But "efficiency-enhancing" corruption cases are conceivable only when formal rules defining a public agent's functions and procedural constraints are dysfunctional: institutional reform, not corruption, is the solution to be applied in these cases (Vannucci 1997a). Moreover, as Markovits and Silverstein (1988: 6) observe, "Liberal democracies seek both to ensure the separation of the private and the public realms and to overcome (or hide) their ambiguity over the use of political power. (...) The liberal's inherent distrust in political power is lessened by a political process defined by strict rules, procedures and public scrutiny. (...) To the liberal, the process *is* the public interest." Therefore, in a liberal perspective, one of the fundamental interests of the principal lies precisely in the respect *in itself* of the rules binding public agents' activities, and "functional" corruption would be logically impossible.

just a black market for the property rights over which politicians and bureaucrats have allocative power. Rather than assigning rights according to political power, rights are sold to the highest bidder" (Benson 1990: 159; Benson and Baden 1985). State activity, like market exchanges, modifies the existing structure of property rights. Public agents may use the coercive power of the state instead of voluntary transactions to allocate resources: the corrupters try to modify the structure of the property rights to their advantage with resources that are either public or subject to public regulation. A rent is created through (a) the acquisition of goods and services paid by the private actors for more than their market price, (b) the selling of the licensing of use of public goods for a lower price than their market price, or (c) arbitrary enforcement activities that selectively impose costs or reduce the value of some private goods to public agents (Rose-Ackerman 1978: 61–3).

By means of a hidden transaction, corrupter and corrupted share between them property rights to the political rent thus created.[7] The corrupted official obtains a part of that rent in return for his services (decisions, confidential information, protection), which aim to guarantee, or at least increase the chances of, granting those property rights, usually in the form of a monetary bribe, but also in the form of other valuable resources (della Porta e Vannucci 1999a: 35–7).[8]

In this perspective, we can better distinguish corruption from other political misdeeds. Vote-buying, when illegal as in most states, is a subspecies of corruption in which the agent is the citizen in his public role as elector, selecting the people's representatives, while the briber is the candidate—or the party—who purchases his vote in exchange for money or other valuable resources.[9] Other activities, on the contrary, should not to be confused with corruption. In case of embezzlement, fraud, or conflicts of interest, for example, the agent also abuses the trust of principal; however, there is no third party involved. In extortion there is not an

---

[7]   Property rights do not coincide with *legal* rights and are neither necessary nor sufficient for their existence (see Chapter 2).

[8]   Corruption can be considered a special form of rent-seeking activity that is a negative-sum social game (Krueger 1974). The wasteful competition among public officials and private actors to obtain rents entails high social costs, among which are the bad allocation of resources to unproductive activities, the distortion of market mechanisms, investment in information related to rent-seeking activities, and an increase in uncertainty on the protection of various individual and collective rights (della Porta and Vannucci 1999a; Vannucci e Cubeddu 2006; Lambsdorff 2007).

[9]   In his classical analysis of democratic governments, Bryce (1921: 478) observes that "four classes of persons owing a duty to the public may be thus led astray, viz. (a) Electors, (b) Members of a Legislature, (c) Administrative Officials, (d) Judicial Officials." Bryce concludes that "The bribery of voters is a practice from which few countries have been exempt […] . Uncommon in France, not extinct in Belgium and Holland, and found also in Italy, it is pretty frequent in parts of Canada and Northern United States, where even well-to-do farmers are not ashamed to take a few dollars for their vote, sometimes excusing themselves on the ground that they ought to be paid for the time they spent in going to the poll."

exchange of rents but rather the use of (physical or psychological) coercion to obtain resources for a private actor. In favoritism and nepotism, a "client" (who can be a relative) pushes the agent not to comply with his duties toward his principle, but the relationship is generally not overtly illegal—even when morally blameworthy and therefore not public—and, especially, no tangible resource is exchanged: deference, gratitude, and informal future obligations within familiar, political, or personal networks are at stake here. In clientelism, finally, the relationship is also generally not illegal, while the resources offered by the "client" are often political support or votes.

The informal obligations linked to clientelistic exchanges, favoritism, and nepotism present the potential for defection: like corrupt dealings, the terms of their illegal agreements cannot be enforced by public institutions (such as the judiciary and the police). Distrust in counterparts, pessimistic expectations, and opportunistic attitudes can be fatal to these relationships, provoking their failure. This intrinsic weakness in clientelistic transactions has, in some places, been recognized by opponents: for instance, "in Mexico's presidential elections in 2000, opposition candidates called on voters to 'take the gift, but vote as you please'" (TI-2005: 77), thus encouraging defection.[10]

Several governance and enforcement mechanisms—administered by party organizations and political machines, emerging within familiar linkages or through reputational assets—may nevertheless be available in these contexts, as in corrupt dealings: "candidates and agents make use of a range of strategies to reinforce the pact with voters. Frequently, voters fear reprisal if they don't accept the inducement or don't vote as instructed. In cases where payment comes after the vote, the risk of non compliance is that the voter will not be paid" (TI-2005: 80). But the very illegality of corruption marks the difference with clientelism here, since only in the case of corruption can any mistake, quarrel, disagreement, misunderstanding, breach of trust, or public denouncement produce disastrous effects for a public agent's career: it represents not merely a lost opportunity for profit but also could result in unbearable personal costs. Transaction costs, defined in general terms as the costs of "establishing and maintaining property rights" (Allen 1999: 898), are in fact much higher in the market for corrupt exchanges than in legal (or opaque but not openly illegal) markets. Property rights can be seen as the capability or power to exercise choice over some resource (good or service), and dispose of it— through exchange, consumption, and so on—according to one's will. When such resources are acquired by illicit means, as in the case of corruption, their exchange

---

[10]   In East Asia's clientelistic exchanges, defection and opportunism are frequent, despite the existence of wide networks of "vote-brokers" who make vote-buying "less an explicit contract (as 'buying' may erroneously imply) than a form of gift-giving intended to demonstrate a candidate's compassion, good will or respect." In Taiwan, for instance, at least 45 percent of people who received money did not vote for KMT candidates; in the Philippines, material offers influenced the vote of about 30 percent of those who accepted them (TI-2005: 84).

and allocation cannot be sanctioned through formal legal mechanisms. Therefore, a demand for effective protection and enforcement services emerge. The informal "governance structures" that may emerge in this uncertain environment, and the actors involved in their operation, will be the main focus of this volume.

Studying Corruption: Some Preliminary Remarks

In the social sciences, corruption has been traditionally relegated to research dealing with either the second or third world. In the functionalist tradition, corruption is considered a sign of friction between various subsystems, and in particular of the survival of old values and traditional institutions during transitions to economic development and political democratization. In this approach, corruption is said to have a number of positive functions, "oiling" blocked bureaucratic and political mechanisms that would otherwise hinder development, modernizing the political system, lessening recourse to political violence, and favoring social integration and economic capital formation.[11] It follows that (a) since corruption contributes to the attenuation or solution of dysfunctional political and social processes that are its hidden generators, it tends to be a temporary and self-extinguishing phenomenon; and (b) in more developed countries, corruption is a residual or marginal component of political processes, caused by a few "black sheep," with few adverse consequences. In advanced liberal democracies in particular, the rule of law, the information function of the media, and the political control exercised by citizens should prevent corruption from passing low physiological thresholds.

The benevolent prognosis of "transparent" modernization in third-world institutions, accompanied in their emancipation by corruption-free first-world countries has, however, largely been proved wrong. While corruption is still rampant in many developing states, various international governmental and nongovernmental institutions (such as the UN, OECD, and the EU among the former, and Transparency International among the latter) have stigmatized the activities of first-world countries as *exporters* of corruption to poorer contexts, whereby Western corporations obtain public contracts, and pollute or gain access to natural resources by paying bribes to local elites. Moreover, after the Clean Hands (*mani pulite*) investigations in Italy and similar scandals in many other advanced liberal-democratic countries, the illusion of some natural incompatibility between corruption and democracy has vanished.

If democracies are not corruption-free, levels of corruption vary significantly among different democratic countries and, within them, within different sectors and public organizations. In Figure 1.2 the wide spectrum of perceptions about the diffusion of corruption in EU and G8 countries in 2008, 2009, and 2010 is clear.

---

[11] See among others Huntington (1968), Merton (1972), Leff (1964), Nye (1967), Beck and Maher (1986), and Lien (1986). For a critical review, see Cartier-Bresson (1997, in particular 52–5).

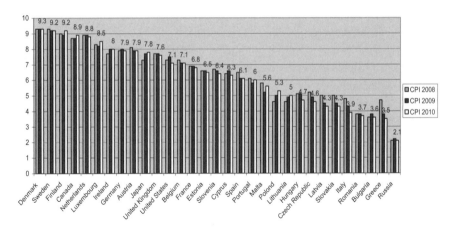

Fig. 1.2   Corruption perception index in 2008/2009/2010 in EU-27 e
             G-8 countries (10=maximum of transparency, 0=maximun of
             corruption - score in 2010 is shown). Source: Transparency
             International.

Considering the wider sample of countries analyzed by Transparency
International (2010b), less "transparent" Western democracies, like Italy or
Greece, are actually perceived as more corrupt than many authoritarian and/or
developing countries, like Rwanda, Ghana, Cuba, Botswana, Jordan, Malaysia,
Namibia, the Dominican Republic, or Saudi Arabia. Significantly, the "quality
index" of democracy uses the variable "degree of corruption" as an indicator for
the quality of the rule of law and democratic processes (Diamond and Morlino
2005).

Unfortunately, quantifying corruption is tricky (Golden and Picci 2005). Like
other crimes nobody has an interest in reporting, the diffusion of corruption is
difficult to estimate, and official police or judicial statistics do not represent a
reliable source of information about its extent.[12] Moreover, statistics are influenced
by the allocation of resources devoted to investigating specific crimes, as well as
by the willingness of parties to collaborate with judges. Finally, scandals do not
necessarily emerge when corruption is more widespread; but when investigators
and judges' activities are unconstrained and not controlled by political power,

---

[12] Corruption is not actually a *victimless* crime, but rather a crime whose victims are
unaware that they are so. The victims of corruption are citizens and taxpayers, who bear
the burden of increased costs and the low quality of public works and other contracts, of
inefficiencies in public administrative procedures, of the delegitimation of public institutions,
of distortions in competitive mechanisms in economic and political markets, etc.

and the media are free to report illegal dealings, public opinion is sensible to this theme and alternative coalitions to the corrupt ones may emerge in society and the political system.

These difficulties notwithstanding, the social sciences have tried to investigate the main causes and effects of corruption, using quantitative as well as qualitative methods. In the search for macro-variables apt to explain the broad observable oscillations in the diffusion of corruption, as well as its divergent impacts on political, social, and economic processes, a considerable amount of statistically significant correlations have been singled out (Lambsdorff 2007). Obviously, the demonstrated association of *perceived* corruption with other social phenomena is important, since it sheds light on some of its hidden characteristics and mechanisms of reproduction. Reasoning about causes or consequences of corruption in general terms may be misleading, however. So many variables should, and actually have been, taken into consideration to explain corruption, each of them interacting with virtually all the others, that it is almost impossible to consider the multifaceted effects of each in isolation from their complex configurations within each specific institutional framework. Some confusion also arises at the boundaries between what *provokes* and what *originates* corruption, most variables being dynamically related to corruption by causal loops, which blend causes and effects. Even casual or marginal factors may then induce vicious and virtuous circles, in a path-dependent process that alternatively favors or hinders the development of corrupt exchanges (see Chapter 9). As in most large-N cross-country studies, issues of multicollinearity emerge, as many and various characteristics tend to cluster (Schmitter 2009). Moreover, overall corruption perceptions in a certain country naturally derive from an average between more "honest" and more "corrupt" local environments, which are all subject to a similar structure of general incentives and opportunities.

Instead of conducting a broad investigation into the causes of corruption operating at a macro-level, we therefore present an in-depth analysis of the set of factors that influence corruption's more or less robust equilibria within certain administrative structures and specific political organizations. From a micro- and meso-level perspective, we concentrate on specific actor's and organizational responses to incentives created by the governance structure of corruption, which are informal norms and mechanisms that regulate and locally reproduce the characteristic features of corrupt exchanges, and eventually expand or adapt them to a changing environment.

Main Theoretical Approaches to the Analysis of Corruption

Since 1995, when it was first elaborated by Transparency International, the ranking of corruption perceptions has highlighted the apparent "Scandinavian paradox." In Northern European countries, the highest degrees of transparency are associated with the most elevated levels of public intervention, which according to orthodox (and naïve) economic perspectives should provide stronger incentives for corruption: when public agents manage the allocation of greater amounts of resources, the widespread recourse to bribery should be induced by the opportunity to covertly bargain their destination with corruptors. If this is not the case, other variables have to be taken into consideration, which should presumably reflect the "moral character" of both the potential bribers and the bribee, that is, the robustness of their interiorized moral barriers and social criteria of recognition of the value of law-obeying behavior.

Even if relevant, the cultural dimension is nevertheless not decisive in shaping the content of individual choices, as the Singapore and Hong Kong cases show. In these two small countries, an opposite line of reasoning can be applied: while presumably sharing similar social norms and cultural atmospheres with their neighbors, which are among the most corrupt states in the world, Singapore and Hong Kong are top-ranking in terms of transparency, 3rd and 12th respectively in 2009. According to several studies, this is the result of effective anticorruption policies, which heavily deter bribery by modifying the cost-benefit calculus of potential corruptors and corruptees (see also Chapter 10). A matrix of economic opportunities, internalized moral costs, and social pressures should therefore be taken into consideration in any attempt to explain the overall diffusion of corruption, as well as its rootedness in specific contexts. The relative importance of these factors, as well as their interaction, is however difficult to assess in general terms. Using a drastic simplification, in the contemporary literature we may distinguish between three main general theoretical explanations of corrupt dealings: the sociocultural, the political-economic, and the neo-institutional explanation.

(1) The first perspective looks at the differences in cultural traditions, social norms, and interiorized values that inform moral preferences and role consideration among individuals belonging to different societies and organizations. Individuals, in fact, are *pushed* toward corruption by the attributes of their internalized values and by social pressures. They tend to be less sensitive to opportunities for illegal enrichment the higher their (or their peer group's) moral standards—and vice versa: "for an individual, the moral cost is lower the more ephemeral circles of moral recognition offering positive reinforcement of respect for the law appear to him to be" (Pizzorno 1992: 46). Key terms associated with the sociocultural approach are *ethical norms, cultural values, traditions,* and *civic culture.* The crucial variables are operationalized in formal models as the so-called *moral cost* of corruption, that is, the utility that is lost because of the illegality of an action. This increases with the sharing of a value system that supports respect for the law (see Chapter 3 for a more detailed analysis).

Individuals will suffer higher moral costs when, from the perspective of their own ethical standards and those of their peers, corrupt behavior involves a violation of values—such as commitment to public service or to business ethics—that have been deeply internalized and constitute shared criteria of judgment. Moral costs in fact mirror social norms and ethical preferences and beliefs, as reflected in the esprit de corps and the "public spiritedness" of officials, the political and civic culture, the political identity and "moral quality" of the political class, the public's attitudes toward illegality, and business ethics. The substantial variation in levels of corruption that may be observed between countries with similar legal systems and formal institutions—that is, comparable monetary incentives and opportunities for corruption—could then be explained by differences in the size (and distribution) of moral costs, since "people in a given society face the same institutions but may have different values" (Elster 1989b: 39). Given similar institutional conditions, levels of political corruption will vary according to the average moral and cultural attitudes of citizens and public administrators, which are in turn influenced by the collective normative and value systems in which individuals are embedded.

(2) The economic approach emphasizes the crucial role of economic incentives and opportunities to engage in corrupt activities. People are *attracted* to illegal practices by their *interests*, that is to say, by the combination of their preferences for monetary gains and the set of institutional opportunities allowing such advantages from the exercise of public authority: "A person commits an offense if the expected utility to him exceeds the utility he could get by using his time and other resources for other activities. Some persons become 'criminals', therefore, not because their basic motivation differs from that of other persons, but because their benefits and costs differ" (Becker 1968: 172).

In this perspective corruption is considered the outcome of rational individual choices, and its spread is determined by the structure of expected costs and rewards: as with other behaviors involving deviation from laws and/or informal norms, the individual decision to participate in corrupt exchanges depends on the expected risk of being denounced and punished, the severity of the potential penal and administrative penalties, and the expected rewards as compared with available alternatives. Political economists have singled out some opportunities and incentives that influence the individual calculus to participate in political corruption (Rose Ackerman 1978): among others, these include the costs of political mediation, the overall level and characteristics of state intervention in the economic and social fields, the size of the rents that can be collected by corrupt agents, the degree of discretionary power in the exercise of public authority, the relative efficiency and severity of various administrative and political controls, and the types of bureaucracy and procedures in which corrupt exchanges develop (della Porta and Vannucci 1999a).

Klitgaard's formula—revisited here—synthesizes the main variables influencing this economic calculus (Klitgaard 1988):

$$C=M+D+H-A$$

Levels of Corruption are proportional to Monopoly (the number of monopolistic positions in both the public and the private sector, implying the creation of economic rents), plus Discretion (the power to decide how to allocate rents), plus Hidden information (the capacity to use as a resource in the corrupt exchange confidential information that can influence the allocation of rents), minus Accountability (the effectiveness of state and social monitoring of agents' conduct).[13]

(3) A third neo-institutional approach, which we adopt in our research, considers not only *external* variables—moral values or economic incentives—but also the *endogenous* dynamics of corrupt networks and exchanges.[14] Once a certain organizational texture and "cultural adaptation" to corruption has developed, governance structures and enforcement mechanisms provide internal stability to illegal dealings in specific areas of public activity, reducing uncertainty among partners in relationships which thus appear more lucrative and less morally censurable. The coevolution of economic incentives and cultural values, in other words, is path dependent. The heritage of corruption in the past produces increasing returns in subsequent periods by neutralizing moral barriers, by creating more profitable opportunities rooted in formal procedures and decision-making processes, and by providing organizational shields and mechanisms of protection against external intrusion by the authorities and internal friction among corrupt actors. The influence of the legacy of bribery operates through several mechanisms, as we will show in the following chapters. Widespread corruption generates "skills of illegality," governance structures and informal norms whose strength is based on adaptive expectations and coordination effects. Moreover, the shadow of past corruption may also influence its spread in the present through the intentional activities of actors implicated in corruption networks, who can obstruct judges' inquiries and strengthen expectations of impunity through reforms facilitating corruption.

What an individual may expect to obtain from his involvement in a corrupt exchange—or from honesty—depends not only on his moral preferences and economic incentives but also on interactions with other individuals' choices, and their effects on social judgments of his actions. The more widespread corruption is, for instance, the lower the risk of being denounced by those who decide to engage in illegal practices; the lower the perceived moral barriers and social stigma of corruption, the higher the cost to be paid by those who try to remain honest, since they become marginalized. Vice versa, when corruption is sporadic,

---

[13]   We added an element to Klitgaard's original formula: the list of potential corruption generators here also includes H, standing for hidden (that is, not publicly available) information. Bribes can be paid not only to influence the exercise of discretionary power but also to gain access to confidential, privileged information. The agent can sell this information, which has a value for the briber since it increases the probability of gaining access to an economic rent. Take, for instance, a public contracting procedure that guarantees an additional profit (an economic rent) to the winner but where no public agent has the discretionary power to decide who will be the winner (D=0). In that case there should be no corruption, unless some agent has access to confidential information (on the characteristics of the project that will be preferred, for example) that can be sold to a briber, who can therefore increase his chances of securing the public contract.

[14]   A neo-institutional approach to the analysis of corruption has been adopted, among others, by Husted (1994), della Porta and Vannucci (1999), and Lambsdorff (2007).

the search for a reliable partner becomes difficult, reciprocal honesty becomes dominant thanks to self-fulfilling beliefs, and the value-system sustains transparent behavior.[15] Multiple equilibria—with ample variations in levels of corruption— are then possible in similar institutional settings, reflecting divergent beliefs and the reciprocal adaptation of choices and preferences.[16]

Our Research and This Volume

Our previous studies on corruption (della Porta and Vannucci, 1994, 1999a, 1999b, 2007) were based on a comparative analysis of relevant cases, reconstructed on the basis of trial records and in-depth interviews, as well as the analysis of existing literature. Our focus was manly on the resources exchanged and the actors exchanging them.

In this work, we address our analysis of governance structures in the market for corrupt exchange by using empirical data and examples derived mainly—but not exclusively—from the Italian context, before and after the "Clean Hands" investigations that, at the beginning of the 1990s, produced a (apparently significant) turnover in the political class and the party system. Due to a quite rare combination of two factors—the large-scale diffusion of corrupt networks and their unprecedented exposure, thanks to judicial inquires—the Italian case seems particularly well-suited for a study of different models of regulation in corrupt networks. We make use of trial records, including interrogations and documents, from about 100 cases of political corruption, 400 requests of judicial action against Members of Parliament, articles from Italian newspapers (with a specific analysis of the national and local chronicles of *La Repubblica*—coded as R in text—since 1996, and other official acts (Parliamentary and Authorities' Reports, etc.).

We believe, nevertheless, that this approach has a more general value and can be fruitful in a comparative perspective. To locate the dynamics and internal equilibrium of corruption in a broader perspective we also refer to some relevant cases of corruption in other liberal-democratic and industrialized as well as developing countries, on the basis of both secondary analysis and a systematic

---

[15] As Andvig (1996: 18) notes, in fact, "one of the major reasons why corruption frequency stays low, when it is low, is the transaction cost involved if one tries to bribe in a society where bribing is rare. Think of a situation when the developer knows that only one of a hundred officials is likely to ask for a bribe. If he then offers a bribe he would have to expect a long search before he met the one to bribe. Given the expected search costs it will not pay to offer a bribe. Looking at the other side of the market: if only one of a hundred developers is willing to bribe you, why then ask for it? In this case only one of 10,000 meetings between officials and businessmen is likely to give rise to a bribe."

[16] The possibility of multiple equilibria in corruption has been formally demonstrated, each equilibrium differing in the amount of the bribes paid (Cadot 1987), the number of corrupt exchanges (Lui 1985), or both (Andvig e Moene 1990). Murphy, Shleifer, and Vishny (1993) single out a model of multiple equilibria in levels of corruption and income.

analysis of journalistic and—when available—judicial sources. Moreover, the Transparency International (TI) Annual Reports (2001–2009) and the TI daily survey of international news—from 2005 until February 2011—has also been analyzed to gather factual evidence on specific cases of corruption.

In the next chapter, we provide a typology of governance structures of corruption that are then used in the following chapters. We shall then look at the normative dimension of corruption (Chapter 3), before describing the mechanisms of hidden governance of corruption constructed around, respectively, public bureaucrats (Chapter 4), party politicians (Chapter 5), private entrepreneurs (Chapter 6), brokers (Chapter 7), and organized crime (Chapter 8). Finally, we will reflect on the self-sustaining dynamics favoring the diffusion of corrupt exchanges (Chapter 9), as well as on some potential strategies to fight them (Chapter 10).

Chapter 2
The Governance Structures of Corrupt Exchanges

The Italian novelist Stefano Benni paints an ironic but illuminating portrait of Baol, a powerful man who

> is also said to be a briber. But he is an honest briber. In twenty years of corruption no one has ever received an amount less than agreed. On the contrary, sometimes he adds by his own initiative an extra sum to a bribe, to a kickback. How could the joy of the bribee be described when he realizes that he has been corrupted beyond what he deserves? Do you know that there are functionaries who have to wait months to get paid by their corruptors, and are often paid with promissory notes and bad checks? Isn't all this dishonest? (Benni 1990: 143)

Similar worries are common in corruption networks: to what extent, and under what conditions, can a public agent trust his corrupting counterpart? How can a briber be sure that what he paid for will meet his expectations? "Lemons" are a risk to be seriously considered in this murky environment, where partners are by definition unscrupulous and no legal recourse can be sought to sanction eventual frauds, while "honesty" and good faith are highly appreciated virtues in bribery.

Real-life situations seem to mirror this fictional picture. In Niger informal intermediaries virtually monopolize the courts, lingering every day in the corridors, going from office to office to chat with people. As corruptors, according to one testimony, they often did not act "honestly":

> When they see a defendant arriving at or leaving a judge's office, they ask him what he's doing at the courts. He tells them that he's come to see the judge; then the intermediary may say 'but he's my cousin, I know him, if you give me 100000 CFA francs, I'll go and see him. Nothing can be done. If the client is naïve, he gives the money to the intermediary. The latter then goes to the judge's office, greets him, comes out again and then goes back to the client who is waiting and tells him that there is no problem, he will sort out the situation and after that the so-called intermediary disappears […] . You see, the guy who paid the 100000 CFA francs thinks that he has bribed the judge. (Cit. in Alou 2006: 165–6)

An explicit reference to the "honesty" of one's corrupt counterpart is made by a driver in Benin, in this case to stigmatize others' greediness:

> The gendarmes you see here are from Abomey. Unlike their Parakou colleagues, they are honest: if their colleagues are out at another control post, they tell you and only take 2500 francs instead of 5000 so that you can pay the other 2500 to

their colleagues at the next control post. But if they are on their own and there is no other gendarmes in the area, they tell you and charge the full 5000 francs. The Parakou road police charge 5000 francs every time you meet them. They are greedy. (Cit. in Bako Arifari 2006: 179)

In Punjab and other northern Indian states a strong incentive to cheat in corrupt deals has been offered to "fraudulent" dealers by the availability of counterfeit notes, which may be converted into low-cost bribes:

> Recently, a police officer in Punjab state paid close to US$100,000 in bribes to ensure that his daughter secured a job in the government, coveted mainly because of the access it provides to more bribe money. But the beneficiaries, who ensured her enrolment by hyping up her grades in the entrance examination, were soon to discover that they had been paid in counterfeit money. (*Asia Times*, April 4, 2002)

The "once in a lifetime" nature of this interaction between the police officer and the corrupt agent may have encouraged defection, since no realistic retaliation could be feared in the future. Similarly, a senior minister who received a large bribe found that a bank in the state capital Chandigarh refused to accept the cash for the same reason—it was counterfeit. As a cost-minimizing strategy in a context of widespread corruption, where interacting agents change frequently, cheating seems the most profitable strategy: "it seems that bribe-givers, resigned to a well-entrenched system of graft, are now trying to minimize their losses by purchasing cheaply available counterfeit currency to ensure their work gets done" (*Asia Times*, April 4, 2002).

Some questions remain unanswered, however, in this vivid description of a long-lasting bribery equilibrium threatened by the opportunity to use counterfeit money: how did public agents react to the increased risk of being cheated? Did they spend time to acquire the expertise necessary to monitor the notes with which they were being bribed? Did they circulate information on previous interactions, to let colleagues know who could be trusted and who not? Did they find some "tough guy" to punish cheaters, discouraging others to follow their "bad example"? A novelist like Benni could portray a continuation of the story. We instead present a theoretical analysis of some recurrent models of "governance" of corrupt transactions, which reflect some of their basic elements: the expected frequency of the exchange, the amount of resources at stake, and the identity of the actors involved as guarantors of the deal.

The Transaction Costs of Corruption

Like any other legal or illegal, formal or informal social relationship or collective enterprise, corrupt exchanges are facilitated by mechanisms of governance that allow coordination and cooperation among agents, overcoming their tendency to free ride. In this shadowy environment, words can be easily said, promises formulated, and agreements negotiated, but sometimes the most profitable decision is to renege on them whenever possible. Particularly when

(i) the economic advantage of defection is high;

(ii) there is a low probability of meeting the defrauded partner again, or his friends and colleagues, and no stain on one's reputation is expected;

(iii) no particular revenge or retaliation is expected, and even an accusation appears implausible, since the accuser would be involved.

Then, seemingly, the best option for any potentially corrupt agent—whose "moral standards" are by definition questionable—is to cheat. Expecting this, or fearing this, the incentive to renounce to the deal with an unreliable partner, or to cheat first, becomes very high. This outcome of mutual distrust would then lead to a preventive collapse of the corrupt exchange, vanishing all of its potential economic advantage. Nevertheless, corruption, as much evidence shows, exists, and under certain conditions flourishes.

How then do actors come to protect and enforce their illegal exchanges? Or, put in other terms, how is the (bad) social capital necessary for corruption networks generated (della Porta, 2000)? How can some amount of trust be sustained, informal norms and expectations converge to support illicit conducts, and enforcement mechanisms emerge, all of which must diminish ambiguity and uncertainty in corrupt transactions? The answers require a closer examination of the origin and nature of transaction costs in corrupt activities.

Transaction costs, as we have seen, can be defined as the costs incurred to establish, maintain, and transfer property rights, that is, to protect the ability to exercise a choice over such resources (Allen 1991).[1] Such rights are not always legally enforceable, since they simply reflect the individual's expected capability to consume or exchange services. In this perspective, transaction costs are "associated with the transfer, capture, and protecting of rights (...) . The transfer of assets entails costs resulting from both parties' attempts to determine what the valued attributes of these assets are and from attempts by each to capture those attributes that, because of the prohibitive costs, remain poorly delineated" (Barzel 1989: 2–3). The difference between ordinary exchanges of legal commodities and corrupt exchanges is that in the latter case the "property rights" over the resources at stake are more fragile, questionable, and aleatory.[2] Corrupt agents can indeed

---

[1]   More broadly, transaction costs are defined as any costs not conceivable in a Robinson Crusoe context, associated with the uncertain (or ambiguous) definition and protection of rights in formal or informal social interactions, also within institutions and organizations (Cheung 1987).

[2]   In general terms, exchanges in ordinary markets are based on *legal* rights, i.e., "the rights recognized and enforced, in part, by the government. These rights, as a rule, enhance economic rights, but the former are neither necessary nor sufficient for the existence of the latter. A major function of legal rights is to accommodate third party adjudication and enforcement. In the absence of such safeguards, rights may still be valued, but assets

be compared to thieves, who "lack legal rights over what they steal; nevertheless, they are able to consume it and to exclude others from it, to derive income from it, and to alienate it. [...] The lack of legal rights may reduce the value of those capabilities, but it does not negate them" (Barzel 1989: 110). Thieves' rights—as well as corruptors' and corrupt agents' rights over bribes—are less secure than those of legal owners. Not because they lack deeds, but because they cannot expect police or judicial enforcement. This uncertainty provides an incentive to invest in self-protection and to seek guarantees of their precarious position from other actors. As a Romanian informant explains,

> There are for instance people who say that it is natural to ask or to carry out a favour, to take or to give a bribe. Nothing is further from the truth. All naturalness disappears when you start to offer something to a person who is supposed to do something for you. Favours and bribes change you, they distort you, they are gestures that create tension and keep you in permanent fear of maybe not obtaining what you expect. (Cit. in Zerilli 2005: 95)

In corruption deals, in fact, there are both *external* dangers, such as being discovered and punished by control agencies or by social stigma; and *internal* ones, such as buying a "lemon," and more generally being cheated or denounced by a counterpart.[3] Transaction costs are therefore higher in corrupt markets (as well as in other black markets) than in ordinary markets: "Since corruption transactions occur outside the law, there are many opportunities for the parties to take advantage of each other. Numerous situations allow for the systematic distortion of information in order to benefit a particular party in a corruption transaction" (Husted 1994: 19). The "natural" environmental conditions for corruption are therefore secrecy, a lack of transparency, severely restricted participation, and high "exit" costs (Lambsdorff 2002: 222). Activities related with corruption must be performed secretly and cautiously, since—as in other illegal markets—"contracts are not enforceable in court of law; the assets of the illegal operation may be seized

and their exchange must then be self-enforced" (Barzel 1989: 4). Likewise, corrupt and corrupting agents are less secure in their rights over bribes and rents exchanged, since they cannot count on "legal" protection from the government for the assets they illicitly acquire: on the contrary—as in other illegal markets—they are exposed to the additional risk of being defrauded by their partners or sanctioned by the authorities: their assets may be seized, their career ruined, their reputation stained.

3   These two risk factors fuel each other. Potential tensions between actors in corrupt exchanges increase the risks of leaking compromising information to investigating authorities as an act of revenge. For instance, the Wuhan Court bribery case "came to light as a result of an anonymous complaint made in late 2000 to the Central Disciplinary Commission of the Communist Party about corruption and irregularities in the court: a disguised citizen was upset that judges did not review his life-sentence verdict after he gave them 'gifts'" (Brief 2005: 30). In turn, judicial proceedings tend to jeopardize solidarity networks among those actors, reducing the temporal horizon of potential future interactions, and therefore increasing incentives to collaborate with the judges.

at any time that law enforcement agencies identify the operation and the associated assets; all participants are subject to the risk of arrest and imprisonment" (Reuter 1983: 114).[4] While agreements cannot be translated into written and publicly enforceable contracts, the flow of information about one's participation in illegal activities must be kept under strict control.

Every phase of the corrupt exchange entails transaction costs higher than those incurred in legal ones: the search for a counterpart, the gathering of *information* on the quality of services exchanged, the "price" and the potential partner's trustworthiness, the *bargaining* of an agreement and the material exchange of "commodities," the monitoring of fulfillment, the *enforcement* of the "bribery contract," and the protection of one's property rights over assets deriving from corruption against third-party encroachment (Eggertsson 1990: 15). These activities are in fact hazardous and onerous in terms of time and other resources required to carry them out with a sufficient amount of cover-up and security (della Porta and Vannucci 2005a). In a simplified scheme, we consider *research and information*, *bargaining*, and *monitoring and enforcement* costs.

The Research and Information Costs of Corruption

Gathering information is always a costly activity, since "a great deal of knowledge has to be acquired before a business transaction can even be contemplated [...] . The way in which people typically proceed is to expand resources on information gathering until they have acquired sufficient knowledge to risk a decision" (Kasper and Streit 1998: 196). However, when the "business" is illegal, risks multiply, since criminal penalties, personal reputations, and honor, as well as future career opportunities and profit are at stake. In this case, reliable information is even more precious and difficult to obtain. Is bribing, or obtaining a bribe, a viable alternative to consider in that particular situation? What is the real value of the "resource"—a public contract, a license, an avoided fine, and so on—which is obtained thanks to the corrupt exchange? What sort of person is the proponent or the potential target of the proposal? Is he a reliable partner, and how is his trustworthiness to fulfill his contractual obligations assessed? Will he denounce the briber, or try to cheat?

The very nature of corruption generates opportunities for fraudulent offers from both public agents and bribers, promising rewards they will not be able or willing to deliver. As trust is a scarce resource in this environment, direct inquiries become a substitute for assessing the expected profitability of corruption, as well

---

[4] There are exceptions, however: in Benin corrupt obligations between contractors and decision-makers who do not trust each other, since meeting for the first time, have sometimes been translated into written contracts: "This type of contract in writing is made in the form of a discharge, without specifying the object or the nature of the transaction. It is often discharges loans in which the contractor recognizes having borrowed such a sum from the officer and consequently commits himself to reimbursing him following a list of payable bills, which curiously roughly sets down the anticipated dates for the various payments during the duration of the contract's execution" (Bako Arifari 2001: 92).

as the reliability of partners. The Russian corruptor V.R., for instance, spent a considerable amount of time debating with his aides which actors they should corrupt in football match-fixing and how much he should pay them (Hill 2009: 168):

FRIEND: $60,000?! The players want this?

V.R.: Yes.

FRIEND: Fuck . . . well, just give the referees the $40,000—if you don't find the rest.

V.R.: What else can I do, fuck? Faggots! I can give them [the players] $60,000 or $20,000. The most important thing is the effect [fixing the game]. Now I will be talking with them and see and maybe I can make a deal. I will give 40, and then bring the 20 later. Fuck! So then there is a guarantee already?

FRIEND: Yes, of course, *the guarantee is needed* [emphasis added].

V.R.: Well, fuck. They also have enough. Those fuckers [the players] already have too much. This is the situation.

FRIEND: Maybe you fucking give the referees 30 [$30,000] fuck. And say to the players: fuck, if you don't do it for 30, I will give the other 30 to someone else, rather than you fuck!

Establishing a connection, expressing in more or less clear words one's proposal for corruption, is a crucial passage, since it implies the risk of denunciation from an honest—or frightened—counterpart. Evidence on corruption can be collected quite easily, thanks to technological devices, as in a bribery scheme revealed in Ecuador: "the videos, together with audio recordings obtained by businessmen using watches and pens implanted with bugging devices, appear to implicate Ecuadorian officials and political operatives [...] . The recordings indicate that an Ecuadorian political operative was working to obtain $3 million in bribes related to environmental cleanup contracts to be awarded" (*New York Times*, August 31, 2009). Similarly, a Brazilian governor was recorded in a secret video by an entrepreneur while taking an envelope containing R$50,000: "Let me pay before I forget," says the entrepreneur. "Great, give me a hamper" was the governor's reply (*Sunday Times*, December 4, 2009). The actions of some "agent provocateur" must then similarly be feared, as in the case of tehelka.com, an Indian investigative website whose reporters bribed their way into the home of the defense minister and handed money to one of the minister's colleagues, senior army officers, bureaucrats, and even the president of the ruling party, who was filmed shoveling the cash into his desk (TI-2003: 156). In one of the major U.S. scandals of the 1970s, FBI agents disguised as sheikhs from the Middle East videotaped a congressman who, "in one of the more amusing moments of the scandal, asked the 'sheikhs' if the money he had shoved inside his suit jacket left noticeable 'bulges'" (Grossman 2005: 2).

Any information on potential counterparts' receptivity is consequently valuable, even when—paradoxically enough—the source is an anticorruption campaign: "When India's government put online the names of the officials facing trial for corruption, the list became a convenient guide for whom to bribe" (*The Economist*, January 28, 2010).

What to expect in these contingencies becomes a crucial issue in deciding who will make the first approach, if at all. Indirect, ambiguous moves may be necessary to test the other party's approachability, inducing temptation without making one's intentions crystal clear. To involve colleagues in bribery, for instance, corrupt Hong Kong police agents used similar cautious strategies: "The organizers are good psychologists. New arrivals in the Force are tested to see how strong their sense of duty is. The testing may take various forms—sums of money placed on their desks, etc. If an officer fails to report the first overture of this sort he is really 'hooked' for the rest of his service, and he is afraid to report any corrupt activities which may thereafter come to his notice" (Klitgaard et al. 2000: 18).

Cultural or ideological heterogeneity, distance, and the low-frequency of expected contacts are among the factors that increase the risks in this crucial passage, as experienced by a Japanese citizen arrested in October 2003 for trying to bribe a North Korean official—who denounced him—into buying drugs from "a third country"—obviously China—and smuggle them into Japan onboard a North Korean ship that used to sail regularly between North Korea and a Japanese port (*Asia Times*, April 20, 2007). Channels to collect information are often opaque, disguised, and ambiguous; knowledge of corrupt opportunities cannot be exchanged in the setting of transparent markets; no "public" advertising is available (Lambsdorff 2007: 140). In other words, high research and information costs are the first, and sometimes insurmountable, barrier to involvement in corruption.

The careful approach of a broker in a cricket match-fixing deal clearly states his awareness of the danger of this state of affairs. It was a well-founded concern, since his counterpart was an undercover reporter, who later denounced him:

REPORTER: If there's two or three that are on for the other side, the betting side, then good luck—they'll be really happy.

BROKER: There's more than two or three. Believe me. It's already set up. That's already there. I'm very wary speaking about this simply because I don't know you guys. I've been dealing with these guys for seven years, okay? Who we deal with and how we deal with it is very, very important. This is the main thing. I'm only dealing with certain people. How we do it and what we do is very, very crucial.

REPORTER: You're already dealing with another party on this matter? Give us some tips as well if you've got any. Happy to cut us in?

BROKER: Yeah I'll give you tips.

REPORTER: If there's anything we need to know in the forthcoming match let me know. Happy to pay. (*News of the World*, May 23, 2010)

Once information has been collected, its significance and consistency must still be assessed. This cannot be done before its acquisition, and it is therefore logically impossible to define how rational it is to invest in searching for new information. To be sure, in corruption affairs information costs are lower when data can be deduced from previous occurrences, analogous cases, and reported experiences. Similarly, searching for a partner and exposing oneself may appear less hazardous when previous practices and "common knowledge" signal a generalized practice of corruption. Information and research costs are, in other terms, negatively correlated with the overall practice of corruption. If the incentive to engage in corruption is directly related to perceived corruption, a positive feedback mechanism is at work (see Chapter 9).

The Bargaining Costs of Corruption

The costs of bargaining include "the opportunity costs of bargainers' time," as well as "any costly delays or failures to reach agreement when efficiency requires that parties cooperate" (Milgrom and Roberts 1990: 72). Coordination failures—arising when self-interested corrupt agents do not adopt mutually consistent patterns of behavior—as well as measurement costs and private information about preferences, are the main sources of bargaining costs. However, once the information gathered is estimated sufficient by the agents involved to enter into the corrupt transaction, a further difficulty is encountered: the negotiation of the "contractual terms" followed by the material transmission of resources. How large must the appropriate bribe be and how is it to be paid? What exactly has to be given in return by the public agent? An acceptable agreement must be stipulated, but its clauses cannot be written down in formal documents and are therefore not legally enforceable, nor even discussed openly in an explicit way. The need to conceal payments by, for instance, substituting bribes for loans or hiding the bribe in other apparently regular transactions, can confer a semblance of legality to the payments (Lambsdorff 2007: 142). In this case, however, the decrease in the penal hazard is accompanied by higher difficulty in stating and verifying the accomplishment of deferred and mixed dealings.

In general terms, bargaining costs are associated with the problematic definition of the content of the corrupt agreement. Take this example of bribes paid to pass examinations in Georgia:

> "One of my brothers was able to improve his grades in his high school diploma after haggling (literally!) with his teacher on the price. In turns out that the teacher was asking for 4 rubles for each extra point while my brother was only offering 2 rubles. In the end, they have settled on 3 rubles per point. Thus, for example, improving a grade from 3 to 5 on a scale of 2 ('fail')–5 ('excellent') cost my brother a mere 6 rubles." (Levy 2007: 429)

Negotiation may be an energy- and time-consuming process; indeed, finding a reciprocally satisfactory equilibrium in the interplay of expectations becomes even more difficult as the number of individuals involved increases. During negotiations partners typically try to persuade each other to increase—or lower—their evaluation of the "fair price" for the resources at stake. When—as in the case of the former Governor of Illinois Rod Blagojevich—what is offered is a prestigious seat in the U.S. Senate, the symbolic as well as the "economic" value is emphasized, and the possibility of "exiting" the deal is used to obtain a better bargain:

> During the call, Rod Blagojevich stated, "unless I get something real good for [Senate Candidate 1], shit, I'll just send myself, you know what I'm saying." Rod Blagojevich later stated, "I'm going to keep this Senate option for me as a real possibility, you know, and therefore I can drive a hard bargain. [...] And if I don't get what I want and I'm not satisfied with it, then I'll just take the Senate seat myself." Later, Rod Blagojevich stated that the Senate seat "is a fucking valuable thing, you just don't give it away for nothing. [...] I've got this thing and it's fucking golden, and, uh uh, I'm just not giving it up for fuckin' nothing. I'm not gonna do it." (U.S. District Court 2008: 56, 59)

The contracting power of partners is typically related to the time horizon of actors and to the amount of available alternatives. The downside of the need for quick bargaining emerges in this policeman-driver negotiation in Senegal: "It is the policeman [...] who proposes the arrangement. One of them just says to you 'Quickly, pay 6.000'. You say to him 'I don't have 6000'. He says to you, 'Just do it quickly' [...] . So this 'Do it quickly', what does it mean? You just take out 1000, which you give to him. He lets you go" (cit. in Blundo and de Sardan 2006: 127–8).

A stronger bargaining position is there for the taking for agents who, in an impasse, can simply select another more docile partner, or can wait without incurring costs until the counterpart retreats from his pretences or resistance. Therefore, agents with lower discount rates and monopolistic control enter transactions with the reasonable hope of gathering the lion's share of the surplus. Take, for instance, the testimony of a Nigerian supplier, who laments the costs of a time-consuming process lowering his contractual power:

> if you don't know anyone in the Treasury, they'll tell you they don't have the money. They make you come and go, finally you are forced to find someone with whom you'll have an understanding there. You propose a sum to him and it's at that moment that he'll do everything to get your money out [...] . It's a place of high intrigues, otherwise, for a small bill of 2 to 3 million, if you're not careful you can easily spend two months waiting. (Cit. in Blundo 2006: 256)

Actually, for large firms, "the time one loses is much more important than the amount one gives" (ibid.). Public-sector employees can easily menace strategic delays in public procedures to soften their clients' pretences, according to the moves of a game that a Beninian trader decoded:

> The customs officers play out impatience. They know we are in hurry so they do it to make us look for an arrangement. It is rare for a customs officer to request an arrangement explicitly. If they know that your affairs are not in order, they start by making threats to put you under pressure. Then they show that they are willing to help you and this is when you have to understand their game and make a proposition to them. Then you bargain it. If, on the other hand, the customs officer really doesn't find anything having checked, he says: 'give me the cola money' [i.e., the bribe]. (Cit. in Bako Arifari 2006: 192)

Similarly, every truck in Aceh, Indonesia, makes on average 20 illegal payments per trip to corrupt agents (police and military officials at checkpoints, to avoid fines for carrying excess cargo) and organized crime syndicates (to "protect" their shipment from bribes and from requests for extra bribes). Corrupt officials adjust the bribes according to their perceived bargaining power: with a gun visibly displayed, payments increased by 17 percent, each additional officer present at the checkpoint drove bribes up by 5 percent. Drivers of older trucks or carrying low-value cargo were asked for lower bribes than those with newer trucks or more precious freight. These factors also increased the likelihood of active price negotiation, rather than an offhand fixed bribe without any discussion (Olken and Barron 2007).

   Obviously, the existence of alternatives also increases one's bargaining power, since the resources sold—as well as the bribes to be paid—can be "auctioned" to the highest bidder. There is a limit, however, to the amount of "competitive bids" that can be collected from different partners, since each of these contacts increases the identification costs—as well as the risks of a retaliatory denouncement from a disappointed counterpart. For example, the mentioned former governor tried to exploit the competition among candidates for a Senate seat he was to nominate—after Barack Obama's election as U.S. President—to increase the amount of money he could collect in exchange. In a recorded conversation, Blagojevich "described an earlier approach by an associate of Senate Candidate Five as follows: 'We were approached 'pay to play.' That, you know, he'd raise me 500 grand. An emissary came. Then the other guy would raise a million, if I made him a Senator" (U.S. District Court 2008: 72).

   Any quarrel during the negotiation of corrupt deals may be ruinous. An unresolved dispute can spell the failure of the business or, even worse, can degenerate into an open clash, drawing the attention of control agencies to the underlying illegal pact. For example, a tragic conclusion followed the dispute concerning a bribe to be paid to two Indian police officers by a man who attempted to carry his bicycle into a train compartment. Asked for 100 rupees, the man counter-offered 5 rupees, but while arguing the officers allegedly pushed his pregnant wife from the train, and "as she struggled to grab hold of the door, she fell under the wheels of the train and was killed instantly"; the officers were later attacked by a mob that caused them multiple injuries (*Telegraph*, June 21, 2009).

The Monitoring and Enforcement Costs of Corruption

The story is not over once a "corruption contract" is agreed upon. On the contrary, difficulties may arise in the final stage, when monitoring and enforcement are required to police, prevent, and eventually penalize partners' deceptions and misbehavior. The agents involved still have to spend their time, effort, and money to control other parties' respect of the terms of the agreement, especially when performances are postponed and payments spread in installments. Eventually, retaliatory and sanctioning activities may be necessary, if something goes wrong. Is the partner honoring his word? How to check whether he is trying to defect from the agreement? To what extent can partial noncompliance be imputed to him or to external factors independent of his will? How can the cheating partner be dissuaded and punished all the while avoiding this personal conflict from degenerating into a public exposure of corruption? The activities needed to provide answers to these delicate questions are risky: they must be performed watchfully and secretly. Confidential information may also be a valuable resource in this context, to ensure the transaction runs a smooth course toward a conclusion of reciprocal fulfillment.

Protection from external checks and controls is crucial when bribes are inevitably passed from hand to hand during a transaction. This is a very dangerous phase, especially when the money transfer is not concealed in the bank accounts of offshore companies, as is usual in cases of "grand corruption" with sophisticated financial management and specialized brokers (Vannucci 2009). As an example, we may consider the international corruption case of the chief executive officer of the Lesotho Highlands Development Authority: "The Swiss bank records showed that, as CEO, Sole had consistently received large sums of money through middlemen or intermediaries from companies and consortia that had been awarded contracts [...] . Evidence showed a clear pattern of payments [...] using numbered Swiss accounts. Bam [the middleman] took a percentage and then moved the remainder of the money into Sole's account" (TI-2005: 33). In this case only a complex procedure lasting years and orders of disclosure issued to Swiss banks, which contractors attempted to block, allowed judges to collect evidence.

Intercepted money in "lower-profile" episodes of corruption can instead be easily used by law-enforcers as proof of the illegal deal. When corrupt agents are forced to hide or destroy money, they may incur unpleasant drawbacks: "a police constable, who took a Rs 1000 bribe, swallowed the cash after anti-corruption bureau sleuths caught him in the act [...] . 'when [he] noticed that we were running towards him, he tried to flee but we nabbed him. He swallowed the currency notes. We took him to Government Medical College and hospital for medical examination. The stomach wash, stool and urine of the constable were sent for chemical analysis'" (*The Times of India*, April 26, 2009). Another Indian police official caught while accepting a bribe "gulped down the Rs 500 denomination notes to wipe out proof of his crime [...] . The police official was taken to a government hospital where he vomited out the notes after being administered some medicines" (*Thaindian News*, April 28, 2008).

Corrupt agreements—being illegal—cannot be enforced by public institutions such as the judiciary and the police, normally available to punish deviation from legally codified contracts and agreements as a third-party enforcing mechanism that reduces transaction costs (Barzel 2002). Moreover, corrupt transactions are often nonsimultaneous in nature, and one party must rely for a certain period upon the word of the other, while denouncement is always to be feared.[5] This was the case of a former Iraqi deputy minister of transport, who asked for a bribe to renew a contract for a foreign security firm: "the deputy minister was supposed to receive the full amount first, but the scenario was changed into him receiving $100,000 [in U.S. dollars] as a down payment, and the rest of the money would be delivered after the renewal of the contract," but he was denounced before the second delivery (*CNN.com*, September 7, 2009). A similar concern was expressed by former Governor Blagojevich; representing his interests, another lobbyist had pushed the "defaulter," who was late with payments, to pay up: "'look, there is concern that there is going to be some skittishness if your bill gets signed because of the timeliness of the commitment,' making it clear that the contribution had 'to be in now'" (U.S. District Court 2008: 39). If trust is not unconditional, some kind of control must be exerted. In particular, when the time lag between promise and execution is ample, continuous and difficult monitoring efforts are necessary.

In other cases, fulfillment requires a sequence of activities: a bribe can be divided into installments, for instance, or vice versa the illegal assignation of a public contract may require the manipulation of different phases of the procedure. Such situations are especially vulnerable to the possibility of one partner "forgetting," reneging, or trying to renegotiate more favorable terms. According to an entrepreneur, this is the worst type of unpredictable corruption, where "you pay what you have agreed to pay and you go home and lie awake every night worrying whether you will get it or if somebody is going to blackmail you instead" (World Bank 1997: 34).

Faced with the menace of fraudulent misconduct, agents must spend resources not only to monitor, but eventually to dissuade and punish defection. To protect themselves from their partners' potential cheating, corrupt agents have to invest further resources to arrange and manage some policing and enforcing mechanisms.[6]

---

5   Japan has a long record of *amakudari*—or "golden parachutes"—whereby senior officials solicit private corporations for postretirement jobs for higher remuneration. In this case the time lag of the hidden exchange is particularly long, and so the trust in the partner's goodwill has to be proportionally high: "*amakudari* is a major cause of *kansei-dango*, or bid-rigging, by public officials. As recent revelations show, public officials play important roles in awarding contracts in exchange for post-retirement jobs in the company they favour. In other cases retired officials who have been promised jobs in private companies leak the bidding prices to likely bidders, who arrange among themselves which of their companies will win, based on the insider information" (TI-2008: 199).

6   As an alternative, corrupt agents may look for some kind of "supernatural protection." In some African countries where corruption is endemic, there is a proliferation of "marabouts and charlatans specializing in the supply of talismans that supposedly provide protection against the corruption of others and conceal holder's own corrupt practices" (Blundo 2006: 106).

Punishment administration and retaliation are costly, however, in terms of risks and effort, sometimes even more costly than the "stolen" resources. Enforcement is nonetheless convenient if, in a wider time horizon, sanctions are expected to deter fraudulent conduct in the future. As we will see in the following chapters, guarantees can be self-produced and delivered by agents directly involved in corrupt deals, using their political, economic, or social capital, or purchased from external specialized actors and organizations, who substitute the missing public authorities as "third-party" enforcers of corrupt exchanges.

Given its high transaction costs, the failure of the corrupt exchange is a concrete possibility. Various cases emerge in which corrupters and corruptees, with reciprocal mistrust and indignation over the "dishonesty" of the others, try to understand who has cheated them and how. Sometimes, frustration emerges as a result of the only partial fulfillment of a promise, as in the case of a cadre of a public enterprise who declared, "They contacted me to see how to get a public bid, how they could win it; they offered me, if I helped them, 500 million, you know. And I let them tempt me, even if I then received only 300" (PMI-DE, March 14, 2003: 36). Similarly, an entrepreneur laments the duplicity of a member of a regional government who, it was discovered, made agreements with his competitors:

> It is not that someone wakes up and goes and sees him, and he forgets two years, as if nothing had happened. I'll make him remember [...] . It doesn't work in this way. [...] And to me, this piece of shit said, don't worry, everything is ok. This is why I tell you that they are unreliable, because they knock on every door, every church is good for them. (TRBA1: 164)

A case in point is the experience of an entrepreneur seeking to persuade a public agency to buy him out of his failing enterprise: "he made payments amounting to about 350 million to a regional deputy powerful enough to be known as 'the boss'. He turned out to be a 'delinquent' who, after making 'a lot of promises', 'stole the money'" (CD, n. 98: 5). Moreover, the opacity of illegal deals encourages misreporting, fueling mistrust within organizations where corruption is a shared practice. For instance, truck drivers in Indonesia do not truthfully report the bribes they have to pay at checkpoints to their companies: "By exaggerating bribe payments, drivers may be able to extract more money from their bosses to pay bribes than they actually need, and pocket the difference. [...] On average the bribes drivers reported in interviews were more than double the amount of the bribes we recorded by direct observation" (Olken and Barron 2007: 9–10).

As a result of this lack of internal regulation, the corrupt exchange seems doomed to fail beneath uncertainty, reciprocal mistrust, and fears. In fact, where political corruption is widespread, we observe the presence of internalized codes, practices and informal norms, bilateral trust, reputation, brokers, and third parties, all components of a complex organizational architecture that facilitates the implementation of corrupt exchanges, enforcing hidden agreements and reducing transaction costs.

Corruption in Complex Exchanges

Associations of public actors include various figures with different roles, and their coordination in reaching administrative decisions that can be exchanged for bribes is indispensable. On the public side, we find public administrators (both those in elected positions and those with party appointments), career administrators, and party functionaries. On the other side, cartels of businessmen may reach agreements on a series of public decisions they must demand from politicians: they collect money and hand it over to political cartels, in turn the latter offer privileged access to decisions and distribute the money among politicians. Sometimes middlemen intervene to establish contacts within and between the groups of actors, to conduct the negotiations, and to transfer the bribe money. Corrupt exchanges do not, however, involve only the public administrators and private entrepreneurs who directly participate in them, but also other actors, who—although not necessarily directly taking part in sharing the political rent—nevertheless obtain favors in exchange for resources they control. The need of *consensus* of corrupt politicians can be obtained via clientelistic exchanges with voters. The required "cover-ups" of their illicit activities can be secured through an implicit or explicit agreement with bureaucratic actors or control agencies (della Porta and Vannucci 1994). When *coercion* is considered necessary to enforce an illegal agreement and avoid individual exit from the occult exchanges, organized crime can supply the resources of physical violence corrupt politicians need to punish "lemons," free riders, or potential "whistle-blowers." In this more complex web of relationships, a combination of *first-party* internalized mechanisms of self-sanctioning, reciprocal *second-party* bonds of trust, and other forms of *third-party* guarantees is needed that allows exchanges of precarious property rights over political rents to be concluded.

In complex networks of corruption, various actors intervene, supplying the resources necessary not only to the successful conclusion of the hidden exchange but also to guarantee its implementation, protection from risks of external intrusion, reinvestment of illicit capital, and the maintenance of a resilient conspiracy of silence (della Porta and Vannucci 1999a). Additional players cannot easily be excluded from the expected benefits of the "corruption game," since their involvement in public decision-making or their access to confidential information on illegal deals provide them with blackmailing power (della Porta, 1992). In such cases there are also illegal exchanges *internal* to each group of corrupt agents, who have to share the expected bribe benefits.

Often, private citizens, entrepreneurs, and public agents do not act as isolated counterparts in the illicit deal. Entrepreneurs involved in corruption are sometimes the organizers or members of collusive agreements, in which information about public works is shared and bid-rigging is more or less scientifically managed (see Chapter 6). The expected repetition of the game reassures participants that individuals in the cartel receive their share of profits from public contracts, while bribes are paid to administrators or control agencies to guarantee rents, via the acceptance of higher prices as well as the lower quality of the work and services delivered. Cartels can obtain compliance by threatening potential free riders with exclusion from the circle of "protected" entrepreneurs. Moreover, cartels socialize individual entrepreneurs to the norms of corruption by justifying illegal payments as necessary if they are to "stay in business." Finally, cartels reduce the individual risks of singling out the politician or public administrator to bribe, bargaining the amount of money to be paid, and increase the overall bargaining power of the "private side" in the corrupt exchange, since the cartel's representatives can use their monopolistic power in the negotiation with public agents, thereby imposing better contractual terms as well as compliance with the unwritten agreement.

On the other side, political actors involved in corrupt exchanges sometimes simply cannot act autonomously, hiding their illicit activities from an inner circle of their own party's functionaries and leaders whose political support is necessary to enhance their role and career opportunities. Moreover, and especially when corruption becomes widespread, parties can play an important role in organizing and monitoring the collection of bribes. First of all, they ensure compliance through their extensive control on public administration: "rules" about bribes (with a "price list" for different "services") tend subsequently to be applied to large sectors of the public administration, weakening the "exit" option for more honest or scrupulous firms. Parties may also socialize their members and candidates to corruption, framing it as "normal business." They also reduce the risks related with the collection of information necessary to perform a corrupt business deal: among other services, party structures sometimes manage unofficial lists of loyal entrepreneurs, often in contact with party administrators responsible for the collection of bribes.

Corrupt politicians need consensus in order to obtain the informal "property rights" to the official role and its decisional power, a consensus that they can acquire from voters and supporters via clientelistic exchanges. Corrupt politicians are normally very skilled in networking, building up circles of loyal supporters to whom they distribute favors (or even just promises of favors). Economic revenues from bribery are often reinvested in political activities, in a sort of modern "party machine" through which contacts are kept and favors are distributed in exchange for votes that reinforce political power—from which further money is illicitly gathered (see Chapter 5).

All these actors need "cover-ups" and a certain degree of certainty in the corrupt exchange; in other words, they must minimize the likelihood of being reported and investigated, as well as cheated by partners. Using either threats or favors, the corrupt and corrupting agents must erect a wall of silence around their illicit dealings and discourage fraudulent attitudes. This can be done by corrupting judges and/or the local press, but it may also require the involvement of bureaucrats, who are very likely to know about hidden exchanges taking place in their public structures. Functionaries, thanks to their specific skills and competences, as well as the usually permanent nature of their roles, can in various ways influence or jeopardize corrupt deals. They can in fact introduce valuable resources to the networks of corrupt exchanges: information on private partners and technical knowledge on norms and procedures to be kept under control, firstly. In addition, bureaucrats, being more stable in their posts than elected politicians, can indeed reduce the expected risks of defection by maintaining contact with the entrepreneurial cartels in the longer term, sometimes even collecting bribes to be redistributed directly (see Chapter 4).

The relationship between corrupt and corruptor may sometimes be made easier by the intervention of a wide range of brokers, who often specialize precisely in illegal markets where the expected rewards, as well as the risks, are generally higher. Middlemen normally intervene to establish contacts between two parties, searching for approachable and receptive partners, to conduct negotiations, and to handle the material transfer of the bribe money. They play an important role in socializing public and private actors to "illegal" norms, but also in reducing moral scruples as well as hazards by collecting bribes, sometimes disguised in the form of formally legal payments for professional services (see Chapter 7).

When trust, repetition of the game, self-enforcing norms, and reputation are not sufficient to enforce an illegal agreement and avoid individual exit from the occult exchanges, physical coercion may be needed as an additional resource. Organized crime is therefore often an actor from whom corrupt politicians and cartels of entrepreneurs buy those resources of violence and intimidation needed to punish "lemons" and free riders and discourage those who threaten to go to the authorities. In fact, corruption networks are especially robust and durable where mafia bosses enter the game, helping the careers of political actors with the supervision of vote-buying activities and their direct influence over packages of votes, but also by strengthening their reputation of being "dangerous" to cheat. Politicians and bureaucrats may reciprocate by protecting mafia bosses from police investigations, but also by allocating them bribe shares, as well as guaranteeing privileged access to public bids to cartels with criminal protection (see Chapter 8).

Figure 2.1 shows a synthetic overview of the multifaceted web of exchanges that can emerge from the interactions of different political and bureaucratic actors, political parties, cartels, brokers, and citizens in their alternate roles as electors, clients, vote-sellers and bribers, and organized crime. To understand corrupt exchanges, we must look not only at the institutional and cultural constraints impeding the violation of the contract between the public administrator (the agent) and the state (the principal) but also at the involvement of actors skilled in delivering and reproducing the additional resources necessary for the development of corrupt exchanges: trust, illegal skills, protection, informal norms, and consensus being among them. These resources lower the overall cost of illegal exchanges by reducing their material risks as well as their moral costs.

In fact, as the quantity of actors multiplies and the amount—as well as the variety—of resources at stake increases, difficulties in understanding and anticipating possible opportunities and outcomes of illegal deals may discourage individuals from participation. The information, bargaining, and policing costs of corruption are clearly related to the extension of the network of actors involved

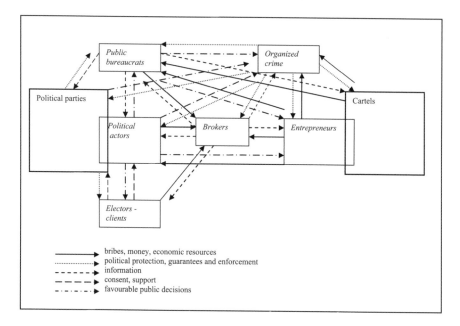

Fig. 2.1   **A complex network of corrupt exchanges.**

and the complexity of the decision-making context, which in a similar environment reflects the vague and sometimes obscure partition of tasks, responsibilities, and personal attributes among wider numbers of individuals. Bargaining turns out to be more complicated and time-consuming, while the complexity of intertwining relationships makes monitoring and enforcement more difficult to perform, increasing the risks of mutual defection.

As in a well-functioning "ordinary" market, however, within the networks of corruption enlargement to new participants may also induce some actors to specialize precisely in the production, "advertising," and selling of resources to reduce uncertainty, favoring the convergence of expectations toward the reciprocally desirable outcome of undetected corruption. Information and reputational assets, networking abilities, social capital, informal norms and constraints, protection, and third-party enforcement are the most important resources that introduce a certain degree of "order" and relative predictability to networks of corruption, that is, the main governance mechanism of corruption.

The Institutions of Corruption: Governance Mechanisms in Corrupt Exchanges

As North observes, institutions are the "rules of the game in a society or, more formally, are the humanly devised constraints that shape human interactions," reducing uncertainty and transaction costs (1990: 3). The complex architecture of formal rules (constitutional rules, statutory laws, regulations, contracts, etc.), informal constraints (social norms, customs, conventions, etc.), and their enforcement mechanisms provide the fundamental margins to the potential unpredictability of human interactions. A rule is institutionalized when actions taken by actors according to their subjective preferences, beliefs, and expectations become mutually consistent over a certain period. In this case the observed reality, created by their choices, tends to confirm their beliefs, which are then reproduced as a guide for further actions: institutions can be characterized "as a *self-sustaining system of shared beliefs* about a salient way in which the game is repeatedly played" (Aoki 2001: 10).

The function of shared beliefs about the nature of interaction and other players' expected choices is crucial for understanding institutional change: when observed actions do not match with anticipated results, a search for new models can lead (more or less rapidly) to the joint adoption of a new and (relatively) consistent system of subjective perceptions of the rules for action and criteria for choices used by others. From this perspective, an institution exists only where agents mutually believe in the summary representation (whether tacit or explicit) of the rules that coordinate their beliefs. Statutory laws and regulations cannot be considered institutions per se, since they are not necessarily observed: "For example, even if the government prohibits the importation of some goods by a statutory law, but if people believe it effective to bribe customs officers to circumvent the law and make it a prevailing practice, then it seems appropriate to regard the practice rather than the ineffective statutory law as an institution" (ibid.: 13). On the other hand, informal practices and conventions can be considered institutions as long as individuals' beliefs converge in considering them as relevant internal guides for everyone's behavior. We may take, for example, the words of some Indian people describing the subterranean "institutions of corruption" regulating every relationship with public agents: "Every day, I see corruption. So, even if we need licenses and all that, it's something you put on the table first and then the license comes," said a marketing executive. And "If you go to a government hospital, you will not be admitted for treatment unless you know some employee or you bribe staff—said a Delhi citizen—your building plans will not be passed until you bribe municipal officials. This has become part of life now" (*CNN.com*, January 20, 2011).

In illegal markets "private-order" mechanisms and other governance structures assume a crucial role. Despite high transaction costs, more or less complex networks of corrupt exchanges can develop, with governance mechanisms that help to meet the "demands" of protection of the fragile and uncertain property rights at stake in the corrupt domain.[7] Such structures can sustain the research and time-consuming

---

[7]   As Turvani (1997: 143) observes: "Prohibition cancels the possibility of referring to a higher, more formal level of institutional orders and sanctions (no court will defend property rights and enforce a contract); it does not cancel transactions. Transactions will take place, but they are now pushed back to another, more primitive institutional environment. A prohibited market is a black market: but the black market is not simply an illegal market, it is a market with a lower degree of institutionalization protecting agents and their transactions."

bargaining activities seen in "honest" trade relationships among different corrupt actors, generating stable expectations that constrain their actions by imposing the fulfillment of illegal contracts. In fact, when *organized* corruption networks prevail, bribe payments are predictable and regulated, resulting in property rights over public resources being allocated as expected (Shleifer and Vishny 1993). On the contrary, the uncertain environment of "disorganized corruption"—where many corrupt government agents operate independently to maximize their bribe revenue—lowers firms' expected profits and discourages their involvement in corruption. A robust body of empirical evidence shows that predictable regimes of regulated corruption—"when the size of the payment is known in advance and when the service that is the object of the bribe is usually delivered as agreed after the payment is made"—increase the frequency of corrupt exchanges (Herrera et al. 2007: 33).

Illicit markets are generally characterized by a variety of different *informal* institutions and enforcement mechanisms, which include self-sustaining illegal conventions, "moral" codes, self-enforcing contracts, norms of reciprocity, reputation, third-party sanctioning, and several organizational architectures (limited in their scope or more elaborate and wide-ranging) whose resources are used to protect illegal deals and corresponding property rights.

Hidden markets for corrupt exchanges are characterized by three different but interlinked enforcement mechanisms, that act upon

(a) *first party control*, when the (illegal) norms and rules of behavior are internalized by the individuals

(b) *second-party enforcement*, when compliance is guaranteed by partners or indirect counterparts in the corrupt exchange

(c) *third-party enforcement*, which relies upon the intervention of external actors, capable of imposing compliance on those directly involved in the exchange

First-party control occurs when the informal norms of corruption have been internalized to such an extent that their violation produces a psychic cost, such as feelings of guilt or discomfort (Panther 2000).[8] Enforcement

---

[8] Paradoxically, as we show in Chapter 3, a moral aspect is acknowledged within the system of corrupt exchanges when, through the internalization of the associated norms, "honesty" (as respect for the corrupt agreements) becomes trustworthiness in illegal dealings. We can consider, for example, the role of Italian *party cashiers*, chosen by leaders precisely for their highly honorable personal reputations in illegal transactions. They managed the flow of bribes and could easily conceal part of the illegal revenues from their party colleagues, as the only ones to possess detailed knowledge of the mechanisms governing their allocation (della Porta e Vannucci 1999a: 97–9). Party cashiers acquired a favorable reputation in the market of corruption thanks to their observance of a peculiar norm of *honesty*, implying complete respect of the obligations assumed in illegal transactions. The national administrative secretary of the Socialist Party, for instance, was considered by his peers "a man of honour who personally saw to his obligations and therefore, for reasons of uprightness and personal prestige, consigned in person the [bribe] money due to the local branches" (CD, n. 202-bis: 12).

here becomes self-enforcement: moral costs are not associated with any violation of the law, but with the moral duty to respect the unwritten clauses of corruption contracts; we could name them *immoral costs* (see Chapter 3). When all partners (as potential cheaters) in corrupt deals share similar internalized norms, exchanges can be successfully concluded. A potential basis for "reliable" corrupt transactions is then the involvement of relatively homogeneous agents who share customs and ideological and cultural values (opposed, or at least autonomous, from those embodied in the respect of state norms) and can produce expectations of reciprocal implementation in corrupt agreements. The corresponding endogenous rule of the game relies on the negative feelings associated with the betrayal of commonly internalized codes of behavior.

The interiorized sharing of illegal codes and norms is, however, rarely so strong and generalized as to discourage free riders. *Second-party enforcement* occurs when sanctions are directly administered or credibly threatened by counterparts in corrupt exchanges (Ellickson 1991). The resources used to perform and enforce agreements generally pertain to the relation-specific expected advantages of a reiterated relationship. The establishment of personal trust can be interpreted in this perspective: when there are frequent bilateral opportunities for repeated interaction, being cooperative (i.e., not cheating) becomes an advantageous strategy, due to the threat of termination (or other forms of retaliation) in the case of dishonesty. Moreover, the acquisition of a *reputation* of "honesty" in illegal dealings, thanks to the circulation of information on previous behavior within the restricted circles of actors involved in the corrupt game, permits the reduction of expected risks in interactions within a wider network of exchange. This is clearly stated by a Senegal contractor: "The commission [i.e., the bribe] is given after being paid, that's my rule, and when you have concluded an agreement, if you have to give 100.500 F., you give 100.500 F., not 100.000 F." (cit. in Blundo 2006: 251). Preexisting networks based on reciprocity and trust, such as *blat* in Russia or *guanxi* in China, may also therefore guarantee an infrastructure in which reliable corrupt partners may be found. Actually, *guanxi* and corruption are often involved in the same actions, that is, exchanges of gifts, favors, and bribes between private partners and public agents: "the distinctive feature of *guanxi* is the way in which it incorporates both genuine sentiment and a series of techniques for getting things done. These techniques include creating a sense of shared identity, invoking obligations and the use of gift exchange to build a long-term relationship" (Smart and Hsu, 2007: 177).[9] Even without any formal sanctions, the enforcement of

---

9   Similarly, as Ledeneva (1998: 46) emphasizes, in Russia *blat* and corruption are distinct phenomena that overlap to some extent. *Blat* denotes the system of informal agreements and exchange of favors which can sometimes—under specific conditions—translate into the payment of bribes: "Although it implies access to public resources and so-called 'workplace crime', as does corruption, *blat* is more legitimate, since it is oriented to satisfying everyday needs and basic necessities. Recourse to blat is normally

corruption contracts generally operates through ostracizing or excluding dishonest actors from future interaction within the network.

As the domain of corruption extends, raising the costs of ex-ante information gathering, identification, monitoring and sanctioning of deceitful partners, the demand for guarantees and "certainty" also increases. Several private-order organizations—such as market intermediaries—may play a role in sustaining illegal contracts: "first, providing information about breaches, and second, organizing the responses to those breaches" (McMillan and Woodruff 2000: 2423). A specialized *third-party*, distinct from those directly involved in the corrupt deal, may then enter the scene, selling protective services. Third-party enforcement mechanisms can in fact secure "private-order" regulation of corrupt dealings. As we will show, third-party enforcement agencies are rarely neutral from the transacting parties: facilitators and enforcers of corruption contracts do not restrict themselves to prescribing or automatically observing and sanctioning rules for compliance, as in the idealized rule-of-law operations of a state. In reality, there are problems of reliability and incentive-compatibility in the activities of actors and organizations involved, as suppliers of protection, in the market for corruption. As we will see, to become reputable and credible guarantors, chosen and trusted by corrupt actors, these actors have to control and exhibit specific resources. Moreover, to guarantee property rights and enforce agreements entails a cost that tends to increase when such dealings and resources are illegal or illegally acquired, as in the case of corruption. At the same time, protection and regulation activities have "public good" attributes that make them, to a certain extent, exploitable by free riders, a dilemma that modern states have tried to deal with through compulsory taxation. But third-party enforcers of corrupt dealings, with the possible exception of mafia organizations, cannot use violent resources to gather compulsory payments for their protection services. They must therefore also police their "extractive" activities to monitor and promote payments of protection-money from the actors involved. On the other hand, since the essence of protection consists in the capability to impose costs, partners in corrupt transactions must also be reassured that the guarantor will not use his power to seize (instead of protect) their resources.

Four Models of Corruption: A Typology of Regulatory Mechanisms

Governance structures vary with some of the characteristics of corrupt exchanges. Corruption may become more or less pervasive, but its *arbitrariness*—that is, the degree of ambiguity associated with the likelihood of gaining the favorable treatments agreed upon in corrupt deals—can also differ considerably in diverse institutional contexts. For instance, corrupt officials may ask for more bribes than originally agreed upon; multiple agents are often involved in decision-making,

enforced by hard conditions, inefficiency of formal procedures and the inability to cope with day-to-day demands."

increasing uncertainty about both *who* and *how much* to pay (Rodriguez et al. 2005; Seung-Hyun and Kyeungrae 2007). In worst-case scenarios, firms cannot anticipate the effects of their bribes, as in Indonesia and Russia: "Before, you paid a lump sum in Jakarta and could be certain you had smoothed things out [...] . Now you pay a lot of small amounts locally, and you can't be sure things will be smooth." As for Russia, "without the structure the Communist Party provided, people didn't know who to pay, and many anarchistic bribe collectors stepped up with their hands out" (Doh et al. 2003: 119). The arbitrariness of bribery—defined thus—is strictly related to its transaction costs: the informal institutions of corruption—that is, the "rules of the game" and corresponding enforcement mechanisms—tend to reduce such costs, persuading hesitant agents to conclude corrupt deals otherwise hampered by distrust.

Two key variables can be used to explain the emergence of different models of corruption: (i) the frequency and expected duration of a corrupt exchange among the actors involved, and (ii) the amount of resources at stake, that is, the rent allocated in each transaction by public agents and partly given as a bribe in return. By crossing small and large resources/bribes with low and high frequencies of bribery, four models of corruption emerge. They represent relatively stable "organizational" patterns of corrupt exchanges: *petty corruption*, *individual corruption*, *structural corruption*, and *systemic corruption* (see Table 2.1).[10]

Both dimensions—that is, the frequency of exchanges and the amount of resources—have an impact on the transaction costs of corrupt exchanges. Contracting parties may then find it advantageous to craft or adapt specialized governance structures to deal with such factors of uncertainty. These costs are, as mentioned, higher in the market for corrupt exchange (and other illegal markets) in comparison with ordinary markets. The interests of the actors involved in terms of reducing transaction costs can explain the emergence and consolidation of informal rules and other regulatory mechanisms within networks of exchange. Several governance structures can be observed in bureaucratic or political structures where there is coexistence between (more or less frequent) cases of corruption and the silence necessary to avoid the circulation of compromising information: "depending on the nature of the transaction, many alternative structures may be available, and these may vary greatly in their complexity and costs" (Milgrom and Roberts 1990: 64).[11]

---

[10]   Other variables—like the number of corrupt agents involved, their degree of specialization, the level of involvement of top-ranking officials, the nature of favors offered, the identity of private counterparts, etc.—could be considered as well and accommodated into subtypologies; we concentrate only on frequency and amounts of resources due to their robust and direct influence on the nature and distribution of transaction costs, and therefore on the characteristics of the resulting governance mechanisms.

[11]   One of the central assumptions of transaction costs theory is precisely that, "except when positive transaction costs block the organisation of some activities altogether, differential transaction costs will give rise to discriminating alignment—according to which some transactions will (for efficiency purposes) align with one set of governance

Table 2.1   Four models of corruption and their governance mechanisms

		Amount of resources at stake	
		Small	*Large*
Frequency and expected duration of corrupt exchanges	*Low*	PETTY CORRUPTION *Individual trust, simple and generic rules of behavior*	INDIVIDUAL CORRUPTION *Brokerage, strong individual trust*
	High	STRUCTURAL CORRUPTION *Reputation, informal norms of reciprocity and conditional cooperation, menace of exit from the deal*	SYSTEMIC CORRUPTION *Third-party enforcement of informal norms, hierarchical subdivision of tasks within corruption networks partly overlapping with organizational roles*

The expected frequency and repetition of deals among the same actors—or with a partial rotation within a restricted circle—have an obvious impact on the stability of any potential "management" of bribe collection. As observed by Becker and Stigler (1974: 4), in the case of repetitive violations, "the substantial transaction cost of ascertaining that the other party is reliable (abides by the contracts) become manageable for both violators and enforcers." Clearly, cooperation among corrupt enforcers, as well as between corrupter and corruptee, is easier when the "game" is repeated, since in that case information can be collected on the other player's past performance simply through experience, and it becomes possible to sanction defection from corrupt agreements in future interactions: "If there are prospects of negotiation further contracts with the same people over time, both the transaction costs and the risks associated with the advertising, gaining trust, and forming a capital of common knowledge are substantially reduced" (Lambsdorff 2007: 215).[12] This is exemplified by a Senegalese contractor in the construction field who shows a precise awareness that "he who sees himself given a procurement and who 'forgets' those who has selected him at the time of payment, will not have the benefit of help a second time. Such an attitude would be equivalent to 'beating a tam-tam with an axe'" (cit. in Blundo 2007: 41). To fail to respect the verbal

structures and other transactions will align with others" (Williamson 1997: 10). As in other illegal markets, however, external risks, information asymmetries, opportunistic agents, limited competition, and other factors related to the absence of official state protection severely weaken any tendency toward an "alignment" of corrupt exchanges with a system of "transaction cost economizing," possibly leading to inefficient outcomes.

[12] This intuitive result can be demonstrated in formal game theory terms as a case of equilibrium between strategies of conditional cooperation in a repeated *"prisoner's dilemma."* Among others, see Axelrod (1984) and Taylor (1987).

contract of corruption "is to close doors to future contracts," observed, in the same vein, a contractor from Parakou in Benin (Blundo 2006: 229).

The amount of resources at stake also plays a crucial role. Higher rents and bribes increase the transaction costs of corruption given that (i) money must be passed into other hands more carefully; (ii) the transactions are easier to detect, since profits from corruption are more difficult to conceal and reinvest; (iii) their eventual subdivision can more frequently generate quarrels; (iv) penal sanctions and incentives for defection are higher. On the other hand, if the bribes collected are large enough, they can induce public agents to put aside the scruples of their consciences and their fear of being detected and sanctioned. Large rents and expected illicit profits furnish the actors involved with a powerful incentive to organize and regulate the corrupt transactions in which they all are involved in a more stable manner, as well as other potentially risky (or fruitful) interactions.

A methodological caveat seems in order here. Although in the reality of corruption various types of governance mechanisms are often interrelated, we can single out some historical circumstances that have facilitated the development of one or the other. We have combined deductive reasoning to define four general and logically consistent models of corruption governance, and an inductive analysis to identify more precisely—on an empirical basis—the content of this typology, that is, which specific "regulatory mechanisms" will more probably be observed in those cases and will presumably tend to emerge, ceteris paribus, in certain contexts.[13] It is not possible, in our perspective, to univocally associate a certain governance structure to its transaction-cost minimizing characteristics without falling into a functionalist fallacy. The existence of informal norms regulating bribe-exchanges, for instance, or the appearance of third-party enforcers in illegal markets, cannot be explained by the positive functions they perform—that is, reducing uncertainty in corrupt deals—unless we arbitrarily relate the presence or persistence of governance mechanisms to their beneficial consequences for corrupt actors (their transaction-cost minimizing role), as an ex-post cause (Elster 1982).

A demand for protection and "certainty" in illegal deals, in other words, is not a sufficient condition for actors to appear specializing in its production and supply, or for impersonal rule to emerge spontaneously. Moreover, an identical request for protective services may be met by several governance structures, whose relative efficiency cannot be defined a priori and does not determine—but can, under certain conditions, influence—their probability of success and survival. In well-functioning and transparent legal markets, competitive pressures and learning processes may represent powerful forces leading toward an efficiency-enhancing evolution of institutional and organizational structures. On the contrary, in illegal markets (as in political markets, and corruption develops precisely a political-criminal market), opacity, a lack of information, secrecy, and ambiguity about the characteristics of the "commodities" exchanged, prevent unidirectional

---

[13] We apply this typology throughout the book, but we concentrate on its empirical accuracy in Chapter 4 on police and bureaucratic corruption, where cases fitting within the four models of corruption are examined in detail.

progress toward "better" governance mechanisms (Pierson 2004). The reduction of transaction costs is not the only driving force toward successfully adapting to specific loci of similar regulatory structures. This instead seems to follow a path dependent process of evolution, with its idiosyncratic, unforeseeable, contingent, and potentially inefficient outcomes (see Chapter 9). We will not then be able to predict whether an "equilibrium" will prevail at a certain moment or not, but only which governance mechanisms could possibly adapt to particular environments within a certain configuration of the corruption network.

Furthermore, this typology is not intended to label, describe or analyze macro-entities. It is not to be applied to predominant models of corruption within states, markets, or societies as a whole. Its defining variables—which are clearly continuous, even if presented as dichotomous for the sake of simplicity—work through subjective incentives, beliefs, and expectations operating at the individual level, and consequently the typology's descriptive and explanatory perimeters are delimited by very specific, locally circumscribed organizational and operative frameworks. In the same country, prevailing models of individual, systemic, structural, or petty corruption will be seen in a haphazard fashion, with a wide range of variation in time and space among offices, organizations, and bureaucracies, reflecting the nature of their decision-making processes, as well as the changeable procedural criteria for the allocation of resources.

The use of "systematic process analysis"—that is, intensive comparison of a small number of cases unfolding over time (Hall 2003)—and comparative institutional analysis seems to be particularly fruitful in this context. Investigating the institutional diversity and complexity of organizational responses to the common problem of reducing the transaction costs of corrupt activities can shed light on the variables influencing the profound differences in the diffusion and characteristics of corrupt networks, also recognizable in similar political and administrative environments: "That is, institutional arrangements can be diverse across economies even if they are exposed to the same technological knowledge and are linked through the same markets. Thus we need to rely on comparative and historical information to understand why particular institutional arrangements have evolved in one economy but not in others" (Aoki 2001: 3). This perspective leaves aside variables operating at the macro-level—cultural attitudes, legal incentives, and so on—which remain in the background. We look instead—and try to compare—the main organizational features surrounding specific decision-making processes where the creation and allocation of public resources (i.e., political rents) takes place, the governance mechanisms regulating corruption which they sustain, and their effects on the uncertain prospects of potential bribers and bribees.

Petty corruption occurs when the interaction between corrupt agents and private counterparts is occasional and presumably unrepeatable, while the rent at stake is relatively small. Since for both partners the profit from the corrupt exchange is small, high transaction costs tend to prevent it. Several factors can nonetheless increase the probability of the successful conclusion of a corrupt deal. A smaller amount of resources to share usually also implies fewer individuals involved, that is, to seek out and monitor, to bargain and exchange with. Moreover, since only small sums of money are transmitted, there are less material risks and difficulties in concealing their pocketing and use. Moral barriers are also weakened, since the bribe can be more easily reframed as a gift, interpreted as a sign of gratitude for a public agent's "understanding" or "kindness." This kind of self-defense emerges in the embarrassed words of a Senegalese policeman:

> It happens that people pay me cola, cigarettes, but there too, I work with them
> [...] I chew cola, I smoke cigarettes. When they give me cola, it is to satisfy
> themselves [...] this too, it is so that they make my job easier. I am obliged to
> take it, even if I do not want [...] . When I am given money, I do not take [...]
> but when the person gives me a cigarette [...] that, to be honest and direct with
> you, I take. I could as well not answer this question. But we are Africans, I am
> with them. (Cit. in Blundo 2007: 42)

Petty corruption is generally characterized by a lower frequency and expected duration of corrupt exchanges *between the same partners*. On both the demand and the supply sides of corruption, agents may be customarily involved in illegal activities, but often they have to face different partners whose reliability is unknown. A corrupt policeman, for instance, is always in touch with different individuals or truck drivers, asking for bribes not to fine them. The problematic management of these situations does not encourage the development of stable coordination devices and hierarchical supervision within the group of corrupt agents, and even less so the intervention of external coordinators. For the same reason, the activity of middlemen is not common in similar contexts unless brokers acquire the ability to capitalize their personal knowledge and trust linkages with corruptible agents, multiplying contacts with a multitude of occasional partners in minor corrupt deals. Petty corruption, therefore, may become a pervasive and persistent phenomenon despite its internal frictions.

In India, a huge variety of episodes of petty corruption have been revealed through an initiative by a nonprofit organization: a website where any recent or old cases of bribes people have experienced can be denounced: http://ipaidabribe. com (Agence France Presse [AFP], November 17, 2010). Between August and November 2010, more than 2,300 cases were reported. Here is a small sample: "My car pollution check-up had expired. I thought I would have to pay a fine of Rs3000. But a mere 300 bucks as bribe and the official let me go. I paid it to get away from the pain of going to the transport office, waiting in queues, paying fines etc."; "At the time of signing the certificate of marriage registration the sub-registrar asked me to pay Rs.500/- his assistant at his left side room, I paid the amount without asking any more questions"; "I have paid 1000 rupees to get the Driving license [...] . I don't know how to drive a car but I am having LMV license"; "I paid both the police man and the writer who issued the certificate. The writer told something interesting 'Did your father tell you about me' with a smile :). I understood the code."[14]

---

[14]   Evidence was collected from the website http://ipaidabribe.com, accessed: January 31, 2011.

In petty corruption a "positive" conclusion of a single illicit deal simply requires a sufficient amount of personal trust among the actors involved. Personal acquaintance, kinship, common ethnicity, political or cultural belongings are obvious facilitating factors here, providing safeguards against the fear of opportunistic behavior.[15] In any case, as occasionally trusting actors meet each other and cautiously conclude their corrupt deal, pieces of information about existing opportunities to gather bribes, favors, and rents through corruption start to circulate in a wider context, shaping expectations. Petty corruption can flourish then through the coordination made possible by spontaneous adherence to some very simple and general rules of "institutionalized" and codified corruption, stating that in certain offices, with certain agents, to get access to certain public resources, a certain bribe has to be paid for things to run smoothly. Elementary norms may become common knowledge—take, for instance, cases of registration flagged on the Indian website, where bribes are "0.1 per cent of registration amount for any property"—but no "external" sanction punishes those who violate them, as cheating only implies the risk of missing a chance for an easy profit, or avoiding an immediate cost. The risk of retaliation/denunciation is remote, nor does it appear as a credible threat against defection in this context: every formal accusation, in fact, imposes a high fixed cost (legal expenses, time, the risk of not being believed, etc.), which can easily exceed the small (moral or pecuniary) expected advantage.

Individual corruption emerges in low frequency but potentially highly rewarding corrupt interactions. The potential corruptor has a one-shot opportunity to obtain a very large benefit, a rent whose allocation depends upon the decision or the information usually at the disposal of a single or small group of public agents, but has to confront two opposing forces. On the one hand, obviously, he has a strong incentive to bribe the decision-makers in order to gain control over the rent (minus the bribe). On the other hand, he has to confront the uncertainty of an unknown and presumably unrepeatable situation, which will increase transaction costs. The risk of being "sold a lemon" or being denounced by an unfamiliar partner whom he will most likely never meet again can be extremely discouraging. In addition, if the transaction is non-simultaneous, one party must rely on the word of the other. The same holds true, on the other side of the corruption market, for the public agent. How can he trust the promises of his private counterpart? The corrupter might denounce him or, having obtained what he sought, may "forget" to pay the promised bribe. The occasional nature of the interaction does not allow for credible threats of retaliation against "dishonest" partners in future exchanges.

---

[15]   Any kind of exchange can in fact be facilitated when counterparts are embedded in a social structure that reduces its transaction costs (Granovetter 1992; Aoki 2001: 208–9). As Lambsdorff (2002: 233) observes, corruption is no exception: "corrupt relationships can be set up with partners with whom some kind of organizational link already exists. [...] Pre-existing relationships can lay the foundation for economic exchange by providing the required safeguard against opportunism."

In individual corruption involvement is generally limited to one or a small clique of public agents—high level bureaucrats or politicians—who control the decision-making process. Since coordination and bargaining problems increase exponentially with the number of participants, it would be extremely risky to organize and manage a broad exchange network for a single, unique occasion for making profit. The nature of the exchange process becomes relevant to define the probabilities of a "happy ending" for the participants. In both petty and individual corruption, in fact, we can observe conditions akin to the ideal type of what North defines as *personal exchange*. The existence of strong trust between partners is a necessary prerequisite here: "personal exchange is exchange in which kinship, ties, friendship, and personal loyalty all play a part in constraining the behavior of participants [...] . All of these factors reduce the need for costly specification and enforcement. A handshake suffices for even complicated exchange. Absent these factors, and the exchange process becomes much more costly" (North 1984: 257). In these cases, therefore, "the identity of the people engaged in the transactions matters. [...] Such cost-minimizing transactions require an initial investment in transaction-specific resources. One refers to this as a specialization of identity. Identity matters because engaging in a certain transaction requires the negotiation of certain rules, norms, or codes of conduct among the related parties" (Lambsdorff 2007: 213).

The relevance of trust is confirmed by the case of the Russian corruptor V.R. He was trying to fix a match with a foreign team administrator when the administrator of a third club allegedly claimed that he had not honored a corrupt deal in the past. He called him, furious, to reestablish his credibility, since his reputation was a major business asset in building trust relationships in occasional meetings with other team administrators (Hill 2009: 171).

> V.R.: Grigori, this is Rubinov. Explain to me this fact! Where or when do I not keep my obligations to your club? What are the times that I have let you down?
>
> ADMINISTRATOR: I don't understand.
>
> V.R.: You are telling Sergei [the Rangers administrator] that I won't keep my promises! [. . .] He told me that you don't trust me. And that I will end up tricking him. This is fucking nonsense! Because when I had to, I solved all the problems [. . .]
>
> ADMINISTRATOR: I told him that you and I made a deal [fixed a match] but nothing else!

In this type of corruption, the relevance of the resources at stake creates incentives for the intervention of middlemen specialized in trading confidential information and building trust relationships between themselves and potential partners. Their function is to ease or "grease" the necessary interactions and to reduce friction in the negotiations between the two or more parties interested in the corrupt deal, as well as acting as go-betweens for the arrangement and collection of payoffs (see

Chapter 7). Generally speaking, middlemen specialize as exchange-facilitators, reducing the costs of reciprocal mistrust. In the illegal market the function of brokers is crucial, since they take on some of the high risks of the exchanges, substituting the lack of trust between the participants and making possible deals that could be advantageous, but impossible to realize due to high transaction costs. In this context, the middleman's services "are necessary [...] because he has special knowledge of the procedures, access to officials, time to spend, and dirty hands" (Oldenburg 1987: 527). Often, mediators in corrupt exchanges are lawyers, brokers, real estate agents, former bureaucrats or managers, personal secretaries, or relatives, who are naturally or professionally more susceptible to creating trust relationships with the providers or recipients of bribes. They invest in specific professional skills (connected with their official job, consanguinity, or related to their previous activity) and furnish the corruption arena with several resources—trust, contacts, reputation, and confidential information—that are useful to win the confidence of those who want to participate in very profitable and risky exchanges, as well as to spread trust and push people to cooperate. By passing on information, however, the brokers also reduce transaction costs and, in particular, the risks of being denounced.

A broker played a crucial role, for instance, in the case involving Cornel Panescu, the owner of a Romanian football team who "is thought to have bribed top referees in order to secure favourable outcomes to his team": accounting documents "show that the middleman, one of Panescu's managers, withdrew funds after rigged matches in amounts equal to what the bribed referees had been promised in phone conversations" (*Southern European Times*, May 6, 2009). A former U.S. congressman and cochairman of the congressional caucus on African trade was also allegedly acting as a middleman: a businesswoman handed him a $100,000 bribe, "which he said he would give to the then-Nigerian Vice President Atiku Abubakar as a bribe to facilitate a business deal"; $90,000 was found by federal officers "wrapped in aluminum foil and tucked inside frozen containers in his Capitol Hill home," in a corruption scheme which also included telecommunications deals in Nigeria and Ghana, oil concessions in Equatorial Guinea, and waste-recycling systems in Nigeria (*Washington Post*, June 8, 2009). Arms deals are generally infrequent, involve a small circle of decision-makers and significant amounts of money: for instance, a middleman allegedly obtained contacts and paid bribes to agents and officials in central European countries "as inducements to secure, or as a rewards for having secured, contracts from those governments for the supply of [...] Saab/Gripen fighter jets" (*Guardian*, January 29, 2010). In the oil business, too, interactions are typically sporadic, involving few individuals (often national leader of less developed countries and a few multinational companies), allowing the collection of huge rents: a context in which individual corruption may flourish. For example, "an American intermediary, J.G., was indicted in 2003 for violation of the US foreign corrupt practice act by allegedly paying US78 million to top political officials in Kazakhstan on behalf of Mobil (now ExxonMobil)" (TI-2005: 69).

There are some features of the activities of judges that also facilitate individual corruption (see Chapter 4). Their decisions are a potential resource in corrupt exchanges, as they can have very relevant consequences in economic terms or in terms of individual freedom. Moreover, the decisional process involves a very limited number of people. A paradigmatic case occurred in Italy, involving only three actors: the judge of a regional tributary commission, a consultant for that very commission, and an entrepreneur. There was one and only one occasion for an exchange, with high stakes, however. Playing a broker function, the consultant asked the entrepreneurs for a bribe (€40,000) in exchange for a favorable decision on the fiscal detraction of a €23 million financing package that had been given to the firm in 2004. The bribe was divided into two parts: the first to be paid, in cash, before the sentence, and the second to be paid as remuneration for a fake consultancy bill by the firm to an English association indicated by the broker. This is the broker's approach to the consultant: "On Friday you'll get the proposal [...] you agree on it [...] and pay half of the amount. Then we'll do the rest." Notwithstanding his cautious behavior and experience, confirming the high risks involved in this type of exchange, the consultant was arrested after the entrepreneurs recorded the conversation and took him to court (*Corriere della Sera*, April 8, 2010). In the African context, the presence of "family brokers" in judicial corruption is diffused: "One doesn't say no to one's family, as not to appear churlish," admits a Senegalese judge (Alou 2006: 150).

Another area where individual corruption may spread is medical care. In these cases, too, the resources at stake are very large, often they are invaluable, as they involve health and life expectations. Decisions of life or death are usually taken by one or a few doctors. As a consequence, they can be sold on the market for corrupt exchanges. In Poland, for instance,

> the head of the Department of Neurology at University Hospital was arrested on charges of demanding bribes for hospital services and arranging for patients to receive immediate care when they should have been put on waiting lists. [...] In February 2007, a heart surgeon at the Defense Ministry Hospital in Warsaw was charged with murder after prosecutors said he turned off the life-support system of a patient whose family refused to pay him a bribe [...] . Patients pay to ensure quality care, to guarantee access to hospital treatment, to skip waiting lists for operations or complicated diagnostic procedures, even to get sick-leave certificates for their employers. (*Krakow Post*, July 5, 2007)

Structural corruption has three distinguishing features:

> (a) All, or almost all activities within a certain public organization are oriented or related to the collection of bribes.
> (b) All, or almost all, agents in the organization are implicated in an invisible network, which is regulated by unwritten norms and a commonly understood allocation of tasks and roles. Its activities include the collection of bribes and their distribution, the socialization of newcomers, the isolation

or banishment of "honest" agents, the camouflage and protection from external inquiries, and the definition of internal rules and their enforcement. (c) All, or almost all, private agents in contact with the organization know the "rules of the game" and are willing to pay bribes to obtain the benefits allocated as a result.

The endogenous dynamics of corruption are drastically modified by the expectation of the regular reiteration of interactions, even when the resources at stake—rents and bribes—are small in size. The perspective of a *repetition of the game* makes confidence, conditional cooperation, and reputational resources crucial in the choice of bribers and bribee to "follow the rules" or cheat, allowing for a growth of scale in the management of illegal deals.

As agents get closer to the ideal of *impersonal exchange*, where contracts must be specified in more detail and more elaborate safeguards developed to enforce compliance, "the lack of third-party enforcement leads to elaborate efforts to establish repeated dealings and clientization, to use kinship ties, and to set the trade within the context of ritual and religious precepts in order to constrain the participants" (North 1984: 259). When hidden exchanges are repeated over longer periods of time, information tends to spread among participants on their past accomplishment of corrupt deals, and similarly their expectations may converge toward a common observance of more punctual and structured norms.[16] Similar norms, codes, and rituals fulfill some basic functions: the identification of trustworthy partners, the weakening of moral discomfort, the socialization of newcomers, and the banishment of honest actors.

The *basic norm* of the invisible order of structural corruption states the unavoidability of bribes, thus generating and confirming expectations that corruption cannot be avoided in obtaining valuable "resources" such as contracts, licenses, concessions, red-tape cutting, information, a lack of checks, or avoided fines from (or within) the public structure involved. As a taxi driver from Kampala, Uganda, puts it, "All I need to know for my work is the name of the traffic officer on duty. Each time they stop me, I just give them something and they let me go" (TI-2001: 70). This type of corruption can overlap with the whole range of public activities. Its pervasiveness may dictate the rules of everyday life for common citizens, as in the case of urban Kenyans, who in 2002 paid on average 16 bribes per month (TI-2003: 242). In this context precise rates of bribe-payment often tend to emerge—a situation captured by an expression used in public contracting, namely,

---

[16] Strategically, as demonstrated by game-theoretical models, the repetition of a "prisoner's dilemma" situation without a certain end may produce different equilibria, including a "conditional cooperation" outcome based on the combination of tit-for-tat strategies (Axelrod 1984). Agents try to cooperate—i.e., do not denounce or cheat in their corrupt deals—and continue to do so as long as others do the same, otherwise they retaliate, excluding "dishonest" partners from future affairs. Similarly, a rational investment in one's reputation of "trustworthiness" may be the optimal strategy in a similar context, allowing for a positive conclusion of particular exchanges (Dasgupta 1988).

the "X percent law"—and this regularity reduces information and bargaining costs, since there is no need to ask and negotiate the amount of the bribe each time. In Lebanon, according to a satirical article in a popular newspaper, "bribes should not be confused with official fees, [which are] usually payable on top of the bribe": an illustration was given about "how much must be paid in bribes for different kinds of bureaucratic transactions. For example, a replacement driving license requires US$7 bribe, car registration US27$, and passport renewal almost US$70. The baksheesh [bribe] for a building permit for a residential house can cost more than US$2000" (TI-2003: 206).

Frequent and small corrupt exchanges lie at the perimeter of what Scott (1972: 89) defines as price or market corruption:

> It is precisely in those areas of government activity involving a large number of small transactions—the issuance of drivers' licenses and permits for village market stalls, the settlement of minor criminal charges, the acquisition of seats or freight space on railway cars, to mention but a few—that "price" corruption is common. Over time, it is also in these areas that market corruption tends to become institutionalized so that there is a widely known and rather stable price for a particular action.

In this case the corrupt exchanges are far from being occasional events in a chaotic and disorganized market. On the contrary, they are *structured* and regulated by a defined set of norms of behavior, establishing who to get in touch with, what to say (or not to say), what expressions can be used as part of the "jargon of corruption," how much to pay, and so on (see Chapter 3). See, for instance, how a shortage in the public supply of water generated a universally adopted mechanism of competitive corruption:

> A group of valve attendants traverses the city every day, opening and closing valves to distribute water—district by district and even street by street. Along the way, rich people bribe them in order to get more water. But they also compete with slum water associations (*comités de l'eau*), which also bribe valve attendants to fill their storage tanks for resale. (TI-2008: 53)

In similar contexts, corruption becomes a sort of self-fulfilling prophecy. The perception that such a norm is widely implemented increases the economic advantages to be had from compliance, as well as lowering the moral barriers against doing so. In the daily reality of Cameroon, for instance, taxi drivers customarily pay small bribes to police officers, from whom they "acquire" the right to work without further problems: "taxi drivers are routinely forced to bribe police officers FCFA 1,000 (US$2) or more for imaginary offences as 'refusal to carry passengers' 'blocking the public highway' or having a 'double windscreen' in the case of drivers who wear glasses" (TI-2005: 124).

Ample empirical evidence of structural corruption has emerged in past as well as in more recent Italian inquiries. To take a few recent cases in a "minor" sector, in Caserta, 32 hospital administrators and undertakers were arrested or investigated for their involvement in a cartel of firms involved in regular payments of "€100 for each corpse to be buried, approximately €5,000 monthly," in exchange for "the immediate release of information on deaths occurring at the hospital" (TRCAS: 2). A similar organization was uncovered in 2008 in Milan, where funerals in eight public hospitals were monopolized by 19 firms, with sales proceeds of €150,000 daily and amounts of between 5 and 10 percent being paid to hospital officials as bribes for each type of service delivered. The bribe money was pooled and subsequently redistributed according to the roles of those involved—these included senior administrators as well as male nurses (R-Milan, October 18, 2008; R, February 4, 2009). In Turin, in 2001, a customary agreement between 35 undertakers, male nurses, and administrators attached to three public hospitals was uncovered. The agreement regulated the payment of bribes of fixed amounts for confidential information about deaths. The group's dealings were managed through a common account for the receipt of bribe money, and records of incomings and outgoings (*Corriere della Sera*, June 21, 2001: 16). In 2007 an analogous situation emerged once again in Turin when eight male nurses and four undertakers were arrested and prosecuted. Administrators took bribes—of between €50 and €300 per corpse—on a daily basis with the money subsequently being shared among the agents involved: "Everything revolves around [...] money: the funerals and literally everything else, absolutely everything " is the comment of one undertaker whose conversation was secretly intercepted (R-Turin, February 7, 2007: 31).

The vulnerability of funeral homes to structural corruption is related to the internal characteristics of the exchange: corrupt agents may regularly get in touch with the same participants in a cartel of funeral homes. Moreover, they do not sell them a decision, but something less compromising and difficult to prove, that is, immediate information on deaths in hospitals. Even if the single bribes are small, they can form a significant flow of income over time. In some cases, corrupt agents were to a certain extent internalized by corrupting firms through a regular monthly fee, becoming their hidden employers. This successful model has been applied in different national contexts ranging from Poland (*Krakow Post*, July 5, 2007) to China (*China Daily*, January 14, 2010) to Hong Kong. In the latter case, according to a statement by the Independent Commission Against Corruption (ICAC), five serving and one former mortuary attendant as well as eight funeral agents were arrested on suspicion of corruption: "Inquiries revealed that the arrested mortuary staff had allegedly accepted monthly bribe payments from a number of funeral agents as reward for giving preferential treatment to the latter" (*Straight Times*, January 20, 2009). Similarly, in Chicago 30 police officers were incriminated for accepting bribes ranging from $40 to $100 for each body by five funeral directors. Policemen were often assigned to transport bodies to a hospital so a doctor could legally pronounce the person dead before being taken to a funeral home: policemen simply bypassed the closest funeral home at their discretion to bring the bodies to the five corrupting funeral directors (*Chicago Tribune*, December 23, 1988).

In *systemic corruption* a fourth condition has to be added to those characterizing structural corruption:

(d) Third-party enforcers monitor and enforce the respect of the (illegal) norms, guaranteeing the fulfillment of corruption contracts and—eventually—imposing sanctions on opportunistic agents and free riders.

The increasing complexity of corrupt exchanges is a corollary of (1) the greater amount of resources at stake, implying a higher rate of returns for free riders, (2) the repetition of interactions with a potential enlargement of corrupt networks, and (3) the specialization of actors in corruption skills, with more assets—whose attributes are difficult to measure and evaluate—coming into play and more agents potentially involved in the commerce in different roles. In this context, the maintenance of a satisfactory degree of internal order and stability requires robust governance structures, while complex contracting activities, as well as objective difficulties in monitoring and enforcing fragile property rights in illegal performances, tend to increase their transaction costs. Neither self-enforcement by the partners themselves, nor trust or reputational assets may be sufficient here, since strong incentives toward cheating and shirking push for the opportunistic violation of the informal rules of corruption. In this case the model of corruption is similar to the "impersonal exchange with third-party enforcement. [...] Third-party enforcement is never ideal, never perfect, and the parties to exchange still devote immense resources to attempting to clientize exchange relationships. But neither self-enforcement by parties not trust can be completely successful [...] . A coercive third party is essential" (North 1990: 35). Third-party enforcement "requires, besides the power to enforce, the commitment to enforce and the ability to adjudicate. Enforcers tend to differ in their ability to adjudicate" (Barzel 2002: 25).

When a third-party enforcement mechanism is in operation, more intricate networks of exchange may develop, since both economic incentives and social forces push toward the generalized acceptance of illegal deals. In systemic corruption, thereafter, "the illicit becomes the norm and [...] corruption so common and institutionalized that those behaving illegally are rewarded and those continuing to accept the older norms penalized" (Caiden and Caiden 1977: 306). When interactions take place regularly and frequently, and the allocation of valuable resources is influenced by public agents, corruption tends to become systemic within the corresponding public organization as soon as norms and third-party enforcement mechanisms emerge.

Systemic corruption is regulated by a system of informal rules of behavior (see also Chapter 3), and thus the building of an informal organizational framework with structured roles that often partly overlaps with institutional roles within public or private organizations, but is also influenced by control over other resources (illegal skills, confidential information, control of illegal funds, etc.) within the corrupt deals. In this case all, or almost all, public and private agents are involved—more or less directly—in the business of corruption, often in connivance with other control structures and agents not directly involved in corruption. In the case of former Soviet countries, for instance, "the informal institutions of systemic corruption are cemented in myriads of networks that pervade the state apparatus and crisscross the state-society boundaries" (Stefes 2007: 6). In the Wuhan Intermediate People's Court in China, investigations uncovered "a network of graft connecting judges and court officials at all levels under the lead of two senior judicial staff." Two judges operated as ringleaders—thanks to their official positions at the top of the Court— managing and regulating all-pervasive illegal activities involving more than 100 other judges, court officials, and lawyers, and pocketing a total of 4 million yuan in bribes: "The Wuhan case exposed a sophisticated scheme of corruption within the court system and demonstrated how multiple levels of judges and administrators were able to form circles of mutual benefit and profit" (Brief 2005: 30). Bribes were taken in exchange for several valuable resources, including evidence for court cases, passing cases to certain personnel, (not) ordering suspensions of business or confiscations of property, beneficial judgments, manufacturing court cases, and so on.

The situation of the Hong Kong police in the 1970s, according to a study commissioned by the governor, was close to the ideal type of systemic corruption, as illegal activities were precisely organized and disciplined. It was called "syndicated" corruption, since whole groups of officers were involved in the collection and redistribution of money:

> It is said that Police corruption is, for the most part, 'syndicated' and that corruption on an individual basis is frowned upon by the organizers of these 'syndicates'. [...] There is a saying in Hong Kong: 1. 'Get on the bus,' i.e., if you wish to accept corruption, join us; 2. 'Run alongside the bus', i.e., if you do not wish to accept corruption, it matters not, but do not interfere; 3. 'Never stand in front of the bus', i.e., if you try to report corruption, the 'bus' will knock you down and you will be injured or even killed or your business will be ruined. (Klitgaard et al. 2000: 18–9)

Systemic corruption is a regulated market activity whose enforcement is assured by third-party specialized enforcers. The protection they provide, which depends on their institutional role, is more valuable when extended from a guarantee of precarious rights in illegal deals to a more general, wide-ranging safeguard against any kind of judicial control or administrative inefficiency. See, for instance, the requests made by the South African deputy president, who "came into investigations for allegations that he attempted to solicit a bribe from Thompson's South African head in return for protecting the company from investigations and giving its 'permanent support'" (TI-2004: 61).

When the corresponding rules become an invisible guide to behavior, uncertainty is reduced. For example, identification costs almost disappear when the payment of bribes is accompanied by widespread—and realistic—beliefs that they are inevitable, reinforced by the bad reputation of public agents who smoothly introduce new entrants (both corrupters and corruptees) into the market. Systemic corruption therefore has the strongest roots and may easily become a self-sustained phenomenon (see Chapter 9). The exit of more honest agents from highly corrupt public and private structures in fact produces a selection process of new members on the basis of their ability and expected willingness to be corrupted and/or to corrupt.

Third-party Enforcers in the Market for Corrupt Exchanges

As we have seen, in the world of corruption, information on illegal deals and opportunities is scarce and asymmetrically distributed: the attributes of the resources at stake are costly to measure, and personal loyalty and other cultural or ideological ties play—at best—a limited role, with risks and uncertainty discouraging participation. In this context, the role of some "coercive" third parties may be crucial to reduce the transaction costs of corruption. On a much smaller scale, and obviously with less effectiveness and more dysfunctional side-effects, corruption enforcers provide *protective services* comparable to those offered by Western liberal-democratic states, which were crucial in the development of wider, complex market economies based on property rights and the division and specialization of labor (North 1990). Besides the state, whose protective services are not available in illegal activities or nonmarket exchanges, "various distinct organizations offer third party adjudication and enforcement. These include, among others, families, firms, religious organizations, local governments, and criminal organizations. Such organizations may be in opposition to the 'legitimate' power-backed third-party enforcer, independent of him, or subordinate to him" (Barzel 2002: 28). Third-party enforcement allows—especially in illegal arenas where potential gains are significant and distributed over long periods of time—for a more precise subdivision of roles to prevent or rapidly solve potentially dangerous disputes over contested rights and irreconcilable expectations, thereby allowing for a peaceful practice of bribe-collection and rent-sharing among individuals and organizations operating within the corrupt network.

A variety of third-party enforcers, as we will see in the following chapters, use different resources to adjudicate disputes in corrupt deals. Both public and private actors can play such a role: public bureaucrats and politicians are among the former, and entrepreneurs and organized crime among the latter. Such actors contribute to enforce the hidden order of systemic corruption, using resources such as money, but also information, favors, and threats.

In this perspective, the definition and protection of property rights over political rents, that is, the sanctioning of corrupt agreements and the resolution of quarrels, require various actors to be able to impose costs in cases of defection (or, conversely, to administer positive incentives for fulfillment). The resources available for the main actors in each type of corruption, as we will see in the following chapters, influence their specific dynamics and the conditions for their development. According to their role and potential access to other sources of influence, enforcers will use different resources to guarantee the fulfillment of illegal deals, imposing costs both by the use of violence and by other means, in particular the threat of terminating long-term relationships. As Barzel observes,

> A third party must be able to impose costs in order to induce each of the principals to an agreement to make one-way transfers to the other. The enforcer induces the parties to an agreement to perform in situations in which they would not be inclined to perform on their own. He does so by threatening to impose costs on them. The amount of cost-imposing power that a third party possesses sets a limit on what he can enforce. Parties making an agreement subject to third-party enforcement will comply only if they think that enforcer is able and willing to impose a cost at least as large as the required transfer. (Barzel 2002: 42)

For instance, a bureaucratic office not only provides the opportunity for receiving bribes but may also supply the "resources of authority" necessary to enforce corrupt deals (Lambsdorff 2007: 223). We may take as an illustration the activities of Mr. X, a manager and civil servant in a third-world country, who works in an office responsible for procurement through international bidding. Through the distribution of benefits and the implicit threat of imposing costs via exclusion from the "inner circle" where rents were allocated, he became the crucial "regulator" of a wide network of people and companies:

> The use of unnecessary intermediaries was designed to spread the profits among persons/companies in Mr. X's circle. Mr. X made close personal ties to the persons owning and running these selected companies. Some of these persons knew each other. Mr. X created a hidden, but to some extent organized, criminal circle where everyone was aware of each other's roles, and more or less dependent on each other, and on Mr. X. The selected companies frequently appeared on the invitation lists, often without any "outsider"-suppliers being invited, at other times together with one or a few more bidders that were almost irrelevant under the circumstances. Sometimes it was clear in advance which of the companies would get the order, even when several of the selected companies appeared on the invitation list. The remaining ones were put on the invitation list only to make sure that the requirement of a certain number of invitations to be sent out was met. (OECD 2007: 81)

Similarly, in a case involving Italian civil defense contracting activities, the leading enforcer was the highest level bureaucrat, who had the ability "to manage his power by distributing favors among several entrepreneurs under his protection, and composing possible quarrels deriving from unsatisfied expectations on public contracts, therefore avoiding potential denunciations by disappointed entrepreneurs" (TRFIR: 64–5).

Summarizing some of the arguments we develop in the following chapters, in Table 2.2 we distinguish several actors that may assume the role of guarantors within the market for corruption, specifying the main resources they can use to protect illegal deals, whether by threatening or applying sanctions, some facilitating conditions for their success, and the weaknesses and strengths of their enduring activities. When they are active in systemic corruption, partners in illegal deals may count on a more precise specification of their fragile "rights" and the expectations at stake in the corrupt exchanges, corresponding to the informal rules

Table 2.2   Third-party guarantors in systemic corruption: Actors, resources, facilitating conditions

Type of third-party enforcer	Structure of the protection system	Resources used to enforce corrupt exchanges	Facilitating conditions	Strengths	Weaknesses
Political party	Hierarchical	Internal appointment, protection of political careers (nomination to public positions, candidacy, electoral support, etc.)	Centralized parties, strength of ideological appeals, clientelism	Exploits party loyalty besides material incentives	De-legitimizes parties
Political-bureaucratic clan	Network	Personal influence, rewards, favors, and exclusion from the net of relationships between public and private actors	Fragmented parties, weakness of ideological appeals, political patronage over bureaucratic structures	Dense network	Localized control; Centrifugal tendencies
High-level bureaucrat	Hierarchical	Control over access to benefits deriving from public decision-making, control over subordinates' career	Hierarchical, formalistic bureaucratic structures; political patronage; weak bureaucrats' identification in the state	Close, robust, and enduring network	Limited in its scale of operation
Political actor/ Boss of the public body	Hierarchical	Power to allocate public resources and benefits, influence over bureaucrats' careers	Fragmented parties, weakness of ideological appeals, political patronage over bureaucratic structures	Personal loyalty of followers and clients	Operating on a low-scale or in circumscribed context, destroying party loyalty and legitimization

Type of third-party enforcer	Structure of the protection system	Resources used to enforce corrupt exchanges	Facilitating conditions	Strengths	Weaknesses
Entrepreneur-Cartel	Market/Network	Economic resources, information, access to cartelized regulation of public markets	Noncompetitive (public) markets, monopolistic rents	Low visibility	Selective operation
Broker	Network	Information, power to exclude from network of exchange	Opacity and slowness in public decision-making, lack of confidence in the state and public agents	Professional and efficient coordination of corrupt deals	Pivotal role of the broker which may produce a collapse in case of involvement in judicial inquiries
Criminal organization/Mafia boss	Hierarchical	Coercive (violence, intimidation), reputation	Lack of trust in public institutions, widespread belief in inefficiency of public procedures, extensive presence of illegal markets, demand for private protection	Very high costs of denunciation and "exit" from the corrupt exchange	Centrifugal tendency and violent conflicts between criminal organizations

and norms of systemic (i.e., institutionalized) corruption, and thus safeguarding themselves from unpleasant surprises and disappointment. The expected costs and risks of the corrupt transaction are reduced; the perception of costs is mitigated by their socialization to the "rules" of corruption; the costs of free riding, opportunism, and defection increase correspondingly (thanks to their control over long-term relationships); and the advantages of compliance with others' corruption increases, due to coordination mechanisms.

As indicated in the third column of the same table, several resources can be invested to induce corrupt agents to comply with the (explicitly or implicitly) agreed terms of the exchange, mainly through the implicit threat of imposing a cost, but also with the prospect of future benefits: the potential use of coercion, deriving from the enforcers' role within a legal or illegal organization; influence over the delegation of public authority; ideological rewards; and information and economic resources, derived mainly from a strategic position within a net of relationships between public and private actors, with the power to guarantee or deny access to privileged knowledge, advice, or profitable exchange opportunities.

To sum up, several resources are used by more or less "specialized" individuals and organizations to enforce corrupt agreements. Third-parties' sanctioning powers may be based on the threat of coercion, the capacity to impose direct physical costs to induce parties to fulfill their obligations in corrupt contracts, as well as ideological appeals. Criminal organizations, for instance, have the power to enforce illegal deals by using force, as well as their reputation of violent guarantors, to adjudicate disputes (see Chapter 8). Party leaders and cashiers (see Chapter 5), bosses in public structures, or high-ranking bureaucrats (see Chapter 4) may use their control over public decision-making processes—whose implementation is guaranteed by the coercive authority of the state—to impose costs on cheaters in corruption contracts. The influence of political bosses, as well as top bureaucrats, over the allocative power of party machines and public structures adds to their enforcement power. They can, in fact, use as an enforcing mechanism their ability to realistically rule out partners in corrupt deals from other benefits derived from repeated *legal* interactions with public bodies or party structures: career perspectives for lower-level bureaucrats, support for nominations to publicly appointed positions or candidatures for elected politicians, awards of public contracts or licenses to entrepreneurs, and so on. Within the party organization, leaders may also appeal to common ideological values to obtain the compliance of corrupt members. Another crucial resource for sanctioning is the control of economic resources and information, which can guarantee profitable long-term relationships (Barzel 2002: 42). The enforcers—which in some cases are also brokers (see Chapter 7) or entrepreneurs (see Chapter 6)—can strategically use their position within a web of relationships, threatening to deprive the partners from the expected benefits of future opportunities.

Chapter 3
Corruption as a Normative System

At the beginning of 2003, a heart surgeon admitted to judges that, in his hospital, "a system of bribes has existed since my arrival in 1982." Bribes were collected by doctors on delivery of "oxygenators, valves, tubes, perhaps even thread, gowns, instruments and scalpels" (R-Turin, February 1, 2003). The scandal spread, revealing a well-developed system at the national level involving pharmaceutical firms and doctors. At the end of the 1990s, another doctor had been accused of distributing money and gifts to colleagues (175 of them were later found guilty) who sent their patients to his private hospital for nuclear medicine for tests; he was also paid as a consultant by the then president of the regional committee for public health (TRMI03). A multinational was accused of offering "travel, books computers, and hi-fis to the doctors that were more active in assigning its pharmaceutical products to their patients (R, February 12, 2003). According to legal investigations, those contributions were solicited by the doctors—"I am not the porter—said one of them—I am the director. And if you gave 40,000 Euros to my assistant ..." (R, February 13, 2003).[1]

One witness described the doctor that directed a center for nuclear medicine in the following words: "he was a maniac as far as attachment to money is concerned"; the witness recalled the frequent aggression against promoters because doctors did not send patients in, or not enough '[...] You can do nothing. Why does the doctor not send? You have to convince him! You have to tell him that we are available to all [...] so, the promoters first tried to convince them, highlighting the scientific aspects and the rapid timing, then started to offer various types of advantages (free examinations for the all family, highly discounted prices for medical machines, travel [...] and then, to those who showed no interest in the general discourse, they offered a sum of money proportional to the number of exams (between 50 and 100 thousand lira)" (TRMI03: 42).

This description of a normative system in-the-making stresses greed as a motivation for illegal actions. The preference for material advantage is so strong that any moral scruple is overcome. Scandals in the health system are particularly

---

[1] In Italy, scandals in the health system proliferated even after the Clean Hands investigations, including fake certificates to cheat insurance companies (R-Rome, January 17, 2003), the prescription of useless tests (R-Milan, January 21, 2003), a preferential fast-track for operations (R, September 5, 2004; R-Palermo, February 25, 2005), the purchase of deteriorated materials (R-Turin, March 19, 2003; R, February 26, 2003), and the promotion of doctors, as well as the nomination of directors (R-Turin, June 1, 2004) or even information on dying patients to send to funeral houses (R, October 1, 2004; R-Genoa, June18, 2004; R-Turin, September 18, 2004; R-Florence, September 6, 2005).

interesting for an examination of the spread of a system of rules that supports behavior so far removed from legal norms as well as from the deontological codes of the professions involved. Starting from these episodes, in this chapter we look at the cultural mechanisms that lie at the basis of the spread of corruption, sustaining a system of alternative but deep-rooted norms.

Among the various factors that can push a corrupt public or private agent to violate legal norms are his ethical standards. These have been labeled in different ways in the various approaches to corruption: moral costs in economic theory, cultural norms in comparative politics, professional standards in constructivist perspectives, and informal constraints in neo-institutional theory. In this chapter, we analyze the different ways of looking at ethical standards, focusing on the role that the enlarged reproduction of certain illicit norms plays in the governance of corruption. In particular, we focus on the ways in which norms have been addressed as negative incentives in the economic approach and national cultures in comparative politics, highlighting some of the limits of both approaches. We then reconstruct the professional cultures of the actors involved in corruption as well as the mechanisms for neutralizing the moral costs of corruption and for strengthening alternative norms. We stress the need for social research on corruption to move beyond not only the methodological individualism on which rational choice approaches are based but also the generic statements about "national cultures" and to look instead at the ways in which norms and institutions that facilitate illegal behavior are created and reproduced through individual corrupt actions and belief-shaping.

The Economic Approach to Moral Costs

A Kuwaiti diplomat committed 249 violations of illegal parking between April 1999 and end of the year; 526 violations in 2000—that is more than 10 per week—and 351 by August 2001. These occurred not only around the UN building in New York, but throughout Manhattan, and especially Greenwich Village and the Upper East Side, areas renowned for wining and dining. This could appear as a rational choice, as the city of New York could not punish diplomats for parking violations: "Just as no rational person should leave a $20 bill lying on the ground, why should any diplomat leave a perfectly good double parking spot unoccupied?" (Fishman and Miguel 2008: 87). However, "Turning from bon vivant Kuwaiti Ambassador X to the Norwegian U.N. Mission staff, we catch our first glimpse of Non-Economic Man. Despite New York's inability to punish diplomatic scofflaws, no Norwegian diplomat accumulated a single unpaid parking violation in New York City during our sample period. The same holds true for their Nordic neighbors, the Swedes" (Fishman and Miguel 2008: 87). In fact, the same research noted a high correlation between a country's (World Bank) ranking on the political corruption index and parking violations by diplomats in NYC, with the average annual unpaid parking violations per diplomat ranging from 11 for low corruption countries to 29 for high corruption ones.

As material costs cannot account for these differences, political economy analysis resorts to moral costs, defined as the utility that is lost because of the illegality of an action, to explain them. These increase therefore with the development of a value system that supports respect for the law. Moral costs reflect internalized beliefs, such as esprit de corps and the "public spiritedness" of officials, political culture, and public attitudes toward illegality. In economic terms, we may distinguish between two concepts of moral cost. In a *macro-analytic* perspective, moral costs are one of the dimensions along which the negative effects of corruption within a certain society can be measured. Besides *economic* and *political* costs (the waste of economic resources in rent-seeking activities, the adverse selection of public agents and firms operating in the public sector, the inefficiency of public actions, the delegitimization of political institutions, etc.), the widespread practice and perception of high levels of corruption also tend to produce *moral* costs, undermining the "moral values" and ethical codes that sustain cooperative and common-interest inspired strategies within public and private organizations.[2]

In a *micro-analytic* perspective, instead, the notion of the moral cost has been used to describe not the *effects*, but one of the factors inducing individual actors to engage in corrupt activities. As mentioned (see Chapter 1) previously, according to economic models, the institutional system of incentives and opportunities explains the choice of corruption as the rational path of action. The probability of being discovered and punished and the severity of the potential punishment (i.e., the *expected* cost), as well as the expected rewards, as compared with the available alternatives, form part of the equation: "In a study of corruption, one can make substantial progress with models that take tastes and values as given and perceive individuals as rational beings attempting to further their self-interest in a world of scarce resources. Information may be imperfect; risks may abound; but individuals are assumed to do the best they can within the constraints imposed by a finite world" (Rose-Ackerman 1978: 5).

These two notions of moral costs—as negative effects and as a factor affecting corruption choices—are obviously interwoven: "The definition of bribes and gifts is a cultural matter, but 'culture' is dynamic and constantly changing. [...] If, however, these practices are imposing hidden or indirect costs on the populace, analysts can clarify and document these costs. Definitions of acceptable behavior may change once people are informed of the costs of tolerating payoffs to politicians and public servants" (Rose-Ackerman 1999: 110).

Moral costs therefore structure the preferences that affect corruption choices: they represent the loss of utility that derives from "engaging in an illegal action" (Rose-Ackerman 1978: 113). Actors still have *given* preferences—they want to have *more* rather than *less* (utility or money)—but their calculations also include this "moral" component. The problematic coexistence between these two distinct

---

[2]   See, for instance, Pasuk and Piriyarangsan (1998), who identify a "moral cost" of corruption in its unequal distributive effects, making a few individuals very wealthy.

sets of motivations is vividly described by a corrupt Christian Democrat local administrator, who as a Catholic frequently silenced his sense of guilt attending confession with his spiritual father (who also absolved): "In me there was a dual attitude: a vocation to honesty, but also the desire to have a career. And collecting bribes for the party was a way to jump to a higher level, to conquer leaders' trust" (*Panorama*, July 12, 1992: 54).

The higher the moral cost for a given agent, the stronger will be his "preference for law-fulfillment" (that is, the kind of *psychological suffering* associated with the violation of legal norms), influenced by his personal preferences as well as by the values and informal codes prevailing in the organization where he has been socialized, and the lower the expected monetary gain from bribery. So, conceived moral costs are expressed in monetary terms and considered a positive function of the bribe.[3] Unsurprisingly, economic models demonstrate an inverse correlation between levels of moral costs and corruption: since moral costs reduce the total expected benefit of corruption, they also restrict the set of acceptable bribes for public agents (Rose-Ackerman 1978: 122). Since individuals have different values, their choices will vary even when they are subject to the same (or similar) institutional constraints.

Given that moral costs influence the individual's choice about violating the law, their distribution in the population influences the overall level of corruption. The assumption that moral costs have a *given* structure within a certain society reflects the attempt of economic models to "sterilize" the influence of cultural factors and social values on corruption practices as a whole, by concentrating on the effects of variation in institutional constraints. As Gambetta puts it, since "the distribution of probabilities of acting illegally within a certain population has a normal form," we will find in every society very few incorruptible or unconditionally corrupt agents, while most will decide if and when to be corrupt according to expected benefits and costs (Gambetta 1988: 240).[4] But assuming the distribution has a bell-form does not provide sufficient grounds to exclude "moral" and other informal constraints from the explanation of corruption. It is the not the relative, but the *absolute level* of such costs, reflecting internalized beliefs (such as the esprit de corps, the "public spiritedness" of public officials, political culture,

---

[3]   The underling hypothesis is that moral costs are either constant, a sort of "fixed cost" of corruption, or increase as the size of the bribe increases (Rose-Ackerman 1978: 121). Johnson (1975) and Alam (1990) employ an analogous concept of "aversion to corruption," defined as the value of the marginal revenue of corruption relative to that of legal activities. Qizilbash (1994) presents a model of "moral character," using a formal definition of temptation to describe agents, who can be continent or incontinent, which in turn influences their corruption choices.

[4]   Aidt (2003: 636), for instance, presents a model according to which "some tax collectors are more honest than others, possibly because of internalised moral costs. To capture this heterogeneity, I assume that a fraction (c) of all potential tax collectors are honest, while the rest (1 - c) are willing—if it is in their personal interest—to misinform the government in return for a bribe."

and public attitudes toward illegality in different societies and over time), that influences the diffusion of corrupt practices (Pizzorno 1992: 43). The substantial variations in the perception of corruption that may be observed among states with similar legal systems and formal institutions (see Figure 1.2)—that is, comparable monetary incentives and opportunities for corruption—can in fact be explained by differences in levels of moral costs (and the characteristics of their distribution).

The practice of corruption in any given country will therefore be affected by a combination of these sets of variables: the expected economic benefit of corruption for individual actors, as well as the characteristics of their interrelated strategic choices; and the distribution of moral costs, which reflect prevailing cultural and social norms. Developed within rational choice approaches, the concept of moral costs reflects the notion that individuals are able to calculate the trade-off between various preferences and maximize their utilitarian interests. Moral costs are therefore just a component of the individual calculation about whether or not to engage in corruption: they are measurable, and they are measured by individuals. This notion is, implicitly or explicitly, challenged by comparative approaches that stress how several mechanisms can induce variations in values and cultures, not only among different individuals but also across groups, social contexts, states, and historical periods.

Comparing National Cultures: God, Family, and Social Capital

> Why did I give to him? He told me he had a bad situation at home [...] he came and begged me [...] . 'I really need help!' So I wrote him those cheques. Just to help him, as he was in a dangerous position. He risked divorce. (PRBA1: 19)

Here, an entrepreneur justifies the payment of a bribe as a sort of sensitivity to the family problems of a public agent. References to the family are frequent in corruption proceedings and are often used as sort of justification for a misdeed. These family (or familistic) attitudes and values are said to be particularly widespread in some cultures. The propensity to corruption observed in different countries—as well as the demand for protection provided by mafia-like organizations (Kawata 2006; see Chapter 8)—has been explained in comparative politics by, among other variables, specific national values, as crystallized in religion, family orientation, or confidence in the state. In this perspective, as Pareto notes, "the differences [between countries] are to be found in the substance, that is in the sentiment of the people; where they are more (or less) honest, there we find a more (or less) honest government" (Pareto 1916: 625). Elster, too, emphasizes the relevance of values: "Although it is hard to prove, [...] the variation in corruption across countries is explained largely by the degree of public-spiritedness of their officials, not by the cleverness of institutional design" (Elster 1989a: 158). And Mény (2000: 213) observes that "corruption is thus more likely to spread in cases where the 'immune defence systems' of the group tend to weaken and the 'moral cost' drops; as will occur when public behaviour is less prized than private, when producing results comes to matter more than observing standards, monetary values more than ethical or symbolic values." In cross-national comparison, it is the general issue of values especially (in particular, but not only, political values), as an aid in the spread of corruption, that has been discussed. Variations in values can therefore explain different individual responses to similar opportunities for corruption. Given similar institutional conditions, levels of political corruption will vary according to the average moral attitudes among the citizens and public administrators.

When looking for cultural traditions, norms, and values that inform the activities and choices of individuals belonging to different societies and organizations, a first observation, fueled initially by comparisons between European countries, points to *religion*. In particular, case studies have indicated that Protestant countries tend to have higher ethical standards, while corruption seems more widespread in Catholic countries, in particular in Southern Europe. From case studies and small-N comparisons, the analysis of the relationship between religion and corruption has expanded to macro-comparisons, using different measures of corruption as a dependent variable (often the TI index) and correlating them with statistical or survey data about religiosity. In research on 33 countries, La Porta et al. (1997: 337) found a positive correlation between hierarchical forms of religion (Catholicism, Eastern Orthodoxy, and Islam) and corruption—although in another piece of research on 114 countries, this correlation is significantly weakened if GDP per head is controlled for (La Porta et al. 1999: 251–2). Similar results are obtained in a macro-comparison, where levels of corruption emerge as negatively correlated with the percentage of Protestants in the total population (Treisman 2000: 428). According to Paldam (2001), corruption is also lower in countries with a large fraction of Reform Christianity and Tribal religions, and higher instead in countries with large influences from Pre- Reform Christianity, Islam, Buddhism, and Hinduism—with a particularly significant impact for Reform Protestants and Anglicans.

Catholicism has been seen to facilitate hierarchical relationships (because of the role the clergy acquires as a mediator between human beings and God), but also the possibility, via confession, to be absolved of guilt and guilty feelings. In the example quoted above, the feeling of discomfort with corruption was neutralized by a politician precisely via absolution of a Catholic spiritual guide (*Panorama*, July 12, 1992: 54). While the Protestant, Weberian "spirit of capitalism" develops individual responsibility, the Catholic religion socializes individuals to the possibility of buying their pardon via a formal act of contrition, which may even include material payments. In both Italy and Spain, the intertwining of spiritual and material powers has a long tradition in the function of the clergy as brokers within a clientelistic machine, where sponsorship of the local priest helps not only in finding absolution but also in terms of material rewards, such as a job or housing (Allum 1995). In Italy, this link between corruption and religious behavior is epitomized in the actions of the Neapolitan politician and former minister who, in order to thank God for the success of his surgery, asked an entrepreneur, with whom he was involved in illicit business deals, to give money to a Catholic charity: "He asked me to make a contribution of 100 million lire—10 million at Christmas and 10 at Easter, for 5 years—to the priest Salvatore D'Angelo for the 'Village of the child' in Maddaloni. He made this request when he came back from Houston where he had had heart surgery in 1984–5, specifying that he had made a vow to help those boys. [...] I objected that it seemed strange to me that I had to pay his votive offering, but he replied that *I* had to pay" (CD, n.344: 4). Personal responsibility for sin in the Protestant culture, on the other hand, is counterpoised to the institutional forgiveness of the Catholic Church, which reduces the moral costs of corruption by allowing cheap forgiveness: "Protestant cultures are less understanding towards lapses from grace and press more urgently to institutionalize virtue and cast out the wicked" (Treisman 2000 : 427). Moreover, Protestant societies tend to have more pronounced separations between the state and the church, and more vivacious civil society, as well as more tolerance for challenges to authority and individual dissent than Catholicism or Islam (Treisman 2000: 427–8).

Linking religious beliefs and political values more or less explicitly, research about *civic culture* has also reflected on the country-specific impact of values on the diffusion of corruption. Banfield, in his research on "amoral familism" in the Southern Italian village of Montegrano, observed that some values and norms affect the political capacity of a community to pursue public goods. According to him, widespread poverty was linked with amoral familism, which is the inability to act in the name of a collective good that goes beyond the immediate, material interest of the nuclear family. Amoral familism interacts with political behavior in so far as it is expected that nobody will pursue the interests of the community, and moreover that citizens will believe that all those in power are self-interested and corrupt. In a sort of self-fulfilling prophecy, the amoral familist in public administration will accept bribes when he does not fear punishment, and all members of society will assume that he is corrupt in any case (Banfield 1956: 92).

Family ties indeed emerge often in investigations on corruption—providing the strong bond of solidarity needed for risky activities. For instance, in relation to Sicily, Michele Pantaleoni has noted that "it is significant that of 18 entrepreneurs in public works [...] two are the direct relations of parliamentarians [...], three married to the children of national-level party leaders, one the son of the director of a regional assessor, another the son of the president of a public body" (Pantaleone 1984: 184). Very often, corrupt deals are justified by the need to secure support for an elderly mother or many growing children. Relatives offer a cover in material terms, but also psychological support, as well as a justification for "minor misdemeanors" in the name of a superior value. One functionary, for example, justified his attempt to collect bribes—by selling information on questions in a television quiz show—with the needs of his mother: "I did it because I wanted to, but I also didn't want to [...]. My mother has a heart disease, and a monthly pension of only 600.000 lira" (R, April 17, 1997: 21). Family loyalty often emerges in the manipulation of public competitions for positions as doctors in public hospitals, as well as in the medical faculties of universities (R-Bari, August 18, 2004), with frequent cases of positions passing as an inheritance from father to son (R, March 3, 2005). Even if these are cases of nepotism rather than corruption, they testify to the development of norms alternative to Weberian bureaucratic neutrality and constitute strong ties that can be useful to grant broad connivance when corruption develops.

Research on different countries has also indicated a strong link between political corruption and *patrimonialism*. In studies dealing with third-world countries, corruption has been linked to their patrimonial character, referring "not simply to the persistence in social relationships generally of personalistic principles of kinship, clanship and clientship, but, more crucially, to their inevitable invocation in dealing with the state" (Theobald 1996: 13).[5] In Spain, where political corruption became "the single most salient issue in Spanish politics" (Heywood 1995: 726; see also Pérez-Diaz 1996) in the 1990s, commentators explained its development with the traditional emphasis on *amiguismo*, involving the use of brokers in relationships with the public administration (Heywood 1997: 70–71). Studies of corruption in Portugal recall the long-standing presence of caciques, "influential local bosses such as priests, lawyers and others who were able to offer to the government in power bundles of votes from their local community" (Magone 1996: 9). Here, a neo-patrimonial structure and culture, inherited by the democratic state, has emerged since 1975. Many political scandals in Greece were labeled under the so-called patrimonial socialism as led by Andreas Papandreou (Magone 1996). As for Japan, another country in which corruption appears fairly widespread, the persistent weakness of the concept of public good, only lately and imperfectly distinguished from that of the private good among those in power (Bouissou 1997), has been often quoted. Corruption in the former French colonies in Africa was facilitated by the development of personalized relationships between the African leaders and their counterparts in France (Médard 1997).

More generally, the hypotheses that in uncivic cultures costs of corruption are lower developed within classical comparative research on political culture, stating that democratic quality depends upon *people's attitudes ves-a-vis the political process* (Almond and Verba 1963). More recently, Putnam (1993) developed similar hypotheses to explain institutional output: when civic values are widespread, politics is perceived as oriented to the public good, and politicians and citizens behave accordingly. In civic regions, citizens trust their politicians as honest, and politicians meet high moral standards; vice versa, in uncivic regions, both citizens and politicians consider corruption the rule and behave accordingly (Putnam 1993: 135). Macro comparisons indicate that generalized and institutional trust (as measured by the World Value Survey) has a significant negative impact on corruption, even when controlling for GDP per head (La Porta et al. 1997:

---

[5]   The survival of corruption, even after democratization, has been explained by the presence of a "soft state," i.e., "a state that fails to supersede personal, family, ethnic and tribal loyalties. Many elected presidents or democratically appointed officers do not perceive the boundaries between state and private finances [...] . This 'soft state' is perpetuated in new democracies because political institutions are usually very weak" (Pinheiro 1994: 38).

336; Uslaner 2005). Similarly, Husted (1999) found a correlation between the acceptance of inequalities and corruption.

Civicness is also linked with the respect for the law—that is, the internalization of the concept of a *Rechtstaat*. Pizzorno (1992: 66–8) focused on the development of public ethics, distinguishing between a political ethic (sense of politics) and a state ethic (sense of the state). The political ethic privileges, in political activity, long-term ends, referring to collectivities that do not coincide with the state territory (classes, ethnic, or religious groups, etc.). Those with a "sense of the state" instead perceive institutions as oriented toward the public good of the community, defined within state borders. In Italy, loyalty to the two political communities— the socialist and the Catholic—prevail over loyalty to the state, thus jeopardizing the development of a sense of respect for the law. Since the 1970s, the "sense of politics" has also diminished, weakening the moral constraints against corruption. As Johnston observes, the very notion of corruption is related to "the rise of a *'system of public order'*: a relatively durable framework of social and legal standards defining practical limits of behavior by holders of government roles, and by those who seek to influence them" (Johnston 1994: 11). If this system is not implemented, or internalized, corruption can develop. In fact, corruption spreads when corrupt behavior is not stigmatized by the elite and/or public opinion, then becoming "white" or "gray" forms of corruption (Heidenheimer 1970).

Like many cultural explanations, the explanation of corruption in terms of values has also been accused of describing its object more than accounting for it. As Heywood (1997: 70) mentions, "one of the most familiar, yet also one of the most easily dismissed, explanations of political corruption in Spain is one which relies on some notion of 'national character'[…] . Just as Germans are supposedly efficient, and the French stylish, so Spaniards are lazy and corrupt." An open question here is, first of all, why should an immoral society produce a corrupt political class? The response that the political class is usually selected from within that population is not fully satisfactory, since specific positions/professions involve specific paths of socialization. A parallel explanation could be that, in an amoral society, politicians do not have to fear stigmatization (and electoral withdrawal) if they are caught in their corrupt deals. Here as well, however, Italian as well as Spanish history (but also the vicissitudes of many regime crises in Southern countries) indicate that scandals do emerge and produce strong emotional (and concrete) effects in societies characterized by weak civicness. In fact, as Banfield (1956: 93) has already observed, in a society of amoral familists, sentiments of law-and-order are widespread.

Investigating the interaction of corruption dynamics and widespread values more deeply, it was indeed observed that a lack of trust tends to interact with the spread of corruption, especially since in such societies citizens (and entrepreneurs) are pushed to "buy" the public services they believe unobtainable otherwise. In turn, corruption confirms the appropriateness of that mistrust, and fuels it all the more. Finally, an appeal to "national character" may even provide a shield against any sense of guilt, as a police officer indirectly admits: "Yes, often when I sort out people's problems on a social level, they come to me with small gifts. But that too is in the nature of the Senegalese. It's how the Senegalese are. If you are satisfied with a guy when he sorts out your problems, eh! ... tomorrow you arrive with a kilo of rice or even a kilo of peanuts, but that's the nature of the Senegalese" (Blundo and de Sardan 2006: 114–5).

Public Class, Entrepreneurs, and Socialization to Corruption

Research on moral costs has addressed the specific characteristics of the actors involved in corruption: the political class, bureaucrats, and entrepreneurs. White collar crime has been explained with reference to *work-related subcultures*[6] that "tend to isolate their members from the mainstream of social life and its construction of reality [...] . Because of this isolation, work-related subcultures are often able to maintain a definition of certain criminal activities as acceptable or even required behavior, when they are clearly condemned by society as a whole" (Coleman 1987: 422–3). Typically, the internalization of norms depends on so-called pride in one's position and the prestige of public service: the more public roles are socially rewarded, the less desirable it becomes to violate group norms. In the Italian case, the diffusion of corruption in bureaucracy may have been facilitated by its traditionally low status.[7] In fact, compared with the German, British, or French public administrations, which have traditionally shown a strong esprit de corps, the Italian bureaucracy is characterized by a generalized lack of sense of state, related to the importance of political protection (or, in the best-case scenario, seniority) in career development. Similarly, in the Russian transition to democracy, a major risk was identified in the extreme weakness of the public bureaucracy, more interested in private enrichment than in providing services to the citizens, incompetent and antidemocratic, capable of protecting friends but unable to take responsibility for the public good (Mendras 1997: 126–8).

Research on local power in the United States had explained the increase in corruption with the emergence of new social groups, what Dahl (1961) called ex-plebeians, that integrated recent migrants through various forms of personalistic use of public resources. These "ex-plebs" supplanted the middle class, which had supposedly brought about a moralization of politics (Banfield and Wilson 1967: 330). In our previous research on the Italian case (della Porta and Vannucci 1999), however, the spread of corruption is not related to the rise of "ex-plebs." Rather, corruption develops when politics begins to attract chiefly those individuals who are able and willing to derive personal benefits from the control of public

---

[6]   Work-related subcultures are "epistemic communities that provide the locus for specialized reality construction in society on the basis of work concerns or ideological commitments" (Holzner 1972: 95).

[7]   A low social status is often sanctioned by low wages. Van Rijckeghem and Weder (1997) show how empirical evidence points to a negative relationship between corruption and wages across developing countries.

resources. We noticed in fact that the crisis of the Italian Socialist Party developed when working-class members abandoned the party, and a new middle class entered it, occupying powerful positions. This new political class was characterized by a "businesslike" approach to politics: political involvement was considered as a way to gain economic benefits and enrich oneself. A similar pattern has also been noted in other times and countries. As Wolfinger observed in his research on New Haven, "Patronage inevitably creates a cadre of activists for whom politics is a way to make money, not a means of striving for the good, true, and beautiful" (Wolfinger 1973: 95).

Business politicians can, however, be described as *homines novi*, whose entry into politics from the Roman Republic onward is considered to have raised the tolerance threshold for deviation from established norms. According to Banfield and Wilson (1967), for instance, in American cities the greater propensity of *newcomers* to involvement in political corruption can be explained by the need of new entrepreneurs and political bosses to break into a world that tends to exclude them. Once they have "arrived," these same social groups become defenders of the new order. Partly taking up these hypotheses, Pizzorno (1992: 45) has suggested that the *homines novi* are more susceptible to participation in corruption because the detachment from prior reference groups entailed by entry into politics lowers the moral costs of behaving illegally: "entering politics, the 'new men' tend to break with what still binds them to their roots or, leaving aside metaphors, to detach themselves from the reference groups in which they were socialized. Politicians who belong to the socially dominant classes and have therefore been socialized in reference groups whose morality is the same as that of legal authority, on the other hand, continue to view their actions as being judged and rewarded according to the criteria of those groups and therefore conform to their norms." Monetary rewards gained through corruption can, in fact, be enjoyed in a socially satisfying manner only if this does not lead to stigmatization by an individual's reference groups.

If "desocialization" leads to greater openness to corruption, it should be added that the environment in which the individual is "resocialized" also plays an important role. In fact, corrupt politicians are stronger in competitions with their noncorrupt colleagues because the former can invest the material resources and networks of clients they have accumulated on the illegal market in their political careers. Using the additional resources they accumulate in illegal markets, the business politicians take over the political parties, prevailing in the competition with their "honest" colleagues. In this way they transform the very rules of politics. Moreover, the actors who move within the corrupt system create and contribute to the diffusion of a set of rules that, accompanied by a jargon confined to the initiated, allows the minimization of risks of denunciation. The party system is in fact transformed into the primary site of *socialisation in illegality*, spreading frames that "neutralize" corruption. As criminologists observed long ago, "criminal behavior is learned in interaction with other persons in a process of communication" (Sutherland and Cressey 1974: 75). As we see in Chapter 5, party organizations may provide mechanisms of socialization to the rules of the (illegal) game, permitting the system of occult transactions to expand. Politicians already "introduced" to the rules of the illegal market introduce others in their turn. Loyalty to the party serves in obtaining appointments, which are then paid for via the distribution of the money acquired through corruption.

Many of Italy's corrupt politicians of the last decade indeed came from the world of business. Political scandals in the 1990s had weakened the existing parties and discouraged individuals with idealistic (or ideological) motivations from party involvement, leading instead to a growing tendency to enter party politics from a career in the private sector. So, apart from the all-too-well-known case of the four-time premier Silvio Berlusconi, media tycoon and leader of the political party Popolo della Libertà, there are several cases of ministers in national governments that own firms or professional enterprises in the market areas they influence with their decisions (*L'Espresso*, November 2, 2006: 87). Similarly, at the local level, politicians have been accused of financing, or letting other entrepreneurs finance, their own firms (R, March 3, 2001; R-Turin, October 21, 2006), or of organizing EU fraud via the organization of inexistent training courses (R, February 2, 2004).

Neutralizing Moral Barriers

In an interview, a surgeon involved in a corruption scandal recalls the testimony of another doctor, who had said, "I was socialized and grew up in an environment that also used to teach corruption," the doctor added that "the system of environmentally widespread corruption made it difficult to give up [...] . Anybody who has a true knowledge of that environment would be able to, I would not say justify me, but at least understand me" (R, February 6, 2003).

As in this case, references to the capacity of the environment to corrupt—to "the mafioso environment which is ours" (R-Genoa, May 7, 2005)—are frequently made in corruption scandals. Referring to Goffman's (1974) conception of frames as a meta-message that specify the context in which the message should be read, Giglioli (1997), analyzing one of the Italian corruption trials, singles out a tendency among the defendants to frame their activity as belonging to a "normal praxis" of politics financing. The administrators implicated in corruption cases tend to present their actions as perfectly *normal*, albeit not conforming to a "utopian" ideal of democracy. Significantly, the public prosecutor observed that one of the administrators involved in a trial in Florence "has always acted on the belief that receiving payoffs for the party was legal, politically laudable and in no way morally reprehensible" (*La Nazione*, February 27, 1986). Looking at the justifications of the defendants, a common feature is their presentation of themselves as "children of the political system," in no way different from their less unfortunate "colleagues."[8]

---

[8]   In a similar way, U.S. Vice-President Spiro Agnew, who had to resign from office in 1973 following allegations of bribery during his time as Governor of Maryland, "protested that what he had done had been normal practice in Maryland for years" (Williams 1996: 7).

Their actions (including bribe-taking) originated in the requirements of politics—not an idealized version of politics but real, actual politics.

For entrepreneurs, too, the decision to pay or not pay a bribe depends on their "moral propensity" to illegal behavior. The condition of illegality may in fact cause a kind of "emotional suffering" that can influence their choice, even when considering it as the result of rational calculation. To explain his final rebellion, an entrepreneur from Bari who had paid bribes for 15 years declared, "I couldn't look at myself in the mirror any more. I felt completely shitty. It seemed wrong, humiliating" (*L'Espresso*, November 18, 1984: 34). Moreover, mechanisms for the progressive and "painless" inclusion in the "rituals" and institutional obligations of corruption exist inside firms. When he was nominated manager of a company controlled by FIAT, an entrepreneur was given "a booklet where all the 'obligations' and payment dates of the company were recorded. A list of names and sums; an inheritance which had to be respected to the letter. *Illegality was so regularized that I didn't feel I was perpetrating a criminal act*" (*Panorama*, April 16, 1994: 86, emphasis added). Thus, managers end by considering their individual contribution to the complex operation underlying an act of corruption—establishing contacts with politicians, negotiating the sums to be paid, creating hidden funds from which the money can be drawn, and effecting payment—as part of a decision-making process that lies outside their personal responsibility. Similarly, skills and knowledge of corruption practices are passed directly from father to son in numerous family-run businesses: "I paid my first bribe in 1966, when I inherited this enterprise from my daddy. We paid for 45 years, since when the Republican Army was founded," stated an entrepreneur arrested in relation to army supplies (R, October 25, 1995: 9).

First of all, parties (or other socializing agencies) provide an *alternative language* for defining corruption as the normal way of financing their activities. In the phase of negotiating the amount of the bribe to be paid, a wide range of terms are adopted: *reimbursement of expenses, compensation, gratuity, bonus, organizational contribution,* and *premium* in the language of public officials; *disbursements, political expenditures, additional costs, obligations, the X percent rule,* and *unspecified expenses* in that of entrepreneurs. In fact, even where corruption is the rule, it is never mentioned openly. The initial approach takes stereotypical forms: "And there's nothing in it for us?" or "speaking of the party's necessities and the usual practice as far as businesses helping to cover them is concerned" (from a businessman's evidence in CDEM: 119). Even when corruption is widespread, the language is never explicit. An entrepreneur reported a conversation with a public administrator: "he started to talk in order to make me understand that one had to give him something [...] . 'You know, all those things to do; I had to control everything myself." I said, 'Mr Engineer, if you have to control what happens, there is no problem'. 'But problems could arise' said he. I opened the dialogue, 'How much?'. He answered, 'Whatever you can do, that's fine by me'" (PRBA1: 26–7). Referring to a request for an electoral contribution, a regional assessor is quoted as having said, "We need 120, like in briscola (a card game)"

(R, October 19, 2000). And an entrepreneur reports meeting a public employee who asked him, "Is there anything for me for Christmas?" (R-Turin, October 26, 2002); while another meeting his mayor was told, "you know the way things go" (R-Genoa, November 1, 2003).

The presence of (symbolically more neutral) synonyms for bribes testifies to the spread of the phenomenon. For instance, one journalist observed that "bribery is so intertwined with the Kenyan culture, there is a code word for it. When someone offers a sly smile after a service and asks for a 'chao', Swahili for tea, that's a cue to slap a bill on his outstretched palm" (*Cnn.com/world*, April 23, 2009). In South Korea, the deep-rooted practice of relatives offering under-the-table gifts to teachers is called *chonji*. "Across the country, one in five parents says they have given chonji to teachers, and one in three in big cities says so," said the head of the bribery investigative team for the national Anti-Corruption and Civil Rights Commission. According to a witness, "Competition in college entrance exams is too intense here. And teachers' subjective evaluations are more influential than objective tests. It is a culture of give and take." *Chonji* do not always come in the form of cash. Sometimes parents sponsor school events or invite the teacher to lunch or dinner without the knowledge of the school. (*Los Angeles Time*, May 13, 2010). Similarly, in Russia, up to 50 percent of university students are said

> to pay bribes to their instructors on a regular basis, and as many as a third of all instructors systematically take them, according to Russian experts who were reacting to a UNESCO report that bribery in Russian higher education now amounts to 150 million US dollars every year. In some universities [...] 'students can choose between studying or paying while in others, everyone is forced to pay up.' [...] Students and instructors know what bribes to give for what outcomes, and both groups know that they have to pay off other staff members, including deans, in order to make this system work. (*Georgian Daily*, June 16, 2009)

Corruption is also often justified in the name of a superior goal. A number of politicians involved in recent corruption investigations stressed their *"efficient"* image as public administrators, a self-representation that also offers a "moral" justification of corruption. The description of an eminent colleague given by a Calabrian administrator makes the point nicely:

> He really is convinced that he always pursued the general interest with abnegation and public spirit. [...] Securing investment, even through corruption, served the interests of the population and contributed to the prosperity of the city. Paris was worth a heap, and public works were worth a bit of bribery even if by doing so the system was perpetuated. He said: 'That's the way it is. Otherwise we have no public works, no employment and no help for the less well-off.' (Licandro and Varano 1993: 71)

Similarly, for entrepreneurs the moral costs of breaking the law are attenuated by what one of them defines as the "ethic of responsibility an entrepreneur has towards his firm and employees" (*L'Espresso*, June 21, 1992: 31) or, in other words, the responsibility "for keeping a firm with a thousand employees going" (PRIM: 15).[9] This is all the more true when the firms involved in corruption—as was often true in the Italian case—specialize in satisfying public demand, thus reducing their opportunities for work in the private sector. The particular location of their plant, the specific skills managers develop through learning-by-doing, or the discrete investments that are made at the behest of the public customer increases asset specificity, rendering them particularly susceptible to opportunistic bribery demands (Williamson 1989: 143). One of the Pio Albergo Trivulzio's contractors stated that "Giving these people money wasn't a result of free choice. Having equipped the firm with sophisticated and expensive machinery and having taken on a large number of highly specialized employees, the firm's survival depends on getting contracts" (Carlucci 1992: 30).

Similarly, in the United States, when federal agents charged 44 people (amongst whom were mayors, rabbis, and even one alleged trafficker in human kidneys) during an investigation into public corruption and international money laundering, the public attorney said that "Corruption among the politicians was a way of life [...] . They existed in an ethics-free zone." In the case involving a mayor accused of having received a bribe in exchange for zoning changes, the accused had, according to the FBI's complaint, told an entrepreneur that "[y]ou can put your faith in me" and that "I promise you [...] you're gonna be, you're gonna be treated like a friend." Supporters defended their mayor, stating "This was a charismatic guy who we thought could get us past all this stuff" (*Wall Street Journal,* July 24, 2009).

Often, the crude essence of corruption is veiled in a language and culture of friendship, which makes reciprocity a sort of perverse obligation. The use of terms such as *gift* and *favor*, as well as the presence of (bad) social capital that facilitates social trust are present in our cases. The terms *gift* or *a sign of kindness* are often used. In one case, a politician who directed a public hospital describes "not bribes but spontaneous offers, gifts, donations. [...] There was this praxis, from before I arrived" (R, December 21, 2002). Gifts might however escalate, including "a golden ring with a diamond" (R-Neaples, June 9, 2000), a Cartier watch (R-Palermo, March 8, 2002), a Rolex watch and travel (R, July 25, 2002), a BMW (R-Florence, January 26, 2001) or Mercedes (R-Milan, November 11, 2002), televisions (R, April 8, 2004), or the restoration of a house (R-Palermo, September 3, 2004). Testing with small gifts and then escalating to bigger ones is a strategy to gradually lower moral barriers. As the Italian broker Zampini explained,

---

9   According to Sutherland (1983), the ideal businessman, as the professional thief, often commits crimes and violations that are not stigmatized within his peer group. In contrast to the professional thief, the businessman defines himself as an "honest man." Corruption, for instance, is an illegal act closely related to activities that are legal and considered socially positive. On those aspects of firms' organization that favor law-breaking on the part of businessmen and other "white -collar" crimes, see Leonard and Weber (1978).

a sort of escalation in this strategy of gift-giving can be a way of testing the moral barriers of potential partners, as well as slowly socializing them to illegality: "The money flowed briskly. Once on the plane, Concorde I think, I spent 3 million lira on presents for everybody. I remember I asked R.G. to draw up the bill and he was astonished by the amount. But he didn't say anything and as far as I was concerned, from then on, he was 'done', compromised, prepared to come in on the game" (*L'Espresso*, November 18, 1984: 45).

A parallel term is that of *favors*. Thus it is asserted that the contributions were "gifts" given not in return for illegal actions but rather to acknowledge "favors." "Gifts" and "favors" are then defined as expressions of "friendship" and "solidarity," terms often used during interrogations. Arrogance thus shades into a particular conception of *generosity*, as the distribution of "favors" to "friends": as exemplified by the words of a corrupt administrator: "I've always given" (*L'Unità*, March 16, 1985). Delays and inefficiencies in the administrative system provided additional justifications: to "speed up the process" for a "friend" becomes a "legitimate defense" against the inefficiency of the system. Indeed, the constant exaltation of "friendship, renders the corrupt transaction ethically praiseworthy. Many of our business politicians would agree with a Sicilian DC "boss" who confessed: "I can admit to having a fault [...] I am human. If I am somebody's friend, I help them" (*La Sicilia*, November 6, 1988). Finally, this conception of politics and of friendship allows those implicated to distinguish between criminal behavior (which is not their case) and a practice described as "unorthodox" or as a "shortcut."

This very language helps make corruption acceptable. A "moral obligation" to accept a tip may even emerge as a sign of "politeness" in corruption, cancelling out its moral implications. A similar process is described by a Senegalese public servant: "Sometimes I provide a service, I simply provide a service [...]. The guy sees that I made a big effort, but all that is a part of my job and I am paid for that. But afterwards he takes out some money, he forces me, he gives it to me, I refuse, but he puts it into my pocket" (cit. in Blundo and de Sardan 2006: 113). Similarly, a retired Indonesian police official admitted, "the cultural acceptance of the logic of 'gifts' in interaction with public agents makes corruption morally acceptable: 'If someone is satisfied with the service he has received and gives gifts to show his gratitude, that is not considered bad'" (*New York Times*, December 19, 2009).

Moral (and Immoral) Norms as Informal Institutional Constraints

A scandal that erupted in Italy in 1996 over medical prescriptions exchanged for money illustrates the development of informal, but efficient, rules that help the governance of corruption. According to the secretary of the firm involved, they knew that "medical doctor X had addressed a certain number of *scintigraphies* to us [...] then we predisposed some lists in which we printed, for each doctor the number of patients that he had addressed to us [...]. The promoters had told us the medical doctors that had been somehow in agreement to receive money in exchange for sending patients [...] so every month we selected from the general list those doctors that received money and we made the calculations [...] on the basis of the type of exams they had prescribed" (TRMI03: 23). "In a white envelope, with the note 'confidential-personal' and the name and address of the doctor already written they put all the dates, with the names of the patients sent and their exams and then the money and a couple of leaflets for the center" (ibid.: 24). The total sums oscillated between 8 and 10 million lira per doctor. A list was also made of doctors that received gifts: "close to the name, there was a *b* for a low cost gift of up to 100 thousand lira and an *a* for more expansive gifts, of up to 200.000 lire, and an asterisk for even more expensive ones" (ibid.: 42).

This detailed accounting of the bribes clearly illustrates how corruption can become a well-regulated system: (immoral) norms reduce moral costs as well as the very perception of acting illegally. On the contrary, high moral costs make anticorruption laws "self-enforcing" independent of expected sanctions and risks of legal prosecutions, sustaining and guaranteeing the honest conduct of public and private agents.

The acknowledgment of a "moral cost" in violating the law implies the attribution of a positive ethical value to its respect. But when there are *strong* alternative sources of loyalty or conflictual subcultures, public procedures and laws can, on the contrary, be subordinated to the pursuance of these private organizations' ends: corruption, where functional to such aims, can ironically assume a positive moral value (Pizzorno 1992: 19). A paradoxical "sense of justice" then accompanies the practice of corruption considered useful to the superior interests of one's party, faction, clan, or family. When, in the clash between two conflicting value systems, such "public" interests prevail, the moral cost of corruption is strongly reduced or can even be reversed becoming a *moral benefit*. In this case, a political agent can proudly claim the right to use bribery to support the purposes of the organization he so strongly identifies with, obtaining both social legitimization in his relevant recognition circle and psychological relief from the perception of acting illegally. For instance, after his imprisonment for corruption crimes, a Christian Democrat leader declared, "I have been strongly and morally helped by the awareness that I was using the bribes that I received in recent years in the interests of the party. It has been decisive in the fact that I can still walk proudly into the Milan headquarters of the party and I am known by collaborators, functionaries and leaders as the one who decisively contributed, for such a long time, to party life" (PM: 23). For an individual, in fact, "the moral cost is lower the more ephemeral appear to him those circles of moral recognition that offer positive criteria for the respect of the law" (Pizzorno 1992: 46). Individuals will suffer higher costs when in both their own and their peers' perspectives corrupt behavior involves a violation of values—such as "public service"—that are deeply internalized. Where corruption becomes a regulated system through a process of informal institutionalization, moral costs are profoundly undermined. Shared beliefs about the tacit rules that govern corrupt interactions with other players reinforce such informal (due to its illegality) institutional frameworks.

Various and interrelated socialization and sanctioning systems may enforce corrupt agreements and reduce their moral costs, which would otherwise increase the risk of being cheated or denounced. When partners share similar internalized norms, the probability of the successful conclusion of a corrupt exchange increases. As we have seen, a basis for corrupt activities is the involvement of relatively homogeneous agents, who share customs, social norms, and ideological and cultural values (opposed, or at least autonomous, from those embodied in the respect of state norms), and who can produce expectations of reciprocal implementation in corrupt dealings. The corresponding endogenous rules of the "corruption game" rely on the negative feelings associated with the betrayal of commonly internalized codes of behavior prescribing "trustworthiness" in corrupt transactions. In this case, then, there is no longer any moral cost in corruption; but a mirrorlike *immoral cost*—so to say—can emerge that is associated with the fulfillment of the terms of the hidden corruption contract. The higher the "immoral cost," the less inclined an agent will be to cheat or denounce partners in corrupt exchanges, since the respect of the "norms of corruption" has assumed an "ethical" value in itself.

In this perspective, the stronger, more lasting, and institutionalized the governance structures guaranteeing the "private-order" norms that regulate corrupt dealings are, the lower the moral costs of corruption will be. Two distinct mechanisms tend to undermine the moral barriers against pervasive corruption: (a) a generalized weakening of the "sense of the state," that is, the civic virtues and public spiritedness in society, due to their substitution with alternate values, more homogeneous with the prevailing norms of conduct that encourage or justify corruption; and (b) a process of adverse selection, which induces the exit from crucial areas of the political, administrative, and economic system of individuals with higher moral resistance against corruption, at the same time attracting less honest ones.

The emergence of the rules of the "corruption game" are in some cases described by the agents involved as a process of progressive and reproduced adhesion to prevailing models of behavior. As a report by Transparency International observes, "In some countries, the payment of fees for judicial services is so engrained that complaints arise not if a bribe is sought, but if the requested bribe is greater than usual" (TI-2007: 4–5). The existence of informal norms eases the potentially dangerous entry of new actors to the market. In most cases, noncompliance is too costly, and efforts at persuasion or intimidation are thus unnecessary. Spontaneous adaptation to the rules in force also allows the reduction of information-gathering costs (Ullmann-Margalitt 1977: 86; Good 1988). As Elster (1989b, 134) observes, often, informal norms "are individually useful in that they help people to economize on decision costs. A simple mechanical decision rule may, on the whole and in the long run, have better consequences for the individual than the fine-tuned search for optimal decision." No hesitation or uncertainty is then associated with offering bribes when such a "constitutional rule" of corruption is in operation (see Chapter 9).

When corruption is systemic, the moral and transaction costs of bribery are further reduced by the widespread belief—intentionally propagated by those seeking corruption rents—that it is *unavoidable*. According to Mario Chiesa, "the tacit rule was that bribery extended to everything, from the biggest public works to the smallest provision of supplies. Bribery wasn't even brought up anymore" (*Panorama*, December 13, 1992: 45).[10]

In fact, when expectations converge in considering corruption pervasive, it is no longer worth engaging in the (embarrassing and dangerous) activity of finding out whether it is necessary to pay in a specific case. A small enterprise was contacted by a Christian Democrat councilor in a public hospital after being awarded a 250 million lire contract: "He approached me in a perfectly normal way and asked for a 'contribution for the organisation', giving me the impression that it was an obligation and the usual practice. I considered it and decided to comply" (Carlucci 1992: 83). The progressive exit or marginalization of agents with higher moral costs in public and private organizations further increases the expected compliance with the rules of systemic corruption. Routinization neutralizes the moral costs of corruption. As a Chinese cadre in a government agency explains, any sense of guilt completely vanishes in routine corruption:

> Even if they don't want to, people will give it to you. It's hard to resolve. Especially since the people sending the gifts are all close to you, really good friends, asking for favors. Can you find a way to help me? And then if you achieve their task, they give you presents. [...] The people giving aren't strangers. Even if you don't want to take it, you can't not take it. You don't even try, and you get rich. You say 'no, no', and wealth just comes. (Cit. in Smart and Hsu 2007: 182)

Far from anomic behaviour, systemic corruption emerges as well regulated. In the words of an African entrepreneur: "In their filthiness, in their corruption, there are still rules of behaviour. There is a line of conduct, a respect for the given word, for commitments, and there are laws governing relations between them. I don't think that on this level there are blunders" (cit. in Blundo 2006: 229).

Concluding Remarks

Different approaches to corruption see ethical standards as barriers against illegal behavior. According to the political economy approach, moral costs can be considered as a negative addendum—reflecting individual's "moral preferences"—

---

[10]   This is confirmed by Maurizio Prada: "The mechanism of enterprises giving us money was so well consolidated that it was no longer necessary to ask. It was well known that the award of a contract required this and it was automatic, once a contract was gained, to quantify the sum to be given to the parties" (Nascimbeni and Pamparana 1992: 148).

that enter the rational calculus of individual actors who must decide whether to engage in corrupt exchanges.

In comparative politics, the moral costs of engaging in corruption have instead been related to cultural values, such as religion, clientelism, civicness, and the "sense of the state." These analyses—either case studies or large-N comparisons—tend however to remain quite generic in their attribution to individuals of some assumed general characteristics of national cultures. The type of linkages between widespread values and individual choices therefore remains unspecified.

In this chapter we have looked at the interactions between moral costs and corruption. First of all, we examined the specific values that characterize the "professional cultures" of public administrations as well as entrepreneurs. Moreover, from a constructivist perspective, we singled out mechanisms neutralizing the moral costs of illegal behavior, which often end up producing "immoral costs" that discourage honest behavior. Within a neoinstitutional frame, we also pointed to the institutionalization of alternate norms that favor corruption. We singled out conditions for the development of a "high-corruption equilibrium": if some professional cultures reduce the barriers to illegal behavior, the spread of corruption subsequently facilitates the diffusion of norms and informal institutions that support alternative rules of the game, thereby reducing the "immoral costs" of corruption. The most widespread corruption, the lower its moral costs, since a growing number of politicians and businessmen internalize new codes of behavior according to which corruption is the supported norm. Political parties and business associations tend, therefore, to work as mechanisms of socialization to corruption.

In conclusion, when governance mechanisms emerge in the market for corrupt exchanges, the latter tends to reproduce itself, along with a system of norms and principles that—while opposite from the legal order (whose supporting values are weakened) and far from being *anomie*—can assume an "ethical" significance of its own. In this way, corruption can seep down from above, as the diffused perception of the involvement of political leaders in corruption reduces loyalty toward the state and undermines the moral costs of followers and the public; but also from below, since "once the incentives for petty corruption have been created, it tends to extend up [...] through interest in complicity. In its turn, by way of impunity, this creates favorable conditions for the growth of corruption" (Cadot 1987: 239). The diffusion of corruption diminishes its costs, reducing the sense of guilt and the risk of losing face, while increasing possibilities of finding dependable partners for corrupt transactions.

Chapter 4
Bureaucratic Corruption

he convinced [...] with the prospect of possible complaints about the legality of checks and final tests carried out in the building [...] others to provide him free services for the monthly equivalent of a sum of one million lira, and an additional sum of 15 million lira [...] as well as the provision of materials for his house (bathroom fixtures, bathroom furniture, a safe, curtains and other goods). (PRBA1: 15)

So the judges describe the case of a high level public bureaucrat in a city in Southern Italy, accused of having accepted bribes in exchange for ensuring mild checks and controls. In general, there are two main forms of involvement for bureaucrats in corrupt exchanges. Alone, they are often involved in minor cases of corruption. Their main resource in such cases is the power to grant a permission, to follow an administrative process, to disclose reserved information, or to soften the severity of an inspection. As one Milanese shopkeeper observes, "the elected politicians make their business elsewhere. They leave this small business to the bureaucracy so that, in exchange the bureaucrats do not jeopardize the bid operations" (Fipe 1992: 65). The threat to block or accelerate some actions is instead the main resource for bureaucrats that have also been involved in more complex corrupt games including elected politicians. To the latter, they often offer precious resources linked to the continuity of their permanence in a certain position (della Porta and Vannucci 1994: 255–61). In contexts of increasing powers handed over to career bureaucrats to the detriment of elected politicians, their role seems to increase accordingly, not only in corrupt exchanges but also in the governance of corruption.

Bureaucratic Corruption: An Introduction

In the first chapter we distinguished *political* from *private* corruption according to the role of the corrupted agent, who either acts within a public organization that delegates discretionary power to him (formally or informally) or who possesses confidential information that may be arbitrarily allocated. Public agents, in their role and status, acquire the power to assign, reassign, modify, attenuate, or cancel property rights (Benson and Baden 1985: 392). In this sense, we can distinguish three general areas of public intervention where rents are created (Rose-Ackerman 1978: 61–3).

The first is *the private provision of goods and services demanded by the state*. In this case a rent is created by the public decision to pay more for private resources than their value for the seller in the most remunerative alternate use. Part of the rent, which is equal to this difference, is then given as a "kickback" to the public agent who influenced the favorable decision. Tenders for goods and services by the state or other public bodies paid above the current market price can be included in this category.

A second area is *the sale or distribution of goods and services administered, produced, or previously owned by the state.* A rent is created by the public agent accepting *less* for the property or resources than the private purchaser or recipient would be willing to pay. In this case, too, the rent is equal to the difference in value, and a share of it can be passed as a bribe to the corrupt agent. The sale of publicly owned goods for less than their market price, or the granting of concessions and licenses that guarantee a profit, can be included here. In certain cases, such as an urban planning program that increases the value of an area, the public measure adopted may be inspired by the general interest, and no official payment in exchange for the land is foreseen: for the owner, the entire increase in value then represents a rent.

The imposition of sanctions or decisions creating costs is the third set of public agents' activities. A rent in this case comes from the power to escape punishment or costs—connected with a violation of the legally sanctioned structure of rights—and is equal to the anticipated loss for the private party (the maximum the private party is willing to pay in order to avoid it). There can be an exchange between the right (or power) of the agent (not) to impose the cost—following state procedures—and the property right of the corrupter of part of the rent that is saved. This is the case of a policeman or a tax agent, for example, who overlooks irregularities, thus allowing the guilty party to avoid paying the fine anticipated by the law.[1]

Following Buchanan ([1975]: 124), we can say that the first two areas of public intervention are related to the operation of the "productive State": "In this role or capacity, the State is not 'protecting' defined individual rights. Government is a productive process," which can secure the net benefits of public goods and services that would tend to be underprovided or not provided at all in the absence of collective governmental action. The third area of public activity is instead interwoven with the functioning of the "protective State": public agents in such cases should protect rights, enforcing rules and property rights. Their task is conceptually purely "scientific": to verify if the terms of the rules were violated or not and apply the accompanying punishment or penalty (Buchanan [1975]: 122). Actually, public agents play a crucial role in determining the effectiveness of the sanctioning of informal rules and, consequently, the level and distribution of transaction costs.

---

[1]   We focus on *voluntary* corrupt exchanges, not on "*extortive corruption*," which entails a form of compulsion, usually to avoid some harm being inflicted on the donor by the public agent (Alatas 1990). Extortive corruption should, in fact, be marginal in well-functioning democratic systems, where public agents cannot employ physical violence to impose compliance with arbitrary requests (with the possible exception, as we will see, of connections between public agents and organized crime), and several institutional control mechanisms—concurrent and impartial— exist.

A wider arbitrary power of public-law bureaucrats (as well as politicians and bureaucrats) simply means a higher level of uncertainty in the political-economic system, that is, higher transaction and protection costs for those property rights that are badly enforced, not fully specified, or subject to regulation or prohibition. For instance, a tax evader or a car driver who exceeds speed limits does not possess legal rights over the money due as a fiscal sanction or fine, but they can nevertheless dispose of such rights if the state's protection efforts are not sufficient (obviously, there are information and control costs that preclude perfect enforcement),[2] if there are errors or inefficiencies in the control procedure, or if the enforcing agents can be induced to "close an eye" to such violations. Corruption is one of the means to obtain this result, passing part of the rent on to the corrupt agents.

Existing institutional constraints determine both the demand for property rights and the investment in the acquisition of knowledge (North 1990). When the capture of uncertain or insufficiently sanctioned property rights is possible and profitable thanks to the collusion, connivance, or inertia of public bureaucrats, we may expect these economic incentives to push more people to violate legal rules, investing time and effort in the acquisition of skills and abilities to acquire and protect such rights (Baumol 1990). If relevant resources can be gained through influence and corruption, a proportional amount of resources will be invested in establishing and consolidating exchange relationships with control agents (to defend themselves from enforcement, to obtain confidential information, to mitigate sanctions, to avoid controls, etc.). In turn, public bureaucrats have stronger incentives to increase the wholesale uncertainty of rights subject to their control agency, since this will permit them to secure (as bribes) greater rents, that is, a greater quota of those potential rights that they—through their decisions (or nondecisions) or the institutional system—contribute to place in the public domain.

Public bureaucrats are not simple "sanctioning mechanisms," as in the Weberian legal-rational model of authority (Weber [1922]). On the contrary, as street-level bureaucrats (Lipsky 1980), they have a discretionary power that can influence the probability of obtaining a contract and being caught and prosecuted, the timing of the procedure, and the severity of the sanction applied, and so on. In other words, they retain a power in their activity that is a valuable asset in the market for corrupt exchanges. The common root of corruption in the public administration is the unavoidable presence of uncertainty in the allocation and sanctioning of property rights, related to incomplete and asymmetric information on the actions and characteristics of the actors involved in social relations regulated by legal norms. Such uncertainty may have different sources, at both the individual and

---

[2] As observed by Becker and Stigler, "We should abandon all thoughts of judging enforcement of laws and rules as simply successes or failures, even if these categories are 'realistically' defined. The society (or a person) buys the amount of enforcement which it deems appropriate to the statute of the rule: more will be bought if the State serves a more valuable goal (protect us from a murder rather than assault) and if a given increase in enforcement is less expensive" (Becker and Stigler 1974: 3).

institutional levels, and there are therefore different private demands for corrupt
services from public bureaucrats:

- When there is a public decision to be made—either a bid to be allocated
  or a sanction to be applied following the violation of a legal rule (penal,
  fiscal, mercantile, civil, administrative, etc.)—the level of respect for the
  due procedures depends on the moral costs of the public employees, as
  well as on the system of institutional incentives and constraints on their
  activity (their remuneration, the system of controls, etc.): "The honesty
  of enforcers will be dependent not only upon the supply of honesty in the
  population, but also on the amount spent to ascertain how honest a given
  person is" (Becker and Stigler 1974: 3). As public *agents* whose actions
  and capabilities are costly to ascertain, public employees can conceal their
  real effort levels from their *principal* (i.e., control agencies), as well as their
  potential corrupt dealings.[3] Weaker "moral barriers" against corruption, as
  well as less incisive controls and lower salaries, will *ceteris paribus* [other
  things being equal] strengthen the incentives for public bureaucrats to sell
  their rights over resources that should be assigned according to the law to
  the highest bidder. Correspondingly, uncertainty concerning the degree of
  concrete protection of such rights encourages a private demand to acquire
  single decisions (or information that produces the same effect), corrupting
  on a case-by-case basis public agents that influence the final allocation of
  valuable resources. Only when the exchange is frequent—for example, the
  violation of rules is repeated, as in the case of criminal activities (the sale
  of drugs, thieves, gambling, prostitution, illegal immigration, etc.)—do
  corrupters have an interest to buy more durable protection for their property
  rights with the revenues of forbidden activities and personal protection
  against arrest and conviction.
- Knowledge about the potential violation of legal rules may also become
  a scarce resource in itself. There may be a "gray area" of *institutional
  uncertainty* concerning property rights over assets that should formally be
  enforced by the state, but are de facto badly guaranteed or overregulated.
  Public bureaucrats, as a consequence, acquire broad arbitrary powers, since
  they can choose, autonomously, *if, when,* and *how* to intervene. Several
  factors may increase uncertainty and transaction costs in the political and
  economic arenas. An excessive burden of norms, as well as their ambiguity
  and contradictions, reduce the availability of information concerning the
  rules of behavior sanctioned by the state: to quote Montesquieu, *useless
  laws weaken the necessary laws.* If and when potential advantages or
  violations of existing rules are almost impossible to detect (or only at
  considerable cost), individuals' property rights are weakened, since they

---

[3]   As Elster (1989a: 157–8) notes: "a system of mutual watching is vulnerable to
collusion. An individual who detects a corrupt practice could profit more from blackmailing
the corrupt parties than from denouncing them."

live under a constant menace of the actions of discretionary enforcers, and incentives to corruption are stronger.[4] Another factor is the *commons* problem in bureaucratic, police, and courts services, which can create an excess of demand in conjunction with an inefficient allocation of limited available and accessible resources (such as time). This can and does result in increased uncertainty in the efficacy of publicly provided protection: "When common pool congestion arises, public bureaucrats have tremendous discretion in the allocation (rationing) of limited bureau resources among competing demands. [...] With such discretion, police can choose which laws to enforce relatively strictly and which not to enforce. Commons problems in the courts generate considerable discretion for prosecutors and judges" (Benson 1988: 74). In addition, the general lack of faith in the impartiality or efficiency of public procedures generates a genuine demand for the protection of property rights against the perceived risks of capture. In fact, such mistrust can make the "official" protection offered by the state to citizens in relationships with its structures or to citizens who expect other services from the government to be ineffective or not advantageous. In this sense, a demand for protection tends to emerge in social contexts characterized by a low degree of trust and confidence in the efficiency and impartiality of public procedures.[5] In fact, mistrust tends to increase transaction costs concerning property rights over "political rents." As we will see, corrupt public bureaucrats can respond to such demands, supplying surrogate protection where a lack of trust in official state protection exists.

Petty Corruption in the Public Administration

One day, after the exams were over, the functionary asked me to take her home. On the way, she told me, stop here, this is my butcher. She went in, came out and told me: "I'm in a hurry. Please, go and pick up what I've bought". I went back, and paid a bill of about 500 thousand lira, cash. She hadn't ordered anything.

---

[4]   Normative inflation is often correlated with the low quality of legislative products and the "obscurity" of their prescriptions (Vannucci and Cubeddu 2006).

[5]   An analysis of the dynamics of corruption (see Chapter 9) indicates that these illegal activities feed off themselves: "the critical attitude towards the non-corrupt in a corrupt society is a main mechanism behind this snowball effect" (Elster 1989a: 268). The generalization of such practices, and the very attempt to combat them through denunciations of the *climate of corruption* (Myrdal 1968: 409), strengthens the idea that where so many others are doing so, it must be correct to engage in corruption. Corrupt agents deliberately introduce conditions of unpredictability and inefficiency into public affairs to facilitate corruption. These conditions are then spontaneously reproduced because those initially hostile to such practices are excluded.

Or:

> Once one of them asked me for 500 thousands lira in cash. Another showed me a telephone bill for 400 thousand lira and asked me to pay for it. Still another told me that he had to visit a sick relative the next day, and said: "We want to give him a transistor radio. You buy it". (R-Palermo, April 6, 2000)

This story was told by the owner of a driving school who denounced the sale of driving licenses for 1 or 2 million lire. In another case, five high level administrators of the driving permission service were accused of having sold driving licenses for a total of about €4,000 for each examining session, and to have then distributed the money among employees and examiners (R-Palermo, May 25 2005).

Those involved in the market for driving licenses represent only a few of the cases of micro-corruption. This is a type that is prevalent in (at least apparently) casual and difficult-to-repeat encounters between public agents and private citizens, characterized by an exchange of small favors and benefits for small bribes. Italian chronicles have revealed in recent years bribes paid to obtain a tomb in a cemetery or certification for a nonexistent accident or disability, to speed up the procedure to evacuate a rented apartment, and to avoid military service (sometimes at fixed prices) or inspections for environmental protection regulations or tax payments (della Porta and Vannucci 2007).

In trading activities, micro-corruption emerged as bribes were paid to avoid inspections of sanitary conditions or with respect to regulations for labor protection in shops, hotels, restaurants, and nightclubs. Bribes were not only paid for certificates to become school teachers but also for dentistry degrees, as well as university exams or even wins in lotteries or television quizzes (R-Rome, February 4 2001). For example, cases of petty corruption were found in inspections of buildings (R, November 7, 1999: 24), commercial inspections (R, November 25, 1997: 21) and labor activities inspections (R, June 28, 2001), as well as in minor fiscal controls (R, November 5, 1998: 27).

In exchange, small kickbacks were passed to each low-level public employee in exchange for their not inspecting and/or disclosing crimes and violations of rules, for reducing fines, or other small favors whose value for private counterparts is in any case limited.

In this context of small-size, one-of favors, transaction costs may be reduced through several factors. First, the risk of accusations from private counterparts is often reduced by their weak negotiation power. In some cases the corruptors are illegal immigrants (R, December 16, 1998: 13), prostitutes (R, February 20, 1999: 25), foreign tourists who have broken speed limits (*La Nazione*, February 14, 2001: 8), or street vendors without licenses (Fipe 1992: 51).[6] Nor can entrepeneurs and

---

[6]   Cases included the payment of fixed bribes for fake medical certificates (R-Florence, March 16, 2000), or even fake fines for failing to pay for tickets on public transport that were then used to prove presence in the country in order to benefit from regularization laws (R-Genoa, March 24, 2005), and of course for residence permits (R, April 14, 2000).

private citizens (car drivers, in several cases) be tempted to denounce corruption, precisely because of the small amounts involved, as denunciation carries high "fixed costs" (in terms of time to be invested, lawyer's remuneration, risks of retaliation or revenge attacks, counter-denunciation for calumny, etc.). If the expected advantage is limited, the most-often chosen strategy is to accept to pay, especially if ethical standards are low.

More generally, the power to bribe is linked to the possibility to arbitrarily impose (or at least threaten) delays and hitches in administrative processes. There is in fact evidence of "parallel offices" for speeding up processes in exchange for fixed prices. Thus goes the approach by a public employee in an administrative office to a citizen: "These are long, very long procedures; you know how the bureaucracy is in these cases [...] But I know a shortcut. You help me out with money and I'll deal with the rest" (R-Rome, March 25 2001). In a similar way, a series of investigations into corruption in Naples revealed what the judges defined as "peculiar bureaucratic-procedural slowness" and "the most various obstacles imposed by the offices" to push the owners of buildings that had been damaged by the 1980 earthquake to pay bribes to obtain the reimbursements they were entitled to. Even porters can become involved in small bribes given their power to speed up, or slow down, an administrative process (VICM: 3). As an entrepreneur explained to Italian investigators, "the porter [...] you think he is the last one, because he is just the porter, he opens the door and says, 'here is the office of Mister X', but he plays a very important role, because all the acts pass over his desk and if he doesn't like you [...] he does nothing [...] and months of your work ends up locked up somewhere" (PMI-MA, February 19, 2003: 34, 36). It is not surprising that low-level officials in virtually every Italian police corps have been found to be involved in cases of petty corruption: local and traffic police, carabinieri, in one case even harbor officials (R, November 14, 1997: 16).

Moreover, public bureaucrats work individually or within very small groups (such as police patrols), so that information on their illegal practices can easily be confined within the boundaries of the group. In this sense, the involvement of top-level officials (who have the power to cover up illegal activities and sanction "whistle-blowers") was neither possible—there were not enough resources at stake to bribe them—nor necessary. Lacking stable coordination mechanisms, public bureaucrats who work together pocket kickbacks that are passed on to them, while the "conspiracy of silence" is guaranteed by their reciprocal blackmailing power. If, for example, one is accused by the other, the victim can easily reciprocate.

Migration police officers have been charged for asking migrants for sexual favors or material gifts in order to avoid expulsion or to get residence permits (R-Palermo, October 14, 2005). We also found cases of migrants asked to pay bribes for trading licenses (R-Milan, March 24, 2002) or to avoid inspections of their trading activities (R-Rome, July 8, 2003) and cases where members of the urban police asked illegal sellers to buy their products back from them after they had been seized (R, May 13, 2000).

Small bribes reduce the moral costs of corruption. The resources that agents receive can be interpreted as gifts or informal remuneration for their "kindness" rather than bribes. The bribe may also be remuneration in kind, such as sexual favors (R, November 5, 1998: 27). In one case, the sexual favor was obtained by a mayor who offered in exchange a job in a public hospital to a poor foreign woman: "I give her a position, which was prearranged for another person [...] . Does she know I must have sex with her?" he said in a taped conversation. Notwithstanding, the woman eventually complied to his request for a "sexual bribe"—the woman declared, "I never did a similar thing. If I accept it's because I'm in despair"— she did not received the promised job: the deal was in fact a fraud (R-Neaples, November 15, 2010).

Structural Corruption in the Public Administration

> The smugglers were hunting for the financial police and after each clash—in the sea or on the road—they were excited. Any act of force was immediately reported to their bosses by telephone [...] . Like brigands they had code names for each man and each vehicle. [...] The carabinieri, which were part of the group, were in the anti-bomb squad [...] . Their task was to offer assistance on the road by informing their bosses about where the police squads were located. (R, February 28, 2002)

This is the description of the activities of a gang of smugglers in Southern Apulia that mobilized the support of some corrupted carabinieri, who were later arrested. As we will see, the internal equilibria change when the exchanges between corrupters and corruptees become more frequent, but the resources at stake remain limited. Repeated interactions allow confidence, or reputational and hierarchical resources to enter the cost-benefit calculation for enlarging the scale of corrupt activities. In general, the private parties ask for some long-term services from the corrupt entrepreneurs, such as avoiding fines on commercial activities or getting regularl benefits. Almost 40 private agencies, for instance, frequently interacting with corrupt functionaries of the driving permission service in Palermo developed long-lasting trust relationships, regularizing the amount of bribes paid for each service (R-Palermo, January 21, 2011). The public agents involved tend to be low-level, as are the small favors they can offer.[7]

The kinds of services provided to corrupters do not usually require any significant specialization or division of tasks among public agents, even if at times there is a "cashier" who manages the flow of bribes to other corrupt agents (R,

---

[7]   E.g., waive a fine (R, February 13, 1996), do not denounce small crimes (R, November 3, 2000; R-Neaples, March 9, 2004), provide reserved information on some police checks (R, November 3, 2000) or judicial investigations (R-Palermo, February 16, 2000; R, February 21, 2001), sell health certificates to prisoners (R-Bari, June 10, 2004).

January 25, 1996: 17). Correspondingly, the involvement of hierarchical superiors is not required: their passive tolerance or lack of checks and enforcement is enough.

The risks connected with the spread of compromising information are reduced, however, by the limited dimension of the group of corrupted bureaucrats (and by reciprocal blackmailing power): from 4 corrupt agents on police patrols (R, November 3, 2000: 27) up to groups of 10. As in the case of petty corruption, transaction costs are also lowered by the small amounts of money at stake.

Quite often, the friendly aspect of the bribe is reinforced by its conversion into what appears to be nothing more than a gift: a ham, champagne, caviar, designer clothes for police women (R, June 7, 1996: 18), even prams (R, June 22, 2000: 25). In a corruption case involving traffic police in Caserta, the nature of the bribe depended on the kind of commodity the truck being inspected was carrying. The approach was very direct: "Are you carrying flowers? My wife would like them," or "A couple of chickens will be enough, for now" (R, July 10, 2001: 22).

All kinds of gifts emerged in scandals that involved the border revenue police in various Italian cities. They included "gasoline, bank transfers, and stipends paid every month by oil entrepreneurs to four public officers" (R-Milan, December 10, 2003), as well as cell phones, gasoline, wine, and visits to luxurious hotels and restaurants paid for by an import-export firm in exchange for fake certification (R-Bari, July 7, 2005). In China, they also included any possible transported good (toys, refrigerators, champagne, olives, shoes, bags, etc.) as well as money (with payments proportionate to the size of the "favor" required) in exchange for avoiding checks on products imported with the fake "made in Italy" logo (R-Genoa, December 8, 2004; R-Genoa, September 21, 2005).

The frequent repetition of corrupt exchanges with public bureaucrats requires customary clients as private counterparts. Corrupters involved in structural corruption were truck drivers in one case (R, July 10, 2001: 21), low-level criminals in other cases. These are individuals who will not presumably be very prone to denouncing corruption in order to avoid the negative consequences of the sanctions that should accompany their habitual violations and their frequent subjection to inspections. They will, at the same time, be interested in establishing and consolidating good exchange relationships with corrupt public bureaucrats, being trustworthy, and respecting the terms of their illegal agreements. Internal and external risks of corruption are thus strongly reduced, as are transaction costs.

Internal controls are weak, however, especially when internal hierarchy is missing in the corrupt network. From investigations into the activities of the urban police in Naples, for example, the "distribution of bribes to those who could create problems" emerged as widespread, but so did the lack of capacity to comply with requests from other voracious members of the same police body. A "Don Carmine" is disappointed in this way: "but how many of them should we pay? [...] . We already paid the first squad, and then the second and the third [...]" (R-Neaples, February 4, 2005).

Potential growth in the scale of corrupt activities is limited under conditions in which

(i) the amount of resources at stake is small

(ii) no complex governance structure of illegal deals exists

(iii) necessary hierarchical roles within the group can not be sustained

(iv) managing a more "organized" form of corruption would presumably have costs greater than their expected benefits (reduced risks of accusation and cheating, etc.)

In this case, bribery is widely diffused within specific administrative units, made up of the sum of single corrupt acts without any relevant organizational texture. Acceptance, or the silent tolerance of corrupt practices among both peers and superiors, is common. There is awareness that even beyond the small group of one's own accomplices the risk of internal accusation is relatively small since reciprocal blackmail power tends to sanction a minimal norm of connivance and bribes-sharing. None of the cases of structural corruption we analyzed emerged as a result of internal complaints or inquiries. Their exposure was due to the dissatisfaction of excluded bribers or the outcomes of autonomous judicial inquiries.

Individual Corruption in the Public Administration

In April 2003, the Tribunal of Milan condemned a judge accused of having received large amounts of money in order to favor a business firm in a judicial proceeding. A lawyer was also sentenced, and two other judges acquitted. The judges spoke of a devastating case touching on one of the most delicate features of the rule of law: the impartiality of jurisdiction, stigmatizing the way in which some judges conceive of their function and their relations with business lawyers, with the "degradation of the judiciary" into a "justice for a private use" (TMBMP: 2).

Beginning in the year 2000, the trial involved only a few individuals, but the stakes were high, as the decision the accused judge had taken concerned a payment of 980 billion lire (ibid.: 145). In this sense, it can be taken as an illustration of individual corruption where the number of people involved in the illegal exchange is very low, but the size of the rent (and, accordingly, of the bribe) is high. The amounts involved can indeed help to overcome moral scruples—as testified in a letter from the accused businessman in the case above to his son: "I attach the *Corriere* [...]. I attach it so that you realize that my 'going to Rome', as you used to call it, proved useful. And believe me, for years, with fatigue but also with great humility and abnegation, with a courage that cost me more than the fatigue: but proud for having won back our name [...] . Sure, I had to do everything on my own, thinking that with the help of a son with a Masters, I would have done better and saved, as you suggested, my weak moral and material health" (ibid.: 234).

In our research we found several cases of individual corruption in which expected benefits turned out to be higher than expected costs, and corrupt transactions took place with no drawbacks. In one case, however, a bribe of 1 billion lire was paid to a carabiniere general without receiving anything in exchange: it was simply a fraud (R, April 12, 1998: 2). In most cases a single high-level public agent was the target of the bribe. In some cases, however, the target had instrumentally built a small network of connivance, friendship, and exchange with other top officials whose decisions could influence the risks of his illegal activities or who could pass useful information on to him (R, November 22, 1996: 11).

In individual corruption, property rights over the "political rent" sold in the black market of corruption are extremely valuable. This was confirmed by the size of the bribes that were paid in exchange for them: hundreds of millions of lire in most cases, and up to 1.5 billion lire in one case (R, December 16, 1998: 20).

Among the categories of "public actors" involved were judges, prosecutors, high-ranking bureaucrats, or police officials. Corruption in courts was sought by rich entrepreneurs, as well as by individual *mafiosi*, to avoid serious sentences or charges or to obtain favourable ones (R, November 16, 1998: 20). For example, according to a state witness, the Mafia paid 600 million lire to a Masonic lawyer in Palermo who had offered "his intervention with the Court President X in relation with a trial in the Supreme Court," and which ended with the annulment of the charges made against the defendants (PP: 253). Corrupt high-ranking police officers provided different resources: protection and confidential information on the police's and other criminal gangs' activities to criminals (R, November 24, 1997: 2), and confidential information concerning future fiscal inspections to entrepreneurs (LR, August 7, 1997: 5).

The costs that public bureaucrats can impose on operators in illegal markets are particularly high, since they include the seizure of illicit commodities and other assets, as well as the loss of personal freedom. Profits from illicit markets open opportunities for corruption, since actors will seek to be exempted from the application of the law or to acquire a "rigid" application of the law against their competitor, thereby gaining a monopolistic position in the criminal activity in question (Benson 1988: 75; Van Duyne 1997). It has also been observed that

> the most important relationship in the criminal organisation, one that can be looked at as a contract, is thus likely to be its arrangements for non-enforcement of the law and mitigation of penalties. Corruption may be easier if the crimes are viewed as consensual (e.g., gambling) by the public and the government; if the criminal activity is an ongoing activity that produces an attractive stream of cash flows; and if the criminal organisation can offer the legitimate political system some benefits, especially cash and votes, which will lead to greater tolerance of the behavior of individual judges or other corruptees who may act favourably to members of the criminal group. (Anderson 1995: 44, see also Chapter 8)

Indeed, cases emerged in areas in which decisions have strong economic consequences, such as judicial decisions in cases of bankruptcy (R-Rome, December 8, 2004) or organized crime, with the release of Mafia bosses costing up to a million lire (R-Neaples, September 9, 2005), and interventions by judges to influence trials costing about 600 million lire (PP: 253).

Several governance mechanisms of corrupt transactions emerged within the context of individual corruption, reducing its expected costs. In the case quoted at the beginning of this section, a network of people (such as employees of the High Court) provided information about the names of the judges who had to decide the case—the judges talked of a structure "ready to act when there was the risk that some judge would jeopardize their plans" (TMBMP: 343).

In some cases, the exchange, although occasional, was not unique. It was repeated episodically, or such a repetition was expected in the future. The corrupt public agent could then be profitably locked in in a long-term protection contract with his corrupter(s). Indeed, *contracts of protection*, by which a public bureaucrat's guarantee of uncertain property rights is exchanged for bribes, are more effective when they are long term.[8] Public bureaucrats became, in a sense, employees of their corruptors, guaranteeing their protective services, which are only actually furnished when occasionally needed and demanded. This was the case for one high-ranking carabiniere, corrupted by a criminal boss, whose monthly fee was index-linked to the inflation rate (R, March 10, 1999: 2) and for a *Camorrista* boss who paid a monthly salary of 3 million lire (plus other valuable fringe benefits) to a senior police official (R, December 2, 1998: 26).

Finally, the figure of a broker emerged in some of the cases of individual corruption analyzed (see also Chapter 6). His function is to ease or "grease" the necessary interactions and reduce risks in the negotiations between the two or more parties interested in the corrupt deal, as well as to act as a go-between for the arrangement and collection of payoffs. In fact, when illegal exchanges are not frequent, paying for the services of a specialized mediator seems more rational than investing in order to build links directly with judges, prosecutors, high-level bureaucrats, or police officials (R, May 27, 1999).

Systemic Corruption

A refined system of bribes developed within the revenue police in an Italian city. According to a manager, "It was known to me, as I had learned it from some entrepreneur friends [...] that when the revenue police arrive, you have to pay. In fact, a police officer, when they started their inspection, told me that the task had been assigned to him for a certain amount of money, penciled on the cover of the file, and that was really the minimum amount that in any case, no matter if there was a contestation of irregularities, he had to bring to the responsible people, I think the power group within the revenue police. [...] he told me that, if he did not give them that amount of money, there would be serious retaliation, he would have been transferred to another office" (MF: 69–70). The bribe was then divided into a fixed quota and another quota proportionate to the irregularities that had to be covered up. According to the manager, "the police officer did not ask me for money, he just said, 'you know very well how it works,' with a clear allusion to the 'entry bribe'. The 100 million, further re-evaluated to meet the inflation rate, was

---

8   This ambiguous nature of protection is not lost on those who trade in it. Intermittent protective services present serious inconveniences for both the protector and the protected. As for the protector, it may become difficult to prevent previously protected individuals from being helped by the protector even when they are not consistent with payments (Gambetta 1993).

the entry tax, the rest derived from a real agreement between the parties, following the observations by the revenue police of existing irregularities" (MF: 70).

In some episodes, including this one, systemic corruption involves broad networks of revenue policemen that collect bribes in exchange for fudged investigations. In this type of corruption, bribes are quite high, occasionally even involving the payment of regular monthly "salaries" of up to 4 million lire to corrupt officers (R, January 31, 1997). In systemic corruption, all—or almost all—the members of a certain bureaucratic unit are involved in corruption. In some cases, more than 40 agents were collectively involved (Davigo 2002). During the 1980s, several hundred revenue police agents, as well as their seniors, were simultaneously arrested in a scandal in which bribes were paid in order to smuggle oil from Saudi Arabia (Turone 1992). Although corruption is not limited to the revenue police, some conditions are particulary favorable to its diffusion in such structures:

> (i) a high expected frequency of controls carried out at economic enterprises
> (ii) the complexity of the fiscal system (which fosters "uncertainty in one's own rights")
> (iii) the high value of the rents at stake (i.e., the amount of fines to be eventually paid)

Systemic corruption of public bureaucrats guaranteed softer fiscal inspections for the corrupters (R, April 18, 2000: 30), a reduction of fines in case of ascertained violations (R, July 8, 1998: 21). Mostly, the *customers* of these corrupt organizations are entrepreneurs and managers of large firms or cartels. Both the demand side and the supply side of the market are then monopolized by a single criminal firm. In such scenarios, reciprocal protection of respective activities can reinforce the effectiveness of sanctions against potential whistle-blowers.

Where corruption is systemic, bribery extends not only to "everything" in the jurisdiction of the law enforcement structure, but precise rates of payment also tend to emerge, which reduces the risk of endless negotiations between corrupter and corrupted. When a common belief arises that a given "price" is known and agreed upon, then what amounts to a rule—the *X percent rule*—may apply (see also Chapter 3). This rule operates both in the exchanges between corrupters and corrupt agents, as well as in the complex exchanges that regulate the internal redistribution of the bribe within the group of corrupt agents. In one case, the bribe was paid as a hidden "salary" of 4 million lira [about $2,000] per month to each bureaucrat" (R, January 31, 1997: 21). Where the probability of obtaining a more favorable price was outweighed by the risks and costs of renegotiation, the tacit repetition of the previously agreed price was the most convenient solution to reduce transaction costs.[9]

---

[9]   This would explain, for example, the annoyance of one entrepreneur with the attitude of an inspector. Unlike the situation with other corrupt officials, it "was never possible to find an arrangement to avoid continual disagreements. For four or five years I had to pay according to his will and inclinations" (PROM: 649–50).

As a consequence, an informal but well-constructed organizational structure emerged within the public agencies. The hierarchical distribution of roles was determined mostly by the institutional positions held by members within the structure, and also by the possession of resources connected with illegal activities (such as blackmail power or illegal skills). In one instance, a private brokerage society was created to facilitate bribe sharing among corrupted revenue policemen (R, December 19, 1997: 19). Top officials within the corrupted structures coordinated both the legal and the illegal activities of public bureaucrats, guaranteeing the fulfillment of agreements. In some cases, they also transferred isolated honest agents who could otherwise have interfered with the customary corruption of others (R, July 8, 1998: 21): their authority was however a guarantee against the risks of exposure. In Milan, every phase of the corrupt exchange was strictly regulated: the collection of bribes, their distribution on the hierarchical ladder, the careers and tasks of more "skilled" agents, and the strengthening of protective barriers against judicial inquiries (MF). Socialization to the bribery rules also followed hierarchical lines, further weakening moral constraints against illegal dealings: "My first kickback was passed to me by my direct superior: how could I refuse it?," is the question rhetorically asked by one bureaucrat involved (I-1).[10]

Bureaucratic Corruption: Some Concluding Remarks

In this chapter, we applied our typology of corrupt exchange (see Chapter 2) to the analysis of corruption within police and law enforcement agencies. Considering corruption as a hidden exchange between a public agent(s) and a briber, we used empirical evidence, mainly derived from the Italian case, to present four specific models of corruption governance. Each can be interpreted as an organizational response to the shared need of reducing transaction costs, mainly connected to severe informational asymmetries and to risks of exposure. We noted several governance structures within the market for corrupt exchanges:

- decentralized market structures, regulated by simple, purposeful, directed, self-enforcing rules of behavior
- brokers who specialized in the reduction of identification and information costs
- "internalization" of corrupt agents within private organizations, through

---

[10] This *top-down* pattern, where corrupt superior officials buy the connivance or the cooperation of subordinates by sharing bribes or other benefits connected with corruption can also be reversed. In "bottom-up" dynamics, low-level officials directly collect bribes, sharing them with their superiors: "In some cases, a pyramid operates—each tier purchases its position from the one above it. If 'street-level bureaucrats' have the most discretionary interactions with the public, the bottom-up pattern holds. Police corruption frequently originates with the power that officials on the beat exercise over businesses—both legal and illegal" (Rose-Ackerman 1999: 82).

long-term "bribery contracts" based on specific investments in trust and reciprocal knowledge
- hierarchical structures with an articulated subdivision of tasks, characterized by the resolution of internal disputes
- guarantee of fragile property rights through the use of bureaucratic power

As we have shown, the models of *petty, individual, structural,* and *systemic corruption* (see Table 4.1) are strictly connected to several characteristics of the illegal transaction, which is made possible by the nature of the powers delegated to public agents.

Table 4.1   Four models of corruption in police and law enforcement activity

Selected corruption foci	Models of corruption			
	Petty corruption	Structural corruption	Individual corruption	Systemic Corruption
Number of public agents involved	One or small clusters	Small groups	One or very few	an 'inclination' for all the members of a public structure
Involvement of senior officials	No involvement or passive tolerance	No involvement or passive tolerance	Active participation as a main actor	direct participation in corrupt exchanges as guarantors, co-ordinators, recipients
Division of tasks among corrupted agents	No specialization	No specialization or very simple division of tasks (a "cashier" who redistributes bribes)	Network of "exchange relationships" with other public agents not involved in corruption	high specialization (articulated rules of behavior guaranteeing corrupt exchange and silence)
Favors delivered by corrupt agents	Lack of control or denouncing illegal and irregular activities, reduced fines	Lack of control or denouncing illegal and irregular activities, confidential information	Favorable sentences and decisions, confidential information, judicial protection, brokerage services	'softened' fiscal controls or non-of denouncing, reduced fines and sanctions, protection of illegal activities
Amount and characteristics of the bribe	Very small "kickbacks," sometimes remuneration in kind	Many small kickbacks, often "gifts" and remuneration in kind	Very high bribes or other valuable resources	high bribes (to be shared among all those involved), sometimes a monthly "fee"

Chapter 5
Political Actors in the Governance of Corrupt Exchanges

Germany. The managing director of Flick Corporation had been granted a lucrative tax exemption by ministers of the Frei Demokratische Partei (FDP) following donations to that party, as well as others (excluding the Greens) advocating a political environment conducive to business interests (McKey 2003, 58). At the end of 1999, former Chancellor Kohl was charged with having received undeclared donations to the Christliche Demokratische Union in a secret bank account. Amongst others, donations had been received from an arms dealer, linked with the sale of tanks to Saudi Arabia. Some indications of corruption—or at least, illegal party financing in return for the acquisition of political protection—also emerged in the sale of an oil refinery to Elf Aquitaine, aircraft and helicopters to Canada and Thailand, as well as the sale at bargain prices of railway worker housing to a company that had financed the CDU. Kohl admitted undeclared donations of more than 2 million German marks, but denied that favors had been exchanged (McKay 2003).

France. In 1989, allegedly, with the protection of part of the Partie Socialiste (PS), Loik Le Floch-Prigent became the president of the public enterprise Société Nationale d'Elf Aquitaine. He was presented in the press as a parvenu, who had acquired money and power thanks to his friendship with Pierre Dreyfuss, a prominent socialist, but had failed to conform to the customs and habits of the class he joined. During his tenure, Elf Aquitaine expanded in Eastern Europe. Said to be fluent in the language of party contributions, corruption, kickbacks, and secret transfers of funds, Floch-Prigent "successfully navigated the uncharted waters of post-communist regimes, where the new spirit of capitalism had been tainted by the ageless quest for personal enrichment" (Yates 2001: 76). In particular, there were rumors of bribes of 256 billion francs paid to German officials for the acquisition of Minol. Once arrested, "Through his trial, Floch-Progent maintained that he was just a cog in an institutionalized corruption machine involving the political and administrative elite of France who profited from an elaborate network of bribes and kickbacks well known to insiders and meticulously documented by them and who also used the public enterprises to provide 'ghost jobs' for cronies with dirty hands" (Yates 2001: 78).

USA. In 1987, five senators were accused of having intervened on behalf of a property speculator from Arizona, Charles Keating, accused of reckless investment by federal regulators. It emerged that they had all received substantial campaign contributions from him (Williams 2003: 69).

Indonesia. In their research on *Economic Gangsters: Corruption, Violence, and the Poverty of Nations*, Fishman and Miguel (2008: 23) describe the economic business of Suharto Inc., as the head of the Suharto family was in government: "Suharto family members had a reputation for demanding a cut of any company wanting to do business with the government. That's how the kids got their fingers in so many pies."

What these very different cases have in common is the involvement of political parties and political actors in complex nets of corruption. While there is agreement among scholars and observers that politicians and political parties play a central role in corrupt exchanges—which usually involve exchanges between politicians and entrepreneurs—there are two different narratives about which characteristics facilitate their involvement or, to put it differently, what pushes politicians and parties to get involved in corrupt exchanges. Simplifying somewhat, we may distinguish between a narrative of strength and a narrative of weakness.

Political corruption, as an illegal means by which money influences politics (Key 1936), is clearly affected by the characteristics of the principal actor in the political system: the party. There is in fact the widespread belief that corruption is favored by the ubiquity and omnipotence of the parties, which are powerful and well-organized political machines capable of controlling civil society and the market.

In the first narrative, political corruption is considered as a sign, if not a consequence, of strong parties, able to dominate society and the market, and distorting the functioning of both. When political corruption scandals emerged in Italy, the term *partitocracy* popped up often to indicate and stigmatize the anomalous power of mass and highly ideological political parties, with broad apparatuses, and therefore a need for money to pay their employees, but also firm control over several powerful positions in public and semi-public enterprises (Pasquino 1990; Rhodes 1997). More generally, international campaigns against corruption by intergovernmental organizations (IGOs) such as the World Bank or the IMF tend to depict corruption as produced by the inappropriate control of the state(s) over the market(s), and the proposed solutions have been privatization and liberalization.

In a different narrative, political corruption derives from the weakness of political parties, not from their power. As Pizzorno (1993: 304–5) noted, "The term *partitocracy* comes from a period in which the parties acted as collective subjects, guided by powerful leaderships responsible, if not to the membership as such, at least to elite circles composed of members. The leadership could answer for their members, parliamentary groups and mass associations before other actors within the political system, represented for their part by other parties. Decisions regarding the selection of political personnel were taken by the party leaderships according to largely pre-established rules." The political parties involved in systemic corruption are instead often divided into personalistic internal factions, in perpetual struggles with one another, under a fragmented and permanently contested leadership.

The development of corruption has been connected to party weakness during phases of growing political participation. Corruption is said to spread in those specific paths to modernization in which popular participation in political decision-making is not immediately accompanied by a strengthening of those institutions that should filter and direct collective demands: "the weaker and less accepted the political parties, the greater the likelihood of corruption" (Huntington 1968: 71). Traditionally, political corruption in developing countries has been linked to a misfit between market development and political underdevelopment, with—within the functionalist perspective—the expectation of a gradual strengthening of political parties, even produced through resources coming from corruption, and a related decline in corruption. For a long time in the United States, the development of democratic institutions has been described as sufficient to overcome the corruption of the "party machine." In Dahl's account (1961), with universal suffrage the "plebs"—who had based their political fortunes on the control of corrupt ethnic factions—lose their power to modern political entrepreneurs.

Clientelism, defined as loyalty to a patron in exchange for protection, has similarly been considered as a sign of strength, and at other times as a sign of the weakness, of the party organization. In Southern Europe—for example, in Spain (Heywood 1997: 73–6; Pujas 1996: 4), Italy (della Porta and Vannucci 1999a), Portugal, and Greece (Magone 1996: 16)—corruption has developed within clientelistic networks, with illegal funds obtained through corruption (see also below). In both cases, clientelism has been observed to be strickly linked to corruption.

The two narratives can be reconciled, but only to a certain extent, if we look more carefully at what is conceptualized as strength and what as weakness. In fact, in the interpretation of Italian political corruption, how the parties' power of nomination (of party protégées to semi-public positions) did *not* go hand-in-hand with party power, not only in terms of identification (that is their capacity to produce collective identities, see Pizzorno 1993) but also in terms of making long-term policy choices (Cotta 1996). As we seek to show in this chapter, different types of political parties can, however, play an important role in the governance of corruption.

Theoretically, our reflections aim at linking different mechanisms of corrupt governance to the different types of parties that have been singled out in the political science literature as moving from mass ideological parties to cartel or electoral parties (for reviews of the relevant literature, see della Porta 2009; Ware 1996), with particular evolutions such as firm-parties à la Forza Italia in Italy (Hopkin 1997; Rhodes 1997). In parallel with the typologies of corrupt governance developed in Chapter 2, we want to look at the effect of party structures on corrupt exchanges, distinguishing centralized versus fragmented political parties. We also consider the amount of material resources a party controls, as well as the difference between ideological parties that mainly appeal to ideals, and clientelistic parties that distribute mainly material incentives.

Political Parties and the Steering of Corruption Exchanges

> For three generations Coesit S.p.A. has paid all those who facilitated our work. Grandfather and father corrupted politicians; after the new laws on public procurement of the 1990s (since it was no longer necessary to pay politicians) the grandson only paid the public bureaucrats. (R-Turin, October 26, 2002)

This is the testimony of an Italian entrepreneur, describing a change in the governance of corrupt exchanges in Italy, where the role of politicians declined, and the role of bureaucrats increased. This change does not, however, imply any moralization of politics. On the one hand, many smaller scandals continued to involve local administrators that had been elected on party lists or nominated by parties to public bodies. On the other, some larger scandals (amongst which was the financial collapse of the Parmalat corporation) confirmed the persistence of illicit payments to parties and party bosses.

What remains relevant in both periods is the importance of parties and politicians in corrupt governance, even though their role has changed. The more centralized the political parties, and the more material resources they can manage, the more they are able to function as agencies of political protection. Acquiring influence within the party is important for a corrupt politician in order to occupy public positions (assigned either electorally or through party nomination), that can then be used to raise bribes. In these cases, the political parties were able to exercise some control over their members in this way, and therefore to enforce some general rules. Bribes were therefore often split in two: with one part going to the politician directly granting the favor, and the other going to the political party, which provided a long-term perspective through the repetition of the corrupt game. Episodes of corruption that see the involvement of parties tend therefore to be of the systemic type, with frequent exchanges and quite significant bribes.

In systemic corruption, political parties may play the role of guarantors of illegal contracts between politicians and private parties (mainly entrepreneurs). Thanks to their powers of nomination, they control the politicians, and thanks to their capillary structures, they can spread the rules of the corrupt game throughout large geographic and administrative territories. In this way, they can act as "trust certifiers," holding instruments to punish free riders on both sides, as well as incentives in terms of perspectives for future illicit business for those who comply (Pizzorno 1992: 31). Moreover, if a political party in government and another in opposition reach various degrees of agreement over the reciprocal protection of corrupt deals, this further reduces the risks of denunciation, helping to further generalize some rules of corrupt exchanges. Political parties also socialize their politicians to the complex skills that must be mastered in a corrupt game. They teach linguistic skills: that is what to say and what not to say during hidden negotiations, how to ask and how to apply pressure. They also help to reduce moral costs by teaching their members what "real politics" is about. Party cashiers, who collect the party's shares of the bribes, contribute to the implementation of the rules of the corrupt game.

Corruption in centralized political parties nevertheless exists in a precarious equilibrium. In fact, the very diffusion of corruption creates tensions within and between political parties. The availability and distribution of additional resources from corruption makes those who are in, but also those who are out, ever greedier. Centrifugal tendencies are fueled by internal conflicts over the distribution of spoils. In Italy, even before the Clean Hands investigations, the political parties involved in corruption had gradually lost control over their political class. The more the party was based on the distribution of material incentives, the less it could control the loyalty of its members, who could always threaten their migration to other parties. Once parties split into fractions, the very logic of internal competition tended to reduce internal loyalty and mutual trust. To be able to perform the function of guarantors of corrupt exchanges, the parties needed to engage in frequent internal negotiations and continuously contest agreements. Socialization to corruption tended therefore to be performed by leaders of the various fractions, and a share of the bribes were to go to them. Personal networks and loyalties external to the parties became more and more relevant in the governance of corruption.

We shall address these differences by looking at the ways in which (corrupt) parties perform governance functions in corrupt exchanges. In particular, we examine the selection of political personnel and their socialization to illegality, and the establishment of (corrupt) rules, guarantees, and coordination.

The Selection of Personnel

A membership card for Forza Italia costs between 60 and 100 thousand lira. And it seems that O. had collected 1.500/2.000 in a few months. He therefore controlled about one fifth of the members in the two provinces, for a total cost of about 100 million. He confessed yesterday that he had received about 90 million ('30 plus 5 plus 30 plus 15, the rest I do not remember). 'And before October 4, when the candid camera started to work? My memory becomes weak.' O. has governed the Molinette since '99. But already at the beginning of the year 2000 the health system was too little for him. It was just before the electoral campaign for the regional election and the *forzisti* aimed at taking over the health ministry from AN [Alleanza Nazionale, a post-fascist party], which controls 70% of the regional budget. Aspiring to that position was B. O. started to collect membership cards for the fraction of his friend G., then already allied with B. Now, in Forza Italia you can only enter with the presentation and signature of an old member. O collected about a thousand membership cards in Turin and 500 in Asti, thanks also to his family connections. He increased his weight and the weight of G. in the party in this way. But, his commitment notwithstanding, he was frustrated. He was not a candidate in the national election, and did not succeed in sending either B. or himself to the regional health ministry. Recently, he was in pole position to be the director of the Regional Agency for Health. (R-Turin, December 21, 2001)

This is a reconstruction of a scandal in the Molinette Hospital in Turin (the third largest in Italy), which involved the hospital's manager and the Forza Italia leader O.—himself son of a Christian-Democratic politician. The same hospital had gone through several scandals: nurses had favored funeral houses, selling them information about dying patients (R-Turin, June 12, 2001); a manager had been accused of having taken money in exchange for accelerating procedures for a transplantation (R-Turin, October 3, 2001), and heart surgeons had been arrested for corruption in a public bid for the acquisition of heart valves (R, November 5, 2002). Arrested while collecting a bribe on December 19 2001, O. attempted to justify himself, saying the money belonged to an aunt (R, December 20, 2001).

The evidence collected for this case offers an illustration of the role played by political parties in the selection of political (and bureaucratic) personnel in cases of systemic corruption. If political parties are still important in the distribution of public positions that are potential sources for bribes, at the same time, the corrupt politicians, through the use of resources collected in this way, help orient personnel selection, favoring those endowed with some specific skills. In a functioning democracy, political personnel should be selected on the basis of their capacity to elaborate general programs, convince citizens that their programs are better than those proposed by their competitors, and implement them. When corruption spreads, the politicians selected are those that are capable of providing material resources for themselves and the party in different ways. Their main skill is not the ability to formulate and implement programs in the public interest, but to increase their opportunities for getting money (Pizzorno 1992: 27). Membership cards become property shares that are used to gain temporary allies within the party, showing loyalty by contributing to general expenses or supporting specific party factions.

The O. case shows how these exchanges work. First of all, a patrimonialistic use of the hospital allowed him to increase his personal clique of supporters in the party organization—and O. was indeed described as "very friendly," "kind, discreet, and particularly able to meet any demand: a bed in the hospital, surgery, hiring people, providing a recommendation for your daughter's exam." The importance of dynamic management is also stressed: "At Le Molinette, he became the Big one, since his desire for grandeur emerged at any occasion" (R, January 25, 2002). At the same time, the boss is also able to arrogantly assess his power over entrepreneurs looking for a public contract. One of them confessed a feeling of "psychological subornation" vis-à-vis O. who, besides collecting bribes, also asked for "340 million lira of work (unpaid) to be done in the 15,000 square meter park of his villa in Nizza Monferrato" (ibid.). Transaction costs were reduced by the development of a system of "fixed bribes"—according to one entrepreneur, O. told him: "Listen, I don't know how it works [there], but here it is 10%" (R, December 22, 2001).

Competition within the corrupt parties is thus influenced by the amount of money a politician can invest to obtain positions of power, buying membership cards, paying the rent for the party headquarters, and paying for party newspapers and party propaganda. The control of membership cards and votes thus became a resource for exchange within the party. As an Italian politician observed, "with the bribes I paid for the membership cards of the members of my section and, on the occasions when various decisions were taken on party positions, I controlled a bunch of membership cards and votes that my reference point within the party indicated to me [...] . And I put my bunch of votes and membership cards on the table of the party when my position had to be renewed and I wanted another position" (Nascimbeni and Pamparana 1992: 160). Another confirmed: "Nobody pays for his membership card here. Let's say, 90% of the members never pay [...] the control of the party is indispensable if you want to be candidate or locate your men in the institutions and the public bodies where there is money. Therefore, you have to buy membership cards" (Licandro and Varano 1993: 123). O. also used part of the cash from bribes for party activities, buying, among other things, 1,600 membership cards for his party (for a total amount of 160 million lire), financing electoral campaigns for his party and its allies (R, January 17, 2002), and distributing generous gifts (70 million lire were spent on "Christmas" presents, including watches worth up to 14 million each) to various fellow politicians. As he himself declared, "I paid for [electoral] dinners, gifts and membership cards in part from my salary and in part from bribes" (R, January 25, 2002). Transferring the membership cards like shares from one party candidate to another, O. could then obtain and consolidate his position as general director of the Molinette. All this, he considered as necessary for the making of his own career. As he explained,

> I wanted to build a career. I was tired of the position as general director of the Molinette, I wanted to grow. And so I tried to build a package of votes for Forza Italia, building about 800 of them between '99 and the year 2000. I spent 70 million on Christmas and Easter gifts for all the influential people in society [...] Mr judge, I spent the bribe money, I spent 160 million to buy 1,600 membership cards for Forza Italia. [...] I gave 8 million for the electoral campaign of Forza Italia, and at the last regional elections I paid 10 million lire for a cocktail event for Berlusconi's party. (R, January 17, 2002)

When the party is centralized, money transfers go straight to the central structure of the party; when the party is fragmented, corrupt politicians form pragmatic alliances with one another, threatening to shift their loyalties if their requests are not satisfied.[1]

By moving their package of membership cards to political protectors, corrupt politicians build themselves careers within the party. Remaining with the O. story, within Forza Italia, he progressed in just a few years from the position of sanitary director of the small Sant'Anna Hospital to the role of general director of the large

---

[1]   Intraparty conflicts, moreover, tend to increase the demand for funds to be invested in electoral campaigns, especially with open-list systems of proportional representation, and therefore encourage the recourse to corruption to finance political activity (Golden and Chang 2001).

and prestigious Molinette. In another case, a former regional minister was charged for having asked for a bribe of €10,000 from an entrepreneur, explaining that he needed the money to influence, through the buying of membership cards, the local party congress. He was quoted as saying "you know, membership cards, they are expensive" (TBSA: 32–3). The lower the transparency and accountability of party decisions (in the last case, the party local congress was held "in a cafe"), the more likely it is that this type of maneuver will succeed.

These investments are important as the parties have nomination powers. The appointment of public positions—especially those that are more useful in terms of bribe collection—lies at the center of complex games and conflicts that are sometimes solved through precarious equilibria.

There are, however, substantial differences in the governance of corruption according to the strength of the party or its politicians. Apparently, similar to the O. case is the first case of the Clean Hands investigations, which involved the Socialist Mario Chiesa, president of the Pio Albergo Trivulzio nursing home in Milan. As he confessed, "In substance, to understand the reasons why I should have exposed myself personally to the mechanism of bribery it is necessary to understand that I did not remain president of an organization like the Trivulzio simply because I was a good technician and a good health manager but also because in a certain way I was a force to be reckoned with in Milan, having a certain number of votes at my disposal. To acquire what amounted in the end to 7,000 votes[,] I had, during my political career, to sustain the costs of creating and maintaining a political organization which could amass votes right across Milan." These blocs of members and votes were then placed at the service of influential party leaders in return for a new term of office.

Unlike O.'s, however, Chiesa's career developed within the Socialist Party through the occupation of elected positions. As he declared, "At the end of the 1970s I was an active militant and a supporter of the party currently led by the then mayor […] . He made a political investment in me by putting me up for the provincial elections. I was successfully elected but found that even minor political positions like the one I had reached were largely empty, simply serving to legitimate the real sources of decision making and power: the party secretariats and their bidding" (Carlucci 1992: 56). In fact, in most of the cases that emerged during the Clean Hands investigations, the career paths of the politicians involved were all of a party nature, sponsored by party structures even though their political activities then facilitated their success in other professional activities, with money from bribes being invested, for instance, in consultancy firms competing for public contracts.

The Party as "School of Corruption"

The corrupt party places its men in various positions of responsibility in public bodies; in return it demands that they conform to the rules, using those positions not only for personal enrichment but also for (illegal) party financing. As a Socialist

MP and President of the Istututo Nazionale Assistenza Dipendenti Enti Locali (INADEL) (a public body) declared to magistrates, "I knew, and know, that the key positions in particular bodies (the INADEL among them) are held by people the parties trust *to take the burden of obtaining contributions for the party itself*; in any case, *I knew that any change of mind on my part would immediately lead to my marginalization and the loss of my position* (TNM: 76, emphasis added).

With the widespread presence of corrupt parties in the various nerve centers of public administration, *corruption becomes the rule*. As a former councilor for the Metropolitane Milanesi relates, "On entering the *Metropolitana* I found *an already tried and tested system* according to which, as a rule, virtually all contract winners paid a bribe of three per cent [...] . The proceeds of these *tangenti* were divided among the parties according to pre-existing agreements" (Nascimbeni and Pamparana 1992: 147, emphasis added). In a similar fashion, Mario Chiesa talked of an "environmental situation" favoring corruption: "My conduct in the PAT," the ex-administrator declared to the magistrates, "wasn't my own invention but the result of an existing *environmental situation* in the Milanese health service (and in the public administration more generally), to which I adapted myself when, beginning my political activity from the bottom, I discovered it to be a source of finance for personal political advancement" (TNM: 27, emphasis added).

Finally, the moral costs of corruption are reduced if corruption is presented as part and parcel of "normal" party life. According to a corrupt politician, "It was the national leaderships of the DC and the PSI themselves that gave me the green light to buy the buildings in question from companies which had shown themselves to be friends of the parties [attentive regarding contributions]" (TNM: 76).

It is often through the parties, in terms of socializing actors to corruption, that the system of occult transactions expands. In general, as Pizzorno has observed, participation in political parties, and politics in general, impacts on the individual's socialization, and therefore their identity and moral principles. The moral quality of life within a party will vary with the criteria for recognition inside it:

> Someone belonging to a political association can receive recognition for: technical or cultural abilities; loyalty, or conformism, in ideological commitment; loyalty to a particular leader; astuteness, aggression or lack of scruples in "taking out" adversaries; capacity for forming links with the wider society and bringing in money for party funds or other kinds of contribution; or, naturally, some combination of these qualities. [...] The more an individual's activity and relations are restricted to the concerns of party life the more the identifications on which identity is modeled will reflect its "moral quality", and on this will depend the moral cost of corruption. The more corruption is diffuse the more political parties themselves function as agencies for socialization in illegality, reducing the moral cost paid by their members for participation in corrupt practices. (Pizzorno 1992: 47)

The politicians already "introduced" to the rules of the illicit market in their turn introduce others. On his role in socializing other administrators to the system of corruption, the ex-mayor of Reggio Calabria writes, "One of the people I initiated into taking *mazzette* afterwards started to make small deals of his own, *gli "assolo"* [solos] as they're called in the jargon" (Licandro and Varano 1993: 48). The more a party is centralized, the fewer the number of party leaders that have to be socialized to these values, as the collection of bribes can be centralized. In these cases, the task is often handled by party administrators, with little diffusion of information. The typical case here is Germany. As McKay (2003: 54–5) observed,

> A distinctive feature of political corruption in Germany is that it is not widespread, low-level corruption, but high-level corruption involving a small number of senior figures. Indeed, it is the seniority of the perpetrators that substantially raises Germany's corruption rating. The most notorious cases in the 1980s and 1990s involved ministers at federal and *land* level and several party chairs [...] . Furthermore, apart from some relatively trivial cases, the beneficiaries have usually been party coffers and not individual politicians. Indeed former Chancellor Kohl, whose dedication to his party took precedence over his commitment to the law of the land, is the antithesis of the "gain politician."

During the reunification period, various political scandals emerged about the selling of public firms and other goods (e.g., the Leuna oil refinery or railway-worker housing), but also about the sale of tanks to Saudi Arabia by an arms dealer and of the sale of aircraft and helicopters to Canada and Thailand. As mentioned above, it was the general secretary of the (very centralized) CDU party himself that admitted undeclared donations of 2.1 million German marks, without naming the private donors. During the scandals, the CDU was in fact accused of having created a network of relations based upon party protection in exchange for loyalty and obedience (McKay 2003: 60).

The more fragmented a party, the larger the number of party members involved in bribe collection and sharing, and therefore the higher the need to socialize a broader number of members to these alternative norms. This is the case, among others, in the episodes of political corruption that have emerged in the United States, such as the "Keating's five" scandal described above. Corruption here adapts to (relatively) weak and decentralized political parties: "In a fragmented political system so evidently lacking in cohesion and discipline, the opportunities for intervention by external actors such as business corporations are plentiful" (Williams 2003: 68). As mentioned, Charles Keating refused to cooperate with the federal regulatory agency and sought the protection of five senators, from both the Republican and Democratic parties, in exchange for illegal campaign contributions.

The Party as Guarantor of Illegal Deals

According to the judicial investigations, the owner of the Parmalat corporation had invested, since 1993, about €12 million to support members of Parliament, city, provincial and regional councilors, and presidents and administrative secretaries of various political parties, as well for advertising in newspapers of different political colors. In particular, he admitted having financed, by paying for publicity, the emergence of the new party, Forza Italia. According to his declarations, he had adopted a bipartisan strategy, financing the electoral campaigns of candidates of different party coalitions (Gomez and Travaglio 2006: 29–35).

Some traditional manifestations of party corruption emerge in this story: in particular the search for some kind of contract of protection. In some cases, parties also help in developing and enforcing the rules of the "corruption game." The establishment of fixed quotas for bribes to be paid on public contracts reduces transaction costs by eliminating the need to negotiate this delicate issue. The development of the so-called X percent rule moves in this direction (see Chapter 3). In France, in a case of collusion among three major French construction firms accused of having formed a cartel for construction works in schools, political parties in the region have allegedly received 2 percent on all contracts in exchange for their intervention to stabilize the cartel (*Le Monde*, October 12, 1998).

General protection of firms is often offered in exchange for (mainly but not only) illegal contributions that were not directly linked to a specific favor. This general protection sheltered the firm from any type of potential problems in dealing with public administration—from the attribution of a public contract to inspections and delays in procedures and payments, as well as requests for bribes—which those dealing with an inefficient public administration learn to fear. To access rights (such as fair treatment) or gain illicit favors, entrepreneurs may then have an interest in obtaining a generalized form of protection. On their side, corrupt administrators therefore have an interest in fostering uncertainty, and then intervening to sell selective, *ad personam* protection to those who pay. Bribes then become—whether intentionally or not—the payment of a sort of insurance against the uncertainties that corrupt politicians themselves help spread in the administrative environment. Advantages are therefore limited to restricted circles of corruptors and corruptees, while costs (such as major uncertainties as well as greater inefficiency for those who are excluded) are widespread (Vannucci 1997a: 109–13). For instance, the Flick consortium is said to have made donations to all German parties at the time (except the Greens) to encourage "a political environment conducive to business interests" (Girling 1997: 17).

A bribe collector from the Italian Christian Democratic Party explained the attempts to centralize the payment of bribes, thereby making them less linked to specific favors, thus:

> The discourse of linking the money we collected to specific contracts started to become less and less sustainable for us; [...] we started a discourse of disentangling. To be clear, the idea was that firms [...] would give us money for X percent on the work effectively done, but as a general contribution that, of course, implied a favorable (or at least not an unfavorable) attitude towards the firm that paid the money. (Carlucci 1992: 10)

This is also confirmed in other episodes where parties were repaid for their capacity to solve controversies and introduce certainties in illegal exchanges. For instance, the national secretary of the party had to intervene when, during a public bid for the construction of a hospital in a Northern town, a conflict emerged between an entrepreneur and local DC politicians regarding the redistribution of a bribe between local and national politicians. "The decision, taken by a sort of committee including the administrative secretary of the party, was that a third of the bribe went to the local level" (*Panorama*, October 18, 1992: 54). Similarly, the bribes paid for seven years by a Sicilian entrepreneur went in part to national level DC and PSI politicians, whose role was "to avoid potential conflicts that could emerge at the local level for the redistribution of the bribe" (R, August 7, 1993). In recent investigations, it has also emerged that some bribes were divided between the periphery and the center—although it was mostly national currents that were involved. This seems to be the case, for instance, of an environmental agency in a Southern region, where bribes (oscillating between 3 and 7 percent) were divided at the regional level between politicians belonging to two allied parties, but half also went to national politicians, considered as the reference figures for the regional politicians (R, December 12, 2005). Unlike a tit-for-tat bribe-for-favor exchange, contributions to national parties like these can be more easily presented as voluntary.

In these cases, the political party is required to be able to control and centralize the corrupt game. So, for instance, party cashiers—sometimes also holding the official position of party treasurer—play an important role in reducing the governance costs of corruption by organizing both legal and illegal financing, and limiting the amount of compromising information:

> Each party has referents responsible for controlling the allocation of contracts, maintaining the contacts with the different companies and collecting bribes, or having them collected. They also try to place trusted politicians on the boards of the various bodies, who then negotiate directly with businessmen [... thus] veiling what are really prearranged deals on bribery with formally legal agreements and legitimation. (*Panorama*, July 12, 1993: 27)

So, according to a Socialist "cashier": "each referent in the party reports to the national administrative secretary who prepares provisional and final balances of receipts, and works with the administrative secretaries of the other parties to control the flow of illegal funding. All this was communicated to the political secretariats of the parties, for the obvious reason that party activity had to be organized according to the resources available" (CD, n.166-quarter: 47). As to their positions being known to entrepreneurs, as several put it, "they didn't ask, and I didn't say" (CD, n.83: 7).

Differently, the more the party system and the political parties are fragmented, the more entrepreneurs have to extend their networks of contributions. The owner of Parmalat also declared that he had constructed a broad net of secret relations with politicians, listing "all the political and institutional relations that I built up during my life, both at local and at national level, that allowed me to realize a system of protection for my financial group and for its development, also with reference to the banking system" (cit. in Gomez and Travaglio 2006: 40).

Similarly, a banker arrested in 2005 declared that he had paid bribes to politicians of various parties to secure privileged access to the credit market— protection here also implied censoring the members of the corrupt parties that represented, with their declarations or actions, a potential risk to his bank. Also in the Parmalat case, it seems these payments formed a sort of generalized insurance policy, disentangled from specific decisions, and aimed instead at a broad, generalized guarantee, sanctioning some expectations that the corrupt system had made precarious, but also obtaining illicit advantages.

This way of paying bribes reduces transaction costs per se as it is more difficult to demonstrate the link between a specific contribution and a specific advantage. In fact, it is not by chance that these types of contributions, when discovered, give rise to charges relating to the violation of the rules on party financing rather than corruption. In the Parmalat case, the widespread payment of political contributions was represented as lobbying by an acquaintance of the entrepreneur involved:

> It wasn't corruption. He just wanted to build friendship and cooperation ties, creating an area of protection for his activities. So he financed various politicians' initiatives, their electoral campaigns, he sponsored this and that, he paid publicity costs, he went into business with those who were close to this or that political leader. Not much money, according to him, between four and six billion in old lira per year. In exchange, he expected attention to the destiny of his enterprise. At a certain point, however, things changed, and he had the impression that he was more and more forced to pay for the politicians' initiatives, for that electoral campaign, for that party or that event. In some way, to use a metaphor, from a spider that produces very subtle threads to construct his net and capture insects, he felt a prisoner in his own net. (R, February 13, 2004)

Adapting to the fragmentation of the party system, corrupt entrepreneurs had less incentives to pay specific parties, balancing their contacts with different party fractions instead. In the latter situation, uncertainty remains high, as internal competition jeopardizes stability of hidden exchanges. In fragmented systems, additional associational loyalties are even more important, as they provide a counter-balance for the declining capacity of the party per se to implement corrupt deals. In Southern Italy, a recent case involved firms known to be linked to Compagnia delle Opere, a voluntary association close to the Catholic organization Comunione e Liberazione. Talking about the latter, an entrepreneur explained to the director of a public health unit that, "in practice, by converging in an association, we attempt some lobbying [...] as the votes are from CL, they are from the priests" (TRBA1: 345). In fact, loyalty here is not dedicated to the party, but to organizations linked to the Catholic Church; according to an entrepreneur, "they are the Catholic, the popolarini, Comunione e Liberazione: They are the same: different forms, different personalities, but identical logics that answer to the bishop, not to the politician; they respond to the bishop, and the bishop responds to Don Giussani, Don Giussani responds to the Pope [...] it is absolutely within the church" (TRBA1: 348). According to the judges, it was therefore within a fraction of Forza Italia, informally organized, that ties of trust based on extra-political loyalty allowed the development of corrupt exchanges. Thus, for instance, after traveling to the Ministry for Innovation and Technologies in Rome, the entrepreneur explained to a collaborator, "we have a contact. I now have to go and see him every week [...] as I used to do with the director [of the public health] unit. It is exactly the same level" (TRBA1: 469). In the most recent examples of corruption, the same idea of an exchange between two partners is somehow overcome by the development of figures of political businessmen who, using their own political positions, assign public contracts and benefits in a direct manner to their own firms.

Party Connivance

In the 1990s, the management board of ENEL (Italia Public society for Electricity) was composed of eight directors appointed by the political parties. According to one, "each director was responsible for procuring his own party money. A tacit understanding was reached: each looked after their own backyard and stayed out of the others' business" (*Panorama*, February 14, 1993: 46). The apportioning of offices among the various political parties therefore gave each political actor control over certain defined areas of public activity, areas that were negotiated or arranged at a higher level.

As public power is usually distributed between the administrators of various parties, it is often impossible for a single agent to offer the service demanded by a corrupter. Therefore, it often becomes necessary to coordinate the actions of a number of politicians and distribute the bribes so that no contention, reciprocal denunciations, or judicial investigation follows when disagreements arise (Dey 1989: 507). When all of the politicians involved belong to the same centralized party, that party's central office can coordinate decisions and resolve disagreements. However, since most public decisions involve politicians from different parties or party factions, alternative mechanisms of governance are needed to avoid conflicts bringing about negative consequences for all the parties involved. Solutions can involve either a consensual and jointly managed division of the proceeds of corruption or a long-term division of public power into spheres of influence. In some cases, for instance, there may be a fixed distribution of public contracts among firms based on the color of their political protection (or to consortia whose composition reflects the relative weight of the various power centers); in others, payoffs are distributed according to the electoral strength of the parties involved (TRIB: 81). For instance, a former Italian communal assessor said,"what I can confirm was the division of major public works among the parties, the construction of car parks was considered a sphere of influence of the Liberal Party" (CD, n.386: 4). Bipartisan involvement in the sharing of bribes was observed in public bids for high-speed railway connections in Italy, with some exceptions. In fact, according to an entrepreneur, "we were told that the Greens and Communists were not included in the sharing" (R-Neaples, January 12, 2000).

When parties are strong, they can negotiate the sharing of bribes at the national level. In Germany, for example, it has been observed that corruption affairs "are often cross-party affairs: sharing out benefits, both legitimate and otherwise, among parties in proportion to their strength" (Johnston 2005: 75). In the late 1970s, the special tax exemption granted to the Flick consortium on the sale of a major block of shares to Daimler-Benz has been said to have been favored by large subscriptions (a total of 25 million German marks) not only to two FDP ministers but also to the other two big parties, the CDU and the SPD. In the late 1990s, the tank manufacturer Thyssen-Henschel was accused of having paid DM 1 million to a former CDU treasurer in exchange for help with the selling of arms in Saudi Arabia; illegal subscriptions were also suspected to have been paid to the other two major parties (Johnston 2005: 75–6). Later on, political protection was also offered in public contracts with major political parties accepting large donations by contractors: "the political parties were active from the beginning, with certain politicians lobbying vociferously for the garbage plant. They used their influence with E. [a civil servant] to strategically place major construction firms as subcontractors in the project. The parties could count on quasi-legal contributions, known as 'thank-you' donations, from forms that won public contracts through the parties' lobbying efforts" (TI-2005: 52). In Greece "slush funds had been donated to political parties in exchange for contracts related to the 2004 Summer Olympic Games." Very large contributions were made to the electoral campaign of the Pasok Party prior to the 2000 general election, but also later on "the ruling party [was] also implicated, as, although most of the contracts were secured before it came to power in 2004, contracting did take place at the last minute, and there was speculation that 'gifts' may have been offered 'to ND people to keep the wheels turning smoothly'" (TI-2009: 340). In France, an extensive case of corruption was uncovered in relation to procurement contracts for the construction or renovation of 300 schools in the Ile de France. All major political parties were suspected to have received contributions in exchange for the regional council's decision to upgrade school facilities, signing 114 10-year construction and maintenance contracts (for about €1.4 billion in total), with only five multinational companies: "It was alleged that these companies made an unofficial and secret deal, involving the payment of 2 per cent of the value of the contracts to various political parties: 1,2 per cent to the ruling Rassemblement pour la République, and 0,8 per cent to the Socialist party, with smaller allocations to the Republican and Communist parties. The payments took the form of apparently legal gifts to finance the parties' campaigns" (TI-2006: 159).

In the centralized, but more personalized, South Korea Democratic Republican Party, party officials "cultivated specific firms, collecting *chaebol* contributions that came to be known as 'quasi-taxes'" (Johnston 2005: 108). Some of these bribes are said to have gone to the president himself for his own personal projects. In the

Italian case, particularly in some phases of the development of systemic corruption, party cashiers of the main parties in government coordinated bribe collection and sharing. According to testimony,

> Senator C. instructed him to keep an eye on what was happening in the environmental sector in order to ensure that a satisfactory equilibrium was maintained between companies 'friendly' to the DC and companies 'friendly' to the PSI and also in order to guarantee that there was a satisfactory division of the money coming from companies operating in the sector between the two parties. (CD, n. 210: 10)

The weaker and more fragmented the political parties, however, the more the governance of corrupt exchanges involving several parties is externalized. It then becomes necessary for entrepreneurs to balance their financial contributions, sharing them between parties. In a recent case in Italy, in order to satisfy all parties, entrepreneurs confessed they had offered to hire personnel in exchange for public contracts—and to "equally divide the hiring between the regional councilors of the government and those of the opposition, as those in the opposition could tomorrow once again be in government" (TRBA1: 54). The presence of weak parties does not discourage the collection of bribes, but corruption further fragments weak parties, favoring their splitting into various fractions with low loyalty toward the party and even less loyalty to the party system. This situation is illustrated by the Japanese LDP, whose various leaders have often been involved in bribes for public works (for 3% of the value of the contract), with a huge 500-million-yen kickback allegedly paid by Lockheed to the then prime minister and leader of a party fraction (the criminal case was ended because of the death of the defendant). Similarly, the Recruit Cosmos real estate and investment firm was accused of distribuiting stock to politicians from different parties and high-level bureaucrats in exchange for various favors (Johnston 2005: 79).

Concluding Remarks

Political actors and political parties occupy a central role in corrupt exchanges as well as in their governance. We have, however, argued in this chapter that the often debated question about the presence of either weak or strong parties as a cause of corruption is not the most appropriate. Rather, we have seen that different types of politicians and parties may play a role in the governance of corruption, adapting to different equilibria.

This explains why we have seen corruption spread in all possible types of parties (della Porta 2009). In the notables parties of the past (Weber 1974) as well as in some recent evolutions of "base-less parties" (della Porta 2009), corruption and clientelism have been used by various local bosses to foster their careers, and they have also governed corrupt exchanges within their feuds. The Japanese Liberal parties provide the best illustration here. In the mass ideological party

(Weber 1974; Duverger 1951), corruption has sometimes been used as a welcome addition to internal financing via membership fees in the attempt to cover the high expenses of the party apparatuses. In this type of party, centralization allows for an efficient governance of corrupt exchanges and ideological commitment sometimes helps overcome moral scruples, especially when illegal financing comes from the party's main constituencies (e.g., cooperatives in the case of socialist parties). Catch-all parties (Kirckheimer 1966) have also sometimes been prone to participate in corrupt exchanges to secure money to invest in electoral campaigns, as well as able to govern corrupt exchanges through their apparatuses even without strong ideological cohesion, albeit also with less moral scruples (the Italian Christian Democratic party is an example here). Even if internally fragmented, cartel parties (Katz and Mair 1993) have accepted private and public contributions as well as legal and illegal ones, helped by strong tendencies toward reciprocal connivance and so potentially able to govern corruption through interparty agreements.

Thus, to a certain extent, all the main resources of the main types of political party and individual politicians could be used to participate in and govern corrupt exchanges, albeit in different ways in the different parties.

As we have seen, political corruption and its governance interacts with *parties' power of nomination* in the public sector, especially concerning positions in which bribes can be more easily collected. The influence of parties in areas beyond public administration—from banks to newspapers—leads to the occupation of civil society, thereby further lowering society's defenses against corruption and mismanagement. In these conditions, political corruption spreads and parties acquire an important function as organizers of political corruption. The more centralized the parties, the more corrupt exchanges tend to take place at the center, and the party apparatus is best suited to drive and govern them. In decentralized parties, the power of nomination is instead fragmented and contested, with the accompanying need for agreements between local and national bosses to be negotiated and renegotiated both at the center and at the periphery. Nomination to important positions in elected and unelected public bodies forms the basis for very personalized party fractions and is used to collect bribes as well as to negotiate within the party and implement a localized governance of corruption.

When corruption is systemic, the parties and party fractions not only socialize members to illicit practices, reducing the moral costs of involvement in corruption, but also secure a kind of *continuity* in the corruption game through its diffusion to every geographical area, throughout the various public bodies and different sectors of public administration. Whoever respects the unlawful agreements can continue to do business with the public administration; anyone who opts out on a given occasion will be permanently excluded from the market for public works. The forms and extent of this socialization may change, however, for different types of parties. Centralized parties can confine corrupt deals and their governance to a few people. These tend to partially overlap with official roles in the party hierarchy (secretary general, treasurer), but often specialized "hidden" positions devoted to the governance of corruption develop (e.g., party cashiers). In decentralized parties, instead, illegal skills tend to be widespread as they represent a crucial resource in forging political careers that rarely follow the traditional *cursus honorem* within the party structure, being driven instead by pragmatic but precarious alliances.

Those who control nominations to public bodies can generalize the kickback, transforming corruption from a circumscribed practice into a customary activity with accepted norms, at the same time guaranteeing the continuity of the system over time despite changes in the political personnel of the public administration. That is to say, the parties or party bosses assume the *function of guarantors of the illegal bargain*, participating in those operations demanding a "certification of trust: in other words, the promises of others, required to be guaranteed in some way, are used to obtain a benefit" (Pizzorno 1992: 31). Moreover, by reaching an agreement between themselves, majority and opposition parties reduce the material risks connected with identifying suitable parties and negotiating the bribes. Here as well, we notice differences within different types of parties. The more centralized the party, the more the role of guarantor of the illegal exchange lies in the party apparatus, and is usually paid for with bribes that are cashed directly at the national level. In decentralized parties, the number of guarantors needed increases, and the governance of corruption is spread out among various fractions and political bosses that build their networks within the public administration. This is usually reflected in the fragmentation of the bribe, with shares going to different political actors who control resources to invest in corrupt exchanges and their governance.

If corruption adapts to various party formats and vice versa, we may add that corruption per se (as much as organized crime) has an inherent centrifugal tendency. In time, corruption tends to weaken the organizational structures of the political parties, which become more and more internally divided and based upon the distribution of selective—and often illicit—incentives. The visible party apparatus tends to lose control of a hidden party structure devoted to the management and governance of corruption. Often, the populist, antiparty discourse that follows political scandals favors access to party positions for personnel that are not endowed with any conception of public service and are mainly interested in business. In this case, however, the governance of corrupt exchanges is affected, with higher transaction costs in terms of risks of defection and denunciation. The socialization to illegal norms, as well as the development of alternative rules of the game, is then externalized to subparty or extra-party actors: party fractions or associations external to the political parties are therefore called on to integrate the weakening loyalty within and toward political parties.

Chapter 6
The Entrepreneurial Management of Corrupt Exchanges

On July 31, 2002, two administrators of two companies operating in the road works sector, M. and A., discussed by phone—unaware their conversation was being taped—the possible inclusion of the former in a collusive agreement the latter was the organizer and guarantor for. In the face of the perplexity of M., the arguments of A. depict an image of absolute normality in the practice of forming cartels to agree offers in public tenders, as an informal rule operating in the whole of Italy and beyond.

> M.: And what have you asked me for in exchange for this, what are you giving me?
>
> Let's talk straight, whether we win or you do, or if nobody wins, I want to know to a certain extent what I'll pocket from it.
>
> A.: I'm telling you the general rule that works in the whole of Italy and that's how it is for the whole of Italy for all these kinds of issues, which I've never disputed.
>
> M.: Or else I'll make the offer and what does it matter.
>
> A.: Exactly, it's the same thing—that's what I wanted to get round to saying to you or else [...] I mean I'm giving you an opportunity if you, I mean it's an opportunity for me.
>
> M.: But what's the opportunity for me, sorry but can you explain what opportunity I get?
>
> A.: That it's in your interest not to go it alone [...] a bit more than going it alone, I mean going it alone, I don't know what you can get done or what you'll manage to get done, you could even succeed in everything you want to and [...] I'll send you my compliments, what I'm saying is: I'm not alone, I've got an army with me, I can't promise the army anything because I'd have to promise 20 people, isn't that right? I mean that's the reasoning, I'm not saying that I only make arrangements with you, I make them with the other 19 and I don't promise the other 19 anything until [...] when this happens you say: ok! [...] I mean there aren't that many things to discuss, I mean I've got the cupboard full of jobs with my name on them that others, completely other people, are doing, I'm not getting—I'm not getting into arguments. (CCA, September 9, 2002: 15–7)

A clear picture emerges from this conversation. A *general rule* exists that all entrepreneurs with contractual relations with the public administration know about, and nobody calls into question or else they will suffer blame and derision from others.[1] To sell goods and services to the state, efficient facilities and competitive methods of production are not necessary—at most, they are a facilitating, but not an essential, factor. What really matters are *good relations* with other entrepreneurs who organize and coordinate the respective "armies," the cartels, as well as, eventually, public administrators who are to be paid in order to avoid the success of the agreements being endangered. The recognition of reliability in collusive agreements or corruption actually increases the possibility of success more than any technological innovation or capacity to satisfy public needs can.[2]

The "Entrepreneurial" Organization of Corruption

The above case is only one example of the many possible incidents within the "business culture" that favor entrepreneurs adhering to corruption. Indeed, the image of a civil society and an economic system characterized by ethical behavior and honesty, in contrast with a corrupt political and bureaucratic system, seems misleading. The world of corruption is immersed in the dimension of *voluntary exchange,* where private citizens are beneficiaries and often promoters of such practices. The practice of corruption, as is the case with other illegal behavior models, from tax evasion to unauthorized construction, can extend deep into society in both developed and developing countries.

In corruption scandals, mass media and public opinion tend to focus their attention on the public administrators involved rather than on the corruptors, usually entrepreneurs, who remain sidelined. While politicians have been targets, at least in the first instance, of public abomination that in more than one case has undermined their public images and jeopardized their careers, entrepreneurs have enjoyed a kind of "reputational immunity." Private-sector managers, even

---

[1]   Another Italian entrepreneur, in explaining the diffusion of collusive agreements to a judge confirms, "Let me say something. In all the bidding processes in Italy, not just these [...] I could go on listing them for twenty years. Not just in those I take part in, in dams, in [...], in plastering, in [...] in all of Italy. You should take us all and make a jail for us. No, I'm telling you, that's how it is, that's how it works" (PMI-LP, February 28, 2003: 25). In Italy, entrepreneurial cartels were found—to give only a few examples—in the provision and disposal of railway materials (R-Bononia, October 25, 2001), in school canteens (R-Milan, July 18, 2000), in providing fruit and vegetables to the armed forces (R, March 15, 2000), in waste disposal (R, September 10, 2004), in public housing construction (R-Turin, July 20, 2002), and in the provision of health materials for diabetics (R-Florence, June 1, 2004).

[2]   The characteristics of this cultural model, an orientation that makes economic actors more inclined to corporative collusion than risk, also surface in the words of an entrepreneur from Milan: he adhered to a cartel according to a design that was "finalised to subdivide the market *without having to submit to extenuating competition rules*" (Carlucci 1992: 46, emphasis added).

after strong conclusive sentences, are often not subjected to reprobation, blame, or censure for their conduct by their colleagues or the public. No news is made public about punitive measures applied by company auditors toward administrators blighted by corruption offences or of sanctions applied by respective professional associations.

The world of corruptors, from large companies to the vast undergrowth of small and medium-sized businesses specializing in satisfying public demand, seems confined to a kind of moral limbo that makes illegal behavior justifiable—to themselves, their social recognition circles, and even public opinion. This attitude of widespread self-justification can come from different sources. First of all, there is a tendency not to consider corruption as an equal exchange, but as an act of extortion that entrepreneurs are subjected to. In the words of the Italian Premier Silvio Berlusconi when justifying the illegal payments by his company to Revenue police officials, "I am the victim of a great injustice, because the events I am accused of are extortion. Anyone subjected to these accusations is a victim twice over: for being forced to pay bribes, just like thousands of entrepreneurs who just wanted to keep on working, and also for the unfounded accusations" (*La Stampa*, November 24, 1994: 3). Another possible explanation is connected to the kind of relationship that binds politicians to the public, with their mandate to represent collective interests, which contrasts directly with the act of corruption. The specific aim of entrepreneurial activity, on the other hand, is to obtain profits, and if its path takes in corruption, it is in the interests of shareholders to whom the manager is responsible.

In general, the preponderant significance or weight of public demand in some sectors (if we think, for example, of the road-surfacing market, large-scale infrastructure, and hospital provisions), as with the technological backwardness of companies operating therein, make recourse to bribery (when it isn't necessary) more convenient. By influencing the outcome of contract allocation procedures, the success, or at least the survival, of economic subjects who would otherwise be destined, in terms of competitiveness, to a marginal role or exit from the market is therefore guaranteed. Corruptors thus load the costs of their inefficiency onto the community and the public balance sheet by accumulating profits by providing public bodies with low-quality goods and services at exorbitant prices.

In this chapter we concentrate on *private regulation* models of corruption, summarized in Table 6.1. In these cases, entrepreneurs or other private-sector individuals take on the responsibility of regulating the smooth workings of corrupt exchanges. They hand out sanctions to cheaters and assign roles to various participants in the system, which in some cases do not foresee any material payments. In private corruption and cartel settlements, bribes are—eventually—withdrawn from a rent that is autonomously created by private sector individuals through exploiting public market distortions or information asymmetries in market relations. In the case of entrepreneurial protection and situations presenting conflicts of interests, the rent is instead created in the context of public decision-making processes. In the case of a conflict of interests, there is no visible transaction between the briber and the bribee, roles that coincide in the same person.

Table 6.1   Models of private organization of corrupt practices and rent allocation

	Material transaction between briber and bribee	
Decision-makers in the rent creation process	*Always present*	*Not necessary*
Public actors	Entrepreneurial protection of corruption	Conflicts of interest
Private actors	Private corruption	Cartels and collusive agreements

In particularly robust cartel agreements, a corrupt exchange with public agents can also become useless, since the entrepreneurs coordinating their offers manage to accurately prearrange the outcome of the procedure without any need for interventions by public agents. Corruption, in other words, becomes *immaterial* and *facultative*, even though the nature of these practices and the extent of their economic and social costs remain unchanged. In this chapter we examine these four different self-organizational entrepreneurial corruption models in more detail, looking in particular at the nature of the resources invested in the exchange.

Corruption and Collusion: Enforcement within Cartels

A limited group of companies can ensure the allocation of public tenders and contracts to the detriment of competitors by reaching an understanding when drawing up their offers. Profit margins guaranteed by fixing award prices are then split between different participants in the agreement, with immediate or deferred compensation, by rotation. Generally, no express or written agreement regulates price fixing, bid-rigging, or other forms of market division: since it is illegal, a similar "contract" would be too dangerous to stipulate, becoming evidence of the deal. Despite their informal regulation, collusive agreements may represent very stable allocation schemes for participants. Price fixing implies the coordination of firms in maintaining (or raising) prices through several mechanisms aimed at reducing or eliminating discounts, adopting a standard formula to compute prices, establishing or adhering to predetermined price discounts, and so on. In many cases, some policing and enforcement mechanisms are also established, to ensure that everyone adheres to the cartel. Through bid-rigging, firms can effectively raise the price paid by public purchasers for goods and services by soliciting competing bids. They agree in advance who will win the contract, avoiding the competitive bidding process, thanks to (i) bid suppression, that is, one or more competitors agree to refrain or withdraw from bids previously submitted, (ii) complementary ("cover" or courtesy") bidding, that is, some competitors agree to submit bids that are too high, to create the appearance of competition or to contribute to the calculation of a final average value that will assure the adjudication of the contract to the preselected firm, (iii) bid rotation, that is, colluding firms alternate in submitting the lowest (or winning) bid, according to terms of rotation that—as we have seen—may vary (size of the contract, customer, geographical location of works, product characteristics, political orientation of the decision-maker, etc.), (iv) subcontracting, that is, generally as a part of a bid-rigging scheme, competitors who agreed to submit losing bids receive in exchange subcontracts or supply contracts, which allows a division of the rent obtained thanks to higher prices paid by the public organization (U.S. Department of Justice 2009).

We found a similar case history in the more than 130 corruption episodes that emerged between 1999 and 2003 within the publicly owned road transport company Anas in Milan. As the investigations highlighted, entrepreneurs had successfully addressed this difficult *intertemporal trade-off* of favors by means of a wide range of behavior, among which

> reciprocal commitments with regard to the future division of awards, the future concession in subcontracts on the part of future jobs, the future employment of other companies' workers in carrying out awarded jobs and, in that case, in promising the reciprocal giving and receiving of sums of money as compensation in the case of a lack of direct involvement in the carrying out of jobs which were the object of the awarded bids. (TMAR: 40)

In some cases the type of tender facilitates the common recognition of a natural division criteria as a sort of "focal point" in the agreement. Companies that have road works closer to their headquarters, for example, incur lower costs and can therefore convincingly plead their "right" to be awarded respective bids. In an entrepreneur's brutal simplification, these are the reasons why they work with a variable number of between 20 and 100 companies, depending on the kind of job: "Well, me at my house, I help you at your house, that's the way it is, it's the only way to be able to live and work in Italy" (PMI-MA, February 19, 2003: 129).

This model of collusive agreement regulation is based on a norm of reciprocity, which prescribes a strategy of conditional cooperation. Every participant adheres to the rules that regulate the sharing of contracts and price allocation in the cartel as long as others do the same. In case of defection, those who cheated are excluded from future cooperative interactions. Let us take the description given by an entrepreneur from Milan:

> Over the years, when tender bidding processes are called, those of us from the interested firms meet on the instructions of those of us most directly interested in the problem to discuss and try to agree a fair distribution of tender [...] . I was contacted and the tender I could aspire to was prearranged. As a consequence, the other companies would not impede me by putting in an offer lower than mine. At the same time, I was committed, as far as other tenders to be awarded to other companies are concerned, to not getting in the way of their wishes. (Carlucci 1992: 45)

In collusive agreements, however, conditions favoring the formulation of a genuine demand for protection do occur. The profits that can be obtained through cartelization are consistent, but the costs of information, coordination, and enforcement, which increase uncertainty over the "rights" exchanged, should also be taken into account, hence the importance of trusting relationships, the continuity of relationships between various participants, and reputation. In tender bidding processes, entrepreneurs coordinate their own offers so as to exclude the intrusion of external competitors, a prospect that is always possible given the formal openness of the procedures, but is in practice warded off or triggered through various techniques. For this reason cartels are generally founded on precise rules for sharing out bids, including territorial criteria, rotation, and the division of customers. But this does not eliminate problems.

In the first place, as we are talking about illegal exchanges, there are difficulties in terms of finding and communicating reliable information, with additional problems flowing from the risks deriving from the frenetic round of intertwined contacts. Intercepted phone calls, private encounters, and large meetings follow one another in a frenzy of activity during which each person tries to test the intentions and credibility of the plans of the others. A note discovered among the papers of an entrepreneur from Verona offers an account of a vertical round of contacts in a tender bidding process for maintenance services for hedges on a motorway:

> in the corridors I hear that X will win. I wait for developments. X phones me on the instructions of Y asking me to get in touch with Z while he gets in touch with Y and A. I phone Z, he tells me he's already sent the offer and that it's very high, 2.5 million/km. X tells me that A isn't participating, he asks me to support him because he has 15 workers without work, he suggests making an offer of 1.9 million/km, he asks me how things are going with Z, he reiterates that he (Z) knows everything but that it's better for him to stay out of this tender [...] . We fill out the offers. He promises me money upon the first payment. (GFV: 18–9)

This is a process that requires suppleness and adaptability throughout, as the following entrepreneur witness testifies:

> To make a cartel, then [...] it isn't like a cartel gets set up in a day [...] if there's a bidding process in a week's time, it gets set up today and it'll remain unchanged. No, because there are a lot of conditions which can change it, by that I mean the several people who phone saying 'Give me instructions', and you have to give them a figure, the several people who say 'Yes, I'm in', and then the next day say 'No, it's no longer right for me.' (PMI-MA, March 6, 2003: 66)

This form of coordination requires then a certain technical capacity to calculate the figures of the lowered prices in order to formulate the winning combination of price bids, given that it is unlikely that all the competing firms can be included. There are also external participants to be taken into consideration:

I mean, I had a real intuition, as far as figures are concerned, for the famous 'schedules', they're called 'schedules' which is to say, they can't be learned, it's something that [...] in any case I can't imagine what figures you'll come up with [...] . But I have my own figures, then I know [...] that person there in the last three bidding processes in ventilation knows that it was won that time with that figure, so he'll throw himself in there because he knows everybody will throw themselves in there. So I also consider hypothetical cases, because we *only had a limited number compared to the total number of participants*, and the calculation doesn't mean figures which I had put in the list, the various upper and lower limits, and the infiltrators, who are the hypothetical cases. (PMI-MA, March 6, 2003: 75–6)

Even after agreement has been reached and the terms perfected, the incentives for disloyalty have not yet been exhausted.[3] Collusive agreements, being illegal, present risks similar to those of a corrupt exchange. And they are founded on *promises*: company X today agrees not to participate or to arrange offers in favor of company Y, in exchange for the commitment of the latter party to repay them in the future with similar conduct, or to pass on some of the profits, or to subcontract them a percentage of the work. Here, an entrepreneur describes the collusive agreement: "I need you one day, you need me another" (PMI-MA, February 19, 2003: 132). It is possible, however, for company X, after having devised the offers, to ignore the promise made and award itself a bid intended for others. An entrepreneur promising a colleague that he will intervene to the advantage of an offer by another potential participant in the collusive agreement, who wants to "hold onto" the bidding process—with the danger of the latter disregarding the instructions received—regrets the difficulties of drawing up a cartel:

it's because ... because ... people don't trust ... I mean they don't trust ... well ... I mean he says: ok, tell me then? Even if at the last moment it's 'I'll come in person, but I'll take care of it [...]'. So you take care of it and fuck off, you taking care of it like being left with nothing [...] . Do you understand? But, I mean, I don't know ... now I'll speak to them and we'll see what we'll do ... it seems like a bit of a *mission impossible*. (CCA, September 12, 2002: 69)

Here, an entrepreneur complains about a colleague who has just informed him of his decision to defect from the cartel, speaking to him in these terms:

'don't ask me for anything, I'll do the Milan works, I might be an idiot but I'll do all of it'. Instead, this was divided half and half, 50/50 [...] . Because the figures were half for one, the cartel was made up half mine and half his, so the work was

---

[3]   When collusive agreements have a single bidding process as their object, the probability of the cartel failing because of distrust over reciprocal intentions is higher. Robinson (1985) shows that stable agreements do not exist in highest-bid auctions with secret offers, while an equilibrium takes hold in the case of public offers, when respect for the agreements can be verified during the bidding process and any defection can be punished immediately.

> half mine and half his. And he told me at the end: 'No thanks to your figures, I'll
> do all the work', and what do I do? [...] Because in any case this wasn't the way
> to behave.' (PMI-MA, March 6, 2003: 74)

Indeed, the risk for those entering the cartel, or preferring collusion to competition, is that company *Y* will "forget" to repay the favor received tomorrow, or surrender their turn or compensate in other ways, or maybe forward an anonymous denunciation to the judiciary, while company *X* cannot demand the favor be repaid before a judge. This is what happened, for example, in a tender bid announced in Southern Italy Vieste. A member of the cartel decided to "play for himself," trusting the purchase of materials to a provider different from the one arranged when the offer "scheme" necessary to win the 10 billion lire contract was prepared. The stake was worth more to the cartel member than the reputation of his reliability, despite the attempt to solve controversy, as described by an entrepreneur:

> And so my father acted as a go-between, rightly so because he always has to be
> the judge in these affairs, he says: no, let me sort out Y for you; in that if those
> were the agreements there's no way that Y won't stick to them, I know him as an
> honest person and yet my father gauged that Y didn't care [...] about the figure
> they gave have him and he took home the 10 billion lira award. [...] And these
> are the famous traitors. (PMI-MA, February 19, 2003: 181–2)

The costs that *X*, along with the other companies in the cartel, can impose on *Y* to sanction the "rights" *Y* violated in this relatively "spontaneous" collusion lie in the break in their relations with the betraying company, from the diffusion of information on its unreliability, from its exclusion from the cartel with its expected advantages: "you should know that, given that I've already been ripped off so much by Y, I no longer want Y to participate"—comments an entrepreneur in the phase of defining the cartel participants for a roadworks bidding process (PMI-MA, March 6, 2003: 72).

However, a climate of distrust can also mature in response to ambiguous requests, uncertain obligations, and unsatisfied demands overlapping over time. In the case described above, the version of the entrepreneur accused of the "rip-off" is in fact conflicting. He reverses the accusation, claiming that his conduct was actually a retaliation for a previous defection on the part of the competitor:

> And then that job, which I wanted to do because I had no work, he told me that
> he was doing it. I say: 'Right then, bury yourself with it all, and when later it
> bursts out from some part [...]'. [...] I'm somebody who gets his own back, in
> time, I must say, the time will come to ... to get my own back. And in fact you
> can see I did get my own back. (PMI-LP, February 28, 2003: 18)

Information on irresponsibility are circulated: "if someone cheats, cheats once in his life, that's enough,"—as two entrepreneurs stated when referring to the exclusion of a colleague from a cartel (CCA, October 4, 2001: 14–5).

In general terms, factors that increase the probability of a successful collusion are

(a) the limited number of potential sellers and providers: the fewer there are, the lower the identification and information costs, and the easier it is for them to get together and agree on prices, contract sharing schemes, bids, and so on;

(b) the frequency and duration of public purchases, since the expectation of future contracts make bidders confident of the opportunity to share them peacefully, at the same time offering the opportunity to sanction cheaters by excluding them from the benefits of future collusion;

(c) the acquaintance of competitors, through social, friendship, ethnic, religious, and political links, as well as through previous economic relationships;

(d) the existence of communication channels among bidders;

(e) the standardization of the product, which may depend on low levels of technological innovation, reducing bargaining costs in the search for a collusive pricing scheme; in fact, as other profiles (design, quality, etc.) enter into the negotiation, an agreement among competing firms becomes more difficult to achieve;

(f) the difficulty in finding substitutes for the product required or the presence of restrictive specifications, which restrains the range of potential external competitors.

In a game theoretical perspective, the conditions listed above are those that favor the emergence of a balance in conditional cooperation strategies in a repeated «prisoner's dilemma» among *n* players (Vannucci 2005). Therefore, the public bodies favoring the formation and success of cartels are those that publish frequent tenders relating to standardized goods, with demands that can be satisfied by a limited number of companies. Similarly, collusion is easier when formally competing companies have strong relationships with one another, have been present in the market for a long time, and are characterized by low levels of technological innovation—a factor that could give an incentive for a more "innovative" company to defect.

If the same companies anticipate staying in business together for quite a long period of time, the collusion's success seems more likely on the basis of conditional cooperation strategies, provided that the expected profits exceed the immediate payoff of defection. For instance, more than 100 low-scale public procurements for equipment and agricultural services in several projects in developing countries were enough to maintain an equilibrium within four distinctive collusive schemes, involving both individuals and companies: "foreign suppliers responded to price quotation invitations by submitting collusive quotations to ensure that contracts were awarded among themselves at artificial price levels" (OECD 2007: 90). A sanctioning mechanism's effectiveness is facilitated by the existence of a consolidated relationship network among companies. This is the case, for example, of the public procurements published by Anas, as emerges from the words of one entrepreneur during an interrogation:

> Yes, we all know each other, all the firms in Italy. When we go to public procurements, there are about a hundred, a hundred and twenty of us; sometimes some aren't there, sometimes others, but we know [...] on paper we all know each other, or by telephone; face-to-face perhaps many of us don't, but we all know each other because we all do the same job. At the end of the day, the firms going around are always the same. (PMI-LP, February 28, 2003: 14)

When marginalization from a cartel or damage to one's reputation are strong enough deterrents against betrayal, the cartel can hold out over time independently of the intervention of any "third party" sanctioning the stability of internal equilibria.

This form of "informal" cooperation does, however, give way to more centralized coordination and security structures in some cases. In the late 1990s, thanks to the intuition of an entrepreneur and Forza Italia politician, a service provider for the acquisition and management of information relating to public procurement was set up. A private document found by judges sets out its real function:

> the establishment of a group of 90–100 companies in order to 'be able to influence the bid awards' and thereby reverse the tendency of increasing the offers in the auction [...] . The document then looks at the problem of how to reach this objective and, through mathematic models, they anticipate 'bringing the bid award percentage below the 20% threshold' and, through this system it can be supposed that a group of 100 offers can purchase 90% of tenders.'

With regard to the allocation of jobs, "the companies closest to the place the tender will be carried out [...] will be favoured," while "the institution of a kind of 'solidarity clause' [is] anticipated by which, in the case of a company being excluded erroneously, even if they are participating in the bidding process, this company is in any case taken into account during the subdivision of the work." Finally, the establishment of a kind of executive committee composed of 5–10 companies was proposed, "which sets out the operative action lines and [is] provided with disciplinary and sanctioning powers" (PRREMI98a: 13, 83–4).

When autonomous cartel enforcement works, corruption becomes superfluous or *not entirely necessary*, provided that the companies succeed in agreeing on award prices, or rather the sum of revenue derivable from public tenders and its redistribution within the cartel by respecting the agreements:

> Together with companies, we get together—states one entrepreneur—and we create the group, but functionaries have no power to arrange things [...] . Once they have made the call for tenders they have no other function. No power to change anything. Because I make arrangements with my competitors, in practice. (PMI-LP, February 28, 2003: 51–2)

Bid-rigging may therefore also be practiced successfully in contexts where corruption is perceived as (and is expected to be) a marginal phenomenon, such as in Scandinavian countries or the Netherlands. A diffused expectation of "transparency" in procedures and the honesty of public agents may then push entrepreneurs seeking higher rents from public contracts to collude among themselves in hidden agreements. There is increasing evidence, for instance, of Finnish companies forming cartels: in the tarmac market, seven companies controlling 70 percent of the market had agreed on prices, participation in public tenders, customers, and geographical sectors from 1994 to 2002 (TI-2006: 155). In Norway, "four large companies were under investigation for price-fixing and collusive tendering in both public and private works contracts [...] . NCC Construction admitted to 'illegal cooperation' with its competitors, issuing false invoices and compensating competitors who lost the tender" (TI-2005: 181). In the Dutch construction industry:

> companies systematically made agreements among themselves relating to the procedures of submitting tenders for contracts. Companies would agree on who would be awarded the contract and for what price. [...] Hundreds of ostensibly legitimate construction companies were heavily involved in price-fixing, cartel forming and secretly arranging the allocation of projects [...] . Similar cartels are formed along geographic lines (regional/town), or on a vertical principle— where supplier or sub-suppliers are integrated within the chain. (CSD 2011: 182)

In more transparent environments, however, collusion becomes more risky, since honest administrators are able to notice warning signs and unusual patterns in bids. For instance, procurement officials at the municipality of Steinkjer, in Norway, denounced two construction firms for illegal bid-rigging in connection with a public contract to restore five bridges in North Trøndelag in 2007. The two companies shared price and other information before each submitted its own bid in the competition, which was indeed considered suspect since both were abnormally high: the cooperation between the two construction companies had in fact led to a common understanding of who would submit the best bid (*Norwegian Competition Authority,* news archive, July 16, 2009).

The consequences of cartels in terms of raised prices paid by the state, and in terms of the fall in the quality of goods and services provided, are identical to those of corruption. The economic rents derived from bid-rigging in public procurement can be quite high. In Korea, for instance, an empirical study demonstrated that contractors usually engage in complementary bidding, with all except one party submitting higher bids so as to lose, with an estimated overcharge on total expenditure of 15.5 percent (Lee and Hahn 2002). In Sweden, cartels pushed up the prices of public procurement by 20 percent (*Swedish Competition Authority,* press release, June 1, 2010).

In competitions for the award of tenders, entrepreneurs (alone or within a cartel) with few moral scruples (and eventually also low production costs), effective political and judicial protection, and better liquidity conditions (when bribes are requested before the payment of compensation) hold a competitive advantage. Cartel agreements, in the same way as corruption, restrict competition, raise prices, and lower the quality of goods purchased by the state, and stall greater efficiency on the part of companies, who have fewer incentives to improve their production techniques (Reuter 1987: 7).

For example, the inquiry into a cartel of companies operating in school cafeterias in Milan was launched on the basis of a report by the judicial police on rotten or out of date food: "for a number of years a cartel of forms had been in an agreement to manage [...] all public tender bidding processes and they recouped these 'management costs' by providing extremely low quality products" (R, July 18, 2000).

The presence of more than one collusive agreement, rather than one single monopolist cartel, could lead to the reintroduction of some form of competition by, to a certain extent, restraining the final prices paid to public bodies. Or at least, this is the justification given by one cartel coordinator: "It isn't like Public Administration loses out, it earns more and more because the more cartels there are the more the price [...] the more the bids increase" (PMI-MG, February 27, 2003: 87). The few organized cartels, on the other hand, do not despise the use of impropriety in the competition to charge lower prices. Far from a transparent bidding process, as one entrepreneur from Turin observes: "I wasn't aware of other cartels' offers. I did, however, manage to figure out their offers through my intelligence service. I had spies [...] . In one case I made a totally different figure. In another I smartened up with the help of a few tip-offs. They have lots of enemies within" (R-Turin, September 8, 2002).

In the absence of corruption, however, politicians and bureaucrats could be excluded from rent sharing. Politicians and administrators can still come back into play in a number of ways, however, and this can explain why often corruption and collusion go hand to hand in public tenders. The uncertainty deriving from the necessity to establish criteria for the sharing of tenders, secure enforcement, and discourage entry of external firms, in fact, can be reduced by corrupt agents: "A corrupt auctioneer can contribute to solve some of this problems, for example by providing means of retaliation to secure enforcement or creating barriers to entry" (Lambert-Mogiliansky and Sonin 2006: 884). Among the factors facilitating a cartel's smooth functioning is the possibility of influencing the decisions of the public administrators supervising procedures with a bribe. For example, here a public company's newly appointed president received a visit from an entrepreneur:

> X let me know that he was the leading figure of a group of entrepreneurs [...] in agreement to subdivide tenders among themselves according to their interests and they clearly wanted to avoid the new board upsetting the old equilibria. (CD, n.266: 4)

The success of a collusive agreement is made easier by measures or information provided by complaisant public administrators. Cartels typically operate in the changing environment of public procurement, in which political demands and bureaucratic red-tape overlap. Such uncertainty can—at least to a certain extent—be kept under control through recourse to corruption or favoritism: a public agent tailoring the selection criteria in tenders in the interest of colluding firms, for instance, may assure the success and increase the expected profit of the in-turn winner (Lambert-Mogiliansky and Kosenok 2009). The former can increase cartel cohesion with various techniques by deterring competitive potential: for example, by arranging focused "thresholds" in calls for bids, by passing on private information on participants and on award dates and criteria, by setting aside generous and constant funds for sectors of interest, and by creating—through manipulation of tender rules—larger opportunities of gain for the firms of the cartel, therefore reducing internal problems in the sharing of spoils (Vannucci 2005). A Sicilian entrepreneur explains,

> Another important role of subcontracted organization functionaries is to provide the entrepreneur with the list of other invited companies in advance. The entrepreneur will thereby have time to contact them to ask them to behave non-competitively (which can occur either by not participating in the bidding process or by presenting a 'supporting', or agreed, offer). (CD, n. 417: 4)

In the previously quoted case of international aid-procurements, too, cartels were supported by corrupt public officials "because of the continuing scheme of collusion which could not have occurred without the active participation of the purchaser" (OECD 2007: 91–2). In the Dutch case, construction companies within the collusive ring protected themselves through corruption: "bribes are used to corrupt construction oversight bodies at the regional level" (CSD 2011: 182). In road network tender in Milan, "there was conscious condescension from public functionaries in ratifying the results of *informal bidding processes by market research*, which often resulted in collusion between interested entrepreneurs" (TMPAM: 12, emphasis added).

Corruption and collusive agreements thus become complementary to each other. While the companies in the cartel consolidate their exchange network thanks to corrupt politicians and bureaucrats, the former, with cartel managers as their sole contacts, are given an even higher share of revenue thanks to the elimination of any competitive process resulting in higher prices paid by public bodies. It is also for this reason that, as a former public company president remembers, collusive agreements between companies are mirrored in tight agreements between political representatives of different parties sitting in the boardrooms of public organizations, which continue to share out bribes in the new composition according to preexisting rules:

> When I took up the role [...] I had the opportunity to notice that even in the water utility sector a cartel of companies subdividing maintenance, provision and installation among themselves was operating. These companies also looked up to a 'reference entrepreneur' who I also spoke with and we agreed that the cartel would deposit 5 per cent of tender value. I also spoke about this with

political representatives [...], and board members [...] and we were all agreed
that I would receive the money collected and would share it out in the same
proportions. (CD, n. 263: 6–7)

In a cartel dividing up contracts in Lombardy, the central role of organizer and
promoter was played, according to the judges, by an entrepreneur and regional
councilor for Forza Italia:

> this person organises meetings with other entrepreneurs to allocate contract
> tenders, decides himself which tender will be allocated to his own companies
> [...] he asks to be sent the list of companies to be invited in each of the bidding
> rounds, he sanctions entrepreneurs who do not respect the agreements made
> beforehand (*they knew from how I acted at the table the other day that this
> time I really was pissed off, seriously, I mean! Using the tools at hand to do
> them in! Because now I've had enough fooling around*). His role as out-and-
> out illegal cartel promoter and founder is recognised by all entrepreneurs in the
> sector, who in fact contact him to reach agreements and explain their problems.
> (PRREMI98a: 85)

Also in France there is a growing evidence of the close links between corruption
and cartels. In a video tape he left to be distributed after his death, one City Hall
official described the praxis of corruption in the Paris City Hall over a decade (1985–
1994) in which he managed and enforced collusion in tenders for construction and
maintenance contracts, with bribes paid to political parties. A recent judgment in
another case provides another vivid illustration: "Detailed evidence revealed the
ways in which corrupt politicians and procurement officials used to initiate and
arbitrate collusion in the allocation of maintenance and construction contracts."
According to a judge investigating a major corruption case in Paris, "it is a rare
exception that a large stake collusion in public procurement in France goes without
corruption" (Lambert-Mogiliansky and Sonin 2006: 884).

The risks of criminal involvement are also allayed when the numerous
treacherous contacts between aspiring corruptors and public administrators are
replaced by a single stable tie to the cartel representative. In some cases the services
provided by public agents stretch as far as actually drafting the offers on the cartel's
behalf. According to an employee of one organization, "the relationship between
Anas functionaries and the companies' cartel was so close that the companies
presented their offers as blank cheques, the envelopes were given to the head of
the sector and it was up to him to sort out the contracts" (R, February 14, 2003).

Conflicts of Interest

A conflict of interest arises when there is a "conflict between the public duties
and private interests of a public official, in which the public official has private-
capacity interests which could improperly influence the performance of their
official duties and responsibilities" (OECD 2003: 15). The presence of a conflict

of interest indicates the weakness of institutional mechanisms—both legally and in terms of societal values—that separate *economic power*, deriving from the management of resources produced in the market, from *political power*, which stems from control over acts of public authority. A conflict of interest arises when individuals holding positions of power in a public organization overlap the functions of office with interests (personal or family) that they maintain in the market or social system.[4] A confusion of roles emerges, making the reality of corruption more elusive. Indeed, no *exchange* is carried out between briber and bribee, given that these roles coincide within the same individual (or are balanced out within family relations), although the nature of the activity remains unchanged. A political administrator with economic interests can pursue personal profit given the inevitable vagueness or ambiguity in the content of referable decisions to any notion of general interests. There is no longer any need to pay bribes, which would amount to shifting money from one pocket to another. Following the principal-agent scheme of corruption presented in Chapter 1, in a conflict of interest the agent and the client-briber coincide in the same person. Corruption is thus *sublimed*, it no longer leaves any trace, nor is it criminally indictable. As shown in Figure 6.1, conflicts of interest have in the last decade become a concern in OECD countries, inducing most to adopt restrictive regulations to prevent confusion between the public and private interests of public office holders, especially in centralized governments.

Every close and unregulated nexus between politics and business may induce an overlap between public and corporate interests: "politicians or their families may have direct financial stakes in the industry they are supposed to regulate, or set their sights on lucrative private sector posts when they leave office" (TI-2009: 34).[5] We may take as an example the councilmember of the Latvian Privatization Agency (LPA) whose vote was decisive in a decision concerning the privatization of the Latvian Shipping Co. (sales price and application deadline); the decision was made while the councilmember also served as the shipping company's councilmember (*Baltic News Service*, September 4, 1999). A "familiar" case of conflict of interest involved a senior Chinese fire officer, who was sentenced for having assigned contracts to companies owned by his relatives' to organize a costly ceremony (*South China Morning Post*, July 6, 2007). In Romania "several EU Sapard projects in Suceava had been marred by conflicts of interest because of links between the civil servants and the boards of the winning companies"

---

[4]   A strategy often used by public agents to minimize conflicts of interest is the handing over of property to relatives, which means that the politician ceases to appear as a direct beneficiary of decisions made in his role of public administrator.

[5]   *Politically connected firms*, whose controlling shareholders and top managers are members of national parliaments or governments, are widespread in the sample of 42 countries considered by Faccio (2006). Indonesia, Russia, Malaysia, Thailand, and Italy have the highest percentages of politically connected firms, which correspondingly enjoy easier access to debt financing, lower taxation, and stronger market power.

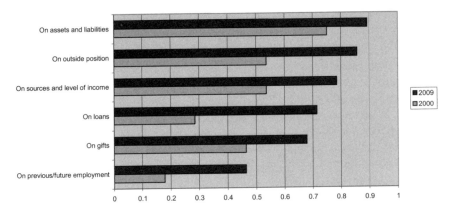

Fig. 6.1   Percentage of OECD countries that require decision makers in the central government to disclose conflict of interest (2000 and 2009). Source: Government at a Glance, Oecd 2009.

(TI-2005: 198). Figureheads or friends may also be the recipients of benefits from the public decision-maker: a former British Columbia premier has been charged for "unintentionally" breaking conflict of interest rules in connection with his handling of a friend's casino license application, allegedly receiving an indirect benefit in return, in the form of free home renovations (*Toronto Star*, November 20, 2002).

In Italy, discussions of conflicts of interest are interwoven with the political-entrepreneurial affairs of Silvio Berlusconi, three-time president of the Council of Ministers as well as the country's richest man and owner of an economic empire ranging from communications to insurance, football to banks. Since 2001, in particular (the decade following his second and third government mandates), several "short-circuits" have occurred between his public and private roles, thanks to government decisions allowing Berlusconi the entrepreneur to enjoy consistent economic advantages by virtue of measures imposed by Berlusconi the Prime Minister and his majority.

In particular, in the presence of a rapid turnover in political and administrative personnel, spaces are opened up for new individuals to enter the electoral market, including those coming from the professional and commercial worlds. Public distrust in the political class, fed also by scandals and investigations, has led to a more frequent alternation in power—also at the local level—among competing leaders and political coalitions: nevertheless, new administrators also have the possibility of using public powers to satisfy their own old, yet never forgotten, economic interests (whether personal or family). Another example of a conflict of interest concerns an Italian political leader who founded a consultancy company (which his wife was also a partner in) that used to pocket generous contracts on behalf of companies benefitting from the public contracts whose allocation he could influence (della Porta and Vannucci 2007). This kind of mechanism, based on the deposit of money not with a politician but with a services company owned by the politician's relatives (with the possibility to overcharge for any services provided), represents the outcome of a process of learning more effective techniques for concealing (see Chapter 9). For the judiciary, it becomes more difficult to prove how this is an illegal exchange.

Entrepreneurial Protection of Corruption

In some cases entrepreneurs assume the task of protecting the organized corruption system. Even if the "production" of decisions and information exchanged for bribes stays in the hands of public agents, some entrepreneurs guarantee the fulfillment of commitments by punishing any impropriety or awarding—economically— "good practices" in corruption. Facilitating conditions here are the presence of public structures with fragmented organizational architecture and an uncertain allocation of responsibility, and of companies with high contractual and market power, if not monopolistic, regarding public demand for their goods and services. *Entrepreneurial protection* thus derives from the power of some influential private actors to cut defectors out of the advantages of the "fair play" of corruption repeated over time, for instance, by turning to other equally corruptible functionaries for the same services. Moreover, some politically connected entrepreneurs may also have the capability to reward their trustworthy corrupt partners fostering their career or vice versa to punish their defection, "causing troubles" with hierarchical superiors or colleagues.

An instance of entrepreneurial protection in corrupt deals is that of Mr. Z, a peddler who in a third-world country secured—almost monopolistically— equipment contracts, licenses, permits, and contract payments for potential foreign bidders:

> Before bid opening, a Mr. Z, claiming he had government connections, approached these two bidders as well as other companies that he thought intended to bid. […] A noteworthy feature of this case is that a single individual (Mr. Z) controlled access to all the project bidding and contract opportunities (up to and including payment of invoices during contract execution) through his government connections. Mr. Z. was seemingly able to sell his protection to the companies involved in the project, while at the same time obtaining subcontracts or consulting assignments for the shell companies he owned. This Case contains an unusual combination of pervasive forms of misconduct engaged in by a single individual (it is worth noting that one person was killed in connection with the implementation of that same project). (OECD 2007: 87)

Another is the case of an entrepreneur who, over two decades—until the early 1990s—paid bribes to get countless contracts from the Italian state railways (which he was a former employee of) by knowingly building a mosaic of relationships with several functionaries at every level. His dominant position contributed to a growth in his negotiation power with individual public agents, who received his bribes in the form of black-market monthly wages. The bribee thereby received demands for goods and services on behalf of the body to be gauged on the characteristics of his company, to the point of becoming the "single maker of his own decisions [...] he makes suggestions to the company by dictating the respective prices" (PR: 101). The simple fear of being marginalized from this exchange network, where the entrepreneur pulled the strings, caused employees to respect the corruption pacts. It is the same entrepreneur who acts to suggest and coordinate the supply of punitive measures against reluctant employees, such as in the case of the transfer of one functionary whom he did not manage to recruit among his "black market employees," despite holding a prominent position (PR: 231).

Similar scenarios are also seen on other occasions. An Italian functionary observes, "The power that companies and bribers have is even more incredible. In fact, it is the companies who choose the functionaries who will have successful careers. Their presence is obsessive" (R, 14 February 2003: 15). In a paradigmatic case, a Neapolitan entrepreneur played a crucial role in systemic corruption, allegedly being the regulator in a large exchange network of politicians and officials—including center-left as well as center-right parliamentarians; regional, provincial, and municipal councilors; criminal and administrative justices; and administrators—thanks to his control of several resources: money (bribes, as well as subtler forms of political financing through pseudo-consulting contracts, etc.), political and administrative careers, the recruitment of relatives, and the subcontracting of public-procurement work. As explained by the judges (PRNAP: 2–3), he

> was the organiser of a veritable 'committee', composed of public officials, professionals, councillors and public-sector managers who, with him at the centre, used their power and duties to help him obtain public contracts for construction and the provision of services, receiving in exchange the rewards that he could distribute (the recruitment of selected people; consulting contracts and assignments; money). They assured him that in contracting procedures public invitations to bid would be planned to meet his requirements, these actually being written by [him] and his staff, his bids later being accepted by the public bodies involved.

During a tapped telephone conversation, the entrepreneur asked an MP to "obtain credit" for a public contract that was unjustifiably awarded to a competitor: "They excluded me because of a friend of his [...] they managed the deal." "If you want, I can stop the procedure." "No, it is not necessary; let him have it, poor guy. But they will have to pay for this." According to the investigating judges, in Naples public contracts and procedures were shaped to match the characteristics of his firms "with the purpose of guaranteeing him the award of contracts worth billions" (R, December 18, 2008).[6]

---

[6] Similarly, a Taiwan entrepreneur was the regulator of a wide network of corruption in China, aimed at smuggling cars, luxury products, oil, and other goods into Fujian's Xiamen city, cheating the state of about $4 billion: "thousands of government officials were involved: Lai Changxing, the chairman of Lianhua group, had corrupted them by such

Corruption in the Private Sector

Relationships between private sector individuals are just as vulnerable to corruption as those in the public sector. Corruption, as shown in Chapter 1, is related to the delegation of power and responsibilities from a principal to an agent; this contractual relationship is altered by the intervention of a client/briber, who in turn enters into a hidden—corrupt—exchange with the agent that interferes with his activities. The sphere of private corruption includes cases in which the principal "betrayed" is a private actor, individual, or collective (a firm, a trade union, an association, etc.). In these cases, a "contract" is violated because of the briber does not foresee any delegation of power on behalf of the whole community, as in the case of corrupt politicians or bureaucrats, but only from one private sector individual to another. Nevertheless, this form of corruption is extremely harmful and sometimes more widespread than that in the public sector. This is the case in Finland, for instance, where businessmen "find dealings with other businesspeople more prone to corruption than dealings with the authorities. [...] The private sector appeared much more prone to corruption than the public" (TI-2009: 320).

First of all, corrupting private agents hide information useful for assessing their contractual performance, distort and misrepresent the competition process, and reward agents with less moral scruples, and thus introduce elements of inefficiency into market relationships. Diffusion is made easier by the transnational dimension of commercial exchanges in globalized markets that, together with the privatization processes of the last few decades, have notably increased opportunities for private sector corruption in contexts with weak public regulation.

Private sector and public sector corruption contain a level of contiguity. Entrepreneurs and economic operators with a tendency to resort to bribes when conducting their private affairs have fewer moral scruples and greater "technical skills" in illegal activities when it comes to dealing with their relationships with politicians and bureaucrats, and vice versa, with the same means. The practice of corruption, which nestles in market exchanges or public organizations, actually generates a web of relationships and a pool of connections, making it easier to apply in other contexts.

Therefore, when a company employee or a professional sells their services to a briber, instead of defending the interests of the company they are employed by or the clients they are representing, we encounter a situation of corruption similar to the one in the public sector. Such cases include, for example, a referee selling himself to a football club chairman, a purchasing office manager for a company receiving bribes from providers to allocate contracts, a lawyer betraying the orders of his client in exchange for a gift in compensation, a journalist hired by the secret

---

means as wining and dining them, hiring their children, or secretly filming them cavorting with hostesses at his "underground palace," known as the "Little Red Mansion" (*Asia Times*, May 6, 2006).

services to write manipulative articles, or a trade unionist softening his demands after secretly being paid by an entrepreneur.

There are, in fact, countless examples of corruption of trade unionists by their employers in exchange for social peace (*Corriere della Sera*, August 30, 2010). For instance, several leaders of a Carpenter's Union have been indicted in recent decades because they allegedly served the interests of contractors who bribed them, instead of protecting union members (*New York Times*, August 5, 2009). A Volkswagen (VW) labor leader has also been sentenced for receiving €2 billion in bribes from VW executives in exchange for supporting their decisions: this was part of a broader strategy of VW managers, who had bought the support of union representatives with secret bonuses, luxury holidays, jewelry, and fake consulting fees (TI-2009: 17). Journalists are vulnerable to corruption as well, since the "commodity" they professionally provide (or fail to provide) to the public—that is, information—may be valuable to private actors who bribe them, yet its qualitative profiles are difficult to ascertain: therefore, pieces of information can be easily manipulated or disguised. In China, for instance, developers in the housing estate industry "are often protected by the press. They bribe journalists to write regular ads to hype properties, an industry insider in Beijing pointed out" (*Asia Times*, December 19, 2003). In Thailand, according to a former news editor, bribe-taking among reporters was an enduring and consolidated tradition: "It has been this way for decades. The practice, which began with simple handouts of cash and gold ornaments, had now become more sophisticated. [...] Companies, politicians and even government agencies offered a variety of gifts ranging from mobile phones to overseas trips in exchange for favourable coverage" (*Asia Times*, March 10 1999).

Private sector corruption is considered a crime in some countries, but not in others: "Though it constitutes perhaps the largest component of corruption in the value chain and has adverse consequences for the working of the markets and economies, private-to-private corruption has received surprisingly limited attention from lawmakers" (TI-2009: 22). Even when unfaithful managers or professionals pocket bribes, they risk only mild sanctions, in some cases only those accounted for in their contracts. Obviously, individuals who work for private firms and negotiate contracts with suppliers, subcontractors, or clients on behalf of their companies may accept bribes in exchange for decisions or information that favors their corruptors. A case of corruption in private purchasing arrangements between two supermarkets giants—Wellcome and ParknShop—emerged in China in 2005, in which 27 people were arrested. Nine staff of the two supermarkets, among them a senior executive, were accused of having taken bribes—more than $100,000 per month—in return for giving preferential treatment to suppliers. The corrupt exchange was managed by two alleged middlemen, who introduced 16 food and flower suppliers to supermarket staff they knew and negotiated agreements: "It's a very competitive market and it is difficult to get your goods on the shelves of a supermarket," a source familiar with the investigations explained (*South China Morning Post*, November 5, 2005).

Finally, virtually all sports—where performances are subject to unpredictable variations and referees' judgments are often decisive—are vulnerable to private corruption. Several match-fixing scandals over the past decade demonstrate how the cricket circuit is conditioned by bribes: for instance, "the South African captain, Hansie Cronje, confessed to his involvement in the largest match-fixing scandal in the sport's history. He admitted taking bribes of up to £150,000 ($414,000) a time to throw games from a man introduced to him by the Indian captain" (*Independent*, March 24, 2007). An ideal context for private corruption is represented by the football business: the amount of economic (and emotional) interests and resources at stake, the arbitrariness of decisions taken, the natural variation of individual efforts and performance—that is, the pervasiveness of information asymmetries—make players and referees a perfect target for corruptors interested in match-fixing. The result of the match in itself, but more often the gains made from gambling on it, is usually the object of corrupt deals. Examples abound (*Reuters*, May 16, 2007; TI-2009: 360). In all such cases, the possibility of cheating must be taken into consideration on both sides of the transaction. A conversation secretly tape-recorded in April 2006 between the "corrupter" and a football goalkeeper shows how difficult it is to manage this "unique" deal, in a suspicious and distrustful atmosphere:

E.: I have spoken to all the other players about the fix. The others know about it.

O.: What? The whole teams knows?

E.: Don't worry about it! [...]

O.: Can I trust you?

E.: The money is in the car. Let me show you.

O.: You mean it is betting? Or do you have an arrangement with the other team? Does our team management know?

E.: If you talk about your arrangement you won't get a single lira! I am trying to do you a favour. These guys are trying to bet 500–600 billion lira. There are two hundred thousand Euro in the bag and there will be more. Just get the score we want. (Cit. in Lambsdorff 2007: 170)

The goalkeeper finally refused the proposal, due to the inability of the match-fixer to appear reassuring and reliable. A successful strategy was instead adopted by a Malaysian fixer, who—according to a former national team player—contacted him and, speaking his native language, guaranteed him his control of the entire team, then showed his determination to enforce the agreement: "He then asked me to inform XX that if he (XX) did not cooperate, he will break his legs. I told XX. He agreed to fix the match. The fixer then asked me to inform the rest of the group. All of them agreed" (cit. in Lambsdorff 2007: 171).

Some Italian investigations into the world of professional football, beginning in May 2006 shortly before Italy's triumph in the World Cup in Germany, reveal a cross-section of an effective, *privately* regulated, system of corrupt transactions. The stable sharing out of advantages was guaranteed through a government structure consolidated throughout years of practice, precise in its roles and internal hierarchies. According to information emerging from the investigations and telephone interceptions, M.—Sporting Director of Turin club Juventus—provided, with the collaboration of a Juventus board director, a control room and a clearing house for the relations between many of the individuals involved in the affairs. Actually, M. "was the master craftsman of a favour bank. The covert tapes of his transactions reveal he not only coerced and bribed people, but far more often he enacted a constant series of favours that were either repaid or withdrawn with a large network of internal sport actors" (Hill 2009: 172). Therefore, he was also the guarantor of the organized working of the exchange network when it came to referees, with whom they used "broadly speaking, disciplinary and media control procedures" by influencing suspension sanctions provided for by referee designators and opinions expressed by journalists (PFD: 26). The so-called "M. system" provides a coordination mechanism between football clubs and individuals involved in the underground favor market that, from the 1990s up to 2006, influenced the outcome of league championships, the fortunes or adversities of sporting directors, referees, managers, and players. With patience and dedication, M. regulated the workings of this "consolidated relationship network" on a daily basis with referee designators and some referees (PFD: 22).

In a spiraling plot of meetings and conversations, M. smoothed out disagreements, reassured waverers, and generously compensated accomplices and supporters (*Corriere della Sera*, May 22, 2006). As a guarantor, M. rationalized conflicts of interests, which allowed the internal compensation of favors between referees, sporting directors, and sports agents of the GEA group, a brokerage company which became a kind of clearing house. This included—as partners and consultants—M.'s son, the son of Juventus's manager, who would go on to become world champion with the national team, the daughter of the president of Capitalia Bank and financial backer of Roma, a club in serious financial difficulties. Just after a loan was granted to Roma, "a thaw in relations with the dominant club in the football system, Juventus, occurs," in the words of the former sporting director of the club, which materialized in the reciprocal exchange of players and managers (*L'espresso*, May 25, 2006: 38). Moggi commented, "but now the situation (Roma's) there is in order, because they want to speak to the bank. I got them to sort everything out, so they should be willing to comply" (*Corriere della Sera*, May 18, 2006). Referees who do not align themselves with the agreements are punished: "This behaviour develops in two different ways. One is realised by threatening sanctions on referees or asking the designator directly to apply them. The other is realised in inspection by some journalists with the aim of protecting the position of referees considered as friends and, on the other hand, attacking 'non-aligned' referees" (CAF: 87). The concerns held by referees about their careers, related to the exhibited capability of "enforcers" to influence them, played a major role in the multiyear success of match-rigging (Boeri e Severgnini 2008).

Concluding Remarks

In the corruption market, private actors are not only beneficiaries of public sector decisions that create profit-making opportunities and fuel the flow of bribes. When political parties or leaders, as well as other potential enforcers of corrupt exchanges, grow weaker, entrepreneurs in particular can assume a more active role. In many cases they try to autonomously protect what they see as their "rights" over the resources at stake in their visible or underground relationships with public administrators: by concluding agreements limiting competition in public tenders or holding personally positions of public power in conflicts of interest, they actually make bribery superfluous. A well-organized cartel is in fact capable of autonomously determining the identity of the winners in calls for public tender, award prices, and the criteria for internal shares. A politician who is at the same time a beneficiary, in his role as entrepreneur, of his public choices internalizes the two sides of the corrupt exchange within the same person, and in this capacity he also eliminates the risk of "rip-offs" and therefore also the demand for protection and enforcement.

Even when the money from bribes flows from bribers to public agents, it may still occur that economic power or influence over public decision-making makes the entrepreneur the guarantor of the repetition of the exchange, and in some cases the arbiter of a functionary's career—and the latter are often sensitive to economic incentives—based on their trustworthiness, particularly in weak and internally divided administrative structures. The same logic is then applied to a wider set of social and market relations, revealing corruption networks branching into civil society that are consolidated over time. Even if confined to the private sector, corruption reproduces the same negative effects as observed in the public sector. Indeed, private sector corruption also hides and distorts information, blurs agents' responsibilities and introduces elements of waste and inefficiency, and discourages useful skills from being gained to improve productivity.

Nevertheless, some factors challenge the equilibria of corruption involving private actors and may increase instability. When some information on illegal deals spreads, excluded actors (from the rents made possible by cartels, private or privately regulated corruption, decision-making influenced by conflicts of interest) may have an interest in exposing and denouncing them; alternatively, such blackmail-enabling information may be used to impose inclusion within the restricted circle of beneficiaries. The first strategy can determine a sudden collapse of the system; the second, a subsequent increase of internal conflicts for the redistribution of profits and gains within a larger set of corrupting/corrupt subjects. A second possible source of pressure on the "private corruption" equilibria can emerge due to the free-riding (i.e., defection) strategies of *internal* actors in the cartel (or participants in the corrupt exchange). If, for instance, their time-horizon shrinks—due to contingent financial difficulties—and they evaluate the expected profits of repeated cooperation with a higher discount rate, they may adopt an opportunistic strategy of low-term maximization, reneging on their previous agreements with corrupt or corrupting partners. In both cases the stability of cartels (and private bribery) requires protection, that is, an informal regulatory framework that—through more or less centralized mechanisms—can assure benefits (reciprocal support, anticipation of future profits, etc.) and threaten costs (exclusion from the system, blackmailing, etc.) to induce generalized compliance with the general or "contractual" rules of corruption.

Chapter 7
Brokers in Corruption Networks:
The Role of Middlemen

An Italian engineer regularly obtains contracts for consultancy services from a provincial councilor valued at around €50,000 a year. In exchange, he pays the councilor a bribe equal to half of his profit. The deal is still convenient, and the engineer is not tormented by any moral scruples. He is faced with another kind of headache however. Here are the words he used to vent his anger in a blog:

> I'm an engineer, what the hell do I understand about these affairs? I've never been interested in political ideas, I don't care at all, but I can't go on this way. The problem is that to make friends, with these cowards, it isn't enough to pay them: you have to speak to them too and get on well. But apart from construction techniques, I don't have any hobbies. I'm not even particularly interested in women. What can I say to them? What can I talk about? I was born here, but it's as if I didn't know anyone. I've always minded my own business. I don't go to dinners, and now I have to. I don't know the names of wines. I don't even have a tie, for Christ's sake! Grappa di mirto, cars, football, family histories, mushroom dishes, tenders, cheats and concussions, jokes, trends [...] none of that, I don't know anything. Why is money not enough? What do they expect from me?[1]

The bribing engineer has experienced firsthand the fact that corruption does not always peter out into an aseptic passage of money. Corruption also requires other types of investment—of time, knowledge, social relations, and friendship—which, given his character, are the source of his personal unease.

This "briber's drama," described in such vivid terms, gives us initial food for thought in understanding the nature of the demand for mediation services that can spring up in corruption relations, analyzed in detail in this chapter. Indeed, the most useful asset for our engineer-briber would be a reliable "professional friendship" with politicians, whose demand for sociability and recognition he has problems satisfying. He needs a professional middleman: an individual to take responsibility, in return for suitable compensation, for looking after the unpleasant (as well as risky) relationship aspects required by the illegal exchange, removing the arduous fatigue from the complaining party, and leaving him the same earning opportunities, and perhaps opening new windows of opportunity for him. Under certain conditions, professional middlemen come into play as pivotal ties in corruption networks by contributing to and widening the networks' size and reinforcing the intensity of the trust connections among the actors involved.

---

[1] Cfr. http://lotta.blog.excite.it/permalink/138154, accessed May 25, 2006.

Resources and Skills of Middlemen

Marriage brokers, estate agents, financial consultants, and lobbyists are examples of individuals and activities of mediation. Indeed, the middleman is a kind of social lubricant, able to conciliate connections and agreements that, in his absence, would be impeded by inability, mistrust, and the lack of information on the partner's features and the quality of resources exchanged.

Agreements regarding valuable and durable goods, whose quality is difficult to verify since experience and information are scarce, require expensive research activities that do not however exclude the risk of being ripped off or buying unsatisfactory "merchandise." To carry out these exchanges, a large dose of trust in the partner is needed, but what can be done when one's reputation is unknown and there are no precedents to base an assessment of intentions on?

Under these conditions, there is a risk that the deal will not come off without the intervention of a "third party"—the middleman—who *professionally* takes on the responsibility of some of these costs. The mediator acquires and deals with the information necessary to disentangle relations in these opaque or unstable markets. He forms social connections, develops skills that will help him in persuading clients to trust him, and looks for direct contacts with potential counterparts. His activity makes it easier to exceed the critical trust threshold necessary to initiate transactions that it would otherwise not be possible to carry out, but he naturally constitutes a cost for the interested parties in the shape of his "fee."

As may be expected, the mediator's activity is often crucial in illegal markets. In these contexts, reasons for distrust and uncertainty are amplified by (i) the lack of *official* courts to sanction the observance of agreements, (ii) the risks taken in identifying counterparts interested in agreeing deals, (iii) the fact that these counterparts are unscrupulous and willing to break the law, and (iv) the difficulty of collecting reliable information. Similarly, the mediators, by being granted the trust of their associates, incur many delicate tasks and specialize in the "dirty work," thereby favoring the success of the illegal exchanges.

The corruption market is no exception. For instance, in India the recourse to middlemen to gain access to some public agents' favors in specific procedures is commonplace: 70 percent of those who obtained a driving license hired "agents" or middlemen, who then bribed bureaucrats; "most were approached by the middlemen, usually more than one, in competition—and only about 2 per cent paid bribes directly to bureaucrats. Hiring a middleman was noted as a common practice for those seeking other sorts of government outcomes, such as passports, ration cards, or land titles" (Khanna and Johnston 2007: 153). In many cases, bribers and bribees delegate some of the tasks required in concluding affairs to various intermediaries and fixers. The middleman's services "are necessary [...] because he has special knowledge of the procedures, access to officials, time to spend, and dirty hands" (Oldenburg 1987: 527). [2] Brokers reduce research and bargaining costs, identify willing partners, and decrease the risks of offering or receiving a bribe, since they know which private agents are prepared to pay and which public agents are corruptible. Moreover, they may be familiar with (or discover) the "minimum price" for corrupt services, thus minimizing the risk of denunciations or the rejection of the deal (Bayar 2005: 278–9). They also lower transaction costs, providing information to potential clients with respect to the capability of the agents to actually deliver the promised service, that is, trustworthiness and ability to fulfill the corrupt agreement (Hasker and Okten 2008). As Lambsdorff (2011) observes, "intermediaries offer *insurance* against opportunism, detection and conviction [...] . Intermediaries may have repeated contact with public servants, providing a deterrent against opportunism."

As shown in Chapter 2, middlemen may provide particularly effective regulation mechanisms when interactions between bribers and bribees are not frequent. In such cases, few learn to trust one another, but the value at stake is high enough to make an intervention characterized by specific abilities and specialist skills *useful* for counterparts and *convenient* for the middlemen themselves.

After all, since each intermediary operation has high fixed costs, even more so if the issue dealt with is illegal, it is worth saving one's services for those cases where the stakes involved make active participation convenient. Middlemen essentially manage four kinds of interrelated resources:

a) *social capital*, the network of personal contacts and relations that controls their sphere of operations;

b) *trust*, the capacity to generate and cultivate trust in their clients, which generates expectations of reciprocal fulfillment and transforms those contacts into exchange opportunities;

c) *reputation*, related to their ability to create and maintain profitable exchange relationships with their clients over time;

d) *information*, on the characteristics of the corrupt exchanges, which can be used to generate, enlarge, and strengthen their network of trust relationships, to individuate and signal profit opportunities to their clients, to reduce the risks of illegal dealings, and to enforce pacts and agreements.

To initiate their activities, the mediator must arrange an initial endowment of social relationships, information, and trust, or invest in acquiring them.

---

[2]   As the magistrates observe in the investigations surrounding one corruption case: "the use of one individual in the role of bribe-collector, the only interface between the world of political administration and the entrepreneurial world, makes direct contact between the parties superfluous; it limits the risk of informants or information leaking; it also makes investigations extremely difficult by identifying all subjects involved" (TRMBL: 45).

Social Capital

Intermediaries operating in the corruption underground, just like their colleagues who operate in the open, are entrepreneurs who extensively use *social capital*.[3] In their case, social capital does not favor generalized cooperation or reciprocity, nor is it associated with the good performance of public institutions (Putnam 1993); instead, it is used *instrumentally and selectively* among those who interact by establishing corrupt relationships.[4] The middleman therefore places crossroads for the passage of information, signals, money, and anything else useful in negotiating and bringing hidden transactions to completion within a relationship network of public and private actors. As one middleman recalls,

> thanks to this knowledge, I discovered that I was able to get favours for friends who needed them [...] . Naturally, the friend I helped out would give me a gift, which could also be a considerable amount of money. I therefore set out to obtain brokerages of a higher level, practically conducting my professional activity just from that. (VPI, April 14, 1989)

During a tax audit, upon the request of the entrepreneur being audited, an accountant-middleman activated his own connections in the Guardia di finanza (the Italian revenue police) for the payment of a bribe: "I made sure the officer knew that the auditors would have to consider that *there was a friend in the partnership, and that friend was me.* By this, I meant that it would be easy to reach an agreement with me concerning a transfer of money" (TMIMB: 121, emphasis added).

It is however also essential that a successful broker in corrupt deals distinguishes those relationships that are potentially more profitable, investing time and energy in cultivating them. When introduced to a politician, for instance, an Italian middleman decided to please him, since—in his words—"I was introduced to an extremely important man, with plenty of funds and countless connections. When I meet an important person, I attach myself to him, and I believe that XXX deserved this kind of interest [...] . Meeting people and having relationships with important

---

[3]   Studies that use the concept of *social capital* are based on the recognition of the importance of interpersonal relationship networks in generating chains of solidarity and trust, cooperatively orientating expectations, favoring economic exchanges and social relations: "Like other forms of capital, social capital is productive, making possible the achievement of certain ends that would not be obtainable in its absence [...] . Unlike other forms of capital, social capital inheres the structure of relations between persons and among persons" (Coleman 1990: 302).

[4]   The connections and exchanges made possible by the presence of social capital do not always produce positive consequences for the group they appear in. When it favors the coordination of members of a terrorist organization, a Mafia group, a syndicate of entrepreneurs, or a gang of bribees, making the pursuit of their objectives more effective, *bad* social capital produces costs that fall on the whole of society (Putnam, 2001; della Porta 2000).

people is something which interested me, it interested me then and it always will" (*Corriere della Sera*, July 7, 2010).

The middleman can recycle relationships built up beforehand, or inherited from family, for corruption purposes. Take the case of the *enabler* B., for example, who said his father "left us in a good position and with a store of connections and relations" (TMLB: 2). According to an Italian vice-Ministry, B. "is a friend of everyone, he is the most known person I know. He is a 'man of relations'" (R, June 20, 2011).[5] Similarly, the Duchess of York Sarah Ferguson was said to try to profit from her enduring relationship with her ex-husband, Prince Andrew, to sell an introduction to him in his role of ambassador for trade:

> FERGIE: I could bring you great business. I'd like to think that if I, for example, if I introduced you to ...
>
> REPORTER: Andrew for example?
>
> FERGIE: Andrew for example . . . and he opened up doors for you which you would never possibly do. Then, depending if it was a very big deal with I don't know, I can't imagine, then each deal you and I discuss the percentage of it. (*News of the World*, May 23, 2010)

The case of middlemen reinvesting communication channels and relationship networks deriving from their ordinary professional activities into illegal practices is also very frequent. *Agents d'affaire*, for instance, ordinarily act as intermediaries in opaque dealings with judges and functionaries in the Senegalese legal system. According to a local clerk:

> These are actors who have experienced the legal system, who have worked in the courts or in the administrative departments of the courts, they have retired, you know these people have a certain profile, they have a human capital, that is to say, they know lots of people, they are extremely resourceful individuals, they have developed a familiarity with the courts over the years, so they now come along to their colleagues [...] . So if they ask a favour of them, those people cannot refuse and generally they have most success with people who are unaware of how the legal procedures work. (Alou 2006: 164–5)

As emerges from the different examples quoted in this chapter, certain professional intermediation activities with the state are particularly vulnerable, such as those of accountants or lawyers, encouraging the acquisition of specific connections in their field and the striking up of regular relations with eventual recipients of bribes

---

[5]   The development of social capital depends on different "social network" properties, yet it is favored by, among other things, the presence of "relationship fabrics which can be orientated in the direction of purposes different from those for which they were originally formed" (Sciarrone 1998: 47). Indeed: "as well as the skills and unscrupulousness, there is also the aspect of network access. The deal intermediary's activity favours the acquisition of being familiar with all kinds of surroundings" (Becchi 2001: 53).

on the one hand, and the beneficiaries of their decisions on the other.[6] In New York, an 85-year-old tax consultant, who, after the end of his 30-year career at the tax assessor's office, started bribing tax assessors in exchange for cutting property taxes, was at the center of a real estate tax fraud ring: "His good contacts with the tax assessors and the landlords allowed him to link up the two sides and arrange corrupt deals that would otherwise have been unenforceable" (Lambsdorff 2011).

Certain professions linked to commerce also allow reusable links to be established in the corruption market. This is the case of a luxury car dealer, one of the principal middlemen used by one entrepreneur to legally pay sums of money to politicians under the table. The entrepreneur states that,

> I established a friendly relationship and I noticed that he had close, strong connections with the political and institutional world [...] but he also introduced me to all the generals in the Revenue Police who passed through Bologna and, subsequently, I also noticed that he had close relationships with a number of politicians. (Gomez and Travaglio 2006: 58)

The same is also true of many former public body employees who, once retired (or having resigned with that purpose in mind), are recycled as middlemen in trafficking bribes addressed to their former colleagues, with whom they retain connections built up over many years of work. This is the case of a former official of the Guardia di finanza, who managed contacts with his former companions on request for tax audit recipients:

> after asking me if I knew the official [in the Guardia di finanza], who I had known since back in 1972, despite him never having been a direct employee of mine, and having received an affirmative answer, [...] he then asked me to contact him in order to check if it was possible to stop these threats (the lieutenant even threatened to make the audit last for several months). (TMIIF, May 19, 1994: 17)

From the 100 million lire paid to the official, the middleman keeps 10 million as a personal fee for his actions.

Connections accrued in entrepreneurial operations can also be useful for launching intermediation activities. Once retired, for example, a former director of a company operating in the hospitality industry set up a business consultancy company for businesses operating in the tender sector, acting as a middleman on behalf of hospitality companies participating in calls for tender for cafeteria goods: "he had always enjoyed 'important introductions into the world of facility

---

6   In Indian corruption "*Dalals*—who typically are fellow farmers—constitute but one type of middlemen in land consolidation. There are also lawyers who specialize in land consolidation cases; office boys, lower-level clerks, and the lowest level of officers (the "scribe" and the "consolidator" [*lekhpal* and *kanungo*]) all take money for some services they provide, as 'tips' or they may claim to provide a channel for bribes to their superior officers" (Oldenburg 1987: 527).

providers [...] in the world of political bodies' even where he was often on commission" (TRMBL: 8).

In other cases, however, the investment of this relationship network in corruption is intentional and reflects the professional decision to operate in the intermediation of illegal affairs. Masonic affiliation, entering exclusive clubs and associations, and membership in a political party may, for example, bring a dowry of a chain of connections and relationships that can be converted for the pursuit of one's own affairs.

According to fixer Adriano Zampini, one technique consists of frequenting places where politicians and entrepreneurs meet (the directors' box in a football stadium, for example) and identifying a *passe-partout*, an established professional who can introduce people to the people in charge.

> The *passe-partout* must become a close relation [...] . It's done. The fixer deals with everything and everybody. It isn't necessary to be part of the CIA to know private things. Information agencies can be found anywhere in any city. Therefore, with only an information note and with the *passe-partout* entering the political circle is the easiest thing in the world. The right way can then be found to join the Lions, Rotary and any other Masonic lodge. (Zampini 1993: 112)

A sporting circle can also become the backdrop where contacts between corruption protagonists intertwine (TMBMP: 272). In cultivating relationships, the middleman must not be too fastidious in terms of the quality of "human material" he deals with, since each contact can unexpectedly prove useful. Here is the advice bestowed by Greek shipowner Aristotle Onassis to Francesco Pazienza, which is then taken on as a life rule:

> Never look down on anybody, even those who, in the moment you meet them, you think will never be useful to you. Remember: humanity is like a library. Having a beautiful collection of books composed only of art volumes or Greek classics is not enough, it's a mistake. In fact, the moment can arrive when you have as a guest an ignoramus or a boor, who you are however negotiating an important deal with. It can happen that, before going to bed, he asks you if you have erotic or pornographic stories. In that case, what do you do? Do you give him Socrates or Thucydides? [...] Keep relations even with those who seem useless to you. One day or another, even these people can be useful to you. (Pazienza 1999: 158)

Once built up, contacts are maintained and cultivated, as an Italian middleman recalls:

> I had an accurate logbook of the dates of sons', wives' and even girlfriends' birthdays, and then I also sent greetings for Easter and summer holidays. It's a glaring error to think that everything's solved just by paying. Spheres of friendship and good manners, which have nothing to do with business, remain more important. You need to know how to weave a web so that the relationship

is reinforced day after day [...] . Otherwise the relationship becomes sterile and forming relationships is not easy. (Zampini 1993: 166)

The fatal attraction of Masonic lodges for many middlemen in illegal affairs can thus be explained, since they are among the places where the quantity of *private* relations and the quality of their "content of trust" appears most, given the common affiliation, entrance selection, and membership rituals. The broker Pazienza pragmatically describes the reasons he joined the Masons:

> What particularly struck me and made me curious was the fact that belonging to the organisation provided the great possibility to increase the variety and quantity of my own connections throughout the world. Should I have joined, I thought that this 'circle' could allow me to widen my interests. (Pazienza 1999: 168)

The Masons are only one of the reasonably secret associations used as social capital "reservoirs" to recycle for the purpose of corruption; there are others where the privacy guaranteed to members' actions is both more effective and greater. The broker Zampini (1985: 92–3) thus describes his membership of the Knights of Malta: "It's the usual structure where all the members are kept secret and for connection operations between brothers, you have to 'pass' from the area boss [...]. In each case it wasn't the connections which made the organisation interesting, but the possibility for business."

Masonic leaders are not immune to the temptation of investing connection capital in illegal intermediation activities. In a telephone interception, one former Worshipful Master of the Grand Scottish Orient of Italy explains the effective nature of his functions as a *middleman* in illegal operations:

> As always happens, they don't have the ability or the desire to speak boldly because they are afraid of the other party squealing, of speaking and their real intentions coming out, and they turn to somebody who acts as a middleman in these operations. And that's our capacity, our possibility to intervene, which I think is required anyway, isn't it? It isn't like it was me who invented it out of the blue. Since I am quite familiar with these environments, unfortunately, and they know that we are middlemen for good or for evil. (R-Florence, September 24, 1993)

Trust

The land so laboriously plowed by the middleman, looking for meetings and making promising connections, risks remaining uncultivated without the availability of a "fertilizer" capable of making the most of these contacts: that is, the *trust* of others and a reputation. In each relationship of trust there are two individuals: one who trusts the other—allowing him to complete certain actions or putting resources at his disposal so that he can use them to his own advantage (as long as this trust is repaid)—and the recipient of his trust, his "trustee" (Coleman 1990: 91). The middleman is successful when he manages to become a trustee of bribers and bribees who are willing to enter into a deal with one another, but are not willing to bear the full corresponding transaction costs.[7] Interpreted in this way, the problem of a person having to decide whether to place his trust in a middleman seems like a kind of bet. The probability threshold attached to the good intentions and skills of the middleman, enough to encourage aspiring bribers and bribees to trust him, must be higher the greater the potential loss in relation to the possible gain; hence, the central role of trust and the delicacy of the role of middlemen in illegal relations where there are good profit-making opportunities. But at the same time, the negative consequences of betrayed trust can be catastrophic.

The presence of a structure of transparent and competitive exchanges reduces demand for trust to a minimum, since market selection processes favor those agents who have proved most reliable and efficient, and worthy of the good reputation that follows them. The corruption market, however, just like other illegal markets (and also indeed some legal markets), is opaque: expected gains and losses are neither easily preventable nor calculable, the probability of the trustees actually being worthy of their reputation is more uncertain. This explains the importance of any information able to reduce the risk of unexpected consequences of individual decisions. And it is precisely through the acquisition, manipulation, and professional use of *information* and *connections* that the middleman can acquire the capital of social relations and trust necessary to conclude his deals.

Trust becomes more important when relationships involve agents who have not met before, are geographically or culturally distant, or do not have reciprocal information on previous conduct. In international transactions, therefore, both demand for intermediation services and risks in searching (and paying) for them increase. Brokers are often considered necessary to enter into a foreign, unknown, and obscure net of procedures, codes, and relationships, but information on their reliability is similarly difficult to obtain. In an exhaustive review of the universe of cases of corruption prosecuted under the U.S. Foreign Corrupt Practices Act of 1977, there is a regular presence of middlemen, who can assume a variety of more or less official roles: consultants, agents, companies, distributors, fictitious "sales representatives," even relatives or friends of government officials—in the case of the daughter of an official in the Tourism Authority of Thailand (Shearman and Sterling 2009). Middlemen may supply the required assistance and guarantees, but they also have to be trusted, and—for exactly the same reasons—this is not always the case. The use of a middleman may provide a shortcut to knowledge of local facts and expertise, but when bribers do not have information or experience, especially in foreign enterprises, the risk of being cheated—even by would-

---

[7]   There is a time delay between the trusting agreement and the trustee's future actions, and the illegal nature of the relationships makes it difficult to use contractual devices (surety, guarantees, contractual clauses) that attenuate these kinds of problems in ordinary market relationships.

be brokers—is high. In a Middle East case, a defense service company was approached by a would-be intermediary "who claimed to be a close relative of a local ruler. He promised to use his connections to help win a large contract. The company made due diligence enquiries. It established that the would-be agent was indeed a relative of the ruler, but had fallen out with him some years preciously. His services would have been useless" (Bray 2005: 119).

As explained by an Italian middleman, several techniques can be adopted to strengthen trust relationships with potential clients: for instance, paying for trips—in formally "official" contexts—as a strategy to share intimacy, familiarity, and habits.

> Of course, you don't always talk about work, hardly ever actually, but rather a bond is created just like those men who go to the sauna together as naked as the day they were born. All the walls of formality crumble. And, once they have returned home, that profound familiarity remains in regard to roles which are, after all, those of giving and receiving. (Zampini 1993: 121)

We are talking about a scientifically calculated investment that is pursued even at the cost of some personal sacrifice:

> I remember that, during one trip, I got up every morning at seven to go to the sauna with one of them: it was a way to become his friend, bring our relations closer and show that we were available [...] . Nobody, of those who participated in the trips, restrained from letting themselves go and, in that way, played the same game as me. For me, these trips had a precise objective: to go from a friendship bond between those who do business together to a more solid one, where you go swimming together, get drunk together, lapse into bad jokes or things like that. (*L'Espresso*, November 18, 1984)

Middlemen and corruptors in general may be instrumentally very generous when they start a new corrupt relationship:

> This phenomenon has also be described as a kind of 'feeding', that is, giving favors in order to place the other side at one's mercy. This may include gifts without requesting any return in the beginning. Yet acceptance of the gift becomes the first step to dependence. Some time afterwards, rejecting a genuinely corrupt agreement suddenly becomes more difficult since declaring acceptance of earlier gifts may be "troublesome", while partners in corrupt exchanges come to be "hostages" to each other. (Lambsdorff 2007: 158)

Similarly, brokers in the contracting activities of the North Sea oil industry usually recruited insiders—from whom they received valuable information—using a technique of conviviality and comradeship, in order "to create an atmosphere of friendship within a setting of parties, dinners and alcohol [...] . Great efforts were made to develop an 'insider', and when first established, he is normally used many times" (Andvig 1995: 309).

A powerful generator of trust rests in shared common identity features among the middleman or his clients, such as belonging to the same ethnic or religious minority. By extending a peculiar "cultural mediation" function to their illegal activities it is often individuals from the same ethnic bloc who pull the strings in exchanges between members of the group and public agents, whom they turn to in order to obtain a number of services, such as work permits or residence permits. This is the case of an Albanian with regards to bribes paid by his co-nationals to employees of the Foreigners' Office (R-Florence, May 10, 2005), or a Sinhalese man in his relations with Immigration Office functionaries (R, November 20, 2004).

By entering the corruption system selectively, middlemen must ward off the dangers of trust spreading among bribers and bribees as a kind of freely available "public good" by favoring spontaneous agreements. For this purpose, they have to maintain *exclusivity* in their social contacts to the greatest possible extent to avoid other actors bypassing them and putting their "crucial" function in corruption networks in jeopardy. This is why Licio Gelli, according to Francesco Pazienza, adopted a sort of *broker-spider* strategy: he spun a web of bilateral relations, taking care not to transform his own estate of relations into resources freely available to clients, but rather to capture each of them individually in his web:

> What seemed rather curious and unique to me from the start was that the members of the P2 lodge, in most cases, did not know one another. Gelli had evidently found it much more convenient to avoid them meeting one another or, at least, trying to avoid this happening in order to keep his central role and make himself indispensible in that crossroads of interests, deals and power. (Pazienza 1999: 213)

Reputation

The reliability of middlemen is unknown to those who get in touch with them for the first time, and the possibility of being sold a "lemon" is not to be excluded. Brokers may be fraudulent, especially when they have a strong preference for immediate profit and do not expect to meet their clients again. In Duisburg, Germany, an intermediary took DM 141,000 from a private construction firm for arranging contracts to build school pavilions: "In reality, the official did nothing but name the firm once to those in charge of awarding the contracts. But he continuously requested more money, arguing that he was supposed to pass the money on to others" (Lambsdorff 2011).

A line of tension exists along which the middleman must maneuver, a trade-off that he has to balance between the need to be recognized as powerful and trustable and the necessity to act covertly. One middleman, when contacting an entrepreneur preparing to participate in a call for tender, reassured the former: "I'll add my clients [...] and I'll look after for you because I know them well, because I'm in the know [...] . He let me know that he had good connections [...] so he could resolve any problem in 24 hours" (TRMBL: 35). An Italian broker, to justify the requested fee of €1.5 million, emphasized to an entrepreneur—in a transcripted phone call from February 2008—the value of his capital of personal contacts, laboriously built over 10 years of cultivating relationships with high-ranking officials in the Italian Departments for Civil Defense and Public Works: "I built my background over ten years of throwing blood available to you and your men [...] because I'm convinced that we can get things done together [...] I'll benefit from it and you too [...] I've risked ten years of all kinds of pain in the backside investments, do you understand?" (*Corriere della Sera*, February 15, 2010).

The demand for middleman's services then augments following the success of a deliberate strategy of reputation-building or the spontaneous circulation of "positive" information on him. This is the revealing portrait of the middlemen B., traced by an entrepreneur: "I know that B. is a very influential and powerful man, closely tied to institutional circles, who exercises an unlimited power to maneuver in all branches of the State and the semi-state bodies [...] . I think that the enormous power of B. is based on his network of relations with both the current leadership of the Italian State and of foreign States; concerning the latter, I know that B. is very closely tied to the Queen of Jordan and to Israel" (CD-2: 196). In a way, middlemen need something similar to advertising to attract and reassure clients about their reputations of power and reliability, yet in another they must avoid news that might compromise their illegal activities from circulating outside the circle of bribers and bribees as this could get them into trouble with the authorities. However, giving ground in regards to discretion means feeding their own reputation by letting elements that make their services more desirable filter out: their influence over decision-making powers, large numbers of valuable contacts, trustworthiness, and "honesty."

To show the possible friction between "coming across as powerful" and operating in the shadows, typical of middlemen in illegal markets, we can take the interviews given by Licio Gelli to *L'Espresso* and *Corriere della Sera*, in which the revered master of a "secret" Masonic lodge (the so-called P2) extols its power, crediting it with 2,400 members in the leadership of institutions and the economic system, or the dialogue with the Socialist leader Craxi, during which he boasts of "being in the vanguard of an organisation which could influence the head of State" (CP2: 137). In another case, a broker was a step away from printing business cards certifying his role as a secret service informer (Pazienza 1999: 128).

The would-be middleman T., who developed an official link with the Italian Prime Minister Silvio Berlusconi, was similarly tempted by the opportunity to advertise his success, in order to increase the value of his reputation and market for intermediation services. In the words of one of his clients:

> The head of the government was his 'business', and he was never a reserved person, everything but. They say that the secret of success is the secret, but T. has never followed this motto. He couldn't keep the joy of having set up this

relationship to himself, and there was now a path to speak with him. Obviously to have a connection with Berlusconi. (*Corriere della Sera*, June 24, 2009)

Intermediaries expecting to "stay in business" for a sufficient amount of time in any case have stronger incentives to build a reputation of "integrity" and reliability in business, even—and especially—when their activities are illegal. Therefore, some official certification of the quality of their services is more precious: "The fact that intermediaries are prominent in the marketplace and themselves have a reputation to maintain gives them an incentive to carry out this certification honestly" (McMillan and Woodruff 2000: 2428).

Information

Information is useful or crucial to establish contacts and relationships with counterparts, who it is convenient to know as much as possible about—bad habits, qualities, powers, weaknesses, virtues—in order to weigh up the possibilities, value, and tenor of future requests. A good middleman knows how to sniff out more prestigious news, news that is more reserved and also compromising and useful for blackmailing. Francesco Pazienza (1999: 350), when contacting a former collaborator of an investment bank, was aware of that:

> he bore a grudge, he wanted to take revenge on the bank which had shown him the door, and he was a potential and marvellous source of private information, if he had been approached by the right people and had been adequately compensated for his collaboration work.

With a selective use of information, the middleman can therefore resolve one of his most pressing problems, convincing potential clients to trust him. The repertoire of behavior deliberately used for this purpose is surprisingly widespread, given that it is based on some understanding of the reasons that influence the decisions of interlocutors, whether of an instinctive nature—a positive first impression and self-confidence—or rational, as in the case of the reputational capital built up over time, or through a show of professional skills and abilities. This is what happened to one middleman, nicknamed the "great trafficker" by his interlocutor, who nevertheless gained credit by showing himself to be a "very competent person from a technical point of view, he knew clients and competitors in the sector" (TRMBL: 11).

A middleman who confirms access to confidential news, shows confidence with even the most complicated decision-making processes, or flaunts important contacts becomes almost automatically worthy of credit in the eyes of his clients. One middleman, meeting an entrepreneur interested in a tender, "proves a profound expert in all aspects of the tender, even showing him the specification and naming the other firms interested in the tender bid." In another exhibition, "a list of jobs which could interest him [...], The document of question was even more up-to-date than that of the councillor himself" (QGT: 377, 381). Another mediator X, when approaching the entrepreneur Y,

> informed him beforehand of the bid, considered important because every lot foresaw a sum of around 5 million lira for 3 years, and the bid conditions to be followed [...] . With the call for tender published, Y confirmed the quality of the 'introductions' boasted by X at the office of the public body, since his information proved precise [...] . X only made allusions, never specific names; nevertheless, Y was convinced not to brag about, which he could have done on a thousand other occasions [...] and which he had never done. (TRMBL: 5–6)

Similarly, in Senegal the role of middlemen—low-level politicians, businessmen, commission agents—in public procurement is crucial, especially when a bribe is required:

> One can dress it in all possible and imaginable kinds of ways, but it's always the guy who'll say 'good morning' to the minister who will be at the cocktail; in short the guy who knows his way in and out. [...] [He] will always need junior officers to supply a small piece of information, to know where such and such a file can be found, to follow it and so on. And if this person is pleasant and allows me to have access to information regularly and normally, I will call upon him regularly. (Cit. in Blundo 2006: 241)

Dynamics and Mechanisms in Illegal Intermediation

We have concentrated until now on the resources, skills, and mechanisms useful in carrying out illegal intermediary activities. In this section, we examine instead the mechanisms that generate and reproduce this "capital" of information, contacts, reputation, and trust, developing the above analysis into a dynamic perspective. Indeed, it is clear that decisions aimed at acquiring the trust of others and concluding relationships or handling information useful to conclude deals can intertwine, generating "virtuous" circles—from the middleman's point of view—that increase reputation and capabilities for accessing and influencing decision-making processes over time. Figure 7.1 provides a schematic description.

First of all, a bond exists between the extent of the middleman's connection network, conveniently produced and transformed into social capital, the signals made toward possible purchasers of his services, and the interest of the latter in establishing business relationships with him. If these are concluded, the trust that arises thereof favors new relationships, allows new useful information to be gathered in that context, and enhances the assets of social relationships that can be used to table new deals: "I've been in this sector for many years and I have a lot of connections, so I had the potential to corrupt people to get tenders myself," claims one middleman who paid bribes in exchange for information necessary to win a tender called by EniPower (R, November 8, 2004). Thus a lawyer-middleman, in an intercepted conversation, guarantees the manager of a company interested in a

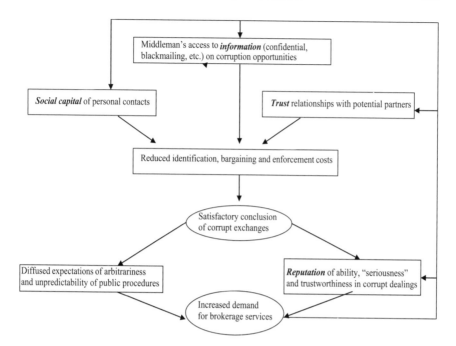

Fig. 7.1   The process of the reproduction of resources in corruption brokerage activities.

tender for the construction of 25 new prisons a wide array of services, made even more attractive by the fact that the proponent is the lawyer of the then Ministry of Justice: "As far as our connections are concerned, we do our best for our clients, to put in touch, exploit [...] . We make a turnkey [...] an annual membership, which is always a substantial amount, but is all-inclusive of contracts, legal issues and advice." As for the money, continues the mediator, "we deserve it in terms of professionalism, but also in terms in connections, which cannot be denied. But this is neither an offence nor a crime. The fact is that by being lawyers of three ministers of the Republic, etcetera" (*L'Espresso*, November 22, 2005: 70).

As for relations, they provide a mine of information that opens up new opportunities to a skilled middleman—such as the one speaking—in terms of attracting the attention of other interlocutors and earning their trust:

> It's precisely thanks to the confidence of so many people that I managed to build a web of connections. I said to one person what another told me, I always knew everything about everyone and in order to gain the trust of people I was interested in I even ended up inventing news. But I did it all very cautiously, calculating the right moment and the right news: a corruptor who talks too much has a very short career ahead of him. (*L'Espresso*, November 18, 1984: 42)

By establishing relationships with communication professionals, such as journalists, middlemen have access to valuable sources of information and contacts (Pazienza 1999: 157). In some cases, journalism even becomes a trampoline for an autonomous career in intermediation. This is the case for a journalist who was one of the mediators in paying bribes on behalf of one entrepreneur: "At that time I worked for ANSA [national agency for press information] which is a terminal for a thousand news stories; X was extremely interested in knowing the news before others" (TMLB: 3).

The meeting between two middlemen, both "professionals" in handling information and contacts, became an opportunity to check the quality of their respective stocks of social "capital." Thus, one of these individuals remembers meeting another, who magnifies his own relations and is subjected to cautious examination by the other, and finally has to admit that

> the splutterings, not requests, affirmations over important relations which he claimed to cultivate were not boasting but reality: from the Great Mason and politician [...] up to the Christian Democrat MP, today head of the Forza Italia group. (Pazienza 1999: 252)

The strategies of middlemen who deliberately try to widen their market are, under certain conditions, supported by factors that both stimulate a spontaneous demand for their services and improve their quality. The more widespread the spectrum of social relations of the middleman and the greater the ease with which he establishes new ones, the more probable it is that the agreements propitiated will be concluded. From this follows a positive effect on his reputation, which increases the desirability of his services. Thus, when one entrepreneur asks for access to public tenders, his political interlocutor refers him to mediator X, who "was a well-qualified person. In short, I knew that X had good relations with the directors of that structure [...] . It's therefore clear that the intervention of X could help him to obtain the tender [which invariably occurred]" (TMISL, April 16, 1993: 4).

A vicious circle also ties together the *qualitative* dimensions of social links, that is to say the strength of the bonds of trust the middleman creates with his clients, and the chances to increase their range of activities. When information circulates over the ability, trustworthiness, and expertise of the middleman, interlocutors are encouraged to turn to him and have greater incentives to respect the commitments undertaken. In this way, one entrepreneur justifies his requests to a middleman: "I know that he's a person who is well introduced into political surroundings and it's possible that I've asked him, sometimes, to provide me with information or introduce me into certain environments" (VPI, March 3, 1987).

The successful conclusion of corrupt exchanges, in turn, positively affects the middleman's reputation and the capital of trust with which he is introduced to interlocutors. This dynamic is summed up in the words of one Sicilian entrepreneur who is involved via a middleman in a problematic collusive agreement: "Who has trust gives trust as well [...] that's how it is, isn't it?" (TPSC: 154). A reputation for "honesty," effectiveness, confidentiality, and unscrupulousness then becomes an excellent business card for intercepting the demand for intermediation services, and at the same time makes them more valid and inclusive.[8] According to one mediator (Zampini 1993: 113),

> The giving and receiving of favours and the coherence with the first commitment will allow your relationship to develop in the future [...] . Being coherent means resting on rational foundations and this emits trust and security. Never think, not even for fun, about manipulating others, its eventual unmasking will lead to the loss of the relationship.

In one way, this *good relationship* means the middleman avoids tiresome deals and extensive checks on good conduct in individual exchanges, and in another creates favorable expectations about the success of the transaction. After one mediator earned the complete trust of the top manager of Eni (Italian Oil Company), the autonomy with which he handled contacts with corruptible politicians became almost total:

> In short, he was the trustee which is why he went over the operations of the entrepreneurial group in respect to the party system. He enjoyed wide discretion and there was no check over the quantity of money he effectively managed to claw back from the outside jobs which the group's company managed to obtain. (TMISL, March 13, 1993: 4)

What matters for middlemen is above all the possibility of being an object of trust again in the future, on behalf of current clients or other individuals whom news of their deeds might reach. Naturally, middlemen are "rationally" better off being reliable (a) the more their relations with their clients are continuous and repeated,[9] and (b) the more information on their past actions circulates and is passed on to those they depend on for future deals.

An often desirable personal quality for a mediator in the corruption market, given the nature of their business, is confidentiality. A similar reputation is fed intentionally by the directly interested party by assuring clients of their discretion, but is also formed thanks to their previous behavior, which certifies their propensity for reserve and privacy for aspiring clients. This is how one mediator, in conversation with an entrepreneur, on the one hand declines a proposal to corrupt a Supreme Court judge despite having done so in the past, and on the other extols his virtues of privacy:

---

[8]   Given that our analysis is concentrated on illegal mediation, a certain degree of unscrupulousness of mediators can be taken as given, even if—assuming that some deals are "dirtier" than others—a certain amount of competition can also occur in this field between mediators who are willing to do just about anything to attract interested clients.

[9]   As observed in the Indian case, in the presence of middlemen, corrupt transactions "are more likely to be regular; the donor's office boy, say, becomes an expert at bribing the postman to censure prompt mail delivery; he thus develops knowledge and access along with his dirty hands" (Oldenburg 1987: 428).

my practices or those of my friends, I've helped some of them. At the Supreme Court there are a series of proposers: there are honest *relatori* [members of the panel of appeal court judges who set out the facts of the case] and dishonest ones [...] . I'm willing to help everyone eat, but I don't want to try it out in a scientific environment, because helping everyone eat means that afterwards you engage in the problem of blackmail [...] . But have you heard me, since you've known me have you ever heard me speak without thinking? No, never! Don't worry, I'm somebody to trust on delicate matters, they never hear me speak. If somebody on the planet says I've spoken with you or about our matters, you have to ask yourself if there's something wrong with them. I was born not to speak. I haven't opened my mouth since I was a child, otherwise I'd be dead. (*Corriere della Sera*, February 9, 1998: 2)

When the combination of these factors, added to pessimistic outlooks on public sector decision-making processes, multiplies the demand for a mediator of corrupt exchanges, they increase their bargaining power and persuasive capacities. Both the collection of information and the network of trusting relationships at their disposal expand and the positive effect on their reputation occurs in parallel to their ability to provide better quality services. Ostentatious contacts approached by middlemen within centers of public sector power spread the idea that corruption is a workable strategy and profitable thanks to them.

A Typology of Middlemen in Corrupt Exchanges

In the corruption market, middlemen put a reserve of trust, contacts, and other specialist knowledge at the disposal of interested parties. Thereby, they reduce the counterparts' identification costs, provide information on possible deals and enforcement, and make possible agreements and exchanges that would not otherwise have occurred. Different types of middlemen establish themselves, depending on the overall size and kind of "openness" of their relationship network, on whether they specialize in awarding trusting relations with public service actors, private sector subjects, or both indifferently (see Table 7.1). When his contacts with one side of the corrupt transaction are frequent and close-knit, with strong and exhibited trust relationships with a few (or only one) public or private agents, the middleman may use these assets as a signal of his capacity to open a covert "channel of communication" with potentially interested counterparts. Moreover, when corrupt exchange opportunities are not sporadic and involve the same subject(s) with significant political and economic resources, there is a common interest—for both the middleman and his more stable clients— in the *internalization* of his brokerage services. The middleman then resembles the informal employee or consultant of the private entrepreneur, or the "right-hand" man of party and bureaucratic bosses. In what follows, we look at different types of middlemen and the specific resources they invest in the governance of corruption.

Table 7.1   Types of middlemen

		Contacts with private agents	
		Few	*Many*
Contacts with public agents	*Few*	Occasional broker	Public body/party-broker; "right-hand" man
	Many	Broker consultant/ employee	*Enabler*/broker-enforcer

Occasional Middlemen

In some cases the middleman incidentally finds himself embodying the role of the "right man at the right time." When an opportunity to carry out an agreement between a briber and a public sector agent (or a small number of agents) occurs and an individual has the right connections in both directions, the latter can carry out the function of a channel of communication and exchange. Even if this is an isolated event, in unrepeatable borderline cases, the central position of the *occasional middleman* turns him into a desirable "man of trust" for both parties (Figure 7.2).

In this case—following the "individual corruption" model (cfr. Chapter 2)—the economic sum at stake is usually high, at least enough to counterbalance the high "fixed cost" (the identification of a reliable partner, the risk for one's reputation, the moral cost, etc.) of an occasional involvement in illegal trafficking. Even when not specialized in these affairs, the middleman very often reinvests in the management of the corrupt exchange connection networks deriving from other professional relationships, developed in their role of lawyer, accountant, estate agent, or even family contact. This was the case of the presumed involvement of the Philippine's "First Gentleman" in the scandal surrounding the US$329 million National Broadband Network (NBN) deal with China's ZTE Corp., a project to electronically wire the country's bureaucracy. According to a losing bidder in the project, the "First Gentlemen" urged him to "back off" from the project during a meeting at a golf course, and quoting another businessman he claimed that he was set to receive a $70 million "commission" from the project: the project was overpriced by at least $130 million to allow for the kickback, including the "First Gentlemen's" alleged $70 million cut (*Asia Times*, September 5, 2009). In South Korea, too, "tales of presidential corruption, or corruption committed by president's wives or older brothers or sons or daughters or in-laws" are commonplace. Several relatives of a former president, for instance, may have acted as professional brokers to allow corrupters to influence decision-making processes:

> X is a shoe manufacturer who allegedly passed a bribe through the President's wife, Y, as a time-honored entree for influence in high places. The figure everyone talks about has been US$6 million, but now prosecutors are claiming more money found its way into the hands of President's son and daughter. The President's brother, meanwhile, has already been indicted for allegedly taking

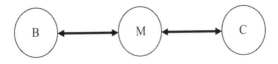

B = briber
M = middleman
C = corrupt agent
x $\longrightarrow$ y = strong trust relationship (x trusts strongly y)

Fig. 7.2   Occasional broker in individual corruption.

bribes to win an appointment for one of shoemaker X's friends as chief tax official. (*Asia Times*, May 14, 2009)

The occasional nature of the mediation service, or rather the low frequency with which it is carried out, does not mean it is less significant.[10] On the contrary, the middleman and his clients often take the opportunity to conclude occasional but highly profitable deals. The case of Duchess Sarah Ferguson shows the importance of family links for successful brokerage. While introducing a fake businessman to her former-husband—asserting that "We're the happiest divorced couple in the world"—she signals the range and profitability of contacts she can channel access to. But she needs money in exchange for her brokerage services to reach such a high-level, aristocratic target. This is the transcript of a tapped conversation, as reported in the media:

FERGIE: Next! On to the next thing, £500,000, when you can, to me . . . open doors.

REPORTER: It would be Prince Andrew?

FERGIE: Yeah.

REPORTER: Is that a deal?

FERGIE: Yeah.

REPORTER: But I've got to give you $40,000.

---

[10]   The importance of the transaction is not only measurable in monetary terms. For example, take the case of one lawyer who acted as an occasional mediator in passing on a bribe of 25 million lire (negotiated after an initial request for 50) to the president of the Molinette hospital, in exchange for the placement of one of his clients on the kidney transplant waiting list (R-Turin, January 9, 2002).

FERGIE: Yeah.

REPORTER: Which I've got now as a deposit. Which is in my safe. But how am I going to give it to you? I haven't got a bag.

FERGIE: Yeah OK but then if you want to go and do a big deal with Andrew, then that's the big one.

REPORTER: I do. Of course. OK, no, of course. So you need 500,000 in pounds.

FERGIE: But that's in wire transfer. [...]

REPORTER: If you give me the bank account details I'll arrange that, no problem at all.

FERGIE: Then that, is then like, then you open up all the channels whatever you need, whatever you want, and then that's what and then you meet Andrew and that's fine. And that's, that's when you really open up whatever you want. And as Andrew said, 'Listen, if he's (our reporter) going to be kind enough to want to play, then Andrew will play.'

REPORTER: Let's play!

FERGIE: And he (Andrew) says, 'Let's play, we'll play' as long as it's nothing to do with him [. . .] . But you will be his friend. I will listen to the friendship talk between you two. And then I do it.

REPORTER: OK.

FERGIE: You two talk.

REPORTER: Right.

FERGIE: I listen.

REPORTER: OK.

FERGIE: Then I activate . . . he meets the most amazing people. And he just throws them my way.

(*News of the World*, May 23, 2010)

This model of mediation is frequent, for example, in corruption for tenders of substantial value that will not however be repeated, or for corruption in legal procedures, when bribes are used to buy the decisions of magistrates. As an example of corruption in government contracts, take the sale of French submarines to Pakistan: according to some witnesses a businessman was the middleman in the corruption scheme—receiving commissions worth 4 percent of the 5.4-billion-franc (€830-million) contract that finally led, as a result of a quarrel over missing final payments, to the bomb attack in Karachi that killed 11 French naval engineers in 2002 (see Chapter 1) (*Dawn.com; AFP*, May 5, 2010).

An Austrian count and former confidential agent of the defense giant BAE Systems also allegedly reinvested his capital of relationships—in particular his familiarity with a former Austrian government minister and a leading figure in the center-right OVP Party, and the enduring contacts with his former employee—into a small set of very profitable corrupt relationships. He is accused of having operated as a broker in the payments of bribes between 2002 and 2008 to agents and officials in Austria, the Czech Republic, and Hungary "as inducements to secure, or as rewards for having secured, contracts from those governments for the supply of [...] Saab/Gripen fighter jets by BAE Systems" (*The Independent*, January 30, 2010; *The Guardian*, January 29, 2010). Closer to a model of "individual corruption," costly military allocations of contracts are sporadic and very lucrative junctures, involving relatively few potential corruptors and corrupted agents. Conditions in this context are favorable to corruption—secrecy, qualitative differences among offers, restricted competition, high and uncontested prices—especially when specialized middlemen ensure that "things run smoothly."

An instance of corruption in a legal procedure is the Jakarta trial on graft allegations that involved a middleman who had offered a bribe to officials of the Corruption Eradication Commission (KPK) to secure the release of the brother of an entrepreneur. According to the middleman, he simply passed the entrepreneur's bribe—US$561,000—to another middleman, without knowing its final destination (*Jakarta Post*, July 10, 2010). Some uncertainty about the bribe's destiny seems to have worried the entrepreneur also, who, according to a witness, sometime later tried to get introduced to one of the officials. He "said he wanted to check whether KPK officials had received the money he had sent" (*Jakarta Post*, July 21, 2010).

In what was called "the greatest case of corruption in Italy and maybe even the world" (TMBMP: 254) by one of its protagonists, lawyer and middleman Cesare Previti, a bribe of 67 billion lire was paid to three lawyer-middlemen and then handed over to a magistrate in exchange for a sentence recognizing a huge public sector rebate of 1,000 billion lire, 678 billion after tax (the bribes amounted to 10 percent) in favor of the heirs of a chemicals manufacturer. Middlemen in the affair acted in common agreement, with strong interest connections uniting them:

> The three always appear together on the scene of the court case, when they appear before the inheritors to demand the credit; when they accept payment for the outcome of the lawsuit without batting an eyelid and without guarantees (it could hardly be any different); when they are in touch with them and the judges; when they finally receive the illegal compensation in their Swiss bank accounts. (TMBMP: 344)

The three lawyer-middlemen boasted close friendship ties that extended to their families, who also invested in the professional sphere, as well as consolidated friends in the judiciary (TMBMP: 335).

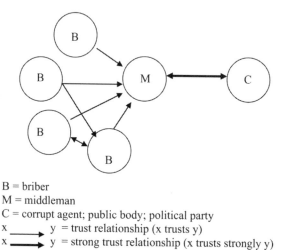

B = briber
M = middleman
C = corrupt agent; public body; political party
x ———→ y = trust relationship (x trusts y)
x ———→ y = strong trust relationship (x trusts strongly y)

Fig. 7.3   Political party or public body's middleman.

Public Body and Political Party Middlemen

A different type of middleman cultivates relationships with a restricted number of public sector or political agents with whom he has created close and trusting ties by offering them his services in the shape of a large number of possible private sector clients. This is the case, for example, with middlemen who become privileged referents of corruptible functionaries in a particular public sector structure. By becoming a sort of monopolist gatekeeper in the bribee's relationships—or those of a small group of bribees—with the outside, the *public body middleman* takes care of keeping external communication channels open and organizing and recording the trafficking of bribes: "Insider middlemen in the recipient's office clearly have the advantage of complete access and knowledge. The donor's problem lies in identifying who, precisely, will take the bribe. If he expects to have to pay off the same department regularly, he can move slowly and delicately to discover the venal officer he needs. Once a regular channel is established, the use of middlemen minimizes costs and risks" (Oldenburg 1987: 529). As shown in Figure 7.3, there is a double asymmetry here. The middleman has a strong trust linkage with one side of the transaction—the corrupt agent—while at the other end of the market many bribers may have an interest in "getting in touch"—a transaction that requires a certain threshold of trust—with the broker in order to get access to his services, which involves opening his channels of communication and exchange with the corrupt agent.

According to judges, a corruption scheme

> was based in the Kazakh president and oil minister demanding that international oil companies pay fees to a middleman. This arrangement, the indictment alleges, helped the middleman to skim money from the deals and send some US$78 million in gifts and kickbacks to the Kazakh president and others through dozens of overseas bank accounts in Switzerland, Liechtenstein and in the British Virgin Islands. One 'gift' was matching 'his and hers' snowmobiles for the president and his wife. (TI-2009: 55)

In some cases middlemen are former public body employees who have maintained good relationships with their old colleagues and use them as trust connectors to introduce their clients to corrupt exchanges. This has been observed in large-scale international business transactions, in which "the bribe-taker may trust the intermediary because he or she is a former colleague" (Bray 2005: 118). In another case of corruption in Italy, the middleman was a former Enel (Italian electricity company) director who, after retirement, became a specialized "consultant" in managing contacts between managers from his former company and businesses interested in tenders (R, November 8, 2004). An analogous role may also be played by individuals who still work in the company, who supplement their salary or improve their career perspectives through mediation. According to its former president, the head of the Technical Office at the Molinette hospital in Turin "acted as a middleman, introduced me to entrepreneurs, every so often an envelope arrived on their behalf' (R-Turin, December 21, 2001).

Every public administration in which practices of some value are dealt with becomes a hunting ground for this kind of middleman. To give some examples, in Italy similar figures appear in the exchange between three officials in the Milan army recruiting office and the parents of boys who want to avoid military service (R-Milan, December 15, 2000), between foreign workers in need of false work-history documents and three employees of the Inspectorate for work (R-Milan, November 17, 2001), between some entrepreneurs seeking to cover up irregularities and inspectors of the provincial labor directorship (R-Florence, June 28, 2001), between lorry drivers who wish to falsify or speed up audits and license processes (R-Rome, July 5, 2002), between council employees of funeral services and entrepreneurs in the sector who are interested in getting information about the deceased before their competitors (R-Milan, September 9, 2004), and between university professors and students who pay to pass their exams (R-Rome, August 4, 2004).

These processes might be institutionalized, to a smaller or larger degree. In Russia "informal bureaucratic mediation is currently going through a process of institutionalization, which means that it has become a generally accepted, autonomous, and profitable activity in the business sphere," as exemplified by the case reported by the director of a construction firm:

Ok, as for the custom ... they [the customs brokers] solve the problems in another way. They do not have ... how would you say ... these direct relationships like 'bribe-decisions'. Everything is rather covert there, and, they have, say, parallel custom structures that guide all the operations with your cargo and solve the problems with customs officials. (Olimpieva 2006: 7)

Socialist Georgia offered a peculiar case of "organized intermediation" in bribery. When officers in charge of monitoring the accounting affairs of government-owned businesses—the *kantora*—visited a town, they audited different stores over two to three weeks:

> The entire process was corrupt, and nobody had interest in devoting too much time to haggling about what would be the right and fair bribe rate for each individual store. Such haggling could compromise the discretion of the entire process. The *kantora* officials, therefore, did not negotiate individual store bribe rates. Instead, the management of the stores that were raided/visited, would quickly meet, collect a large sum of money [...] and a designated person— typically someone who personally knew one of the *kantora* officials—would take the money to the official at the hotel as a 'gift and token from the local business community.' (Levy 2007: 434)

In Brazil middlemen specialized in specific public procedures are called *despachantes*, that is, "fixers" specialized in obtaining driving licenses or sorting out visa problems: "*Despanchantes* know the bureaucratic ropes, and can work their way round difficulties. It is generally understood that they may make payments to ensure that their clients' papers move swiftly from desk to desk, but the amounts paid are low [...] . The role of *despanchantes* is socially recognized in Brazil: many operate from offices where their profession is openly proclaimed by their name-plates" (Bray 2005: 116). Similarly, in Benin,

> nearly every customs officer has at least one *klébé* working for him. *Klébés*, or 'banknote rippers' in the swindlers' jargon of southern Benin, help customs officers 'control fraud'—and take a 10 per cent commission on seizures as they do so. [...] The *klébés* function as middlemen, acting as screens between the givers and takers of bribes, who do not want to be identified. [...] Their expertise is knowing the topography of corruption and the short cuts that only the bribe or secret fee can reveal. (TI-2003: 221)

In Indonesia so-called *markuses* work in the shadow of police stations, courts, and attorney generals' offices:

> they are middlemen who can persuade corrupt police officials, prosecutors, and judges to drop a case against a client for the right amount of money [...] . In dealing with the police, the *markuses*—who are typically relatives of police officials, lawyers, journalists or everyone with contacts in law enforcement agencies—bribe police officials on behalf of a client in trouble with the law [...] . Each stage—the police, the attorney general's office, the courts—has

its *markuses*. But there are *markuses* that are so dominant, they can arrange everything in one package. (*New York Times*, December 19, 2009)

When the permanent referent of the mediator is a political actor, we enter into a category that includes both *secretary–bag carriers* and *party middlemen*. In the first case, the middleman works in symbiosis with a politician, in whose name and on whose behalf he deals with dirty deals, in corruption and other underground contexts. For instance, in an informal speech with a newly reappointed manager, a former governor of Illinois replied to his thanks "that XXX should only talk with 'Tony' or [Kelly] about the Planning Board, 'but you stick with us and you will do very well for yourself'" (U.S. District Court 2008: 19).

In the case of the private secretary to former parliamentary minister Gianni De Michelis, the status of bag carrier is perhaps an understatement, given that according to one manager, "He is a sort of prosthetic aid of De Michelis, if you can't get an agreement with him, there's nothing you can do" (cit. in Gomez and Travaglio 2006: 619).

By establishing a lasting and organic relationship with a political party, the middleman can present the employment of the powers exercised by directors in different decision-making fields to the advantage of private individuals as a bargaining chip. A Malaysian broker was chosen by an Australian firm precisely because of his political connections to corrupt high-ranking officials: "The middleman was engaged by the RBA firms due to his claimed high-level connections in the country's ruling UMNO political party. He has also been a broker for a Pakistani government weapons-making factory" (*Sydney Morning Herald*, July 22, 2010).

Depending on the range of deals negotiated, middlemen might obtain an investiture directly from the higher echelons of the party. For example, in relation to a difficult agreement between three public service insurance companies resolved with the payment of a bribe, arise the figures of two middlemen commissioned by the administrative secretaries of the Christian Democrats and the Italian Socialist Party as representatives of their parties' interests in the insurance sector; the middlemen deposited a sum in compensation for the mediation (TMENI: 25).

For middlemen, flaunted contiguity with leading politicians has remained a precious resource in recent years. A former Italian member of parliament describes his relationship with a middleman responsible for depositing illegal funds with public administrators by an entrepreneur in this way: "I've known [...] X for a while, having introduced himself as centre-right, a dynamic entrepreneur, very close to my party's positions [...] . X is a very expansive person and it was he who interweaved a more regular relationship, calling me often" (cit. in Gomez and Travaglio 2006: 73).

The roles, activities, and fortunes of party-brokers as gatekeepers for corrupt dealings follow the fate of the party organizations that they are connected to. If—as in the Italian case—traditional parties enter a crisis, these middlemen's functions and responsibilities also tend to decline or to assume more complex features.

In "light" parties, however, the lack of internal controls may lead to an overlap between organizational roles and brokerage activities. A fusion between party roles (national coordinator of the Popolo della Libertà Party), private activities (as president of a bank), and brokerage functions, is exemplified by the case of a leader of Forza Italia. According to the transcript of a telephone conversation, the intertwining of these roles, which allowed him to reinvest resources in other contexts of activity—political influence, the power to allocate public as well as private funding, information, contacts—derived from his changing roles as politician, bank executive, and middleman and increased his influence in other spheres of activity. Particularly important as a networking asset was his political role, as he explained to judges, "In the period we were talking about I was Forza Italia's only coordinator, now I'm one of the People of Freedom Party's three coordinators [...] . I'm at the party headquarters from morning until night and so, despite being in this triumvirate, I'm actually always there. And so everyone calls me, everyone looks for me" (*Corriere della Sera*, March 6, 2010).

Middlemen-Consultants or Employees

The mirror image of the middleman–bag carrier is the figure of the *middleman-consultant* or *employee*, who looks after one or a few private sector individuals' relationships with all the public sector agents identified as possible recipients of bribes. In the Telecom abusive telephone interceptions scandal, for example, a female mediator used by her business to manage external relations described her role as follows: "My job could be described as a cobbler who attaches herself to the different parties I manage to bring together in a friendly and proper climate"; according to magistrates, payment for her services also helped create a black-market fund to be employed for corruption purposes (R, September 25, 2006). As Figure 7.4 shows, the consultant or employee middleman represents a sort of gatekeeper that allows private clients—with whom he is connected through a very strong trust relationship, and in some case also by a formal contract that subordinates him within a hierarchical structure—to enter into corrupt deals with a wider number of unspecified and changeable public agents.

"Kickback brokers" are often observed in transnational corruption, when companies starting to operate in an unknown environment are typically approached by an individual or entity who offers to be their "local representative," with knowledge and networks, and also to assist them in illegal deals (Ware and Noone 2005: 34). In one of the hundreds of cases of enforcement of the U.S. Foreign Corrupt Practices Act, for instance:

> From August 1994 until June 2004, Kellogg Brown and Root LLC and its partners in the joint venture authorized, promised, and paid bribes to Nigerian government officials, including officials in the executive branch, employees of the government-owned Nigerian National Petroleum Corporation, and employees of government-controlled Nigeria LNG Limited, to win and retain

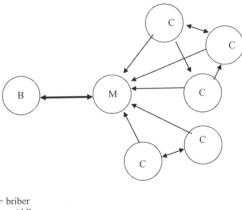

B = briber
M = middleman
C = corrupt agent
x ——————▶ y = trust relationship (x trusts y)
x ══════▶ y = strong trust relationship (x trusts y)

Fig. 7.4   Consultant or employee middleman.

the EPC contracts to build the Bonny Island Project. To conceal the bribes, the joint venture entered into sham consulting or services agreements with intermediaries. The joint venture hired one consultant to pay bribes to high-level Nigerian government officials. That consultant received over $130 million for use in bribing the officials. Another consultant, hired to bribe lower level Nigerian officials, received over $50 million to use for that purpose. (Shearman and Sterling 2009: 17)

An Australian reserve bank currency firm had, according to a federal police witness, hired middlemen to create contacts useful to win contracts for the supply of polymer banknotes to foreign Asian governments bribing their central bank governors. A middleman told the witness in 2007 that the "governor would be very happy if the commission [payment] was increased." One of the most senior managers told him to arrange an Asian prostitute for a visiting deputy governor of a foreign central bank:

> Next time that this official was in town, [I was told] that I was to procure him a bodyguard, and with raised eyebrows and a wink ... a particular type of bodyguard being an Asian woman. He was suggesting I might like to procure a prostitute for one of the central bank officials on his visit to Melbourne.

In a 2008 diary entry, the witness recorded that a consultant employed in Asia told him that to win contracts, the firm needed to hire someone to bribe officials or "to pass white envelopes for you." In another diary excerpt an employee is recorded as telling him the RBA firm paid very high commissions to middlemen to secure a contract in Nigeria because so many people were "feeding off it": "A range of senior government ministry officials and central bank officials would've been getting a slice of that 20, 25 per cent commission," the witness said (*The Age*, May 24, 2010). A middleman operating in Malaysia has admitted his role as a link between the firm and "at least one person closely connected to a senior Malaysian government official" who received kickbacks from the commissions of about $4 million that the middlemen received from the Australian firm (*Sidney Morning Herald*, July 22, 2010).

Another broker carried out the function of an "institutional" trustee of ENI—informally and underground—in international contacts and the payment of bribes to parties in government, acting as a "clearing house" for debts cropping up in different areas. The confirmation in office of the ENI's higher echelons, and therefore the persistence of trusting ties with this group, depended on this flow of bribes:

> In practice, he directly took on the burden of depositing money to the parties so that, in so doing, the governing political party system would not change the directors of ENI or companies in that group. In fact, he found the possibility of carrying out the role of middleman just because it was the structure of directors of ENI or other controlled companies who gave him it, though these responsibilities were in trust and informally attributed. It therefore occurred that he could also pay funds to parties out of his own pocket because he had direct interests in his director friends remaining in their key positions in the ENI group companies. (TMISL, March 13, 1993: 4–5)

Brokers who paid bribes to ensure their clients won contracts in the North Sea oil industry were in some cases "agents" of the corrupting company: "the advantage of an agent compared to an independent information broker is that he is more likely to be trustworthy in the sense that he will normally only represent you and may not at the same time represent your competitors as well. [...] In addition to transferring the contact between the briber and the bribee, the agent may also arrange the payment, and assist in the money laundering" (Andvig 1995: 308).

In the borderline case where the middleman is continuously compensated for lending his services to a private sector organization—usually a company—he is in fact "internalized" within it as an employee (whether recognized formally as such or in a de facto sense).

> Instead of employing costly and potentially unreliable intermediaries firms may opt for producing intermediation services themselves. They vertically integrate their foreign sales units, writing long-term employment contracts with those who submit bids for local contracts and concessions. [...] They aim at inducing a high degree of loyalty and dependence of their representatives, reducing the risk of whistleblowing or even extortion. (Lambsdorff 2011)

Scientific informers who, on behalf of their respective pharmaceutical companies, paid doctors a small bribe—up to 2,500 lire for each prescription—

for each pharmaceutical product requested by patients also fall into this category (R-Florence, July 1, 2000). A similar mechanism was applied on an even greater scale by a pharmaceutical company, with bribes of 5 to 50 million lire for medical consultants—"if I corrupt him I'll hit the jackpot," commented one informer—that involved over 2,900 doctors all over Italy (see Chapter 2). In an internal memo, the technique for approaching the recipients of bribes, the doctors, is explained to representatives: "with the money we have to give to doctors we are close with, we should adopt uncompromising language" (R, February 13, 2003).

The "Enablers"

By limiting their range of activities to just a few actors—in the public or private sector—with whom they establish close trusting bonds, or high "density" social capital, middlemen can attenuate some of the risk factors connected with their illegal activities. Each illegal middleman must in fact look for a point of equilibrium in the uncertain balance between *profit-making opportunities* and *dangers* (of being denounced or cheated) deriving from the expansion of their own contact network, and between the *quantity* of relationships to draw from to propitiate agreements and the *quality* of those trusting connections that are their internal glue.

The greater the frequency of opportunities to enter into deals, and the higher the number of interlocutors and the value at stake, the more the middleman will become interested in extending his own circle of stable clients. He thus becomes increasingly autonomous as a *professional mediator* who, without exclusive bonds to politicians, political parties, companies, or public bodies, provides his services to just about anybody enters "the right circles" and formulates demands, willing to extend his greedy dealings whenever and wherever the opportunity presents itself, or actively creating opportunities by himself.

The "enabler" assumes a pivotal brokerage role in a wider network of corrupt exchanges, as the target of trust relationships for a large number of both potential bribers and corrupt agents. It is essential for him that autonomous trust does not develop among bribers and corrupt agents (even if it is possible, as shown in Figure 7.5, that contacts with a trust content bind together some agents on both sides of the corruption market), who could otherwise bypass him, carrying out their transactions without recourse to his costly services. As clearly stated by a high-level bureaucrat, who describes the practices and habits of the well-known "enabler" B., "Take into consideration that B. is a 'triangulator'; about the matter, B. hardly says anything concerning himself to anyone else; he doesn't let the others communicate with each other" (CD-2: 254). The "enabler" will accordingly manage contacts and channels of communication and exchange in order to maximize his positional rent within the web of corruption that he actively contributed to build and expand.

In North Sea industry, for instance, *information brokers* played a fundamental role in the management of bribe payments to corrupt employees of firms allocating

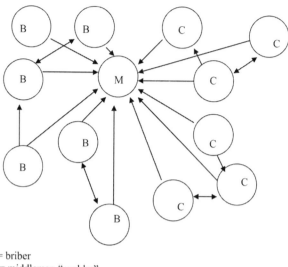

B = briber
M = middleman-"enabler"
C = corrupt agent
x ———→ y = trust relationship (x trusts y)

Fig. 7.5   A network of corruption mediated by an "enabler."

contracts, and in gathering and selling useful information to the highest bidder, thereby reducing research costs at both ends of the illegal market:

> The information brokers are independent agents who do not have any long term commitment to any particular supplier. They normally start collecting as much information about the development of any given field as possible, legal and illegal, and may sell it to any interested supplier, their sellers or agents. [...] With a broker, the employee of the oil company need not undertake the costly and risky process of reaching the relevant employee of the relevant supplier himself. Seen from the point of view of a supplier, the advantage with an information broker is that he usually has established a network of contacts in different oil companies and in different parts of the same company. [...] It is clearly advantageous for a firm to relate to an information broker with a large network, since it may then relate to a single broker for many different assignments. (Andvig 1995: 309)

The Italian figure of the *faccendiere* provides a good representation of the role of the "entrepreneur in illegal intermediation" that some individuals occupy in the corruption market. Pazienza (1999: 210), for example, proudly asserts his own independence, refusing to be tied down exclusively to any single purchaser of his services: "I had never been anybody's employee and so I would have operated on the basis of a 'commission' calculated for each operation I managed to conclude."

As an example of the density of the networks built by the *faccendieri*, we may take the list of how Sergio Cusani's role has been defined by various witnesses and accused parties during the court case surrounding bribes paid for ENI contracts:

> Cagliari's trustee, Cagliari's consultant, Ligresti's trustee, connecting official between Cagliari and Craxi, Ligresti's consultant, Ligresti's trustee, Craxi's trustee, Grotti's trustee, sixth Committee member, Craxi's family friend, derailleur or obstructor of decision-making processes, mediator in political mix-ups, area boss, has power of controlling and disabling, [...] shadow consultant. (TMENI: 209)

By combining resources and professional abilities, from a lack of scruples to a defiance of danger, the "enabler" becomes a kind of "clearing house" between the interests of many subjects who enter into deals through them. As a *generator of social credit*, in some cases the "enabler" weaves a network of obligations of various natures (economic or noneconomic), which could be linked non-contextually (with deferred payments), or indirectly: if Z has a debt with X and X has a (more or less) equivalent debt with Y, the "enabler" makes sure that Z pays Y and that everyone is satisfied. The trust that they inject into the corruption system works as a kind of currency, facilitating exchanges even when reciprocal obligations are not easily definable or quantifiable.

The variety of resources employed affects the ways in which middlemen accommodate different parties' interests. According to Coleman (1990: 180–85), the simplest and most widespread intermediation model is that of the *advisor*, who merely provides information that the parties consider reliable and through which trust is earned. His commercial capital is resolved in the credibility of the advice and information that he provides to clients, inducing them to overcome reciprocal mistrust. If reassurances over the information prove misguided and the deal does not go through, the middleman's reputation is negatively affected; on the other hand, the success of the exchange increases his credibility in future transactions.[11]

The middleman can decide to employ resources that he will risk losing in the case of failure, for example, by advancing the bribe from his own pocket, toward the success of the transaction. In this way, any betrayal of trust carries a cost for the middleman; this does not, however, affect his trustworthiness in the eyes of those who judge his actions. He thereby cushions the mishap caused by real and proper rip-offs dealt—to him and the counterpart—by the less "correct" client, which would otherwise risk putting a spoke in the wheels of his business. This is the role played by one accountant, a middleman in the payment of a bribe to Guardia di finanza officials on the occasion of a tax audit of a company:

> Since the company did not have funds in the black, I had seen to advancing, by withdrawing from my personal finances, 150 million in cash, which I saw to

---

[11]   See also Dixit (2004) on the function of middlemen who record information on previous defections, as an instrument of *governance* in economic relations.

depositing directly in the account under the name of the Friends' Association of Medjugorje. Subsequently, when I paid the remaining 100 million, I withdrew it directly from this account and X reimbursed me afterwards. (TMIMB: 16)

Another Italian "enabler" put a similar system of deferred clearing in place by counting on his financial means tied to his banking activities:

> Moreover, I must tell you that with X's insertion into these kinds of financial relations with ENI the question of funding the Socialist party also increased because, with X being in banking, he often advanced amounts which the party political system needed and then evened it out over the funds which the ENI-controlled companies allowed him to obtain. X could do this because it was guaranteed by a trusting personal relationship with the ENI group's management in that he was a close friend with some ENI company administrators who guaranteed him the return of however much he shelled out. (TMISL, March 27, 1993: 6)

A model of brokerage "from many to many" clients may appear economically profitable—in terms of the amount of rents allocated—to sustain an "official" and visible, even if camouflaged, entrepreneurial activity. This seems to be the case of a consultancy firm, which operated as a mediator between more than 100 German senior academics—significantly, not those holding long-term appointments—at a dozen top universities, and hundreds of mediocre or unqualified Phd candidates. Students allegedly paid bribes of €4,000 up to €20,000 after being told by the consultancy firm that the money would go a "long way" to ensuring that their doctorates "were in the bag." The importance of reputational assets is confirmed by the duration of the business: the company at the center of the investigation had been operating for 20 years, formally offering to help students obtain Phds and to *get them in touch* with suitable senior lecturers or professors (*The Independent*, August 26, 2009).

By operating on a large scale and exclusively in markets and social contexts in which counterparts have a significant economic value, in some cases "enablers" assume the function of the real and proper *regulation* of corrupt markets. This is not limited to propitiating the safe conclusion of deals, but includes safeguarding the participants in corruption, who are induced to respect "contractual terms" to avoid punishment, usually consisting in their removal from the relationship network controlled by the "enablers." An *enforcement intermediary* accompanies his clients to the trade and finds out whether they have been cheated. He "does not merely keep a record of cheating; he inflicts immediate punishment on the trader who cheated his customer. [...] If the punishment is drastic enough, and Enfo's [the enforcement intermediary] threat of inflicting it credible, then it deters cheating [...] . But credibility has to be based on acquired reputation, which requires a substantial up-front investment" (Dixit 2004: 107).

Middlemen therefore use their capital of information and social contacts as resources to inflict costs on those who defect from corruption pacts, excluding them from long-term profitable relationships. Dealing with several "customers," intermediaries have an effect similar to that of an information repository, publicizing the cheating, generating punishment, "certificating" partners' capabilities, and "honesty" (McMillan and Woodruff 2000: 2428). Being able to dissuade those who do not intend to respect the commitments assumed in corrupt exchanges transforms the mediator into a *guarantor*, who ensures the fulfillment of obligations by handing out sanctions, particularly exclusion from further deals, accompanied by spreading information on perpetrators' incorrectness.[12] For example, one middleman, among the various functions carried out in terms of trafficking bribes for ENI tenders, "has the task of avoiding black-market deals from causing troubles and quarrels" (TMENI: 209).

The effectiveness of the enforcement middleman's dissuasive strategy thus depends on the expected repetition of exchanges. It is completely unproductive in the case of occasional middlemen, while for middlemen-consultants or party political middlemen it can only work with reference to their most stable referents, with whom their ties have already matured, making the risk of defection small in any case. Otherwise, the punishment for nonfulfillment requires the collaboration of the centers of power whom their fortunes depend on. For example, in the case of opposing entrepreneurs who interrupted the flow of bribes addressed to some directors of the Public Agency for Labour Insurance—using the arrests of functionaries that had occurred at one of the body's other locations as an excuse—a middleman and one of the recipients of the bribes agreed on revenge. The director urged the middleman, "you can already spend the guarantees today [...] What I'm telling you is : put the people who are being idiots in line [...] tell them clearly [...] I'm going to start a war with them. Meanwhile I'll give them real shocks [...] I mean letters will go out, letters, don't worry." The middleman comments, "They have to feel like they've been buggered [...] they'll realise I was right" (TRMBL: 41).[13] It is, above all, the professional mediators and "enablers" who occasionally assume these kinds of enforcement functions.

---

[12]   A "contractual intermediary" applies external enforcement: in fact, he "records information about the agents' past productive actions; in particular, the intermediary can verify the occurrence of deviations from the cooperative outcome. Further, when such a deviation occurs, the agents may call in the intermediary to engage in the costly process that culminate in official certification that the dispute has been resolved. [...] The intermediary can also enforce contracted transfers between the agents" (Ramey and Watson 2002: 363).

[13]   The mediator does not hand out sanctions to entrepreneurs who have stopped paying bribes, but stops at giving them warnings and threats agreed on with the functionary. In other words, he is also an intermediary in relation to exchange *protection*, in fact self-assured by the very same bribed administrators. The cartel coordinators examined in Chapter 6 also carry out a similar function, using their intimidation potential derived from their contacts with Mafia organizations to ensure that collusive agreements stick.

Concluding Remarks

Public and private sector agents interested in striking corrupt deals do not always translate their intentions into practice. Discouraging them, as well as possible moral scruples, are the costs—heightened by the illegality of the relationships—of the activities they must undertake: identifying a willing counterpart, informing themselves over their trustworthiness, negotiating an agreement, and guaranteeing that the pacts will be respected.[14] As has been shown in this chapter, middlemen in corruption professionally assume a part of these costs, contributing to the success of otherwise fragile exchanges.

The instrumental employment of information and its circulation allows middlemen to produce *trust* and *contacts* that link bribers and bribees through them by transforming the trust and contacts into a fruitful social capital of "good deals" for all the individuals involved. Once it is ascertained that the intermediary can be trusted and that he is not just a big talker, a time waster, or a rip-off merchant and has not been boasting about nonexistent friendships, he keeps what the news of the good quality of his services promises and feeds demand for his services, widening his trust base and relationship network. With his reputation won, he encourages other individuals with similar positions and interests to turn to him.

Furthermore, the more middlemen exercise their professional activities with continuity, the more they are sensitive to their reputation and careful not to tarnish their intangible assets. Intermediates and "enablers" therefore contribute to make participants' conduct in corrupt exchanges more safe and predictable, since *(a)* they make advantageous agreements for "well-intentioned" individuals, *(b)* they create disincentives for the betrayal of agreements among those with bad intentions, and *(c)* they limit the damage caused by eventual defections (to their reputation and the *organized* workings of the corruption market) by assuming costs and inflicting punishment on those responsible.

Two consequences follow from this: "honest" (in corruption) subjects' voluntary participation in the exchange network is encouraged by increasing the internal cohesion within corrupt circles, and the risk of controversies deriving from uncompensated rip-offs coming to the attention of watchdogs is reduced by increasing protection against the outside.

Finally, the prominence assumed by mediators in some contexts of political-administrative activities can be ascribed to some features of the decision-making process. The hypertrophy and complexity of public sector regulation, for example, promotes widespread distrust toward the effectiveness of the procedures. As expressed by the director of a Russian construction firm, "In such a situation,

---

[14]   The risk of being involved in legal investigations, as well as being an independent variable, which increases the cost of illegal relationships, also affects other dimensions: if there is a misunderstanding or a quarrel caused by a rip-off, or if the negotiations go on longer than planned, the danger of attracting the attention of the judiciary and incurring related sanctions increases.

with the real state of things, constantly, whatever you do, you always violate the law. And you always feel yourself a criminal and, in fact, you are forced to make payoffs" (cit. in Olimpieva 2006: 3). Corruption was indeed one of the workable paths to bypass these obstacles (Vannucci and Cubeddu 2006). The perception of invisible "entry barriers" in relationships with the state encourages recourse to the services of individuals who, through their connections and technical skills, promise to professionally dissolve these sources of uncertainty. This appears to be a generalized problem:

> Bureaucratic rules, permits, licenses, etc., in many countries lead to the occurrence of intermediary sectors. These sectors are usually established around the bureaucratic services involving heavy red tape. Formally, they are established to earn clients' valuable time, to follow up the bureaucratic procedures, fill in forms, give required documents. However, behind the scenes, these sectors may be a way of serving corrupt transactions. The sector may decrease the risks involved in the corrupt transaction by separating the briber and the bribee, playing a mediator role. (Bayar 2005: 295–6)

As well as impeding the formation of or unhinging eventual autonomous trusting ties, mediators in illegal exchanges must also avert the possibility that aspiring bribers trust institutionally foreseen procedures for getting in contact with public agents, instead of demanding their services. As Kahanna and Johnston (2007: 156, 163) note,

> The middleman himself [...] is, therefore, not just a conduit for exchanges; rather, he shapes citizens' and officials' expectations in important ways. He has a stake in maintaining an image of officialdom as remote and impossible to manage without his help, in persuading the official that he will deliver clients and maximize income reliability, and in assuring *both* sides that he can be trusted to deliver on his commitments and to reduce costs. Clearly, such perceptions and reputational capital take *time* to become credible. [...] The middleman has an interest in maintaining the perception that officials are arbitrary, unpredictable, unapproachable, and that little can be done without his help. This perception also helps maintain his credibility, for a time, should he fail to produce results.

For mediators, it is therefore convenient to perpetuate the belief that corruption is omnipresent, since this multiplies the demands for their services. For this purpose, they tend to intentionally project to members of the public and entrepreneurs an image of public sector decision-making processes as a kingdom of corruption, arbitrary and unpredictable: the middleman

> has the clearest interest in maximizing the belief that corruption is pervasive. [...] The *dalal* [middleman in Indian land consolidation process] preys on ignorance. He has a clear interest in keeping the process of land consolidation as mysterious as possible. [...]. He also claims to have special access: only *he* can reach the official: after all, they have indicated to *him* that money is to be paid. The *dalal* has the time to spend on seeing the transaction through, and he lets it

be known that he is willing to dirty his hands; not only is he experienced (knows the subtle hints, knows the techniques of passing money), but making use of him also allows the briber to distance himself from the transaction. (Oldenburg 1987: 526–7)[15]

Whatever their aims and intentions, the simple active presence of mediators implicitly confirms the most pessimistic expectations of those who turn to them—their clients—and those who do not purchase their services but observe their fortunes. Once they are up and running as an informal channel for accessing benefits and public resources, both the delusions of those excluded and the successes of the privileged feed distrust toward impartiality in decision-making processes and the expectation of being able to bypass this through other means, both factors that increase demand for intermediation services.

Paradoxically, the success of actions to tackle corruption can increase demand for illegal intermediation services. When, in a context of systemic corruption, perceptions of the risks of corruption increase (as is the case during particularly incisive legal investigations; for example, Clean Hands in Italy in the mid-1990s), these new beliefs do not necessarily lead to a significant reduction of the phenomenon. If occasions remain enticing (and moral barriers weak) a growth in the prices paid to public agents—the bribe—can occur to compensate for the perception of danger, accompanied by more frequent recourse to intermediaries, who professionally take responsibility for cushioning these risks. Moreover, changes in the political class—at both regional and national level—caused by scandals rips the tissue of trusting relationships uniting political actors and economic subjects in corruption. In this "vacuum," mediators can become central figures, precisely by virtue of their capacity to cushion the uncertainties associated with the illegal nature of the exchanges.

---

[15] See also Kahanna and Johnston (2007: 163).

Chapter 8
Organized Crime and Corruption: Mafias as Enforcers in the Market for Corrupt Exchange

On a *pizzino*—a slip of paper passed between Mafiosi to communicate with each other, minimizing the risk of the message being intercepted—from Sicilian godfather Bernardo Provenzano, the Mafia's ambivalent attitude toward politicians emerges clearly:

> Now you're telling me that you have a high-level Political contact, which would allow us to run many large jobs, and you want to know what I think before going ahead with it: But not knowing him, I don't know what I can tell you. We'd need to know their names and what their arrangement is. Because the way things are just now you can't trust anyone. They could be fraudsters, they could be cops, they could be infiltrators, and they could be novices and they could be very calculating, but if somebody doesn't know which path to take he can't walk, so I can't tell you anything. (TPMA) [1]

The allure of the "many large jobs" to be obtained thanks to contacts with politicians is counterbalanced by the lack of confidence in their trustworthiness because of their *professional* persuasion in responding to multiple interests, and spending their words freely. This caution also lies at the root of the difficulties experienced by politicians seeking to enter Mafia organizations. "It's difficult," comments the Mafia informant Antonino Calderone, "for a politician to become a 'man of honor'. Cosa Nostra is very cautious towards them because they're disloyal and don't keep their promises, always trying to be 'wise guys'. They're people who break their words and have no principles" (Arlacchi 1992: 208–9). Another informant, Tommaso Buscetta, confirms: "I've never been attracted by politics and I've never liked politicians: due to their opportunism, their inability to keep their word and their flippancy in the principles they claim to stick to. To a 'made man' such as myself [...] they seemed untrustworthy and third-rate"

---

[1]   This is a "plain" translation of the godfather's very colorful and dialectal lexicon, with many grammatical mistakes and slang terms. Those familiar with the Italian language will appreciate the original: "Ora tu mi informi che hai un contatto Politico di buon livello, che permetterebbe di gestire molti e grandi lavori, e prima di continuare tu volessi sapere cosa ne penso io: Ma non conoscento non posso dirti niente, ci vorrebbe conoscere i nomi? E sapere come sono loro combinati? Perché oggi come oggi non c'è da fidarsi di nessuno, possono essere Truffardini? possono essere sbirri? possono essere infiltrati? e possono essere sprovveduti? e possono essere dei grandi calcolatori, mà se uno non sa la via che deve fare, non può camminare, come io non posso dirti niente."

(Arlacchi 1994: 101). Besides, it is clear that the qualities required for the role of arbitrator in private controversies, a blend of authoritativeness in mediation and willingness to resort to bullying and violence that characterizes successful Mafiosi, differ from those important in facilitating the career of a politician, who works in the public eye and is obliged to compromise, make pretences, and walk the political tightrope. Politicians' lack of reliability and trustworthiness in fulfilling promises made in the electoral market and their unscrupulous behavior in generating (and sometimes manipulating) the trust of the electorate and political partners only serves to feed the contempt of Mafiosi. For Mafiosi, getting involved with politicians without the assurance of a preliminary meeting or information encouraging the formation of a faithful bond seems a gamble. As Woody Allen has joked: "Politicians have their own ethics. All of them. And it's a notch below that of a sex maniac"; and also below that of Mafiosi, we could add.

Despite similar (and presumably reciprocal) diffidence, exchanges between political actors—at the individual, faction, and party levels—and criminal organizations are a natural consequence of the former's control of valuable exchange resources. The cooperative interactions between politicians and Mafiosi have, however, often been crucial to mutual success in the spheres of political and criminal activity. As judge Giovanni Falcone observed,

> The Mafia does not willingly commit to political activity. It isn't particularly interested in political problems unless it feels that its power or sources of income are being directly threatened. It is content enough with getting 'friendly' councillors and politicians elected, and sometimes even members of the organisation. This is done both to steer public spending and so that laws primed to favour its income opportunities are passed and others primed to put ominous repercussions on its business activities in place are rejected. (Falcone 1991:165)

The crossover domain between political and criminal actors' activities is a subterranean market where the major resources at stake are public decisions, ranging from single administrative acts to general laws and regulations, favorable sentences and judicial acts, the omission of inspections, information, and political protection on the one side, and private protection, violence and intimidation, electoral support and votes, bribes and financial contributions on the other. As we show in this chapter, the problem of confidence and the mechanisms that, in its absence, allow relationships of political exchange and corruption to be nurtured, help us to understand the nature and specific qualities of Mafia-fostered "regulation" in the political market, in corruption and collusive agreements.

Organized Crime and the Political System: A Typology

Mafia-like organizations carry out countless kinds of criminal activities, but the *qualifying* component that characterizes them is the employment of a series of resources—violence and intimidation, reputation, information, relationship and acquaintance networks—to provide services guaranteeing property rights where the protection of those rights is fragile and uncertain (Gambetta 1993). The demand for *protection* is in some cases vigorously promoted by the Mafia itself and in others actively formulated by "clients," particularly when self-protection or protection provided by "third parties"—such as the state—is not available, or proves more expensive or ineffective. In India, for instance, the general public's distrust in due process fueled by long delays in the judicial process has created a market for private protection and illegal methods to solve disputes: "people hire thugs and criminals to bully and threaten their opponents, thereby forcing a settlement" (*UPI*, May 26, 2009). To give another example, similar conditions were observed in the transition toward a market economy in post-Soviet Russia, where the demand for protection in legal and illegal activities was only partly— and ineffectively—met by state authorities, and a supply of people trained in the use of violence and weapons became available (Varese 2001).

Illegal markets represent one of many fields where the *genuine* demand for protection services is more intense, given the unavailability of "public" services to resolve disputes and enforce contested property rights. The uniqueness of Mafia groups, as compared to other criminal organizations, lies precisely in their ability to stimulate and satisfy a demand for protection in contexts of unstable property rights, uncertain expectations over the outcome of agreements and fragile or nonexistent trust. When state enforcement, social norms of reciprocity, or confidence networks are weak or absent, the existence of a "market" for private protection can be the necessary condition for the emergence of new domains of exchange. Mafia groups enter these contexts as providers of private protection services and controversy settlement by employing specific trademarks, including Cosa Nostra, 'Ndrangheta, Camorra, Yakuza, Triads, and so on. Moreover, the internal cohesion and solidarity within Mafia-like groups is strengthened by the use of ceremonies of initiation and affiliation rituals and by the extensive application of different rules of interaction: "Through the rite of institution, the new affiliate is called on to become a 'man of honor', and to behave as such in both his private and public life" (Paoli 2003: 73). Nevertheless, unlike the liberal-democratic state, the Mafia does not recognize general criteria and impartial procedures in exercising its activities of controversy resolution, which are enforced following the personal authority of leading bosses and may thus prove arbitrary and unpredictable in the applying of sanctions.[2]

---

[2]   The Mafia's supply of private protection does not exclude, as in the case of other "social dilemmas," socially disastrous outcomes as a result of interaction between Mafia organizations—demolishers of both confidence in the state and trust as a "public good"— and the institutional structure of the societies in which they operate. The Mafia private protection *industry* suffocates possibilities for economic development and worsens social living conditions. The presence of private protection companies induces a "vicious cycle" in the development of institutional constraints, as a consequence of both deliberate decisions (the Mafia "rationally" injects doses of distrust into the social and economic system to increase demand for its own services) and unintentional effects (impersonal distrust and distrust toward the state, once they have passed a critical threshold, breed by themselves) (Gambetta 1993; Vannucci 2001).

The demand for Mafia protection is not limited to illegal markets such as those associated with the formation of cartels and corruption. For the regulation of public contracting procedures to be effective, it is necessary for one of the key actors in the system—the political administrator—to be sheltered from the uncertainty that makes his role unstable and thereby risks undermining the stability of the collusive agreement. Budget allocations, decisions regarding works to be carried out, the formation of decision-making committees, the identity of decision-makers and the availability of information on proceedings actually depend on the exercise of public power placed in the hands of actors who cannot be completely trusted. Politicians exercise "rights of control" over the public authority, used as bargaining chips in the corruption market, which in democratic systems are by definition provisional—"fixed term"—and uncertain, since they respond to the mechanisms of electoral representation and the dynamics of the political market. When a *demand* for the protection of rights of control over resources at stake in political and electoral exchanges emerges, Mafia organizations might have both an interest in and the resources to satisfy it. They thus contribute by mobilizing consensus and manipulating the vote market for the election—or reelection—of "reliable" candidates, thus strengthening the political counterparts with whom they expect to manage business in the market for corruption.

In some contexts, then, where equivalent services are not universally offered, the Mafia ultimately holds a kind of monopoly over protection services, exercising a crucial function in settling disputes in illegal exchanges in particular: "It is not clear if a monopoly will emerge in this case. [...] But the incentives for monopoly appear to be strong. Monopoly in the market for dispute settlement service would seem to offer a particularly efficient means for taxing other illegal enterprises" (Reuter 1983: 155). As Gambetta (1993: 155) states, "we can define the mafia as that set of firms which (1) are active in the protection industry under a common trademark with recognizable features; (2) acknowledge one another as the legitimate suppliers of authentic Mafioso protection; and (3) succeed in preventing the unauthorized use of their trademark by pirate firms."

Mafia groups are capable of enforcing their use of a specific apparatus of symbols and brands, protecting them from appropriation by competing criminal groups, and at the same time defending their evocative power with the use of violence and the reputation to be able to use it. Trademarks are in fact crucial, since their use signifies and represents control over an ambiguous commodity like protection, with its elusive and potentially ominous qualities.[3] The collaborator Antonino Calderone describes this role clearly: "Our reputation as Mafiosi was of being above parties,

---

[3]   The boundary between protection and extortion, between voluntary exchange and imposition induced by a threat from a Mafioso, often proves uncertain or unpredictable (Tilly 1985: 170–71; Pizzorno 1987: 197). If we consider the employment of violence for the aim of extortion as a key, if not exclusive, determiner of the demand for protection, the latter does not exist independently from the offer, which thus assumes an entirely predatory and parasitic character (Catanzaro 1991).

above all of these underworld groups on the periphery who trusted us and accepted our intervention in their controversies" (in Arlacchi 1992: 153).

A direct link between *violence* and protection certainly exists. Guarantors of property rights must create expectations and, if necessary, demonstrate their abilities in terms of getting people to respect their decisions in the disputes proposed to them. Protection requires that enforcers be capable of discouraging agents from defection or of sanctioning them: "The essence of enforcement power is in the enforcer's ability to punish (i.e., to impose costs). These costs can be imposed both by the use of violence of by other means. [...] Different third parties impose costs by different means" (Barzel 2002: 38–9). Threatening behavior or the use force is the most effective instrument in assigning contested property rights to one of the litigating parties. The informant Calderone highlights this point:

> At the end of the day, any Mafioso knows perfectly well where his power comes from. People are scared of being physically thumped, and nobody wants to even vaguely risk being killed, whereas a Mafioso has no fear and takes risks. (Arlacchi 1992: 200)

For Mafiosi, the need to resort to violence is inversely proportional to the availability of another resource, that is the *reputation* of having the skills and resources to carry out enforcement activities. Some credible evidence of their ability to enforce their decisions must sustain arbitrators' activities, in order to create the expectation that they will carry out enforcement in cases of noncompliance: "The critical factor that accounts for the Mafia's apparent monopoly as settler of disputes in illegal markets may be the Mafia's reputation, itself a function of the durability and stability of the group. The reputation is a matter of no controversy" (Reuter 1983: 158). This reputation is indeed the result of a credible demonstration of their capacity to employ violence in arbitrations over disputed property rights: "This is why the *reputation* for being capable of violence is important. It allows you to obtain what you want—or, generally, to exercise influence—by economising on violence. Domineering or aggressive behaviour shows the capacity for violence and therefore increases prestige" (Pizzorno 1987: 198).

When a criminal organization such as the Mafia delineates and guarantees rights, it becomes less risky to exchange "commodities" in corresponding markets—the market for narcotics, for corrupt exchange or collusive agreements in public procurement, or the market for votes, and so on—since it enforces the buyer's agreement to pay as well as the seller's promise to deliver, and adjudicates eventual disputes:

> This enhancement of economic rights over banned commodities is of exactly the same nature as the enhancement of economic rights over legal commodities brought about by the legitimate protector's enforcement. Though these organizations are illegal, they rely heavily on their brand name, especially on 'honor'. Like the legitimate state, they can gain by adjudicating disputes impartially. The more that people believe that the enforcers adjudicate disputes impartially, the higher the demand for their services. (Barzel 2002: 231–2)

This is also why the asset of *protection* is from some angles impalpable. When protection provided by the Mafia is considered credible and effective, individuals spontaneously adapt to the rules of conduct that define fragile and potentially contestable rights. All the Mafioso does is to collect the proceeds obtained by "taxing" the exchange of these resources, the effective availability of which would otherwise be obstructed by mutual distrust.

In this manner, the offer of protection results in the *prevention* and *composition* of conflicts and controversies, as well as the eventual sanctioning of breaches of confidence, whether they relate to specific agreements or the observance of the rules of conduct that define property rights in general. Let us take, as an example, the role of the boss in Lercara Friddi's Mafia family. In the words of his son, "It would often happen that people implicated in a controversy would turn to my late father as arbitrator. In these cases, he always made every effort to get them to reach an agreement, never failing to put in a good word" (TPAZ: 588). This is a rather delicate activity of "clarification," which requires authority, credibility, the capability to enforce one's word, as well as a certain degree of social legitimacy.

There are circumstances in which Mafiosi, like other criminals, find it convenient to resort to corruption in order to consolidate their monopolistic position in an illegal market, thereby obtaining higher profits, as well as other specific benefits from public agents—information on investigations, operations, criminal competitors—or to increase their chances of impunity (CSD 2011: 15). Buying protection from the state may in fact become a necessary condition for the growth of criminal organizations.[4] By paying politicians, functionaries, magistrates, or police officers bribes to overlook their hidden trade, they aim to reduce the risks of being discovered and to squeeze competition. For this reason "corruption has a centrality in illegal markets that it does not have for legal markets generally" (Reuter 1983: 123).

Law enforcement officials are in fact the main targets of bribes paid by organized crime (Abadinsky 1990: 401). For instance, "a rising number of U.S. border enforcement officers are being arrested on corruption charges as Mexican drug cartels look to bribes as a way to get around tougher enforcement" (*USA Today*, April 24, 2009). The bribing of customs officials is a common feature of transborder organized crime networks involved in the smuggling of drugs, arms, or human beings: Mozambique, for instance, "has become an international transit-point for narcotics through widespread collusion between criminal groups and state officials" (Transparency International 2008a: 3). Similarly, in southeastern Europe, "The elites in the Yugoslav republics were actively involved in the development and organization of smuggling channels, and they protected and

---

4   Buscaglia and van Dijk (2005: 10) confirm the strong correlation between organized crime and public sector corruption with a quantitative analysis based on a large sample of countries: for instance, lower levels of effectiveness in customs systems and higher levels of political interference in the appointment, dismissal, and promotion of civil servants are positively associated with the stronger development of organized crime activity.

assisted those who were directly involved in their exploitation. This prosperous 'business' was controlled in close collaboration between politicians, their security forces lobbies and organized crime structures" (CSD 2003: 9), In similar cases, criminals or Mafiosi act as common corruptors. Their partners, however, have good reason to abide by the deal, since they know they run the risk of violent retaliation.

Yet the "regulatory" activities of the Mafia also allow them to reduce other costs that would otherwise present obstacles to the positive conclusion of deals. When the market for corrupt exchanges enlarges, problems in obtaining reliable information tend to increase, as do the risks involved in making contact with unknown counterparts of dubious trustworthiness, and the difficulties in punishing eventual swindlers. In exchange for a "price of protection," the Mafia adopts the role of guarantor of the mutual respect of rules and "contractual clauses," sanctioning the boundary between acceptable conduct and unacceptable breaches of faith by corrupt and corrupting individuals. If the workings of the market seem *orderly*, then expectations of the common observance of the "obligations" taken on by participants in corruption are reinforced. In other words, in some areas the Mafia performs the role of a "third party," controlling the activities of various individuals who share promises, signals, information, bribes, and other resources.

In Table 8.1 we propose a very general (and simplified) framework for the analysis of four ideal-typical modes of interaction between criminal and political organizations, stressing their relation with prevalent practices of irregular political financing.[5] Key variables are the characteristics of organized crime (distinguishing a relatively centralized, hierarchical, and monopolistic structure versus a more dispersed and competitive criminal network)[6] and those of the political actors (a party—or a faction—rooted in the territory with its locally prominent and influential candidates versus weaker and de-structured political subjects).

For different reasons, both Mafiosi—in a broader sense—and political actors are subject to severe uncertainty concerning their ability to *remain in business*. Political uncertainty is a logical consequence of competitive democratic politics, in which the right to occupy certain elected public roles is by its very nature precarious and derives from the variable outcomes of electoral and political processes (Moe 1990: 227). The "life-expectation" of criminals—as well as of the organizational structures within which they operate—is even more insecure and unpredictable due to the illegal and often violent nature of their interactions. The "Mafiosi time horizon is in turn influenced by the struggle against the State

---

[5]   See Morlino (1991) for a typology concerning the relationship between interest groups and political parties, partly adapted in modeling the exchange of political actors and organized crime. An analogous model is presented in della Porta and Vannucci (2012).

[6]   This is obviously a radical simplification: structural features of organized crime could be better analyzed as a continuous variable ranging from a more hierarchical to a polycentric network (Williams 2001).

and by the competition among Mafiosi: both factors, when they become more intense, provoke the disappearance of protectors, generating instability, as we know" (Gambetta 1992: 267–8). A demand for *protection* clearly emerges in this context, especially where there is a broader-spectrum "contract" available to actors, guaranteeing the favorable solution of disputes in which their uncertain expectations and "rights"—matured in the political as well as the criminal arena—are challenged, contested, or quarreled.

We suggest the degree of institutionalization and organizational strength—as expressed in elementary form by the variables in Table 8.1—is associated with the time horizons of political and criminal actors leading or operating within them, and the influence of "shades of the future"—the discount rate they apply to future payoffs—over their actions and prospects, which, in turn, affects their bargaining power, and the nature and content of the resulting relationships. As their time horizon extends, their credibility as guarantors increases, and they become more trustworthy as potential providers of reliable protection. On the contrary, "if the future looks uncertain, protectors will maximize present over future income. They will be more likely either to sell bogus protection or to charge extortionate prices, or both. [...] . Finally, if customers know that the mafioso's 'life expectancy' is short, they will be more reluctant to buy protection" (Gambetta 1993: 33). The same holds true for customers—criminals, for instance—seeking political protection, but discouraged by the perception that their would-be political guarantors do not appear destined for a long and brilliant career.

Generally speaking, criminal organizations' influence over political decision-making may be obtained by political actors using several means: (a) political resources, that is, organizing votes and consent, or regulating the market for votes, (b) economic resources, that is, providing money and financial support to political actors, or simply bribing them, and (c) violent resources, that is, intimidation or the elimination of political rivals.[7] Here, we concentrate mainly on (a) and (b), when such influence does not imply any direct application of coercive means.[8] If organizational features, reputation, and the historical legacies of collective actors create expectations of profitable long-term relationships, then predatory strategies—that is, choices maximizing short-term profits—as well as defection are discouraged, monitoring and enforcing costs are lowered, and trustworthiness assets come into play. This facilitates the evaluation of the qualitative attributes of those intangible resources at stake in the exchange that are otherwise difficult to assess: political authority, which can be bought with financial support, or is used

---

[7]   Obviously violence and threats could also be used by Mafiosi to directly intimidate public decision-makers. In such cases, however, we enter the realm of extortion, which we do not take into consideration here, concentrating our analysis instead on *voluntary* exchanges between politicians and organized crime that influence the political process.

[8]   An analysis of the interaction between criminal organizations' violence and the electoral process in Southern Italy is developed in Sberna (2011).

to provide consent, pressure in electoral campaigns, policy making, and particular acts or omissions.

When long-lasting relationships are expected on both sides, political resources—which require time to be organized and mobilized—can be used more profitably in transactions between politicians and criminal organizations, substituting (or complementing) direct financial support. What emerges is a *symbiotic relationship of reciprocal protection* between political and criminal actors.[9] No exchange-commodity is specified in order to reciprocate the deal; instead, a wider and more durable protection contract is flexibly applied to unforeseeable circumstances to guarantee both sides' interests. Take, for instance, this statement by the Mafioso collaborator Tommaso Buscetta:

> Every family head in the Mafia selects a man whose characteristics already make him look approachable. Forget the idea that some pact is reached first. On the contrary, one goes to that candidate and says, *'Onorevole*, I can do this and that for you now, and we hope that when you are elected you will remember us.' That candidate wins and he has to pay something back. You tell him, 'we need this, will you do it or not?' The politician understands immediately and acts always. (R, November 18, 1992: 2)

The mobilization of political resources by criminal organizations requires a previous long-term criminal investment in the acquisition of social connections, information, intelligence, and territorial control. These resources are also necessary for criminal organizations if they are to operate convincingly as guarantors in the cumbersome market for votes, where those demanding ballots— that is, political actors—are confronted with issues of scale (to negotiate each vote individually would increase transaction costs enormously), trust (it is difficult to verify the fulfillment of the agreement), enforcement, and payment (Gambetta 1993: 184).

Moreover, the authority of a criminal organization over local votes for their affiliates, families, and supporters—which may in certain contexts represent a significant slice of the total electorate—is in itself a valuable resource that would otherwise be wasted. In a tapped conversation, a boss of a Calabrese 'Ndrangheta family explicitly expresses his intention to avoid this regrettable outcome in regional elections: as a consequence, a demand emerges for politicians willing to be the target of the electoral support gathered by local families ('Ndrine) in the same geographical areas (*"locali"*), naturally balanced by the expectation of "getting something in exchange" in the near future (TRCOS, I: 5).

We may expect that electoral support will, ceteris paribus, substitute financial support as a means of exchange, reflecting pragmatic considerations. Used

---

[9]   Symbiosis is the outcome of a *cooperative exchange relationship* between strong criminal and political actors, one we analyze here. Obviously, this is not the only possible ending to the story: open contrast and conflict is the opposite result, where interactions are punctuated by homicides and intimidation on one side, and strict regulation and prosecution on the other.

as a commodity in implicit or explicit contractual agreements with politicians, the mobilization of votes can have the same effect as a financial contribution for a criminal organization, but with lower economic costs: the circulation of information on the Mafiosi choice for an election may be enough.[10] Moreover, it guarantees a long-term influence over the political counterpart, as criminal groups have resources of intimidation at their disposal should they need to enforce the deal, thus minimizing risks of cheating.

Being a reliable partner in political exchanges or a guarantor in the market for votes requires resources that tend to be at the disposal only of socially rooted and long-established criminal organizations with a relatively centralized internal apparatus, and that have some "dominance" over territorial spheres of licit and illicit activities and act as agencies for the provision of private security in a manner akin to the *power syndicates* described by Block (1983). Moreover, the capability of criminal organizations to guarantee the functioning of some troublesome markets where politicians are involved—the market for votes, or corruption, and so on—may generate flows of money in unexpected directions. In the market for votes, for instance, Mafiosi usually collect the price for their guarantee of electors from politicians; in corruption, the rent derived from public contracts is shared in fixed quotas among several actors, while criminal actors regulate the whole business.

When symbiotic and cooperative relationships prevail, political and criminal actors operate as reciprocal protectors in their respective spheres of interest and activity. Therefore, they may strengthen each other in an "increasing-returns" process, reducing uncertainty in their future prospects in political and illegal markets. The resulting equilibrium may be quite robust, as the decades of fairly peaceful and mutually fruitful exchanges between Cosa Nostra and Christian Democratic factions and leaders in Italy seem to attest. Actors seem to be aware of this potential "virtuous circle" in their hidden interplay, as confirmed by a Camorra turncoat, the "white collar" consigliori of the Bidognetti clan, who describes the reasons underlying his campaign in support of a politician: "In a meeting with the candidate I reassured people that he would have compensated our support in the future, since '*if he will grow, we will grow too,*' for instance getting public contracts from other Municipalities" (TRNOC: 23, emphasis added).

The scenario changes when there is a higher level of uncertainty about the stability of political actors' authority over decision-making due to the scarce institutionalization of parties or the weakness of their candidates. The reason for

---

[10]   The rumor that a politician enjoys the protection of organized crime may in turn be enough in itself to guarantee a competitive advantage in electoral terms. As reported by the Parliamentary Anti-Mafia Committee: "Support from the Cosa Nostra can also involve supplying constant 'supervision' of the candidate, who, as he makes his rounds in his electoral constituency together with members of the [Mafia] family, is not only protected in terms of personal safety, but shows voters that he is backed by 'men who count'" (CPMF: 16).

this may be an "exogenous shock," such as the collapse of the party system in Italy following the Clean Hands inquiries into corruption in the 1990s. Different strategies are available for relatively strong and "stable" criminal actors lacking trustworthy political protectors. First, they may try to replace missing parties by promoting the founding of new political organizations, or to colonize destructured parties with members of the criminal organization. Second, they can continue to operate as guarantors in unsteady markets and exchanges where political actors are involved as purchasers of votes or providers of corrupt services, or seek some kind of external enforcement for their precarious political agreements. Finally, criminal actors can simply demand specific services when needed, bribing politicians or party administrators.

As we will see, the symbiotic and replacement/colonization models are consistent with the criminal traditions of two Italian criminal organizations, the Mafia and 'Ndrangheta, and in certain phases also with those of the Camorra and Sacra Corona Unita. Moreover, when criminal groups operate as protection agencies, they may also enforce exchanges in the market for votes: as a camorrista told judges, "I do not solicit politicians. They solicit me at election time. They need me, I don't need them" (APN: 8). The selling of votes to politicians, which is forbidden by Italian law, has assumed noteworthy proportions, particularly in southern regions of Italy, where they are regulated by criminal organizations.

When criminal structures are more unstable, competitive, and decentralized, Mafiosi are less credible in mobilizing electoral support, since this requires enduring commitments and roots in local society. Their political partners cannot fully rely on them as effective guarantors in the market for votes, since their more ephemeral existence fosters incentives for both cheating and predatory strategies, thereby nourishing instability. Moreover, they are less effective in safeguarding their partners against uncertainty in the electoral and political processes. Nevertheless, akin to enterprise syndicates, criminal organizations can reinvest some of their illicit profits in political financing and bribes in order to obtain specific privileges, administrative and legal acts, favors, and more general political protection against their "professional risks." How often, and with what results, critically depends on the characteristics of their political counterparts.

If their political counterparts are expected to be long-lasting and reliable partners, criminal actors have a stronger incentive to buy all-purpose and stable political protection from them, for instance, to reduce uncertainty about and the severity of legal enforcement, to lengthen the "life-expectations" of their criminal careers, to obtain competitive advantages against competitors, and to influence the allocation of benefits in public decision-making. Money flows here can be frequent and intense. Financing is not necessarily bound to a specific favor, as in corrupt deals, since it is reciprocated by political actors via a sort of "insurance" policy against potential troubles and inconveniences in their criminal activities. Political actors may contribute by helping them avoid or settle these. Politicians guarantee a kind of (cautious) gate keeping for criminal organizations as regards access to a wide-ranging set of political decisions, which is reciprocated mainly by economic resources, and occasionally also by other rewards.

Finally, when both political and criminal actors suffer a lack of solidity and organizational strength, they are unlikely to be in a position to supply each other with more durable safeguards against uncertainty. They may coexist with limited interaction; even so, they can still enter into occasional mutual advantageous exchanges. In this case, as time horizons shrink, transactions will likely involve more limited, contingent, and well-defined resources. Money will normally be preferred to the doubtful recruitment of voters in the political exchange, since reciprocation in such a case would require trust in the counterpart's lasting authority. This is the ideal setting for corrupt exchange. Bribes are more frequently at stake here, as a quid pro quo for precise political favors, but not as general financial support for unspecified future rewards. Actually, corruption is a sort of natural substratum in every arena where criminal and political actors interact. To pay politicians, officials, and magistrates, or to corrupt police agents so that they close their eyes to illegal trafficking, is often necessary for criminals to reduce the risks they run during those activities and to crush competition: "Organized crime almost always involves corruption" (Malts 1985: 24).[11] If bribery is observable in all four models presented in our typology in Figure 1, it is only in this context that it tends to become the prevailing, if not exclusive, mode of interaction.

Mafia protection, although sold selectively as a private asset, could assume the features of a "public good" that would make it, at least to a certain extent, appropriable even by free riders. If their conviction that everything will run smoothly is strengthened, corrupt and corrupting agents benefit from the shared observance of the rules controlling their conduct without paying any charges to the Mafia guarantors, who are the invisible authors of the successful conclusion of their affairs; hence, the Mafiosi's need from time to time to affirm their own "extracting" capacities, if necessary with intimidation and violence. Furthermore, corrupt and corrupting individuals must have some reassurances that the Mafia guarantor will not use his power to rob, instead of protect, their precarious "rights" over exchanged bribes. The protection market, in other words, also exposes its protagonists to the risks of friction and complications that may provoke a crisis, attract the attention of judiciary bodies, and thus disrupt the unstable balance of beliefs and expectations it is founded on. In the rest of this chapter these dynamics

---

[11]   Profits from illicit activities can be reinvested in corruption in order to exempt them from the application of the law or to acquire more rigorous enforcement against competitors (Benson 1988: 75). Corruption can then contribute to the creation of a "monopoly" in illegal markets. Efforts to regularly corrupt enforcement agents "can be undertaken only by a fairly large firm that has reason to expect that it can enjoy most of the market and get a satisfactory return on the investment" (Schelling 1967: 66). In fact, "this expectation of mutually profitable contracts between repetitive violators and enforcers [...] explains the development of organized crime: an organization is engaged more continually in violations than its individual members are, and can, therefore, make arrangements with judges or police that would not be feasible for these members" (Becker and Stigler 1974: 4).

Table 8.1 Four models of exchange interaction between political actors and organized crime

		Organized crime	
		Criminal protection firm (centralized monopolistic organizations)	*Gang/group operating in illegal markets (competitive criminal networks)*
Political actors	*Political guarantors (structured parties/strong candidates)*	**(I) Symbiosis** Criminal organization as stable, long-lasting consent organizer, support collector, guarantor in the market for votes; money-sharer in a wider bribe collection activity regulated by Mafiosi (public contracting procedures, public licensing), e.g., relationship between Cosa Nostra, Christian Democrats and some of its leading figures (Ciancimino, Lima, Gioia, Andreotti's faction) in Sicily from 1987 to 1992	**(III) Gatekeeping** Political parties/actors as gatekeepers for various criminal actors seeking immunity and protection; money, as well as other exchange resources, used in medium- and short-term relationships to influence political/administrative decision making, e.g., relationship between political leaders and criminal organizations during destabilizing conflicts in a fragmented and competitive criminal environment (as in Campania and Apulia in limited periods)
	Political actors not capable or willing to provide durable protection (de-structured parties/weak political candidates)	**(II) Replacement/Colonization** Criminal organization as founder-organizer of parties, Mafiosi entering political competition directly through their influence over selection of candidates, criminal organizations as guarantors in the market for votes or enforcers of political alliances, criminal colonization of local governments and party structures, e.g., project for autonomous parties after the World War II and after 1992 in Sicily, political career of Mafiosi, and the pervasive control of local administrations in Southern Italy by criminal organizations	**(IV) Neutrality/Occasional exchanges** Mafiosi as occasional partners in short-term corrupt exchanges of different resources (contingent protection, favors, etc.) with political actors, e.g., interactions with public administrators in northern and central Italy, generally mediated by accomplished entrepreneurs, following the expansion of organized crime's illegal activities and economic interests outside their areas of territorial control

are analyzed with particular reference to the evolution of the illegal regulatory system of exchange mechanisms between organized crime and political systems in public procurement and the market for votes.

The Symbiotic Nexus: Reciprocal Protection between Organized Crime and Political Actors

When both criminal and political actors' expectations converge toward stable, long-term contractual relationships of reciprocated protection, the symbiotic dimension prevails. Besides the direct support of criminal affiliates during elections, Mafiosi can guarantee the accomplishment of political agreements regarding the formation of public bodies, bargaining processes within otherwise unstable alliances, and the market for votes and corrupt deals. In short, their services serve to contain *uncertainties* that would otherwise worry unprotected political subjects.

A turning point in the relationship between the Mafia and politics in Sicily took place during the 1950s when the "rural Mafia" turned into the "urban Mafia" and a demand emerged for new exchange relationships with politicians. Particularly during the years of the so-called sack of Palermo (uncontrolled urban expansion), from 1958 to 1963, with Salvo Lima as mayor and Vito Ciancimino as assessor of public works, according to judges, "a pact was stipulated between the Mafia, the municipal administration, and construction companies that became a model for crime in many areas of the South" (APN: 15).[12] Ciancimino in particular, later mayor himself, "did not stop acting in a general way to promote the interests of private speculators, but in a more specific way was successful in favouring Mafia figures close to him" (TRP: 86).

Criminal influence over political participation is a relevant resource at stake in such exchanges. Criminal groups can organize votes and support for their affiliates, relatives, and friends. According to the Mafia turncoat Tommaso Buscetta, the terms of this political exchange are quite simple: "each candidate sold his electoral availability in exchange for money. That's it" (CPATB: 353–4).

In this electoral market, according to Buscetta, a retrospective approximate calculus on the "political value" of a criminal organization's support is difficult but possible:

> The politician usually knows the votes that he will have, he already has a percentage. He already has an idea, but he knows perfectly well when this percentage will increase [...] . If your quotient in that suburb is one hundred votes and suddenly, when you have reached agreement with me, then, out of

---

[12] Sicilian political life was consequently conditioned by "men of honour." This was the case, for example, in the political ascent of Salvo Lima, "decided by Cosa Nostra, with public meetings of politicians and 'men of honour' in Monreale. [...] Already mayor of Palermo, Salvo Lima was personally accompanied to these meetings by the most noted and authoritative members of the Mafia" (PP: 829).

kindness—not negotiations, there are no negotiations, at least in the Mafia environment—you will see three hundred votes, you will know that two hundred have come from me, from my intervention. So, you know better than anybody that you have to respect me if those votes are to be always yours. (CPATB: 375)

The competitive advantage guaranteed by the support of a criminal organization, especially in contestable political markets, is a strong incentive for politicians to demand safeguards against the uncertainty of electoral results, or contributions to their success, from Mafiosi. As Buscetta states, "the politician looked for the Mafioso because he knew that he could get much more than the one who had put himself forward as a candidate on his own" (CPATB: 374). The long-term prospects surrounding electoral exchanges in this symbiotic context are plainly stated by the ex-Mafioso informer Leonardo Messina. In his description, the politicians seeking Cosa Nostra's support—and reciprocally the Mafiosi who trust them—expect to set up a long-term investment in order to build lasting *political capital*, a durable asset that they will potentially use later without direct Mafiosi involvement:

Cosa Nostra controls a candidate for many years before getting him off the ground. In the first years they get to know him, and then they control him and introduce him. Afterwards he no longer needs the Family because he has made his halo, friends, etc., by himself. However, many politicians have contacts with the top of Cosa Nostra. When the elections take place, stable orders to vote for this or that person arrive but we don't know what agreements they have made or what they have given. Sometimes, at provincial, local or national level, we make different commitments as different families. If the order to support a person came from the Commission [i.e., it's an order from Cosa Nostra at regional level], then fine; if, however, we had to vote for two or three people, one was the person indicated by the Commission and we looked for the others ourselves. (CPALM: 550–51)

Camorra bosses also seem to prefer similar long-lasting protection contracts with politicians, in order to consolidate positive expectations and trust. The repentant camorrista Pasquale Galasso states, "in most cases, these politicians are voted in where there have been, for years, durable relations" (CPAPG: 2279).

The blocs of voters that criminal organizations are able to mobilize in some Italian southern regions are considered impressive in both size and discipline. For example, according to former Mafia member Antonio Calderone,

The family of Santa Maria del Gesù is the most numerous and has about 200 members. [...] We are talking about a terrifying, massive force, if you keep in mind that every man of honour [Mafia member], between friends and relatives, can count on at least forty to fifty people who will blindly follow his directives. [...] If we think that in Palermo, in my time, there were at least eighteen administrative districts, and that each of these areas included not less than two or three [Mafia] families, we can readily understand the significance of Mafia support in electoral competition. (DAP: 39)

The arithmetic of Cosa Nostra's electoral basis is straightforward: the Mafiosi "can play around a lot with the votes. Consider that there are 14 or 15 *mandamenti* [geographic zones of influence], each of which is formed by 2 or 3 families, each of these made up of at least 40 or 50 men, each with wives, children, sons-in-law, fathers-in-law, etc. It is easy to understand how many votes they can bring. When this large packet of votes arrives where it must arrive, it weighs an enormous amount. [...] It is only their vote that they give to politicians" (CPAAC: 319–20).[13]

The electoral strategy of the Camorra clan of Casalesi has been calibrated according to the social characteristics of potential voters, reproducing traditional models of southern Italian clientelistic political machines. According to a Camorra repentant:

> concerning the control of the electorate by the Casalesi clan, I should specify that there was a different administration for directing the votes of the penniless elements of the electorate compared to the one used to direct the more wealthy. In reference to the former, the Casalesi clan [...] —found huge quantities of basic foodstuffs (pasta, tinned tomatoes, sugar, milk, or rather bulky but low cost foodstuffs) which it then stored [...] . Walter Schiavone then went from house to house indicating the name of the candidate they should vote for and occasionally added more precisely "don't take offence, but if you pass by my house. I've got some shopping for you". The poor elements of the electorate then went to pick up the gift packets at Walter Schiavone's house assuring their vote. [...] Obviously, they didn't use this system for the more wealthy electorate (among which businessmen, professionals, etc.), but there was a general mobilisation of all members of the clan to channel the votes towards the clan's preselected candidate. (TRNOC: 188)

Moreover, criminal organizations rooted in the social environment do not need to use overt—and costly—material engagement in electoral campaigns. They can use informal communication channels, oblique signals, and their understanding of social norms to convey the manifest intention to support certain candidates. For instance, as the repentant Mafioso Tommaso Buscetta explains, traditionally the public exposure of contiguity between local Mafia bosses and political candidates is enough:

> I remember that when it was proposed to help a candidate, or a candidate asked for help in a certain district, we all went to that district accompanying the candidate, and we always met the Cosa Nostra representative of the suburb for a coffee, nothing more, so that the people could see that the representative had received a visit from the Mayor, or the candidate to be next Mayor, and so the votes went to the candidate we wanted. (TPAN: 672–3)

---

13   In Apulia, according to the turncoat Salvatore Annacondia, the criminal organization Sacra Corona Unita can also draw on wide electoral support, 30–40 percent of 50,000 inhabitants. (CPASA: 2508–9). Similarly, in Campania, the Camorra used its influence over "blocs of votes" to direct internal relationships among politicians toward their desired equilibrium, causing some trouble when the irreconcilable demands and appetites of competing parties needed to be satisfied (APN: 9).

Buscetta vividly describes that in this context electors always "know it, know it. You have no idea how many bells ring in Sicily, faster than phone calls, these things are known, there is 'u zu Peppino' who wants you to vote for [...] and you do not have to know what this politician is going to do either. Mafia do not intimidate, it is not necessary" (CPATB: 384).

Criminal organizations address the votes they control toward the candidates that they maintain are both useful (in terms of resources controlled and expected permanence in power) and reliable (in respecting illegal agreements). As a repentant Mafioso revealed, "It is important to know which political figures receive electoral support from Cosa Nostra, because, if that is the case, it is possible to turn to them for favors in compensation for electoral backing already given" (DAP: 39). Informal norms of behavior regulate how to approach politicians. According to the repentant Mafioso Vincenzo Marsala, "the fundamental rule was that political propaganda was allowed by members only in favor of the Christian Democrats. [...] However, voting for exponents of other political parties was sometimes allowed; but purely in a personal capacity, to return personal favors, and in any case with a ban on propaganda" (TPAN: 713). Each Mafiosi group's support was conveyed toward specific candidates of the Christian Democrat Party:

> I therefore consider that when the voting orders arrived as mentioned it was a case of politicians which the Mafia had an interest in placing in certain positions. In other cases, votes were given to Christian Democrat politicians who, due to their power, could guarantee the attainment of certain advantages. [...] In reality contact with politicians cannot be maintained by an ordinary member, it is necessarily maintained only by people in the 'family' who, as 'district-bosses', have a high rank in the hierarchy of the organization. (TPAN: 713)

The functioning of this unofficial rule minimizes dangerous contacts and the dissemination of information, as the repentant Mafioso Gaspare Mutolo confirms:

> there was, let's say, a rule which was more than anything else a rule of observance and confidentiality, namely that not everybody could speak with important figures. In that period, those who could speak to, let's say, the Hon. Salvo Lima were Stefano Bontate, Gaetano Badalamenti, Mimmo Teresi, Vitale. [...] It was necessary to follow a kind of practice, because there were men who specifically had contacts with these figures, otherwise anybody could feel authorised to disturb somebody like that. But anybody could need, could interfere through these figures. (TPAN: 760–61)

This does not however mean that the impact of criminal support is always decisive. A repentant Mafioso, Antonino Giuffré, remembered that in 1987, when the Cosa Nostra Godfather Salvatore Riina decided to support the Socialist Party instead of the Christian Democrats, the Mafiosi themselves were disappointed by the limited impact of their indications: "*ci parieva ca nuatri eravamo i padroni del voto* [it seemed to us that we were the owners of the vote] [...] it was quite an ugly situation. [...] Let's say that errors were made." The Socialist Party in the Province of Palermo in fact saw a relatively small increase of only 30,000 votes, from 11.2% in 1983 to 15.4% in 1987 (CPAM-IVX-II: 931–2). The long-term nature of the relationship of mutual protection, which had assumed ideological and identifying characteristics, defused the potential threat of vote withdrawal. In reality, this was just a bluff, and the unilateral and unnegotiated support for the Socialist Party was not reciprocated. The repentant Mafioso Marino Mannoia states: "I must also say that shifting votes from the Christian Democrats to the Socialist Party turned out to be in vain, because the Socialists didn't become colluders. Anyway, this shift was in practice a bluff, because many made men agreed but never got round to voting for them. Starting with me" (TPMP: 108).

When electoral sanctions are ineffective, Mafiosi can nevertheless use their traditional primary assets to sanction violated pacts, that is, violence and intimidation. This is the reason why, according to the repentant Mafioso Giovanni Brusca, the shooting of Salvo Lima was the consequence of a calculation on the expected ineffectiveness of electoral pressure:

> Because if we had only removed the votes, therefore not voting for the Christian Democrats, we would not have managed to remove the strength he had, because the votes were not only Mafia votes, there were votes from many other people involved in politics, plus the votes of the Mafia. So if we had only removed the votes of the Mafia, we wouldn't have got the result we wanted. (CPAM-IVX-II: 932)

Logically distinct from the previous case, even if in practice often overlapping, is the role played by organized crime as a protection agency in the market for votes. Electoral exchanges between politicians and the Mafia, forbidden by Italian law, seem to have assumed particularly noteworthy proportions in Campania, Calabria, and Sicily. In general, in illegal transactions involving the expression of electoral support, a demand for guarantees of reciprocal fulfillment between sellers (voters) and buyers (politicians) emerges. Mafia groups are well equipped to supply such protection: "A more ideal setting for the Mafia can scarcely be imagined. Although the market for votes exists in areas of Italy where there is no Mafia, in Sicily it appears to be larger and more efficient" (Gambetta 1993: 184).

In this context, the direction of money flows in from politicians to Mafiosi, who become middlemen and enforcers in exchanges of money for votes, which are otherwise at risk of being thwarted by mistrust. Examples abound in Southern Italian regions. One of the candidates in the Sicilian elections of 1991, obtained, for a price of 25 million lire from the local Mafia family, "control and protection for its electoral office and leafleting. Even if no violence was deployed, it was understood that those who did not respect the vote suggestion of the family, could suffer consequences" (TPMP: 897). In Calabria, during the 2005 regional elections, €15,000 was the price for an UDEUR (a small post–Christian Democrat Party) candidate suspected of "making an agreement with Y, boss of the 'Ndrangheta, through the intermediation of X by virtue of which they committed to returning money in exchange for votes" (R, March 19, 2010). In Campania, according to several legal inquiries, rates in the sale of votes are quite stable: politicians pay from €30 to €70 per vote to Camorra bosses, with blocks of 100–150 votes on sale for €1,500 (R, May 14, 2006).

On their side, political actors may reciprocate via general concern for the the latter's interests. For criminal organizations, political protection translates into influence over public decision-making, responding to their changeable interests and contingent needs. In this case too, the uncertainty surrounding criminal operations can be reduced thanks to political protection. The first and foremost resource demanded by the Mafiosi, who live in a situation of illegality, often as fugitives or already in jail, is *impunity*. According to several legal documents, Mafia and Camorra members, on the one hand, and political figures of national prominence, on the other, were primarily engaged in obtaining protection during investigations and acquittals in trials; these ends were achieved because political "patrons" pressured the forces of order and magistrates. As a state's witness—Gaspare Mutolo—recalled, "The unanimous belief was that one could usefully influence the action of the courts through politicians and that, further, the function of Sicilian politicians was critical for 'Roman politics' [or national-level political decisions] with regard to Sicilian matters involving the Cosa Nostra" (DAP: 24).

The cases range from a politician who ensures that a house arrest is arranged, to another who negotiated the transfer of particularly disagreeable public officials (TPMP: 38). According to the state's witness Carmine Schiavone, the nonintervention of the police during several summits of the Camorra clan Nuvoletta, that involved "tens and tens of armed fugitives," followed from "the political protection that the Nuvolettas had thanks to the support they offered to Hon. Gava [DC boss and former Minister of Budget, Justice, and Home Affairs] and other politicians" (Barbagallo 1997: 37).

Political protection also extends to the settlement of disputes, assigning contested rights, and the dispensation of "kindnesses" favoring criminal counterparts. The repentant Giovanni Brusca presents a wide sample of situations in which the Mafiosi benefited under the protection of influential Christian Democrat politicians:

> we got funding through the politicians [...] . So when favours were mentioned, which were not necessarily about ... trials or laws, they made themselves available for these kinds of favours. [...] For example, we went to get loans and we didn't get them through the Salvo cousins, like when we ... we acquired land in Contrada Don Tommaso [...] so thanks to his political power. For example, jobs at the Tax Office to employ people. There was a whole series of activities, there wasn't only ... there weren't only trials. (TPAA: 1104–5)

The Mafioso, in his own words, felt secure that possible future difficulties or needs would be guaranteed by this well-established collaborative relationship with politicians. The repentant camorrista Pasquale Galasso, similarly, describes a broad attitude of national level politicians, who "during elections ask these people for their votes promising them any easy favour. In essence, if the last of the criminals needed a passport renewed, he can go to the politician who will tell him to go and see a cop, or others, or he personally supplies it through his secretary" (CPAPG: 2310).

Symbiotic Relations and Mafia Enforcement in Public Contracting Procedures

In addition to the political arena, symbiotic relationships between political actors, entrepreneurs, professionals, and criminal organizations emerge in the market for collusive and corrupt agreements in public contracting. The building industry, in fact, is particularly attractive for organized crime since it allows criminals to expand not only their illicit businesses but also money-laundering. The capability of criminal organizations to "regulate" the winning of public tenders, influencing the allocation of the factors of production (labor, capital, raw materials) in areas typically characterized by high levels of unemployment, also increases their power to gather support and direct votes toward local and national administrators. In turn, the control over significant quotas of electoral consent permits criminal actors to actively promote—thanks to their political and economic counterparts— those projects for public and private construction that they expect to manage more effectively. Moreover, collusion between producers, present in many branches of economic activity, is particularly common in the public procurement sector:

> Relative to private customers, public institutions are fewer, take out long-term contracts, buy fixed quantities, are generally slack about quality, careless about price and corruptible. In short, they are easy to share. The small number of participants as well as the availability of sanctions—they share the same crowded market area and could easily make life difficult for each other—are such that this agreement could in principle do without outside assistance, although some evidence suggests that this is not the case. (Gambetta and Reuter 1995: 123–4)

The degree of autonomy of cartels from Mafiosi protection has changed during different periods in response to several variables. In general terms, the availability of criminal organization's protective services may facilitate the formation of stronger collusive agreements, offering "selective incentives" to the institution or the respect of bid-rigging agreements. In the case of Japan:

> Gangsters (*yakuza*) occasionally help enforce selective incentives. In Sakato City in Saitama Prefecture, a contractor desperately desired the contract for an agricultural waterworks project. Several days prior to the date for submitting bids, he telephoned representatives of the other firms designated to bid on the project and attempted to arrange a meeting at a local eatery. Unnerved by the unfolding *zenekon* scandal, most of the other contractors refused the invitation. As a last resort, the contractor hired two thugs, with ties to a well-known gangster organization, to intimidate the contractors who had declined to collude. (Woodall 1996: 43)

Japanese collusive agreements have also been internalized in wider "cliques," where prominent entrepreneurs, politicians, bureaucrats, and Yakuza bosses interact. Businessmen obtained public contracts in rotation in exchange for bribes and the mobilization of their employees; politicians and bureaucrats obtained money and perks (such as free entertainment in gang-owned or associated bars and clubs) in exchange for their decisions and the flexible application of regulations; yakuza bosses, with their extra-legal expertise, fulfilled the function of arbitrating and enforcing decisions taken within the clique (Hill 2006, 56).

For a long time the Sicilian Mafia's involvement in the procurement sector was limited, in the phase after the award of a public tender, to the collection of extortion money or "arranged" payments, by and large similar to that collected for other economic activities, and at most extending to the participation of other companies protected by the allocation of subcontracted work.[14] This Mafia-company interaction model is defined as *parasitic* (TPCG: 18), since, beyond general protection in relation to other eventual extortion requests, theft, or damages, the price paid to the Mafiosi does not extend to other services. It does not allow award mechanisms to be influenced nor does it allow the enforcement of collusive syndicates. A similar relatively "low level" of involvement seems to characterize the role of triads—Chinese criminal organizations—in the construction industry in Hong Kong, both as regards private developers and government contracts. Triads seem to operate by "(1) forcing building companies to employ their triad brothers as watchmen or workers, although they never turn up to work; and (2) triads setting up their own construction companies and 'persuading' contractors to sub-contract a portion of building work to them, though they are unlikely to complete the work" (Chu 2000: 47). Fearing intimidation, several companies pay protection money in the form of a monthly fee, and "in some cases operators of large construction companies employ a powerful local triad leader in the area to be the protector before setting up their sites" (Chu 2000: 48).

In Sicily the territorial allocation of the power to extract bribes precisely mirrors the regions of influence of each Mafioso group, with occasional conflicts arising only in cases of "uncertain sovereignty." This marks a difference between the operation of the Mafia in Sicily and New York: "in Sicily there is a clear geographic division; individual families have specific areas in which they have sole operating authority. Members of other families can operate there only with permission. Within New York the nature of the division is harder to determine. It is certainly not territorial, perhaps reflecting the lack of small-area local government

---

[14] The *pizzo* (a bribe paid to the Mafia) is, according to Giovanni Brusca, equivalent to the "so-called 3%, which was actually 2–2.50–1.50" (TPGB: 120). As collaborator Antonino Giuffrè observes, "The arrangement money [...] is when at the moment a company is awarded a job, before going to start work on that specific job, they need to make arrangements, meaning that they have to go looking for somebody who answers for the company, guaranteeing that at the end of or during the work they will pay the bribe to the area where the company does the job" (TPSC: 60).

that would permit the use of corrupt government authority to establish monopolistic criminal enterprises" (Gambetta and Reuter 1995: 119).

As often occurs, entrepreneurs have also drafted collusive agreements autonomously in Sicily, often sheltered by an umbrella of political and bureaucratic protection. By eliminating competition, entrepreneurs involved in the cartel can dole public contracts out, fictitiously increasing the prices of the adjudication through playing off prearranged offers, and thus also increasing their profits. In collusive agreements, however, a demand for protection emerges, as we showed in chapter 6. This is tied to the need to coordinate the offers among the entrepreneurs who divide public tenders by sticking to their turns, on a territorial basis or on the basis of contracting bodies assuring the observance of the "rules" of the division. Presented with a proposal to agree on offers or abstain from participating in procurement bids, each entrepreneur must have a certain amount of trust in the future availability of the applicant to return the favor.

The prospect of a frequent reiteration of exchanges and access to a series of additional "services" (information on bids, invitations to bid on "barrier grids," selective invites, etc.) provided by politicians and functionaries in exchange for bribes facilitate the success of the cartel. A company intending to defect can in fact be dissuaded with threats of being excluded from the benefits of prolonged cooperation. A Sicilian entrepreneur reconstructs this "autarchic" phase, in which cartels were upheld by the simple expectation of an exchange of favors over time:

> Up to a certain point there was just a fellowship among us entrepreneurs, where we exchanged envelopes, we did each other favours, which means that if there was a job which I was maybe interested in, in managing to get a hold of the list of companies participating in the tender by hook or by crook, I went round all the businesses asking some of them for the favour of abandoning their participation and others to help my bid by putting in a reduced bid at the amount agreed by myself beforehand. (TPSC: 68)

The entrepreneurs who organize the cartel in procurement for road building contracts in Sicily, since they have done the same job for generations, have accumulated a vast network of relations and interests shared with other individuals: "These people," states Giuseppe Lipari, "have been really tough businessmen for 50 years doing the same job, with parents and offspring, and therefore—this is the only job they have done—they were well-regarded and deep-rooted" (TPSC: 422). The long time horizon they operate in allows the entrepreneurs to develop, from one generation to another, a sound belief that their colleagues will fulfill their commitments, from time to time calibrating the credibility of opposing parties and marginalizing those who have shown themselves to be unreliable. This fabric of shared trust makes it easier to make new agreements and schedule deferred exchanges in support of the cartel's arrangement. In this setting:

> Cosa Nostra does not invent the system of dividing contracts up at the 'small table', Cosa Nostra has since the mid-eighties introduced and managed a system

of the pre-arranged awarding of public tenders which was previously the exclusive domain of entrepreneurs and politicians. (TPCG: 19)

A similar form of control over construction contracts seemed to characterize the role of "twenty or so largest contractors in New York City who, from time to time, through collusive bidding, decided among themselves who would get a particular project" at least until the 1980s. When a winning bid was formulated: "either an emissary of organized crime or a union official [...] approaches the contractor and tells the general contractor who his suppliers will be, who his subcontractors will be, from whom he will purchase materials and at what price those materials will be purchased" (PCOC: 71–2, cit. in Abadinsky 1990: 377).

In Sicily, between the end of the 1970s and the beginning of the 1980s, an initial leap in quality was achieved. As the repentant Mafioso Giovanni Brusca recalls:

> Then some of the men from Cosa Nostra started getting directly interested in procurement, in the management of construction work, even if on being awarded [...] the work is set right properly. Being business, it wasn't personal affairs, so people paid what the sums due [...], which means respecting the rules of [...] Cosa Nostra, except that then they had no personal relationships, and they could therefore elude this particular detail. (TPGB: 22)

In those years, the eclipsing of some centers of political power traditionally contiguous to the Mafia organization, such as that led by the former Christian Democrat mayor of Palermo Vito Ciancimino, opened up spaces that other individuals attempted to occupy. As collaborator Angelo Siino, coordinator of the cartel, explains:

> it's not like the Mafia noticed my competence back in '87. It was a coincidence. The cornerstones the running of Mafia procurement was based on, which wasn't just my business, had passed away; Vito Ciancimino had been arrested, just when I got my first contact for this affair with Honourable member Lima, and he told me that none of the Palermo guys were capable of adequately running the procurement sector, meaning that in Agrigento there were figures who already managed procurement. (TPAN: 778)

In 1983 the end of the so-called second Mafia War confirmed the success of the Corleone faction, which coincided with a change in the equilibria between Mafia protection "companies." From an arrangement based to a large degree on the autonomy of the families and local bosses, and characterized by area-by-area criteria assuring each family control over all relative illegal and legal activities (including procurement), they now adopted a centralized system where the dominant Corleone group firmly occupied the higher echelons of the organization (TPCG: 18; CPAA: 199). Between 1986 and 1987, this change in power relationships was also reflected in the procurement market. The Corleone faction of the Mafia organization appointed itself guarantor of the enforcement of rules in allocating the prices of bid awards.

Nevertheless, the identification of a promising "market" for protection services largely unexplored (that is, the market of collusive procurement management) was not a sufficient condition for it to extend to Palermo and the rest of the region. This transition required the presence of a criminal entrepreneur capable of combining the scattered resources and skills necessary for such a move through the coordination of the several actors to be involved: entrepreneurs, professionals, bureaucrats, politicians, and Mafia guarantors. In the New York concrete industry, for instance, a critical role was assumed by Avellino, a leading figure in the cartel, member of a Cosa Nostra family, and active entrepreneur with a prominent role in the industry. Thanks to his "coordination" efforts, the amount of money delivered to Mafia families increased drastically: "A striking feature of Avellino's performance was the fact that he persuaded so many others of the carters that he was seeking, almost altruistically, arrangements that benefited all. Repeated references were made by others to how much their lot improved after Avellino entered the industry" (Reuter 1987: 36).

In Sicily, similar organization and intermediation activity required the preliminary purchase of a specific protection contract by the Mafia's "Godfathers." Angelo Siino—another entrepreneur with friends in Cosa Nostra—planned a system of tender-sharing where "everybody had a share," thanks to the accurate planning of the offers, which ensured an internal subdivision of profits. We find parallels here with the role of the Mafia in New York's concrete market: "Cosa nostra families established a club of concrete contractors who decided which contractor would submit the lowest bid on each project; other cartel members prepared their complementary bids accordingly" (OCTF 1990: 11). The cartel among the main concrete construction companies working in New York was regulated within a club—that is, a cooperative venture among the Cosa Nostra families—which set rules and settled major disputes arising within the scheme:

> The rules of the Club were: only such construction companies as the Commission approved would be permitted to take concrete construction jobs worth more than two million dollars in New York City; any contractor taking a concrete job worth more than two million dollars would be required to pay the Commission two percent of the construction contract price; the Commission would approve which construction companies in the Club would get which jobs and would rig the bids so that the designated company submitted the lowest bid; the Commission would guarantee "labor peace" to the construction companies in exchange for compliance with the rules of the Club; and the Commission would enforce compliance by threatened or actual labor unrest or physical harm, even to the point of driving a company out of the concrete business. (U.S. Court of Appeals 1991)

In Sicily, Di Maggio was first involved by Siino in the new business:

Siino came to me, I already knew him [...] and he told me: 'there are public contracts awarded by the Province which are lost, out of control, contractors offer price reductions of more than 25, 30%, if we get control I know politicians who can give me the list of works, we can manage tenders and try to get some profit for ourselves. (TPBA: 7)

Authorization was requested from the Godfather Totò Riina, who finally accepted with some hesitations: "Siino could get into some trouble, like Ciancimino [...], but if he is aware and accountable for them, then he can go on" (TPBA: 7).

The introduction of the new enforcement mechanism in collusive agreements was founded on *rules of conduct* that partly changed the previously accrued expectations of entrepreneurs. To defuse, at least in part, the possible risks of misunderstandings in transactions, Siino saw to the diffusion of information on the changes introduced by the Mafia regulation in a series of meetings:

> The new rules imposed by Cosa Nostra are communicated by Siino to some of the most important entrepreneurs in Sicily over the course of several meetings specifically convened in almost every province. These are entrepreneurs who, though not belonging to Cosa Nostra, are considered 'dependable' by the Mafia organisation and who, due to their weight in the business environment, can actively collaborate in making the system work by intervening with their influence when necessary. (TPBA: 10)

Companies ready to participate in a bidding process already settled by the cartel in favor of an internal winner expected a request to "coordinate their envelopes," that is to present an agreed offer or withdraw altogether. For example, an entrepreneur could be approached by a colleague and a surveyor who ask him for his support in two public tender bids that will soon take place:

> Rather, he asked me to make myself available, to submit the envelope or not to participate in this job. [...] Submitting the envelope means preparing the bid, giving it to them or putting the number they said was more convenient, more suited to them mediating the bidding process as they liked. The number which helped them most to mediate the bidding process and ensure it ended in favour of who they wanted, the discount imposed or the reduction imposed on the bid offer. (TPSC: 72)

In this context, the role of the Mafia organization, as Antoniuno Giuffrè observes, is essentially that of a "behind-the-scenes-supervisor":

> if at the moment there were some companies in the cartel or other companies from outside the cartel, we intervened to advise this or that company not to disturb, not to enter into certain issues which didn't concern them with threats of damage. When the cartel went around, they went around promoting the name of Provenzano [a "Godfather"] in particular. Do you get what I mean? (PPTO: 1053)

Consequently, Siino started to keep 5 percent of the value of the public contracts: initially, according to Baldassare di Maggio, 3 percent was taken by the Mafia organization, and 2 percent was handed on to politicians who, in turn, guaranteed the smooth advance of procedures. The role of politicians and public officials, even if peripheral, was also useful in making cartels run more smoothly in the case of the carter industry in New York, enforced by Cosa Nostra: "What was remarkable was the ubiquity of the favor-giving. [...] The officials provided three kinds of favors: Favorable ruling of the industry as a whole, coercion of dissidents, and non-enforcement of rules for favored members" (Reuter 1987: 48). A similar percentage was paid in a Mafia-run concrete cartel in New York: 2 percent from the winning bids was charged by a Mafiosi family for its services in fixing prices (Gambetta and Reuter 1996: 132). In another case of a concrete cartel in Long Island, the collusive bidding scheme was coordinated by a union official, who took 1 percent of the contract's value, and then funneled a portion of the money to the Lucchese, Genovese, and Gambino Mafia families (OCTF 1990: 35).

Dissuading any vague temptations to defect from the collusive pact, spontaneously giving into and observing the rules of the cartel and showing signals that allow for the rapid correction of misunderstandings and errors *costs* the Mafia guarantor—in terms of "professional" risks and commitments—much less than settling arguments and applying sanctions once problems appear. The possibility of staying in the backseat, limiting oneself to collecting protection money, is highly connected with the importance of reputation, which, as in the case of other immaterial assets, almost becomes a substitute for real goods. By spreading the name of the Mafia guarantor, the cartel effectively discourages defections and intrusions without the person directly referred to even lifting a finger: "the job of concluding agreements, which is to say going round other entrepreneurs, is normally carried out directly by the designated company and thus the real Mafioso can stay, or in fact does stay, in the shadows" (TPCG: 28). As long as no conflict or external competitor emerges, violence can be spared while actors remain voluntarily in collusive dealings. In the carter industry in New York, for instance, collusive agreements were enforced by Cosa Nostra without any apparent coercion: "There was little evidence of either threats or actual violence, but it seems reasonable to infer that the racketeers provided a credible continuing threat of violence that ensured compliance with the rulings of the committee" (Reuter 1987: 11).

However, when there are internal quarrels or intrusions by unsatisfied competitors, the request for arbitration services is made more explicitly to the Mafia guarantors:

> the authentic Mafia face of the organisation unmistakeably emerges in what I would define as moments of crisis in the workings of the system. This regards cases in which it is necessary to bring entrepreneurs into line who don't adapt, or don't adapt immediately, to the observance of the rules as outlined before. (TPCG: 28)

Occasionally, when reputational assets are not sufficient or recognized, violence becomes a necessary resource to maintain order and reciprocity within the cartel. A similar condition was observed in New York, where "violence can also be a tool used by racketeers to discipline uncooperative contractors." An intercepted conversation between a Mafia boss (Scopo) and a contractor (Costigan) shows how Cosa Nostra operates in the enforcement of collusive agreements:

SCOPO: If I tell you stories about contractors that you know, that's supposed to get hurt, that I protected ...

COSTIGAN: Why would any, they get hurt?

SCOPO: Well, we ... for doin' what they're not supposed to be doin ..." (OCTF 1990: 33)

Collusive agreements have to be protected both from the risk of internal defection and from external competition. The enraged tapped reaction of a Mafia boss against a Sicilian entrepreneur who was submitting lower bids without due authorization, causing protests from disappointed colluding competitors, demonstrates the risks of "free riding": "If there's this lunatic, then hurry up and make him see sense— the boss shouts—but at the same time tell him—if he's acting alone, tell him ... let him know nicely, because our legs are getting broken the way he's carrying on, tell him never to go back there again" (*Giornale di Sicilia*, May 13, 2009: 5).

When the Mafia coordinator gets to the bottom of the cartel's coordination mechanisms, in-depth technical knowledge on public procedures is necessary, as is "possession of a solid relationship network with the business community, with political representatives, public functionaries and good mediation skills" (TPBA: 5).[15] As Angelo Siino observes, in the Mafia's procurement regulation system, Cosa Nostra becomes: "a guarantor ... a guarantor who had the power to set contracts, it has its powers of intimidation towards everybody, which put everything right. People were afraid of the 'scupetta' [the gun] and so in practice they had an interest in respecting the agreements" (TPGO: 157)

The competitive restriction of procurement and the diffusion of corruption generates advantages and profits for many people: companies in the cartel are awarded tenders at a discounted price, while the rotation system reduces uncertainty; politicians and administrators collect larger bribes, with less concerns over the reliability of the mediator; Mafiosi get a percentage of the rent generated at the expense of the public budget, and by widening the range of protection

---

[15] As well as a prerequisite, the acquisition of "social capital" is one of the objectives pursued by Mafiosi with procurement sector regulation. As Sciarrone observes, Mafiosi "in such a way manage to accumulate the advantages deriving from weak bonds (network extension and diversification) and those deriving from the high-density networks (control of relations). Mafiosi are interested in obtaining the cooperation of other individuals, which is why they tend to favour, more than the acquisition of new and exclusive information, the control of relations transmitting it" (Sciarrone 1998: 51).

services offered to other actors, they increase the number of resources requested in compensation (TPBA: 8). These conditions are at the root of the progressive enlargement of the range of "Siino method" of enforcement:

> it first spreads randomly expanding from the public tender bids invited by the Province of Palermo to those invited by other public bodies and then, as a system, tends to transform in the late eighties into a top-down global public procurement control system over the whole area of Sicily. (TPBA: 9)

In the late 1980s, Siino was partly substituted by other guarantors, since entrepreneurs from Northern Italy had become involved in the public procedures and a "cleaner face" of the Mafia had to be presented. Another factor to be considered, according to the repentant Antonino Giuffrè, was the dissatisfaction of some Mafiosi:

> Siino's 'small table', at a certain point, did not work anymore, since Provenzano had received many complaints from mafiosi close to him who had been excluded from the 'cake'. So a new 'small table' was created [...] which allowed us to share public contracts among entrepreneurs and bribes among politicians and mafiosi families responsible in the area of the works. And the whole cartel was promoted by Provenzano. (R, October 18, 2002)

The agreement between Mafia leaders and entrepreneurs is defined by the protagonists themselves "at the small table": as well as taking the management of large-scale procurement, that is amounts higher than 5 billion lire, out of Siino's hands, a later sum of 0.8 percent of the value of the contract, the "Riina Tax," alongside the bribes paid to politicians and local Mafia families, was scheduled to be directly channeled to the organizational nucleus of Cosa Nostra, to cover the "central" expenses of the criminal organization, tied to arms purchases, detainees' legal expenses, "subsidies" to their families, and so on. Antonino Giuffrè reconstructs this succession, when

> the bidding processes of a certain importance were taken out of Siino's hands and the power was transferred to the so called Tavolino [small table], which was where we find the people behind the scenes who I spoke about a short time ago, Pino Lipari, as well as others [...] . This table had the specific function of sharing out jobs from the beginning by guaranteeing bribes, once the bidding process was accomplished and jobs contracted, to politicians on one hand, and to the area, to the Mafia family where the work was based. Now let's say that in this moment we were behind-the-scenes- supervisors, this job was accomplished by a cartel of companies who met with each other and brought forward the division of jobs with our consent, and when order needed to be kept. (PPTO: 1053)

The reasons for the handover from Angelo Siino to the new "small table" are the result of a *learning process*. The strict rules of the previous system with its near unitary management delegated to Siino created friction with the entrepreneurial system. The Mafia organization settled this by increasing costs. Hence the division among guarantors on the basis of the value of the contracts and the extension of the number of individuals delegated the function of coordinator:

> On procurement—again states Giuffrè—Cosa Nostra had tuned a perfect device with part of the political world and the business community: there was a thorough division on this. After 1988, this mechanism, which had been widely controlled by Angelo Siino, was improved. The so-called 'small table', where very important figures took part, was built. [...] That was the welding moment between the Mafia and the part of politics and entrepreneurs. (CPAM-IVX-II: 129)

Politicians delegate the selection and control of the companies, which take turns in the awarding of contracts to Mafia guarantors, or at least as long as their bribes arrive regularly. Their *trust* in the "reliability" of the Mafiosi, who deal with the flow of bribes, pushes them to become disinterested in the following phases. According to collaborator Gioacchino La Barbera, the secretary of the Sicily Regional council, after receiving a bribe arranged for a contract, he cared nothing for the company who had been awarded the work:

> he wasn't at all interested because he had complete faith, he knew that it had something to do with reliable people in as far as from what I heard he wasn't completely interested in me; anybody, because then Cosa Nostra decided on the company, and so they aren't problems which concerned Mario D'Acquisto, the only thing he was interested in was the 5% which Gioè had to bring him, rather immediately before it happened on the company's behalf, which is to say even before collecting the money he started the work. The moment when the work was awarded, he had to prepare 5% of the amount to give it to the politicians. (TPGO: 215–6)

The centralization in the hands of a few individuals, delegated by the Mafia, of the tasks of identification, information, and guaranteeing the fulfillment of the collusive arrangement reduces coordination problems. On the other hand, a similar "governance structure" of cartels exposes politicians, companies, and Mafiosi themselves to the danger of the system collapsing, as far as a critical junction in the system, the coordinator, accumulates a capital of compromising information on the activities of many public and private individuals involved in the corruption market.[16] In the case of involvement in investigations, the coordinator has an incentive to make this capital of knowledge bear fruit, by "selling" to the legal authorities in exchange for favorable treatment. This is exactly what happened in the case of Siino, who after his capture in 1991 started to collaborate in 1997, and of his successors, arrested thanks to his collaboration.

---

[16] The coordinator's activity violates organizational criteria typical of many criminal companies, allowing them to reduce the "production costs" tied to legal risks: the restraint of flows of compromising information within rigorously delimited "watertight compartments" (Reuter 1983).

In the past few years, the Sicilian Mafia has thereby revised its governance model, redistributing tasks and powers to a wider number of individuals, its faithful entrepreneurs:

> In the field of this submersion strategy [...] 'Cosa Nostra' renounced every desire of direct and centralised management of the procurement system in the phase of their award (just as occurred at the time when first Angelo Siino and then Pino Lipari had a strategic role in this sector): it preferred to leave this task to the reference companies and the 'affairs committee' [...] to influence the award in a discrete and invisible manner. (PPLA: 12–3)

By abstaining from interfering in the stages of selecting and funding works, the prearrangement of the bid invitations and the material management of the bidding process, the criminal organization avoids "the risk of identifying individuals delegated to these offices and of the overexposure of Cosa Nostra" (APRC: 4). However, tenders remain for the Mafia "the substantial area of primary enforcement of their own criminal activities, probably with less authority but certainly with a greater pervading commitment" (CPAA: 202). Coherently with the more general strategy of Cosa Nostra and the Calabrian 'Ndrangheta to recede into their territories, avoiding international competition, "today they obtain a growing and preponderant quote of their revenues by manipulating the tendering process of public works and imposing generalized extortive regimes on all the economic enterprises of their areas" (Paoli 2004: 293). In the tender regulation system, aspirations toward any centralized and "global" control over all phases through a single organizer delegated by the Mafia organization failed after the arrest of Siino and other coordinators. Cartels of companies that share the market for public procurement between themselves continue to exist, however. In the opinion of Antonino Gioè,

> Many years later, I can say that the 'small table' stopped, but the connection with politicians, entrepreneurs and Mafiosi did not [...] . In this way, business competition failed [...] . The Mafia provided security and got 2 percent in exchange. (CPAM-IVX-II: 129)

The cartels are now managed with greater autonomy for entrepreneurs, and no longer with the unified coordination of a mediator delegated by the Mafia from the moment works were funded or awarded. As of the end of the 1990s, there are signs that the "balance of powers" between politicians and Mafiosi in the market for corruption are realigning in favor of the former. Politicians have an ambivalent relationship with Mafia protectors, who on the one hand hang over them with the threat of intimidation, impeding them from managing the tender and bribes business autonomously, yet on the other provide secure and organized funding for the system.

Replacement or Colonization: When Organized Crime Enters the Political Arena

A different outcome may emerge when structured criminal organizations, operating as local monopolies in the supply of protection in more or less muddled markets, face political actors—party, faction, and individual subjects—with uncertain prospects of duration and success, shorter time horizons, and fragile roots in society. In this case there is a change in the nature of resources demanded, the expected duration of the relationship, and the bargaining powers of counterparts, reflecting the different balance of needs, costs, and opportunities for criminal and political actors. Protection is highly demanded by political agents, but their unstable future prospects discourage criminal organizations from postponing payments, or leaving contractual terms too general and unspecified. Nonetheless, criminal organizations are often required to stabilize wobbly alliances and pacts between individual and collective political actors with their enforcement apparatus. Fixing criteria for the occupation of public roles and the allocation of resources, in fact, will contribute to the peaceful and orderly development of illicit markets where criminal organizations are involved as guarantors: corruption in licensing and contracting, cartel agreements among entrepreneurs, and so on. Moreover, under certain conditions, powerful criminal "protection agencies" may try to replace political actors, to occupy their structures, conditioning list formation, and colonizing—especially at the local level—the whole administrative structure.

Different factors can produce relative insecurity in the enduring capability of political actors' to exercise roles of public authority. Extreme cases are the collapse of the party system or some kind of institutional crisis, which tend to generate a state of flux and radical uncertainty in the political arena. Even the ordinary dynamics of electoral competition may induce analogous results, however. If elections are truly competitive, criminal actors can hardly stipulate long-term contracts (stating the allocation of future public contracts, zoning, licenses, guarantees of immunity, etc.) with their political partners: if defeated after the next popular vote, the latter could simply be unable to give what they promised when in charge. This is the case when a competitive party or party coalition not backed by the Mafia contests elections, supported by ideological or ethical commitments.

In this case, however, at least two strategies can be adopted by the Mafiosi. First, they can enter into an exchange relationship with *all* the main competing parties and leading actors, assuming the role of informal regulators and enforcers of hidden consociational pacts among them. There are some drawbacks in this case: criminals could be victims of some turbulence in the collusive pacts among politicians, since the multiplication of counterparts implies augmented transaction costs, also related to the risks of defection and to the possibility that some "moral opposition" emerges among parties involved in this criminal network. Criminal actors may be weakened precisely by their involvement in political affairs, with increased risks of visibility and exposure without any reliable shield against inquiries. Second, criminal actors may use their reputational and coercive resources to ensure a steady competitive advantage in local elections to one of the competing political actors, therefore rendering elections less and less competitive. In a dynamic perspective, in fact, we may expect that if a strategy of colonization/occupation—implying the supply of Mafiosi protection to specific political careers—is effective and successful, the political actor may obtain additional resources of authority and consent in the political market, therefore increasing his bargaining power, and eventually emancipating himself from his criminal counterparts.

In Italy, in two phases Cosa Nostra's bosses cherished an ambitious political project: the establishment of a Mafioso political party as a component of a wider plan for regional independence or stronger autonomy. Both periods coincided with a destructuring of the preexisting party system and, more generally, a dramatic crisis in the preexisting political equilibria. At these critical junctures of Italian history—immediately after the end of the Second World War and in the mid-1990s, when the Clean Hands investigations sanctioned the end of the so-called first republic—the Mafiosi's reaction to a peak in uncertainty in the political realm was a vague aspiration toward complete self-sufficiency in the process of political representation and competition in Sicily. The replacement of traditional parties with a "Godfather party" were never realized, however, since new political actors came onto the scene as partners for possible cooperative interactions with Cosa Nostra (CPAM-XIV-II: 518).

In several countries criminal figures have occasionally pursued a strategy of substitution of political actors, when the latter are perceived as weak or totally unreliable, or when criminal actors are in search of social legitimization and respectability. Cases of direct penetration of the political sphere, involving open participation in the electoral process, are clearly limited to contexts where the criminal-political nexus has not become public. In Colombia, direct connections between politicians and drug traffickers who financed the campaigns of both Liberal and Conservative candidates, have been observed since the late 1970s. Members of criminal trafficking organizations or their close relatives would run for office directly through traditional political parties, or occasionally through parties of their own. For instance, the criminal boss Pablo Escobar, after a long period of criminal training in which "he had spent more than a decade building his local criminal syndicate and learning the ways of bribing officialdom" (Bowden 2001: 26), financially supported the career of a politician who in 1982 won a seat in the lower house while Escobar became his alternate. Escobar enjoyed some popular support from marginalized segments of society thanks to his populist stance and assistance offered to the residents of marginal barrios in his adopted hometown of Medellin.

Also in Ukraine, during the post-Soviet transition, a criminal-political nexus emerged involving criminal organizations, members of the former party elite and of the law enforcement and security apparatus. In the vacuum of an emerging but still de-structured political system, "the infiltration of Ukrainian legislatures by criminals became a serious problem. More than 20 members of the Parliament would be tried on criminal charges if they were stripped of their parliamentary impunity [...] . Forty-four legislators, elected to local political bodies, also have criminal background" (Shelley 2001). In the uncertain political scenario of the Bulgarian town of Dupnitsa, "two former special services officers [...] accumulated their capital through violence in the 1990s and then, using racketeering methods against local entrepreneurs, formed a political structure that won the local elections. In this manner they gained direct control over local administrative power. [...] Similar cases of direct participation of criminal entrepreneurs in local politics were observed in some smaller resort towns" (CSD 2011: 213).

When the political environment appears less stable and orderly in its functioning, the protective services of organized crime are even more valuable. Mafiosi's authoritative arbitration can in fact provide some degree of certainty in these murky electoral and political markets. According to the repentant Mafioso Antonino Calderone, the criminal organization may prefer a more "chaotic" and unpredictable political process, as found in ill-functioning democratic procedures, precisely to increase its bargaining power and expectations of impunity: "Why does Cosa Nostra try to give votes not to left-wing parties but parties like the Christian Democrats, the Liberal Party, the Republicans and the Social Democrats? Because, in their opinion, these are democratic parties and when there is democracy politicians tend not to agree: *the more confusion there is in politics the more they gain an advantage* because they are obstructed less. They try to make the most chaos possible to keep afloat" (CPAAC: 284, emphasis added). We may add that Mafiosi may prefer—and deliberately promote—some uncertainty in political interactions as it also produces, as a side effect, an increase in the demand for the protection and the enforcement services they sell.

In Campania, for instance, the political scenario was until the mid-1990s characterized by competitive pressure from different actors to renew a medium-term agreement with local bosses, who could monopolistically decide whom to trust according to previous experiences. As explained by the repentant camorrista Pasquale Galasso,

As far as honourable politicians at national level are concerned [...] when the elections arise, of presenting to the Camorrista group, to Carmine Alfieri [the Camorrista boss], of having passed on that news, of having made themselves available for that tender and this being able to ask to be voted for. The elections are something else completely. About five or six months before the elections, there's a coming and going of all of these politicians who have been in contact with our Camorrista group and come forward to grab our votes. They then point out their unlimited availability and a market is formed in that moment. [...] Eventually, Alfieri and the rest of us from the organisation work out what that honourable politician can offer in exchange, whether it is political power, whether he can be useful in creating a friendly relationship with public institutions, mainly the judiciary and many other things. In the end, we measure whether the honourable such and such has certain political strength. (CPAPG: 2277–8)

The calculation of the camorrista boss is straightforward, aimed at establishing the partner's trustworthiness in future uncertain contingencies: "In the end, Alfieri had reached the decision to perhaps get rid of some politicians and support others after figuring them out and thinking along these lines: 'This person will give me something; what will he give me? If he's elected, what Commission will he go into? If, for example, he goes into the justice Commission, it's gone well, but I want the promise of a man of honour who will follow my judicial problems'" (CPAPG: 2310). While the potential for mutually profitable exchanges between criminal and political actors remains, in this scenario mistrust and suspicion arise: because both politicians' *determination* and *capability* to maintain their promises are difficult to ascertain, since previous experiences are missing, their reputation is ill-defined, and future opportunities are unclear. Essentially, why should Mafiosi trust politicians in this case? The implicit menace of violent retaliation could suffice here, but the application of violent sanctions has a cost and should be avoided whenever possible. In a tape-recorded dialogue, the Mafia boss Giuseppe Guttadauro expresses his worries about the conduct of the future regional president Totò Cuffaro, whom he will finally accord his doubtful confidence:

> What I'm interested in is that a commitment is taken to resolve any problems. When, for example, he says of a life sentence: 'I want to take on all the commitments under the sun'. But if they are taken off him or not, what does he lose from it? [...] In any case, I give my unconditional support to the Regional President and Totò, that's indisputable. Have I explained myself? So now go and find the best way to get less damage and a better return. (Bianchi and Nerazzini 2005: 27)

If political equilibria are expected to be wobbly, criminal organizations may guarantee a safeguard for pacts and contractual terms among parties and political leaders. In facilitating and enforcing political agreements, organized crime contributes to the settling of disputes and the stabilization of local governments, therefore inducing an orderly allocation of budgetary resources and distribution of appointed positions in key public roles. For instance, the repentant camorrista Pasquale Galasso states that, after the election of the town council in Poggiomarina (near Naples), "I was asked to intervene with a reluctant councillor to tell him, with all the weight of my Camorra fame, to ally himself with Antonio Gava [DC political boss], who had promised him the position of mayor." An agreement therefore emerged between the two main DC representatives in the local government. In this account, this agreement only became stable thanks to the presence of the camorrista: "For the duration of that government—Galasso continues—I was the tongue, convincing the one, who didn't want to renounce to his position as Mayor, and the other, who wanted to occupy it, to remain united" (Barbagallo 1997: 149–50). Criminal groups were obviously paid in exchange for their services, with cash or open access to decision-making processes whose stability they had contributed to.

In extreme cases, criminal enforcement requires the application of physical intimidation or assassination against those who perturb the fragile harmony of political actors' expectations. This is the case of the assassination of the powerful Christian Democrat exponent Ludovico Ligato in Reggio Calabria. According to a state's witness, his elimination "should be framed as a moment of the conflict inside the Reggio's business committee," given the fact that Ligato, with his political power and his contacts with a rival Mafia band, had "interfered in the political life of Reggio" (Ciconte 1994: 168). The murder had the effect of consolidating the nascent political coalition in Reggio: "After the assassination, or, better, because of it, the game was made and the new agreements were implemented thanks to a series of very important decisions, that in previous times would have been discussed for months in the city council" (Ciconte 1994: 168). Any element that might have disrupted the coalition and its plans for sharing out public resources was thus eliminated. Thanks to this violent pacification, the market for corruption could expand undisturbed and benefit Reggio's *business committee*, composed of "prominent figures in the dominant political class, who were able to influence the choices of local and central public agencies," of "'favored' national companies that routinely received public contracts," and of "local entrepreneurs who acted in symbiosis with local organized crime and were thus the actual executors of the work" (CD, n. 256: 2).

The repentant Mafioso Gaspare Mutolo accurately describes the ambiguity surrounding Cosa Nostra's pacification role in political disputes: the Mafiosi's protection is both demanded and feared by political actors, but must not in any case be confused with violence. On the contrary, it is aimed at guaranteeing precarious "rights" and expectations in otherwise fluid political agreements. The recourse to Mafia boss arbitration in quarrels was normal even for leading political figures: "I went there whenever he wanted: it was normal, also because these people weren't looked upon as criminals, but as people who acted in the best interest. [...] There were issues, one person had one Mafioso, another had another and an agreement was needed to be found. In the eyes of these figures, they were peacemakers, not assassins" (CPAGM: 1276). Besides, dispute settlement was usually sanctioned spontaneously, relegating physical coercion as a last resort: "Any politician could have a person who could avoid a conflict. At the end of the day, if these people made the effort, they did so in the best interest not in the worst: in fact, the matter was that, if a way of getting them to agree, of being more elastic and mellow wasn't found, everybody would be killed, just us some people have been killed" (CPAGM: 1283).[17]

---

[17] In our typology we do not consider the center-periphery dimension. The local context of interaction may nevertheless be relevant, especially when we consider the relative weakness of "small-size" political subjects and administrative structures when confronted with the "military" enforcement apparatus of an effective criminal organization. Local administration and party structures, as well as candidates for municipal and provincial roles are therefore especially vulnerable to complete colonization by organized crime (Mete 2009).

When criminal organizations can enforce unstable coalitional pacts, settle disputes on political affairs, and colonize administrations, the resulting predictability of "ordered" decision-making may be profitable for several actors. Not only politicians and criminal organizations but also entrepreneurs included in the consequent allocation of public resources and privileges. As the Camorra repentant Pasquale Galasso described it, every Camorra clan had a "prime political sponsor," and together they managed which works should be planned and financed, which firms should stipulate public contracts, and which sites should be earmarked for construction:

> The politician who directs the financing of the contract, and thus its assignment or concession, acts as a mediator between the company (which is almost always from the North or the Center and is quite large) and the Camorra. This mediation occurs by forcing the company to pay a kickback to the politician or his direct representatives, and to accept that subcontracts be assigned to [local] companies, directly controlled by the Camorra. The relationship becomes more complicated since the local companies flank the principal company as equal partners in the job: In this case an overall management of the operation emerges that involves politicians, businessmen, and *camorristi*. (APN: 9)

According to Neapolitan judges, each participant could obtain significant benefits in this "iron triangle":

> The entrepreneur obtains from the politician work and the possibility to make profit, from the *camorrista* [...] 'social peace' and 'credit' in the relationships with the local administration: the *camorrista* obtains money from the entrepreneur, judicial 'protection' from the politician, and social legitimation from both. [...] The politician receives electoral strength and the capacity of illicit influence on public functions, added to relevant economic resources. (Barbagallo 1997: 163)

Entrepreneurial intermediation in organized crime's contribution to political financing has a double advantage: money flows are less compromising in cases of disclosure, even when irregular, as long as there is no evidence of direct involvement by criminal organizations (see table 8.1); entrepreneurs can apply their professional skills and budgetary expertise to conceal or "launder" these financial flows, while identification and transaction costs are lower, since the

---

A stronger demand for protection and support in electoral competition emerges when local political arenas are contestable. This demand could be fulfilled by criminal organizations capable of reinvesting some of their illicit profits in the political arena. Moreover, the presence of organized crime in the territory creates a distorted and inflationary input in electoral campaigns and, more generally, political activity: "decentralization processes open up new arenas of political competition that add to the cost of politics" (Casas-Zamora 2010). An in-depth analysis of the facilitating factors and consequences of the interaction between organized crime and the electoral process in several Latin-American countries is carried out by Casas-Zamora (2012).

politician's counterpart can more easily bargain, gather, and transmit information. For instance, in a Sicilian municipality, according to the decree of dissolution,

> the mayor, having already been elected in the same role in June 1999, has for a while proved tied to the aforementioned entrepreneur, indicated as belonging to the powerful Mafia society of the area with leading functions and administrator of considerable real estate and commercial properties on behalf of that clan. [...] The administrator obtained the support of the entrepreneur for the electoral campaign relating to the Spring 2000 consultation, capable, in virtue of his substantial fortune and the large number of personal staff, of influencing electoral consensus to be directed in a way favourable to the interests of the Mafia clan of which he is a prominent exponent. (Sberna 2010)

Money—as circumstantial bribes or less goal-oriented payments—can become the privileged commodity of exchange in these cases. In local arenas pragmatic considerations prevail, while political actors are approached on the basis of their presumed availability and receptiveness. Interests of criminal and political actors then converge in the cartelized control of local decision-making, where relevant profits—particularly in the public contracting sector—may be shared. Bribes are then paid to political actors, who then find themselves in a weaker bargaining position. Money becomes the precise and quantifiable *numerarie* in these kinds of exchanges, and permits criminal actors to ask for the immediate reciprocation of valuable resources allocated by politicians. In this context the corrupt exchange may not require any "mediation" by less reliable political actors to get access to police or legal protection. Criminals often pay bribes directly to public officials who can offer them information and protection: this is the case of drug trafficking organizations in Colombia, where "police are paid to provide information on planned raids, when arrests will occur, and how investigations will proceed. Prosecutors are bribed not to prosecute, judges not to convict, and penal officials not to detain criminals and terrorists who do end up in jail" (Thachuk 2005: 146).

Bribes could be (and sometimes actually are) demanded of Mafiosi groups by more stable political actors, as a component of "symbiotic" interplay. However, as soon as the time horizon of their interaction widens, there is a common interest among political and criminal actors—who may in the meantime develop good reason to trust each other—in avoiding the risky transmission of assets (such as bribes) that can be fairly easily detected by control agencies. The common long-term expectations of their interaction allow for a wider range of more "elusive," but very important, resources—capacity of mobilization of electoral support, political pressure to be shielded from police action, judicial inquiries, etc.—to become crucial.

Political Gate Keeping and Occasional Exchanges with Criminal Networks

In the previous paragraphs we have considered the effects of the presence of a criminal group that operates as a *protection firm*, a supplier of guarantees and enforcer of the fragile rights at stake in social, political, and economic interactions, tending to be monopolistic in its sphere of illegal activities.[18] In our view, the four main Italian criminal organizations can be located within the first two cells of table 8.1 in terms of their relationships with the political and electoral process in South Italy.

In other contexts, however, the criminal group may resemble a more dispersed network of criminal actors. When in very competitive criminal environments weaker criminal gangs—without the organizational capacity to credibly propose and enforce vote-buying—encounter stable political protectors, there is an incentive for the latter to adopt opportunistic or exploitative strategies. On the other hand, criminals' demands for protection from political actors in administrative affairs or judicial procedures emerge here, and might be paid through bribes (or other valuable resources). Politicians in this case have the power to choose which among competing criminal groups should have the opportunity to benefit from the allocation of public resources, therefore favoring the criminal group they choose as ally with a sometimes crucial supplementary asset. If such a "gate keeping" role, preferentially granted to a criminal actor, operates effectively, the latter may in fact derive from it—besides economic profits—a monopolistic advantage over its criminal competitors that may be used to become a more reliable regulator, also in the political market.

This is the case, for instance, when several criminal gangs manage the production, distribution, and selling of illegal commodities (drugs, imitation goods, contaminated products, etc.), or the exercise of illegal activities (smuggling, prostitution, gambling, dangerous waste disposal, etc.) in a disordered environment, without any "criminal authority" capable of regulating illicit activities and solving quarrels; or when formerly operative protection firms—due to state prosecution or defeats in a criminal war—are paralyzed or ineffective in their activities of contract enforcement, dispute arbitration, and the guaranteeing of contested rights. In this case, too, the time perspective of the criminal organization shrinks, and so therefore does its credibility as a supplier of protection—which usually requires trust in the protector's capability to secure his services in an undefined number of contingencies and in an extended time span. Relationships with public agents and political actors thus reflect a different nature of the services demanded and supplied by criminal actors, as well as an increase in the discount rate applied to future expected payments, cheating becomes more profitable and reputational assets lose some value. While political protection may be more greedily demanded by criminal actors, there are less *political* resources available to purchase it, and political counterparts are presumably less interested in entering into a business involving long-lasting relationships and the consent mobilization of criminal

---

[18] According to Schelling (1984: 182–3), organized crime can be distinguished from other forms of criminality precisely by its tendency to monopolize, regulate—and enforce—exchanges in illegal markets.

gangs, since their involvement would imply extremely dangerous dealings with presumably ephemeral partners.

Faced with political counterparts that are strong enough, criminal networks may try to acquire some form of safeguard for their illicit affairs, offering money, also in the form of contributions to political activities. In Bulgaria, for instance, "violent entrepreneurs" leading small criminal networks (CSD 2011: 205) and political oligarchs managed their corrupt deals in this way:

> Organised crime groups most often employ political corruption in order to ensure freedom from inspections or regulatory oversight for their business operations in exchange for 'political contributions' to parties or individual political actors. These contributions are usually accomplished through legitimate companies and reliable intermediaries. The return on this 'investment' takes the form of appointing to key positions preliminarily agreed individuals designated by the 'investor'. (CSD 2009: 51)

Similarly, in Nigeria and Thailand "organized crime syndicates have allegedly backed candidates from political parties, and their support is sometimes even sought out by the national government," while in many cases party leaders consult with these "godfathers" to determine who should be nominated as candidate" (Thachuk 2005: 145).

This sort of "informal gate keeping" to the advantage of competing criminal groups, each offering economic resources, is possible when political actors show the capability to secure prolonged interactions with public structures whereby they extend their authority. For instance, in the attempt to influence the political agenda, discourage the police from investigating their activities, and influence the appointment and dismissal of judges and chiefs of police, "proceeds from illegal trafficking serve to finance political parties and election campaigns in South Eastern Europe, as the scale of criminal networks in the region requires strong political protection" (Transparency International 2008a: 6). In the most critical phases, politicians may simply wait until a new winning criminal counterpart emerges from a conflict. As stressed by repentant camorrista Pasquale Galasso: "With the passing of the years, I've understood that the entire sequence of murders which destroyed me and my family just like many others in the whole Campania region, ultimately plays into the hands of these politicians, who are prepared to sneak away and wait upon the winner, who he can then ally himself with for the running of business and votes" (APN:13).

A different model emerges instead when both political and criminal actors are unable to offer each other durable guarantees of reciprocally enforced protection contracts. Political and criminal spheres may then coexist with only limited interaction. Pessimistic expectations concerning future roles and strength do not, however, prevent other kinds of "exchange arrangements." In such cases, since both partners do not trust the other's capability to extend their contacts in a longer time span, they will tend to limit their transactions to relatively well-defined resources, possibly with tit-for-tat negotiations of rewards. Corruption is the most natural (and frequent) mode of interaction in this context: with bribes criminal actors acquire specific favors, influence over decision-making or privileged information from political (as well as administrative) agents. A reiteration of corrupt exchanges between several criminal gangs and political actors can represent a relatively stable outcome, however, even if participants do not project the prospects of their relationships beyond the near future. The benefits in this case are mainly confined to the economic dimension, with limited direct impact on the electoral and political sphere: in other words, political and criminal actors will less likely derive from their exchanges—more limited in their scope and in the amount of resources at stake—the "surplus" needed to evolve the more stable and authoritative roles of "protectors" by enlarging their spheres of activity beyond the sporadic advantages of corrupt deals.

When political and criminal environments are perceived as unstable and the time horizon of actors shrinks, contextual exchanges are preferred: economic resources are still available to criminal actors, who also typically need to launder their illicit profits. If all-purpose political financing is less probable, due to mistrust of the future utility of a medium or long-term deal, more circumscribed deals are possible. Criminal gangs in West Africa, for instance, are typically structured in a fluid, *project-based* form of organization: often an individual criminal "entrepreneur" invites junior relatives or dependents to join him as the illegal business develops, creating a network where family or ethnic links play a major role. Corruption is the ordinary way for criminal gangs to buy impunity: there are several examples of criminals bribing judges in Ghana (Unodc 2005: 7), while in South Africa "corruption of police forces is essential to organized crime for investigators to turn a blind eye to specific crimes, destroy evidence, provide information, assist in the registration of stolen vehicles, etc. Groups of warders also cooperate with criminal networks both inside and outside the prison. Many criminal networks run their activity through import/export companies and rely heavily on corrupt customs officials to mis-declare or undervalue their shipments" (Transparency International 2008a: 10). In China criminal gangs have emerged in the past decade, organized around the traditional businesses of gambling, prostitution, and drug dealing: later some set up "regular" companies with godfathers also performing the role of chief executive, and a quota of gangsters hired in each department. Large-scale corruption in sectors of criminal interest—huge infrastructural projects, among others—is one of the consequences. In the city of Chongqing, 4,893 suspected gangsters have been taken into custody, many of them city officials, including a former deputy police commissioner and the head of the city's justice bureau, who is suspected of having accumulated a fortune of over 100 million yuan (£10 million) in bribes, guaranteeing a protective umbrella that shielded the gangs from the authorities (*The Telegraph*, October 17, 2009). Criminal groups also regularly corrupted police officers in Rio de Janeiro: 30 were arrested in February 2011, among them the former deputy chief of Civil Police, in the so-called *Operação Guilhotina*; the accusations include receiving bribes from drugs and weapons traffickers, providing criminals with information, the protection of prostitution and illegal gambling, supporting militias, and reselling confiscated weapons and drugs (*Rio Times*, February 15, 2011). In the Netherlands, where organized crime can be described as "in transit," taking advantage of the country's role as an important logistical hub in several illegal trades and smuggling of goods, "low-level police corruption and information leakage related to drugs occasionally take place" (CSD 2011: 171).

A Triad boss operating in Malaysia in the illegal markets of prostitution, loan sharking, narcotics, and fake goods has a very pragmatic approach toward the corruption of politicians and police officers:

> If I want to operate on a particular street and ask a politician to ask the authorities not to disturb me, the politician might say: 'It's impossible to have zero arrests, so you can operate during certain hours and we will patrol after those hours'—so it's a win-win situation [...] . If someone betrays me personally ... I will get a few gang members together and beat him up until he's paralysed or he's a vegetable, but if the matter is really big then they'll be brought before my tai ko for a trial. If my tai ko asks us to deal with someone, even if we kill that person, we won't be worried, because if the police arrest us, my tai ko will get me out. Last time I was taken in the front door of the [police] lock-up, and right away I walked out of the back door. (*BBC News*, September 5, 2005)

Bribe payments connote more or less sporadic deals between political agents and the corrupting criminal organization, as in the case of northern or central regions of Italy, where criminal organizations export some of their financial assets and economic interests. When criminal organizations have to move in a potentially more hostile and unfamiliar political environment, they may entrust entrepreneurs with recycling their money through real estate and other affairs, or with mediating their relationships with public actors. For instance, an entrepreneur whose firms reinvested 'Ndrangheta capital in real estate in Milan paid bipartisan bribes to at least two center-left and center-right political administrators in a nearby municipality to obtain permits and influence urban planning. The entrepreneur had also paid dinners to a couple of regional councilors during political events (R-Milan, March 10, 2010).

Some Concluding Remarks

In Southern Italy the deep-rooted presence of criminal organizations, with interests ranging from traditional illicit trafficking to public contracting, licensing, real estate deals, and so on, has created a wide set of opportunities to establish cooperative interaction with political actors. A complex system of exchanges developed, involving frequent contacts between the Mafia and politicians, where the Mafia offered votes and protection in return for public contracts and impunity, with money flows also used to buy specific resources. As we have shown, a relevant resource at stake here is protection, that is, services that both criminal and political actors—as "protection agencies"—may supply in order to decrease the other's uncertainty over future prospects, solve disputes, and avoid cheating and the disclosure of illicit deals in their respective spheres of activity. The time horizons of their expected relationships therefore expand, while the resources exchanged can more easily include votes, electoral support, and political participation. Money and financial support are not the only available—and often not even the most advantageous—exchange commodities in this longer-term contractual perspective.

We based our analysis on the Italian case, where criminal organizations are closer to the ideal type of the "protection firm"; as a result most data we found is accommodated within the symbiotic and substitution/colonization models. We have also noted that in several situations, especially in the south of Italy, criminal organizations had a territorial control that allowed them to provide votes, rather than the money to buy them. A relation of reciprocal protection developed between a centralized criminal organization and a centralized party in power. In other cases, however, organized crime intervened in competitive electoral competitions where competition was personalized rather than ideological, and Mafia support did not scandalize the public (it was indeed often displayed proudly by the protected candidates in order to strengthen their reputation of power).

Exchanges between politicians and organized crime are influenced by the types of markets organized crime is interested in. In the Italian case, in particular, the involvement of organized crime in public contracts strengthened the relations between the various Mafia, 'Ndrangheta and camorra actors and the politicians that controlled public contracts. In this context, Mafia activity, entrepreneurs' collusive activities, and corrupt exchanges concern different resources. Mafia organizations produce and sell private protection services in contexts where the pressure of extortion, the weakness of relationships of trust, and the illegal or informal nature of relations generate a demand for enforcing contracts and rules of conduct, sanctioning the acceptable ways of employing the resources at stake in political and economic markets and in social relations.

Two illegal markets in which a demand for protection arises are the corruption market and the market for collusive tender arrangements. In the former, property rights over political revenue, generated by decisions or information connected with the exercise of public authority, are exchanged (Vannucci 1997b). In the latter, a restrictive arrangement for competition is created between entrepreneurs who trade agreed offers, or abstention from bidding processes, against promises for the reciprocation of such conduct in the future. Although they are logically different, the activities of individuals employed in collusive exchanges and corruption do have an area in common, a "common market" in which public administrators, Mafiosi, and politicians offer and demand guarantees for protecting agreements and claims accrued in the different exchange arenas. The availability of the services provided in each of these markets actually increases expected profits and reduces "production costs" in others. This symbiosis is evident in the case of Mafia protection, which attenuates information costs, the costs of enforcing cartel agreements, and the transaction costs of corruption. At the same time, the protection provided to Mafiosi by politicians in exchange for bribes reinforces the Mafiosi's hopes of impunity by increasing the time horizon of activities and improving the quality of services offered, and thus reinforcing expectations of fulfillment among the colluding entrepreneurs.

Finally, the success of the cartels that share out the resources bound for public tenders allows the draining of greater sums from public accounts, by redistributing money into the exchange network and assuring Mafiosi of another channel of communicating with individuals dealing with decision-making hubs in public administration.

The Mafia thereby ensures a regulation of corruption and collusive agreements that allows for the development of transactions along two axis. The first, horizontal, axis ensures that illegal exchanges are commonplace and that they affect every contract without exception. According to Siino, "all bidding processes were rigged, all of them, none excluded, from those worth a hundred million up to those worth a hundred billion" (TPAS). The second line of development, the vertical axis, affects the different phases of the tender procedure. Mafia-like organizations, when operating in the public procurement process,

> act and organize the infiltration before the bidding procedure begins. In fact, they act before the design of the bid and the awarding procedures in order to: *control the businesses* that are to be the winners of the procedure [...]; *control the raw materials* (e.g., concrete) [...]; *set up collusive/corruptive relations with white collars and professionals*, such as lawyers, accountants and notaries, who will acts as facilitators in the setting up of new 'clean' business and the bypassing of legislative rules and obligations: *set up collusive/corruptive relations with public officials* in order to tailor the bids. (Savona 2010: 145)

The Mafia "governance" of exchanges intervenes at the bottom, guaranteeing the stability of political equilibria between individuals who sanction the criteria for allocating resources and delegating roles of public authority (i.e., the presentation of projects in electoral programs or the funding of campaigns), but also in the subsequent award phase, blocking interventions by investigative organs and technicians, to bypass problems in the contract execution or in the quality checks. Furthermore, greater *stability* in the corruption system and collusive agreements is guaranteed, since Mafia protection—as well as incentivizing fulfillment— discourages denunciations and reinforces omertà. As a company's area manager for Sicily observes:

> the system of tender in Sicily works like it does in all of Italy. The difference is that in Sicily there is more discipline. What does that mean? It means that in Sicily, contrarily to what happens in the rest of Italy, somebody sometimes is killed and discipline is a consequence of that. (TPBU:127)

Through this credible threat of violence, which shapes the expectations of cartel participants and potential competitors, "racketeers provide a reputational barrier to entry. Entrants must be concerned that they will not be the target of retaliation by racketeers." Moreover, reputation must be sporadically reaffirmed: "both in New York and Sicily an occasional killing or act of violence has been required to discipline a cartel member. Though these acts are situation specific, they also serve to enhance the reputation of the mafia and augment the reputational barrier" (Gambetta and Reuter 1995: 129–30). In the construction industry in New York, "corruption is supported by intimidation and violence. The presence of so many known organized crime figures in the industry makes the explicit threat of violence credible and the implicit threat of violence sufficient. Actual violence is only rarely necessary; but it materializes from time to time to punish uncooperative contractors, union reformers, or rival racketeers" (OCTF 1990: 31). Strong in this resource, the Mafia regulation of the Sicilian public procurement emerged from the judicial inquiries almost unscathed, making sure that the entrepreneurs involved generally maintained an obstinate silence (TPBA: 5). The protection provided by criminal organizations, in fact, made the corruption market more resistant to both internal quarrels and judicial inquests.

Chapter 9
Snowball Effects:
How Corruption May Become Endemic

The confessions made to Italian judicial investigators by T., whose outstanding career as a would-be middleman was abruptly interrupted by his arrest in 2009, offer a clear picture of how political processes and decision-making can be "endogenously" conditioned by expected opportunities for corruption in a hidden underworld where personal relations and values are shaped by prospects of illegal enrichment. T. describes his consistent initial investment in connections and the building of contacts, which can be particularly expensive when the middleman aspires to the highest levels of intermediation and must therefore satisfy potential partners' secret tastes:

> I wanted to meet President Berlusconi and therefore I had to bear considerable expenses in order to get to be one of his intimate acquaintances. Being aware of his interest in women I introduced girls to him telling him they were my friends, concealing the fact that I sometimes paid them. I asked him to introduce me to the person responsible at national level for civil defense, Guido Bertolaso, since I wanted a friend of mine, with whom I had reached a collaboration agreement, to have an opportunity to illustrate to him the qualities of his industrial group, with the prospect of obtaining future contracts. One evening President Berlusconi introduced me to Bertolaso […] . I want to state that the use of prostitutes and cocaine is related to my project of creating a network of connivance within the public administration, since at that time I believed that girls and cocaine were the key to success in high society. (*Corriere della Sera*, September 9, 2009)

Delivering "girls and cocaine" to public administrators was not an easy business, however. It was a difficult and costly task. The girls should not be perceived as prostitutes by beneficiaries, for instance. Therefore, in a dizzying series of meetings and dates, T. at times had some difficulty in providing new girls. Sometimes, he said, he rewarded the escorts with €1,000 when they stayed the night at the president of the Council of Ministers' residence, or when they were expected to do so. Some other precautions were also necessary: "When I accompanied the girls to Palazzo Grazioli [Berlusconi's house] I got them to sit in the backseat since my car's rear windows were tinted after having had them replaced in September 2008, if I remember correctly. This trick was to avoid journalists and others looking into the car. [...] When I drew nearer to Palazzo Grazioli, I informed a security officer of my arrival and then once I reached the front door the first security guard informed others of our arrival" (*Corriere della Sera*, September 9, 2009).

Just like any other entrepreneur, T.—as far as he specialized in illegal activities—also responded to "profit" signals and perceived earning opportunities in that environment. He invested a considerable amount of time and energy in acquiring skills and abilities—knowledge, trust, friendship, but also the power to blackmail—that would allow him to control key resources in exchanges with administrators and politicians at the highest institutional levels. In his account, he used the same strategy toward the president of the Council of Ministers as he had already successfully applied with public administrators in Apulia, his initial center of commercial interest. In building his series of contacts in Apulia, drugs, as well as prostitution, also played a crucial role: "I admit that I knew that A. was an escort and I paid her to carry out sexual services for third parties. [...] On the occasion of a party at my house I offered her cocaine free of charge." T. expanded his network of contacts thanks to these "sexual bribes," also acquiring *credibility* and *visibility* among future business partners, and in particular consultants in the hospitals his company sold medical prosthetics to:

> The attention [payment of escort's sexual services] I gave to X led to him presenting me to doctor Y, administrative director of the health authority in Lecce. I had told X, the former Vice-President of Puglia, of the reasons I was interested in meeting doctor Y, which was the acceleration of payments for the services carried out by my companies and the fulfilment of a deliberation taken about the purchase of operating tables. I know that X represented my needs to doctor Y several times and I spoke about it in person with Doctor Y himself. The payments occurred, even if late, the same for the resolution. Attending X was especially useful for me in getting visibility in the eyes of the consultants. (*Corriere della Sera*, September 9, 2009)

Middlemen are not selected on the basis of their political allegiances—T. prefers administrators from the center-left in Puglia and from the center-right in Rome—but on the basis of their willingness to enter into the network of relations controlled by the entrepreneur-mediator. His activity is in some ways similar to that of a lobbyist: he makes funds available to business partners, organizes election dinners attended by political representatives and consultants, and provides drivers and cars when needed. The additional resource is his willingness to act unscrupulously, for example, by crediting a health authority official with "a sum of money proportional to the number of patients invited, a series of maximalist family physicians who will send their own patients to the centres of B. for specialist visits in the orthopaedic sector so that she could thereafter send those patients to the clinic presided over by professor P. and therefore provide an increase in our provisions to the clinic" (*Corriere della Sera*, September 9, 2009).

In summary, in this corruptor-middleman's career we notice, (i) the high "start-up costs" for his illegal activity, (ii) consistent investment to acquire the necessary "skills of illegality" and the necessary information capital, contacts, and trust, (iii) the adoption of coherent entrepreneurial strategies with the expectation that corruption—even through "girls and cocaine"—is the most effective strategy to achieve success in that environment, and (iv) the commitment of a series of coordination mechanisms between the several actors involved in the illegal network. As we show in this chapter, this concerns some of the factors that feed the hidden growth dynamics of corruption networks.

The dynamics of corruption

The mechanisms described in chapters 2 and 3 constitute the *hidden motor* of corruption, which, through the transmission chain of many individuals' decisions, simplifies, encourages, morally justifies, and socially legitimizes their choice to pay or accept bribes. Strong economic incentives and weak moral constraints are the combined factors that explain the wide diffusion of corrupt exchanges in some societies and countries. The combination of poor profit-making opportunities and strong public ethics, on the other hand, is the ideal deterrent to the development of corruption in other social settings.

But the "equilibria" of corruption are by their very nature diverse and changeable. Corruption is indeed a dynamic phenomenon. To successfully occur, the corrupt exchange requires the presence of particular social relationships that support the formation of a minimum level of reciprocal trust between partners and guarantee protection from risks. But during the transaction and following its conclusion, expectations change and new relationships develop, the network of complicity and connivance can widen to further circles of individuals, and the psychic uneasiness with illegality can fade. In other words, with a critical diffusion threshold breached and particular decisional centers "won over" thanks to the presence of actors who are sensitive to the lure of bribes, corruption can generate positive feedback effects.[1] For instance, even if some amount of *coercive pressure* may at first be useful to push citizens and entrepreneurs to pay bribes to get privileged access to unpredictable decision-making procedures, the mere existence of corruptors who provide protection to avoid bottlenecks in regulation and some degree of certainty in bypassing red-tape increases delays, unpredictability, and the costs incurred by noncorrupting individuals, who are therefore encouraged to resort to bribes themselves. According to an African informant, "most people will be doing it involuntarily, because if you look at the institutions which are taking the bribes, it's the police which means they are in a situation where they are threatened with some sort of punishment or some sort of pain if they do not pay the bribes. There's a little bit of coercion in it, but there's also the element that people are trying to maybe skip the queue or save time or whatever by paying bribes." A

---

[1] The spontaneous reproduction and adaptation of systemic corruption through positive feedback effects does not exclude that its foundations may be imputed to a different mechanism, for instance, the intentional activities of some corrupt agents who have voluntarily shaped a "corrupt-vulnerable" administrative and political environment. As Thelen (2003: 209) emphasizes, "factors responsible for the genesis of an institution may not be the same as those that sustain it over time."

Ugandan public official explains, "people have this idea in their head that if you are going to that office, you have to pay some money to get a service. Everyone has that, even me. [...] Maybe I am promoting it, but if you don't do it you will lose. It will be at your own cost" (cit. in Perrson et al. 2010, 16–7).

If not tackled adequately, corruption thus ends by permeating whole sectors of government, public administration, civil society, and the economic system. Behind this large-scale reproduction ultimately lie the establishment of values, expectations, and standards of conduct that penalize "honest" behavior and almost explicitly encourage and support behavior favorable to corruption (Elster 1989a: 268).

Of course, an inverse path is also possible. When the presence of corruption is so sporadic that actors' expectations encourage them to avoid the risks inherent in getting involved, a guilty conscience and social stigma reinforce the pressure toward law-abiding behavior. "Honest" government leaders put strict repression policies in place and the convenience of resorting to bribery tends to decrease. In the socially "virtuous" outcome that emerges, the marginalization of corruption is a precondition for avoiding its appearance in the political and social realm. Two opposite dynamics can thus occur depending on the combination of initial conditions or casual factors.

In other words, in the development of corruption, features are present that can make its evolution *path dependent.*[2] Strong discrepancies in the spread of perceived—and practiced—corruption in countries that have similar legal systems, analogous judicial organization, and equivalent levels of economic development can be explained as the result of the progressive achievement of diffusive or deterrent mechanisms, as well as less or more effective governance structures for illegal exchanges. Several outcomes—each with different levels of corruption—may in fact emerge as equilibria within the same institutional setting.

The timing of events or their sequencing—for example, which political figures assert themselves in a particularly uncertain election, or which anti-corruption or corruption-enhancing measures are approved and implemented first—can be of great importance in determining the level of diffusion of corruption. The hard-won victory of a populist kleptocrat, for instance, can generate effects on the social tolerance of corruption and its practice that are difficult to reverse in following decades.

The evolution of corruption is punctuated by particular events that remodel the expectations of important actors and provide a springboard toward a different

---

2   Path dependency does not imply simply that "history matters," and that events that occurred at time t influence in general terms those occurring later, at time $t+1$, $t+2$, etc., but more specifically that the costs of leaving a certain path are higher as times passes: "This conception of path dependence, in which preceding steps in a particular direction induce further movements in the same direction, is well captured by the idea of increasing returns. In an increasing returns process, the probability of further steps along the same path increases with each move down that path. This is because the relative benefits of the current activity compared with other possible options increase over time" (Pierson 2000: 252).

equilibrium during critical moments or junctures. The further a certain path has been trod, the more difficult it is to modify the resulting outcome. For example, the so-called judges' revolution of Clean Hands in 1992 produced hope in Italy—at least in the short-term—that a break with the past of pervasive corruption was taking place, but thereafter the resilience tied to the heredity of beliefs and skills related to corrupt activities won through, carrying the practice of corruption down the same old path (Vannucci 2009; Porta and Vannucci 2011).

A sort of "snowball effect" therefore accompanies the embedding of interests, values, knowledge, and expectations favoring the expansion of corruption, while, on the contrary, the presence of unfavorable conditions increasingly dries up its fertile ground. The effects of widely practiced corruption—or honesty—generate vicious or virtuous circles of self-reinforcing activities, ceteris paribus making corrupt or honest behavior even more attractive for the next round. Some typical aspects of these occult activities facilitate this evolution, making corruption *endemic or systemic* under some conditions and *marginal* under others.

In empirical analysis, different   political, social, and economic macro-variables have been identified that can act as both *facilitating factors* and *possible consequences* of corruption diffusion. Their presence is thereby associated with a possible loop of cumulative causation that invests "overall" levels of corruption in a country, incrementally facilitating or obstructing its diffusion over the course of time. To provide some examples,

1. *Low levels of freedom of information*→ *greater corruption* (weaker controls and political sanctions in the event of exposure to the public)→ *further limitation of the freedom of the press* (to reduce the risks of exposing illegal government activities to the public)[3]

2. High *levels of black economy*→ *greater corruption* (as an instrument for eluding controls)→ *further black economy growth*[4]

3. Shor*tage of social capital and confidence in institutions*→ *greater corruption* (higher demand for particularistic advantages and weak control over public decisions)→ *less public trust in institutions and public administrators*[5]

4. Low *levels of education*→ *greater corruption* (weaker public and political controls over public administrators→ *less public investments in education* (corrupt politicians have an interest in investing less in education than in sectors such as infrastructure, military, etc.)[6]

The mechanisms considered in this chapter are of a different type. More than on macro-causes, we concentrate on meso- and micro-level mechanisms

---

[3]   Cfr. Brunetti and Weder (2003); Besley and Prat (2006). Freille et al. (2007).

[4]   Cfr. Buhen and Schneider (2007); Dreher and Schneider (2010).

[5]   Cfr. Bjørnskov and Paldam (2005); Uslaner (2005).

[6]   Cfr. Arnone and Iliopulos (2005).

to show how some processes of corruption diffusion can display a growing output within *specific* areas and sectors of political and administrative activity, thanks to decisions, expectations, and the learning paths of particular actors and organizations.

A first set of mechanisms reflects the decisions of some actors who, when placed in key positions, *intentionally* introduce conditions to make corruption more convenient and less risky into the political system, into the market, or into some areas of public intervention in accordance with their own interests. In this sense, the consolidation of a high-corruption equilibrium is to a certain extent the result of an "engineering" project. The informal norms regulating it result, in other words, from an "organized order" in which it is possible to identify one or more material makers (a kleptocrat, a corrupt government leader, a high-level bureaucrat, etc.) and which uses its own enforcement mechanisms.

On the other hand, other mechanisms generate a kind of "spontaneous order" in the corruption system and emerge from the combination of actions by self-interested individuals who do not, however, intentionally aim at creating them. In these cases, consolidating the tangle of rules governing the actions of corrupt and corrupting individuals appears to be, in the descriptions of its protagonists, a process of spontaneous evolution of rules, to use Hayek's expression. Conforming to these rules of conduct, they unwittingly gain desirable outcomes *for themselves*—such as the *organized* functioning of the corruption market—from which they can profit but that are not intentionally prearranged. But conforming to the rules is worth it for everyone because, given the (expected) corrupt decisions of other actors, this appears to be their preferred option, which consolidates converging expectations, reduces the elevated "fixed costs" of corruption, and takes full advantage of the knowledge and skills of acquired illegalities. These mechanisms are, in other words, "the forces making a spontaneous order," that allow individuals in corruption networks of different sizes to collaborate more or less consciously (Hayek 1973: 43–4). Thus, an entrepreneur from Milan accused of paying bribes for many years describes, with somewhat twisted words, the development of the system, resulting from the *actions* but not the *intentions* of the individuals involved:

> Here we found ourselves in a really perverse situation, so at a certain point we found ourselves enveloped in the phenomenon, in a system which had become unsustainable. As we left off, it's not like between one day and the next we said 'right, now we need to ... ' The events evolved one step at a time and we arrived at a situation like the one which burst. (*Un giorno in pretura-Rai 3*, February 22, 1993)

Through these mechanisms, a sort of "invisible hand" seems to make corruption feed upon itself, without any conscious design by actors involved, along a path of pervasive illegality. Moreover, the "grabbing hand" of corrupt administrators and private actors fuels these processes, generating additional appropriable rents and weakening controls in different contexts of more or less organized corruption (Shleifer and Vishny 1999).

Intentional Inputs to the Growth of Corruption

The first positive feedback mechanism of corruption is based on the *interests* of administrators who are personally corrupt or collude with corrupt ones, particularly those who are already specialized in such activities, to consolidate the most favorable conditions for the safe and profitable practice of corruption—at the level of regulation, administrative practice, and social values—through their decisions and deliberations. As Pierson observes, "Actors may utilize political authority to change the rules of the game (both formal institutions and various public policies) to enhance their power. These changes may not only shift the rules in their favor, but increase their own capacity for political action while diminishing those of their rivals" (Pierson 2004: 36). Corrupt actors can interestedly produce changes in the rules of the game that enlarge occasions for bribery, and reduce or weaken controls.

At least two paths can be identified, depending on the characteristics of the political regime. In a closed political system void of institutional counterweights and effective controls over autocratic ruler's decisions, there are only weak internal bonds to counterbalance the institutional changes tied to satisfying the corrupt political decision-maker's interests. Corruption then becomes *endogenous*—that is, a constitutive component of the political process.

We thereby move closer to the model of "monopolistic corruption" described by Shleifer and Vishny: "In the case of an economywide bribe-collecting monopolist, such as Marcos, corruption is similar to revenue-maximizing taxation." Similar to a "stationary bandit," the kleptocrat acts like a private monopolist, maximizing his personal profits with a systematic spoliation of resources produced by the economic system.[7] Like any private monopoly, as a consequence, the kleptocratic state restricts the output of the economy. Unlike taxation, however, the illegality of the corrupt kleptocrat's activities produces further distortive effects: "Government officials will use their powers to induce substitution into the goods on which bribes can be more easily collected without detection. For example, officials might ban some imports to induce substitution into others. Or they might prohibit entry of some firms to raise bribe revenues into others" (Shleifer and Vishny 1999: 105).

---

[7]   As Olson (1993: 568) observes, the "grasping hand " of a stationary bandit is rationally preferred by his subjects to the anarchist condition deriving from the alternation of several roving bandits: "If the stationary bandit successfully monopolized the theft in his domain, then his victims do not need to worry about the thefts by others. If he steals only through regular taxation, then his subjects know that they can keep whatever proportion of their output is left after they have paid their taxes. Since all of the settled bandit's victims area source of tax payments, he also has an incentive to prohibit the murder or maiming of his subjects." Similarly, the presence of a monopolistic kleptocrat can be preferred by his victims to generalized "anarchist" corruption, since the kleptocrat has an interest in prohibiting further bribe requests, guaranteeing some degree of certainty on the amounts to be paid, and letting his subjects produce and accumulate assets (a percentage of which will be seized by him).

It is precisely this "distortive effect," the product of intentional inputs into corruption, that takes place in principal government decisions and public policy. Indeed, in these cases the autocratic kleptocrat—as found in many African, Latin American, or Asian dictatorships—can plan the organization of all government activity, or at least its most profitable activities, from tax collection to the concession of natural resource extraction rights, in order to maximize corruption revenue, which he personally takes possession of, at most sharing it with a close circle of family members, oligarchs, and bureaucrats. In the Philippines, for instance, Marcos was not alone in gathering huge profits through corruption: "Entrenched oligarchs, their families, and their personal clients have engaged in pervasive corruption, inhibiting the growth of democratic forces while enriching themselves in both the public and the private sector" (Johnston 2008: 214). Corruption then becomes a systemic device used by the kleptocratic ruler to extract rents from the population. To solve problems of internal cohesion, in fact, "corrupt offices are created to satisfy a leader's desire to foster loyalty through patronage" (Charap and Harm 1999: 5). The entire state structure is managed like private property, in accordance with the patrimonialistic state model, where the government leader's entitlement over the group becomes an absolute personal power, similar to entitlement over any economic good susceptible to possession and realizable in its value (Weber, [1922]). In a "predatory state" the attributes of sovereignty (laws, military, taxes, courts, etc.) become instruments in the hands of the government leader, who can employ them at his pleasure to create rents and confiscate resources produced by the economic system or deriving from the sale of natural resources as personal property (Lundahl 1997).

Only rarely, however, is the kleptocrat able to maximize his personal wealth without constraints, due to several de facto limits on the exercise of his power, such as an imperfect control over the economy, a weak and disloyal civil service, and a vague and confusing legal framework: "The weak kleptocrat is likely to favour a bloated and inefficient state to maximize corrupt possibilities [...] . As the cases of Stroessner, Mobutu, and the Duvaliers demonstrate, a corrupt ruler influences not only the size of the government but also the mixture of taxes and spending priorities. Taxes, regulations, subsidies, price fixing, and privatization are examples of activities that kleptocrats can manipulate for their own benefit" (Rose-Ackerman 1999: 116–7). The former ruling elites of Paraguay, Zaire (now the Democratic Republic of Congo), and Haiti exemplify the tendency of kleptocrats to consider and manage the whole regulatory and administrative system—with its inefficiencies, bottlenecks, and dissipation of resources— as a source of private profit. Nevertheless, the approximate amount of money embezzled into private bank accounts by corrupt political leaders can be large, both in absolute and relative terms. Consider the following examples: Mohamed Suharto (President of Indonesia, 1967–1998) held accounts for US$15–35 billion; Ferdinand Marcos (President of Philippines, 1972–1986), US$5–10 billion; Mobutu Sese Seko (President of Zaire, 1965–1997), US$5–10 billion; and Sani Abacha (President of Nigeria, 1993–1998), US$2–5 billion (TI-2004). After the popular uprising in January 2011, the Tunisian kleptocrat Ben Ali and his wife escaped abroad with gold bullion: the family's wealth is estimated at US$10–12 billion, including real estate and other properties in France, and bank accounts in Switzerland (*Bloomberg*, January 21, 2011).

Milder forms of corruption-enhancing institutional changes may also be implemented in more democratic and pluralist political systems. In this case, the "winner-takes-all" quality of electoral mechanisms comes into play when a leader or a ruling elite has a direct interest, due to his/her personal or party involvement in corruption practices, to foster—even if not openly— rules increasing political or private opportunities to gather illicit profits, as well as guarantees of immunity. The longer the time span over which corrupt political leaders' interests have influenced policies and institutional activities, the greater the impact on the moral costs and the expected benefits of illegal activities. The spectacle of leaders who are suspected of being involved in corrupt activities, and who make such practices remunerative and less dangerous through their government decisions, risks tarnishing the very same moral resilience of those groups who are closest or most sensitive to government leaders' charisma, as exemplified in Gregorio Magno's saying—"Corruptio Optimi Pessima"—*the corruption of the best is the worst*. Moreover, political and bureaucratic careers may be positively influenced by the redistribution of bribes toward hierarchical superiors, inducing an upward expansion of corruption. For instance, in Indonesian police corruption, "because the money is usually distributed to the officer's supervisors, police officers with a good nose for potentially lucrative cases tend to rise quickly in the force" (*New York Times*, December 19, 2009).

In the absence of counterweights, electoral dynamics and the dynmaics of administrative careers thus become vulnerable to the effects of corruption, since the reinvestment of the proceeds of bribes in political competition facilitates the success of aspiring candidates for government or facilitates promotion within bureaucratic hierarchies. Corruption amplifies power asymmetries, whose origins are hidden from public view and scrutiny: "Thus, positive feedback over time simultaneously increases power asymmetries and renders power relations less visible. The allocation of political authority to particular actors is a key resource of this kind of positive feedback" (Pierson 2000: 259). Corrupt political actors may in fact use their authority in critical public roles to generate changes in the "rules of the game"—in public policies, laws, regulation, the activities of control agencies—deliberately designed to enhance their corruption rents, as well as their expectations of impunity, widening at the same time disparities in political, as well as mass-mediatic and economic, resources among contending leaders and parties. The "climate of corruption" is also fostered by explicit statements with a symbolic impact on the framing of corruption. We may consider here the example of a Bulgarian Minister of Healthcare, who publicly announced that "there is no corruption in public health institutions since a bribe up to 50 levs [about 10 percent of a doctor's salary] is a cultural norm and not a breach of any institutional, moral or legal norm," and that "a reform is needed that would allow the money given 'under the table' to be paid 'above the table'" (Dimitrov 2008: 60).

Measures that open the doors to better corruption opportunities are reported as the outputs of democratic political processes in a number of states. In Argentina, for instance, a law approved in May 2008 gave wide discretionary power to the executive branch over the judiciary. As a consequence, "executive appointment may compel acting judges to rule in a way that pleases the president" (TI-2009: 213). In Venezuela, a law on public contracting approved in March 2008 widened recourse to direct procurement— traditionally exposed to corrupt exchanges— beyond defense and national security to emergency cases or cases with a lack of multiple suppliers (TI-2009: 243). In the same year, the Korean Independent Commission Against Corruption was placed under the control of the prime minister (TI-2009: 295–6). In Nicaragua, "control over the legislative branch has enabled the two parties to steer through several laws that make it more difficult to tackle corruption" (TI-2006: 214). Naturally—seeing as the fight against corruption is not only the objective of public policies, but is balanced against other collective needs—it is difficult to directly associate measures of this kind with the interests of a leadership involved in corruption.

However, in some countries the link between corruption-enhancing measures and a democratic leadership involved in bribery scandals seems quite evident. In Italy, a symbolic "dividing line" in the institutional architecture can be drawn with the national elections of May 2001, won by the center-right coalition led by Silvio Berlusconi, who has been indicted for crimes of corruption on several occasions. From then on, a number of measures, often tailored on an ad hoc basis to the contingent legal needs of Prime Minister Berlusconi, were passed to restrain and weaken the impact of legal investigations into corruption (Vannucci 2009; della Porta and Vannucci 2011a). Media and public attention were diverted toward other issues, while the political class began to systematically condemn corruption investigations as a form of politically biased intrusion by judicial authorities in the political realm. The need for anticorruption policies completely disappeared from public debate and was eradicated from the political agenda. At the present time, "Italy does not have a coordinated anti-corruption programme. No methodology is currently in place to estimate the efficiency of anti-corruption measures specifically targeting public administration" (GRECO 2009: 28).

Legislative measures potentially encouraging corruption have in several cases been characterized by broad impact and ambition, as is evident in the general reform of corporate law and related offences that de facto de-criminalizes a number of offences related to false accounting; and in the law reducing the time limit specified by the statute of limitations, which has had a number of significant effects, since "a disquieting proportion of all prosecutions for corruption fail because of the expiry of the relevant time limit specified in the statute of limitations. [...] There was a high chance of the limitation period expiring before the trial could be concluded, even if the evidence was strong. This is a significant shortcoming which clearly undermines the efficiency and credibility of criminal law" (GRECO 2009: 15). The blurred and shifting line between legal and illegal conduct creates expectations of impunity, and therefore pushes toward further corruption: "What happens when politicians (such as Italy's premier, Silvio Berlusconi) change the law so that their previously 'illegal' practices of book-keeping are reclassified as legal?" (Haller and Shore 2005: 4).

On the "demand" side of new "rules of the game," we can instead take into account the activities of interest groups or companies that, as beneficiaries of favorable legislation, subsidies, concessions, or other privileges, invest in activities within the blurred boundary between *lobbying* and corruption, aimed at protecting or extending their revenues, favorable regulations, and privileged positions.

Large Fixed Costs in the Setting-Up of Corrupt Transactions

When there are large set-up costs involved in the start-up of a particular economic activity, whether of a legal or illegal nature, strong incentives are created to keep up investments in order to "spread" these high fixed costs over the proceeds obtained in a greater time span. The actors involved thus end up identifying more and more with the pursuit of this particular option, since the allure of alternatives diminishes and they remain "stuck" with their original decision (Arthur 1994: 112).

In this way, a powerful corruption diffusion mechanism is generated that encourages corrupt and corrupting individuals to proceed down the path of illegality where that path has been travelled in the past. Indeed, the *first* occasion of involvement in corruption has a very high fixed cost, which can be ascribed to the presence of many factors: (i) the expected sanction sharply increases from zero to a substantial penalty at the moment one "yields" to the allure of the first bribe, while involvement in further episodes involves proportionally lesser increases, (ii) the showing of remorse or guilt (the "moral cost" of corruption) is more psychologically linked to the initial episode rather than the "overall number" of acts of corruption, and (iii) the danger of tainting one's own honest reputation, of being branded corrupt or being ostracized by one's own social circle, results from that crucial first engagement in an illegal activity, which exposes a risk that did not previously exist.

A former mayor of Miami describes these sensations of uneasiness and risk by likening the betrayal of his own public duties to adultery: "I took my first bribe in my second term on the city commission. It's a terrible thing, like cheating on your wife for the first time" (cit. in Lambsdorff, 2007: 154). This similitude, indicating high psychological costs, is also used by other participants in the deal: "Corrupt business people habitually compare their habit to having an affair: no sooner have you given in to temptation than you are trapped in a world of secrecy and guilt" (*The Economist*, April 10, 2010). An Indian woman who paid 3,500 rupees to acquire a driver's license comments: "I felt awful that day. And yet the driver's licence was important to me. I didn't know how else to get it. I hate to live in India because I am scared I will come across such a situation again and feel helpless about it" (*AFP*, November 17, 2010). The suicide of Angelo Reyes, the former Armed Forces chief of staff and defense secretary of the Philippines, shows to what point self-justification may collapse after public exposure of involvement in a corruption scandal. In a last memorandum, he wrote,

> I speak the truth not to whistle-blow or to seek neither immunity nor protection
> nor to escape from any form of liability. As a matter of fact, I speak the truth
> to accept responsibility for whatever liability I may have. [...] I did not invent
> corruption. I walked into it. Perhaps my first fault was in having accepted aspects
> of it as a fact of life. (*Inquirer.net*, February 13, 2011)

The former mayor of Reggio Calabria states, "One time, while talking about those who take kickbacks, an entrepreneur theorized: 'For politicians, money is like drugs. Once you take it you can't get by without it. The first time is difficult. Then you need it like heroin, and you go asking for it'" (Licandro and Varano 1993: 47–8). The statement by a councilor from Milan arrested for corruption also describes "the tension and shame" at the time of his (presumed) first bribe: "I received a contribution I didn't ask for which left me motionless, unconvinced and which I clearly made a mistake in accepting. [...] I didn't even look him in the face, I wanted to get it over with, I wasn't accustomed" (*Corriere della Sera*, May 6, 2010: 23).

The repetition of corruption is facilitated by psychological processes of neutralization and self-legitimization, the acquisition of information and professional skills, and the building of hidden channels of communication and exchange. Once these set-up costs have been assumed, individuals are urged to carry on down the path of corruption. The costs of "socializing" for illegal activities, which is necessary within the corruption network at the time an exchange is carried out or else new actors will enter the scene, also lead in this direction. In this critical phase, there is a higher risk of misunderstandings or of being denounced, which can be limited by paying particular attention to contacts who aim to ease beginners' psychological discomfort as well as teach them the art of corruption, or practices and techniques for concealing illegal activities. This commitment initially requires a considerable expenditure of time and energy, both for the beginners and the actors "introducing" them to the rules of the game, but it carries the advantage of a greater ease of coordination, which subsequently bears positively on the pursuit of corruption activities.

A middleman, found guilty of corruption-related crimes in Turin, clearly explained that his attitude and abilities derived from a long process of socialization into the practice of corruption. Day-to-day experiences reinforced a value system that could be seen to be work:

> Having chosen a path you follow it through to the end, right or wrong. On mine I
> found people willing to be corrupted. Indeed it quickly taught me that if you did
> not learn how to corrupt others you would never be anybody, you would never
> be able to do business. One day when I have to explain to my son why his father
> went to jail that's exactly what I'll tell him, and I'll also explain that 90 per cent
> of the people he will find in front of him during any negotiation can be bribed.
> (*L'Espresso*, November 18, 1984: 38)

Once begun, corrupt activities may therefore feed upon themselves, since to cover "first-level" bribes further illegal payments become necessary—and are relatively less costly to manage—to corrupt inspectors and judges. In Turkey, for instance, a legal investigation in 2003 revealed that pharmaceutical companies had allegedly bribed doctors and hospital managers to use and prescribe specific brands. The owner of a "pharmaceutical company implicated in the procurement affair, had allegedly used a group of lawyers to bribe high-level justice officials, to obtain the release of family members that had been arrested" (TI-2005: 213).

Paradoxically, the same effect can accompany social stigma when corrupt and corrupting individuals meet following earlier investigations, denunciations, or convictions. Once labeled as corruptible or inclined to corrupt, they actually benefit from their "bad reputation." In India, for example, an online list of functionaries under trial for corruption rapidly became a useful guide to those who could easily be corrupted again (*The Economist*, January 28, 2010). For corrupt public agents, the expected cost of further involvement is thereby attenuated and career opportunities in aboveboard legal activities decline; on the other hand, incentives to continue their criminal career are strengthened (Opp 1989).[8] The risks of looking for available partners are also very high at the start of their criminal career, when they do not have accurate information on the reliability of opposite parties. Afterwards, however, individuals looking to get into the corruption system know they can find trusted middlemen in these individuals with a "bad reputation." This latter characteristic is indeed a lasting capital, resistant even to a seeming fall from grace. After his arrest for corruption, a fixer reveals, "The most incredible thing is that many people turned up or do turn up to ask me for advice and opinions, to the point where I almost feel like I never committed a crime" (*L'Espresso*, January 18, 1984: 42).

For that matter, entry into the corruption system also assumes an identification factor, such as implicit recognition of belonging to a group that accepts corruption as a "unit of measurement" of reciprocal power. As a politician from Milan observes,

> When your political referee accepts the quota of a bribe from your hands, it means that you have made another jump in quality. That transfer of money seals an unwritten pact, yet one which is at the base of politics [...] . You have entered alongside those that matter in your own right [...] . You feel like a member of a closed group, with everyone backing up everyone else. A kind of palace of power. By and large, the bribe is the consecration of your membership of the group. (Andreoli, 1993: 62)

---

[8] The *collective* "bad" reputation of all public administrators—following the stereotype of "they're all thieves anyway"—creates "stronger incentives for undertaking corrupt activities," establishing a vicious cycle even for new entrants so that new generations suffer from their predecessors' original sin (Tirole 1996: 3).

Coordination Effects in the Market for Corrupt Exchanges

Coordination effects "occur when the benefits an individual receives from a particular activity increases as others adopt the same option" (Pierson 2004: 24). Such effects may contribute to the diffusive dynamics of corruption, since any corrupt activity may be enhanced by its combination and "harmonization" with the corrupt conduct of others, fitting reciprocally. This mechanism configures some sort of indirect "network externality," as long as the expected benefit of corruption for an agent increases when more other agents are involved in it. The demand for corrupt exchanges may therefore be directly related to their diffusion. Over the course of time, a positive feedback loop comes to strengthen individual incentives for corruption and the extent of the network of corrupt agents at the same time.

Norms that regulate corrupt practices and exchanges in fact create an institutional matrix of informal and self-enforcing conventions that reduce transaction costs, make spontaneous fulfillment cheaper, and favor a happy ending to hidden exchanges. The "basic norm" of this invisible legal system sanctions the *unavoidability* of bribes, the rule that recourse to hidden exchange cannot be avoided in return for any "resource" of value obtainable from the public structure within the corruption network: contracts, licenses, concessions, the acceleration of procedural passages, reserved information, fiddled controls, milder sanctions, a range of cases across the whole spectrum of public activities.. An Italian entrepreneur states that "In the Public Society for Roads you have to pay bribes to virtually everyone, I mean from the ushers to the Minister, as well as parties appointing the managers [...] . The stream of bribes has been standardized for at least 20 years [...] . I can say this because I am in touch with countless entrepreneurs, all of whom have told me the same thing" (cit. in Davigo and Mannozzi 2007: 266–7). Similarly, in Bari, "one of the arms employed to induce the various entrepreneurs to fulfil the obligation of bribes is to convince them that no public contract avoided their control [of the corrupt politicians], to the point that the same companies manage to convince them that their economic survival is closely tied to this kind of symbiosis" (TRIB: 546). In the New York construction industry, similarly, "illegal payments flow from contractors to union officers and public officers. [...] Sometimes contractors claim not to know exactly why they pay; experience tells them that payoffs are necessary to assure that "things will run smoothly" (OCTF: 19).

Once established, coordination norms sanctioning the idea that corruption cannot be avoided apply as binding constraints to all those who enter the sphere of relationships with the state, those who promote and support them as well as those who do not. Several enforcement mechanisms, as shown in chapter 2, guarantee the fulfillment of obligations in the corruption market as well as its orderly functioning, pushing toward the "exit" of more honest or scrupulous agents. Some East European entrepreneurs, for instance, were so convinced that personal contacts and informal networks determine the allocation of public tenders in their countries that they did not feel like taking part. "Public procurements [...] I am not participating in these things [...] every second (maybe more) public procurement is not public—it is decided in advance"; "I personally ceased participating and only from time to time—for the sake of 'sport passion'—take part in such events and I see how deplorable the results are"; "There are no real tenders, all the tenders are staged and contacts are used there [...] that is why we no longer participate there—this is not a tender, this is an agreement," are the opinions of a few Czech and Bulgarian managers (Grødeland 2005: 65). In this case, reversal to a more "transparent" environment becomes less probable and more unattractive over time, as the self-reinforcing processes of socialization and selection of corrupt agents and the marginalization of honest ones come into play.

The positive network externality of corruption derives from the increased benefit that an agent may derive from it when the number of other agents involved in the same kind of activity increases (Liebowitz and Margolis 1994). In general, the higher the number of individuals practicing or tolerating corruption in a given context, the more (i) the costs of identifying an opposing party able to pay or accept a bribe decrease, since information circulates on who to pay, how much to pay and how to corrupt (or be corrupted),[9] (ii) the risks of incurring a denouncement from other equally involved agents decrease, (iii) the probability of avoiding sanctions increases—even if denounced—by corrupting a police officer or judge, (iv) the sense of guilt or fear of compromising one's own reputation fades, given the absence or weakness of the social stigma,[10] (v) the disadvantages against subjects trying to stay honest increase, and they thus become marginalized or excluded from decision-making centers, (vi) the difficulty in finding people ready to collaborate in revealing corruption increases, given that illegal activities are often interconnected,[11] and (vii) the countering action of the judiciary, who must initiate widespread controls and spend a growing amount of resources to try to break the wall of silence, is obstructed, making convictions of corrupted individuals less likely.

For these reasons, then, the growth of the extent of illegal activities ensures that even noncorrupt individuals are led to collude, or at least live with the corruption of others, especially if this allows them to gain political or economic advantages: bribe money channeled by political parties may come in useful, for example, for

---

[9]   For instance, in Georgia the diffusion of knowledge about bribery techniques lowered expected risks and shaped beliefs of widespread corruption: "As far as I know, everybody was doing that. In fact, through word of mouth communication, people would often share another information about the market bribe rate, i.e., how much money a particular public official was taking" (Levy 2007: 429).

[10]   In Georgia, where corruption "was *the norm*," "everybody was doing it, and that provided ethical and moral justification for our actions without feeling too much guilt or embarrassment about it" (Levy 2007: 430).

[11]   As Murphy et al. (1993: 409) observe, in rent-seeking activities, there is a natural "strength in numbers": "If only a few people steal or loot, they will get caught; but if many do, the probability of any one of them getting caught is much lower, and hence the returns to stealing or looting are higher."

paying for electoral campaigns—even for those who did not contributed to their collection. If honest administrators are scarce, entrepreneurs also have incentives to resort to these illegal practices.

The effects of coordination become particularly intense in the decision-making centers where corrupt and corrupting individuals have managed to design public decision-making and resource allocation processes that depend on the expected collection of bribes. Corruption must indeed be compatible with mechanisms, favoring the production within the public organization of valuable resources of exchange (favorable decisions, confidential information, protection, etc.) for potential partners. Increased recourse to corruption encourages changes in decision-making—or the preferential allocation of public resources through specific procedures—coherent with the success of illegal activities, which are rendered more profitable and less subject to the risk of exposure. In turn, this evolution tends to attract more corrupt agents within the network. In the words of an entrepreneur,

> It was a kind of habit. There was no particular cause. I considered it convenient, having heard that some others did it, to adjust to this procedure as well because I could have had advantages in terms of work funding and in general [...] . As that's how the system was, I preferred to be a part of the system as well. (*Panorama*, February 14, 1993: 61)

Increasing returns from coordinated illegal activities are not confined within the boundaries of specific areas of public intervention. As emphasized by North, even at a meso- and macro-level, "the interdependent web of an institutional matrix" may produce positive feedback effects (North 1990: 95), favoring the success of organizational structures deeply involved in corruption, which in turn produce new complementary rules favoring coordination and increasing their illegal profits. Organizations like parties, interest groups, bureaucratic structures, firms, and informal cliques are regularly involved in a wide set of political and administrative activities (political financing, electoral campaigns, lobbying, defining procedures for decision-making, etc.), which often induce the creation of new institutional arrangements, that is, original "rules of the game" in political and economic markets. Path dependence here operates at the level of the complementary configurations of these "rules of the game" and organizations. For example, an inefficient, arbitrary, or time-consuming procedural scheme, as well as a regulatory design that strictly limits competition within a certain market, or an opaque political finance regulation, may develop in a complementary and parallel manner with the coevolution of a corruption network due to the organization activity operating in both areas of visible—that is, public—and hidden interaction.

At the end of this process, when people hostile to corruption are marginalized or forced out of the system, and when the selection mechanisms of agents in public and private organizations are coherent with the informal legitimization codes of these practices, corruption seems like the most natural response to conform to the everyday decisions of others. A study on the Chittagong Port in Bangladesh, for instance, found that in 2004, "'tipping' for permission went without objection for so long that it had become institutionalized, with bribes paid in 100 per cent of cases for both IGMs [import documents] and EGMs [export documents]. [...] Importers bribed customs officials to delay the auction in order to take advantage of price fluctuations in the market" (TI-2006: 128). In a similar vein, a functionary from Milan retraces the evolution of his relations with an entrepreneur:

> I then got in touch with C., who I had friendly relations with and who I did favours for, not essentially for money, but out of friendship, even if in actual fact he did give me money [...] . Our environment is corrupt. That's a well known matter of fact. (PMI-DE, March 14, 2003: 3)

Similarly, entrepreneurs surrounded by more unscrupulous colleagues also witness a growth in problems and obstructions in their dealings with the state. An Afghan shopkeeper who pays about $2,000 in kickbacks to the customs office each time he ships a container from China describes the interplay of corrupt activities: "If you want to do business in Afghanistan, you must bribe people every step of the way, otherwise your business collapses. I think it seems almost impossible to root out corruption, because we can't live without it" (*Reuters*, November 25, 2009). Integrity is consequently discouraged: more than 40 percent of 350 CEOs of international firms said that they had lost new business at some point over the past five years because a rival had paid a bribe (*CFO.com*, March 1, 2007). This reconstruction of the real "rules" governing the allocation of public contracts in the cultural heritage sector was provided by an Italian entrepreneur:

> In 2004, four of the first five contests carried out were 'rigged', or in other words they had pre-determined winners, winners who habitually sell poor quality products [...] . Did I report it to the authorities? I tried, in 2000. After 9 court cases, between Tar and the State Council, we obtained a micro-compensation which did not even cover the legal bill. Meanwhile, those who usurped us for the job used it to obtain other contracts, which we obviously lost. [...] Everyone seemed aware of this dangerous moral drift and adapted to it, devising new forms of persuasion. Many of my colleagues resigned themselves to it and invited me to desist since it isn't possible to spend a whole life fighting an unequal war alone. (R, June 24, 2005: 18)

Learning by Corrupting (or Being Corrupted)

The corruption market is by its very nature opaque; contacts and transactions are risky. For this reason, knowledge acquired about its smooth functioning becomes precious and guarantees increasing returns from the continued use of these communication and exchange channels. To the extent that the value of their "assets"—like specialized knowledge, social relationships, and trust developed in illegal deals—are specific to corruption, agents have a strong incentive to continue corrupt activities, since it is more difficult—and costly—to reuse them in different contexts.

Corruption actors therefore tend to acquire and develop "skills of illegality" over the course of their activity:

> It is a case, for those possessing it, of knowing how to act under the threat of sanctions, knowing how to chose the repaired paths, knowing how to cover your own back and how to protect yourself; but even more importantly having the most extensive and direct knowledge possible both of other people willing to participate in illegal transactions and people who, although not getting involved, occupy positions of authority which cover the areas within which the chances of such transactions are more common. (Pizzorno 1992: 23)

As North observes, individuals and organizations adapt to the "rules of the game" that determine a company's profit-making opportunities: "if the institutional framework rewards piracy then piratical organizations will come into existence" (North 1994: 361), and people will consequently invest in becoming "good pirates." And if existing formal and informal institutions provide incentives to become rich and powerful through corruption or illegal influence-trafficking, then politicians, entrepreneurs, bureaucrats, and citizens will invest in acquiring (and transmitting) knowledge, "professional" skills, and abilities useful to become (and meet) "good" corruptees or corrupters. With the repetition of their deals, agents learn how to enter and conclude corrupt exchanges more effectively, and their previous experiences tend to encourage further innovative moves in related activities (Pierson 2004: 24). Signals that large profits can be collected in sectors where corruption is rampant and personal contacts are the determinant of success generate an investment in the acquisition of similar skills, information, and personal relations. This is the testimony of a Senegal construction entrepreneur:

> Now, at the level of Senegal, everyone wants to be a building contractor, even the mechanic, even the shopkeeper [...] . Out of ten firms, only five are legitimate, and even these five, in general, they have problems because firstly the people who created these firms are not [...] in the profession. That is to say, a tailor, one bright day, he wakes up and creates his firm, so now he's a contractor. Of what? Of building. Through his good relations, advisers here and there, he gets hold of a contract. (Cit. in Blundo 2006: 251)

When personal experiences of bribes are not frequent, as in the case of more "transparent" countries, corruption expertise and know-how are not acquired directly, even if such competences would be useful and demanded, particularly to win competitions abroad. This could explain the striking content of the guidebook "A Little of This, a Little of That" published by the Finnish-Russian Chamber of Commerce in 2003 as a tool for Finnish entrepreneurs, which "outlines in detail instances in which bribes may be paid and gives examples of their size and kind" (TI-2006: 156).

Thanks to their previous experience and practice, individuals "learn by doing" in using illegal profit-making opportunities with minimal risk and maximal profit. They thereby introduce "innovations" into corrupt activities: new approach techniques, a coded and specialized language, safer mechanisms of bribe payment, and "concealed" decision-making procedures, which, for example, allow them and their representative to enlarge the scale at which societies of corruption are put into action. Moreover, special practices and covered procedures develop within companies, helping to camouflage their illegal affairs: according to an ex-manager, for instance, allegedly, in Siemens, "managers carefully signed Post-it notes that had been affixed to potentially incriminating documents so that they might later peel away evidence of their imprimatur if necessary. 'In this way, the signatories could elegantly remove signs of their involvement if it came to an investigation'" (*New York Times*, May 27, 2008).

Competence and skills on how to manage corrupt deals successfully are not merely learnt through experience. These abilities are also taught to collaborators and partners in order to spread a common expertise that minimizes the overall risk of exposure. An entrepreneur—under investigation for connections with the Calabrian Mafia—boasts in a taped conversation, "I am the mentor of I. [councillor for public works in a Northern Italy municipality], I taught him to collect bribes, but with grace, preferring more sophisticated rewards to simple kickbacks" (R-Milan, March 15, 2010). The preparation and handling of bribes also require skills in order to minimize the risk of denunciation:

> I opened the bag and bundles of 100.000 [*lire*] notes fell out. It was all perfectly prepared and I should know, I used to work in a bank; all used notes but none too damaged. Bills nobody could ever identify; it would have been impossible to trace them. An expert job. Whoever was responsible was a specialist; they really knew what they were doing. The bands on the money were as anonymous as the envelopes and the briefcase. Nobody could ever have proved anything. The whole thing betrayed solidity of organization, efficiency, shrewdness and professionalism. I thought to myself: 'These people do nothing else'. (Licandro and Varano 1993: 33)

When profitable opportunities in unproductive rent-seeking activities, such as corruption, appear in a society, we can forecast an increase in investments in the acquisition of abilities that can be used in that field. In interviews between two associates involved in the payment of a bribe for public contracts in the health authority in Puglia, for example, the obsessive concern to demonstrate their own ability to cultivate good relationships with politicians emerges, an activity that animates body and soul: "We must do business first and politics second," to recover "an investment made [...] we must move quickly," "this can't be overemphasised," "and there are three billion in there [...] I'm not joking" (TRBA1: 68–9).

Especially in social relationships with high levels of uncertainty and opacity, such as those typical of corrupt exchanges, individuals are heavily biased in terms of filtering information and communication via their existing "mental maps" (Denzau and North 1994). Their comprehension of "how to move," "what happens," and "why" within this hidden arena is therefore subject to positive feedback, since the development of their basic interpretations involves start-up costs as well as learning effects. Shared with others, it also creates network externalities and adaptive expectations. A significant instance is the need for corrupt agents to learn a specific *linguistic code*, a *common jargon* that allows them to better camouflage their illegal dealings and, if necessary, to silence their residual moral scruples.[12] Expressions and apparently innocent words are used to describe—and minimize— the content of their illegal dealings—in the case of bribery, they become "small gifts, tips which businessmen offered me spontaneously," in the words of a corrupt politician (R, January 17, 2002). This secures them a shared view and discourse, favoring the success of otherwise subtle and risky communications. To survive and reproduce themselves in the environment of corrupt transactions, people develop context-specific skills. Contractors in West African countries, for instance, have to "learn how to speak well," and to show unconditional generosity: "He who keeps his hands closed can't do business. If you have money, but you don't say hello to anyone in the family, some even seek to kill you. It's the same in the administration: if you don't give, you'll be stuck till death," explains a businessman from Niger (cit. in Blundo 2006: 257).

At the same time, they provide the foundation for the "justifying discourse" through which the logic of corruption can be reinterpreted and represented as part of an ideological or general understanding of reality. Structured values and tenacious orientations may in fact defend the individual contribution to support— even through corruption—more or less particularistic entities, such as political or faction party belongings or clan and family linkages, according to Banfield's formula of "amoral familism" (Banfield 1958). The significance of these basic outlooks, which is a premise for the acceptance of the practice of corruption, is then individually and socially confirmed and underpinned through time by repeated involvement in risky illegal dealings in a path-dependent dynamic.

Learning the most effective measures for making connections and controlling and guaranteeing the attainment of corrupt relationships hence rewards the most unscrupulous individuals, those who are resolute and creative in starting up or benefitting from corruption opportunities. The contribution of skilled individuals, with their expertise, may be the necessary catalyst for the conclusion of corrupt exchanges. For instance, in a German scandal, the manager of a construction firm indicated, in a delicate conversation with the official in charge of a large-scale construction project, "how badly his company needed the bribe, so badly in fact that they were ready to bribe." As both potential partners lacked the know-how, they needed an experienced partner:

> Although willing, neither knew how to go about it. That was when garbage entrepreneur H. T. entered the game. With his extensive experience, T. was able to recommend conducting bribe payments via Switzerland. He had been playing the political field for years and knew all the right channels. He had shown great

---

[12] In Chapter 3, several examples of linguistic codes adopted in corrupt transactions are presented in detail.

interest in being involved in the waste incinerator project and he was, with his network of influence, an essential partner. (TI-2005: 52)

The capability to effectively organize money transfers, for instance, becomes a valuable skill that reduces expected risks. An Italian entrepreneur in a tapped conversation proudly testified as to how his skills in "well-done" corruption preserved him from judicial inquiries:

> You're either a thief or a down-and-out, just those two things. We have a way of stealing which is sometimes justified and others, on the other hand, are thieves because they steal apples at the market and go to prison. It's harder for them to put us in jail, in fact I got through all of "Clean Hands," with hands pre-cleaned. I got through them all, I was the biggest business group in Rome and I never went to jail, nor was I incriminated because I'm used to doing things well. (R, February 14, 2010)

In another example—a successful corrupt agreement between a senior civil servant and a foreign country that had obtained a contract and sought advantages in its execution—the bribe payment was managed with expertise and competence through a complex transnational scheme:

> The senior civil servant did not come directly into contact with the manager of the Company R. It was a 'double-blind' (double intermediation) system, passing first via the consultant and then via the civil servant. Payments were made by the company R to an offshore company, before being transferred to an account handled by a foreign trust company, and then channelled into accounts opened in the foreign country for the consultant and the senior civil servant. (OECD 2007: 76)

In a process of adverse selection, the individuals less able to develop these abilities are penalized. According to a former councilor convicted for corruption in Milan, his not-so-brilliant political career was "the consequence of being considered a *stupid* by his party colleagues, as he was incapable of stealing" (*Un giorno in Pretura-Rai3*, February 22, 1993). Similarly, in entrepreneurial activities, a lack of experience in corruption may cause the loss of profit opportunities. This was the complaint of a Polish manager when he first received demands for bribes from two clients: "It was like a very cold shower. I asked myself if I could do business in a corrupt environment [...] . Leaving aside the moral connotations, I have no skills in giving bribes, I have never done it before, I don't know how much, I don't know to whom and I don't know in what situations I am supposed to give bribes, so I am losing in that competitive field and I am sentenced to death in the business world" (*news.com.*, April 11, 2001).

Methodically practicing the art of corruption, without blunders or excessive risks, therefore requires specific qualities, the accumulation of necessary skills in moving while hidden, but still effectively, in the complicated undergrowth of hidden relationships that ties together representatives of the worlds of politics, administration, finance, and business. A repentant Mafioso thereby praises the corrupting ability of a "white-collar worker" used by the criminal clan exclusively for the payment of bribes and the maintenance of complicated relationships with corruptible public administrators:

> he was Cicciotto's trusted man: not due to blood connections but mainly due to illegal affairs tied to garbage trafficking as well as the control of relationships with public administrations and for obtaining concessions and authorisation measures; this was because it was he who had the 'right key' for interjecting with public administrations. By this, I mean that he dealt with corrupting public officials and I must also add that he was very good at it. (TRNOC: 14)

The former mayor of Reggio Calabria, Agatino Licandro, describes here the kind of skills necessary:

> You usually think that bribery is the transfer of cash from one pocket to another; something straightforward and easy, theft with the scent of nimble fingers, an obscenity. It isn't like that though. It is extremely complicated to explain what the world of bribery is like. And it isn't easy to understand if you don't have the patience to enter into the diverse, often sophisticated, mechanisms. It isn't an orgy of hijackings, but a reality of rules, relationships, firm agreements, a language where hints and stresses assume the solemnity of a signature on a contract. (Licandro and Varano 1993: 18)

The success of individuals who are more "innovative" or competent in exercising corruption techniques can then have imitative effects, providing models of conduct for other willing corrupt or corrupting individuals.[13] Moreover, having learnt the art of corruption, entrepreneurs have an easy time applying it in countless new contexts and abroad, as an additional resource of spending to beat competition in global markets. The Transparency International (2008b) *Bribe Payer's Index* records the common perception, among directors of multinational companies, that among 22 leading international and regional exporting countries, the companies of some industrialized democratic countries often corrupt emerging countries' public administrators (see Figure 9.1). The hypothesis of a negative correlation between democracy and corruption seems thus to be reverted: companies coming from consolidated democratic contexts do become proponents of corruption in weaker and frayed state and institutional contexts. This process of *corruption exportation* reflects the conditions of economic interdependence and growing permeability of state borders, which make a country's "bad habits" the object of ever greater worries for the security and well-being of other states (Elliott 1996).

---

[13]   Baumol (1990). The innovative skills and capacities necessary for succeeding in one's activity are thus molded by the structure of expected benefits incorporated from the political and social "rules of the game": the structure for corruptors, lobbyists, or fixers differs from that for entrepreneurs and company directors (or at least, it is desirable for this structure to be different) (North 1994).

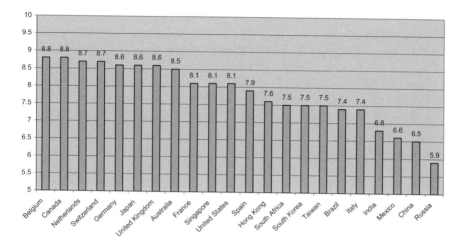

Fig. 9.1   **Transparency International Bribe Payers Index 2008 (10=lowest likelihood of companies from a country to engage in bribery when doing business abroad; 0=maximum likelihood). Source: Transparency International 2008.**

The practical skills and abilities necessary for mastering corruption methods are accumulated over time. In the diffusion of the phenomenon, corrupt and corrupting individuals interact and *learn through practice*, from one another, moving in the shadows and reducing the risks of being discovered. Expertise in requesting and passing on bribes is so precious that a corrupt employee of the Public Society for Roads in Milan who was due to retire was convinced by his superior to postpone his retirement and stay in service "to pass this art on to his successors" (R-Turin, May 31, 2002).

Similar considerations are valid for many other figures, mentioned in this volume, ranging from *business politicians* to *middlemen*, whose card-up-their-sleeve is their professional specialization in the management of illegal affairs and the development of "skills of illegality." In a kind of corruption handbook, one of these individuals describes some useful qualities for success:

> First of all, if you want to become a corruptor with a minimum amount of credit, you need to keep to commitments and be as punctual as a Swiss watch. [...] *Confidentiality* must then be a corrupter's essential feature. You must avoid friendly behaviour towards business associates in public. With the corrupted individual's middleman, you must show you have a kind of psychological subordination; you must position yourself a step below him, especially when talking about issues of his particular area of knowledge. You, the corruptor, must however show yourself ready and informed on the issues he knows nothing about, you must be willing to resolve any kind of problems relating to banks, finance, furnishings, cars and even women. (*L'Espresso*, November 18, 1984: 40)

Incidents (of a legal nature) along the way become the equivalent of *natural selection* mechanisms, which improve the "species" of the corrupt, eliminating the less able and allowing others to learn from their errors.

Adaptive Expectations in Corrupt Networks

The dynamics of adaptive expectations are similar to the effects of coordination, but in this case, more than the *awareness* of the corruption of others, the *expectation* or foresight of possible advantages from corruption is enough to start an avalanche effect. Forming *adaptive expectations* transforms the belief that corruption has become an everyday practice into a reality, as is the case, in a sort "self-fulfilling prophecy with the belief that honesty won't pay." The perceived "rules of the game" within a corrupt environment "cannot be ignored by any agent as far as others do not ignore and thus influence their strategic choices. Agent's strategic choices made on the basis of shared beliefs jointly reproduce the equilibrium state, which in turn reconfirms its summary representation. Thus the institution becomes self-sustaining and information compressed in it becomes taken for granted by the agents unless some events shaking the shared belief occur" (Aoki 2001: 12).

As observed in the case of football match-fixing, "perceived corruption brings corruption: even actors who prefer honest methods will fix in situations where they expect a high degree of dishonesty" (Hill 2009: 176). In places like Burundi, where, according to a 2008 study, 90 percent of entrepreneurs think paying bribes is the ordinary way of proceeding to reduce tax payments, avoid fines, or advance files through the tax service, the "social pressure" toward individual adhesion to the standard practice is almost irresistible (*The Cutting Edge*, October 26, 2009). In a discussion with a reporter at a Ugandan newspaper, this source of individual engagement in corrupt activities is clearly stated: "Anyway that is life… Anyway, you look at the surroundings, it is the circumstances… It is that feeling that if I don't take it, it is going to be taken by somebody else" (cit. in Perrson et al. 2010: 14).

The idea that honest individuals are destined to be penalized in politics and the bureaucracy or to go bankrupt in business, as with the prediction that this process will strengthen in the future, becomes a powerful spring that drives a growing number of individuals to resort to corruption in order to enjoy its expected benefits, or so as not to damage their career. Projections about the future "lead individuals to adapt their actions in ways that help to make those expectations come true" (Pierson 2004: 24): there is nothing like a shared forecast that corruption will become systemic to induce the speedy individual adaptation that makes such a scenario come true. As a Bulgarian entrepreneur observes, the use of kickbacks in his country is so widespread that

> as for the public procurement system, my feeling is that it has been established to promote corruption. There is a zero chance of success if you take part in a public procurement tender in the normal way and you have no access to the person who is in charge of things. And if you are ready to take up things in an

irregular manner (you have to) promise something in exchange for the favour. (Grødeland 2005: 66)

In a sort of bandwagon effect, the practice of corruption spreads and becomes increasingly advantageous when a sufficiently high number of individuals are convinced that it is the best way of maximizing their chances of profit and success over time. Moreover, the same moral barriers to illegality fade when the practice of corruption is expected to become predominant in an individual's social recognition circles. Finally, there is no moral implication perceived in bribery, since "systemic corruption" dictates the rules of behavior: "there are things in which one is obliged; one doesn't have a choice. So one does the minimum, but one is always forced to go through with it," is the explanation of a French contractor (cit. in Blundo 2006: 257).

Besides, an unintended consequence of the diffused practice of paying bribes to obtain favorable treatment from politicians and functionaries—the acceleration of procedures, privileged payments, and so on—is that "noncorruptors" see increased waiting times and uncertainties regarding the outcome of their requests. The time and commitment of public agents is a limited resource, and when they devote their attention to those compensating them with bribes, the quality of their performance toward honest individuals deteriorates. Pessimistic expectations are thus formed, confirmed, or reinforced. From here stems the consolidation of predictions over the inevitability and convenience of corruption, which makes widespread recourse to these practices more profitable or, alternatively, leads to "honest" individuals leaving the public market. This too, however, leads to an increase in the "density" of corrupt agents (della Porta and Vannucci 1999a, 2005a, 2005b).

A businesswoman reconstructs her *socialization to corruption* by her father in the following way:

No, that's how it's always been, [...] there were times my father said 'that's the way life is, it will never change'. My father said these things with a lot of pain inside [...] you must always give something, or else you will be replaced and not ... even if you have everything by the book. (PMI-MA, February 19, 2003: 24–5)

When expectations are pessimistic—as explained clearly by an Indian Inspector in the Finance Ministry—the path to endemic corruption is a ready one: "I am ashamed to say, but in this country [...] I think there are more corrupt people than honest people. People, they are like that, it is their daily life, they get up early in the morning to go find opportunities to enrich themselves and this is regrettable" (cit. in Blundo 2007: 41).

The conviction that "everyone does it" attenuates any eventual sense of guilt and gives a sense of *normality* to corruption, which can be converted into claims of vulnerability: "with the passing of time," a former Italian Minister observes, "the practice of not denouncing bribes was so widespread that it was almost impossible to imagine a formal denunciation" (cit. in Gomez and Travaglio 2006: 622–3). "Our profession does not leave us the space to refuse corruption, still less to deal with it. For if you always refuse, others will take, whatever the price. Better to take yourself as well," are the words of a contractor from Senegal (cit. in Blundo 2006: 257). Paying bribes therefore is often "neutralized" as normal behavior—as an Italian entrepreneurs declared, "My colleagues also told me that that was the way things worked, that everyone did it and in the end there was nothing strange about it" (*L'Espresso*, November 18, 1984: 41). Similarly, colleagues can introduce one another to the system of bribes: one nurse recalls that colleagues had told him receiving bribes from funeral houses "was a system that had worked that way for years" (R-Turin, June 14, 2001).

Hence, there is the motivation to hurry, as long as there is time and space, to establish the necessary contacts for corruption. As the match-fixer for the French teams Olympique de Marseilles and Bordeaux in European Cup matches between 1983 and 1993 testified, he began to help fix matches in 1983 after a match that Bordeaux lost 1–0 to a German team due to a controversial penalty, handed out by an allegedly corrupt referee:

> I said to Claude, 'If you want us to win you've got to make a move, and do something *like the others* [create an illicit fund to bribe linesmen and referees, emphasis added].' He said, 'Okay.' Afterwards, referees started falling over themselves to come to Bordeaux. (Hill 2009: 164)

In the drug industry, paying bribes to doctors and hospitals can assume similarly conventional features: "Bribing doctors and pharmacists is widely considered a tradition among many domestic drug firms" said a Korean industry official. According to the Korean Anti-Corruption Commission, local pharmaceutical firms set aside around 20 percent of their annual revenue for bribes to doctors and pharmacists, and the bribes account for up to 25 percent of drug prices (*Korea Joongang Daily*, June 5, 2009). A pharmaceutical entrepreneur justifies the payment of bribes to functionaries and commission members deciding drug prices in similar terms:

> Having to be in this game was inevitable. Given that all pharmaceutical companies were heading in that direction, if I hadn't done the same my firm would have inevitably been penalised in respect to others. We had arrived at the point where there was a contest between pharmaceutical companies to give "the most possible" to the various interested functionaries [...] . Therefore P. never needed to ask anything of me. Those were the rules. I paid, just like everybody else. (Montanaro and Ruotolo 1994: 60)

A Korean parent involved in the diffused practice of giving a small bribe to a teacher—so-called *chonji*—in order to see their children favored in school evaluations (increasing opportunities to get access to the best universities), confirms the crucial role of similar pessimistic beliefs about others' intentions: "I gave some chonji because of the concern that the teacher might treat my kid differently if I didn't give any money when other moms did" (*Los Angeles Times*, May 13, 2010).

Naturally, these expectations arise not only from a spontaneous adjustment to "rumors" about common rules but also from deliberate efforts to persuade directly interested parties; these expectation may also be the result of previous experiences.

> Objectively, I know I made a mistake—states an entrepreneur to justify paying a bribe—in fact I've never forgiven myself for having made that mistake and having assented to handing over money for the first time in my life, but I'm also aware that I found myself in a moment of great weakness because, in professional education, a lobby, a professional education Mafia, had been re-established. (TRBA2: 33)

A powerful spring capable of making actors' expectations converge toward an equilibrium of endemic corruption is generated by the *symbolic value* the money of the bribe and involvement in corruption can assume. Especially when corruption is perceived as widespread, bribe money can be symbolically associated with the authority of the individual asking for or receiving it, thereby becoming a sort of "unit of account" of the impalpable resource underlying the transaction, that is, the power of the corrupt agent to influence decision-making or to provide protection. As Thomas Hobbes ([1651]: 151–2) observed,

> The Value or *Worth* of a man, is as of all other things, his Price; that is to say, so much as would be given for the use of his Power: and therefore is not absolute; but a thing dependant on the need and judgment of another [...] . And as in other things, so in men, not the seller, but the buyer determines the Price. For let a man (as most men do,) rate themselves as the highest Value they can; yet their true Value is no more than it is esteemed by others.

In the opaque corrupt environment, the genuine *quality* of the otherwise intangible "commodity" exchanged is difficult to ascertain for both the buyer and the seller, but can be quantified approximately in economic terms: the market value of the resources received. Information about the "prices" practiced by public agents spreads in contained environments, orientating expectations of their power and thus, upon closing the circle, directing successive bribery-flows. Bribe quotas passed on from bribers to political actors in fact permit implicit acknowledgment by the receiver, as well as his counterparts, of his relative importance. In many African administrations, "Corruption is sometimes compared to a kind of 'perk of office' and thus represents the natural extension of the official's status [...] . The receipt of money from users [...] is, therefore, merely one legitimate privilege among many others that expresses the appropriation by officials of the space, facilities and materials of the service for which they work" (Blundo and de Sardan 2006: 115). This attitude is confirmed by an Ugandan politician: "In fact, [people] laugh at you sometimes when they find you are at a certain level and yet you do not have as much money as they would expect you to have"; the same holds true in Kenya, according to another politician: "if you get into a state institution and you walk in with one suit and one shamba, and you walk out on your retirement with one suit and one shamba, you will be considered foolish. So you go there and eat. You eat, you yourself, your family, then the whole patron client kind of thing now [is] created." (cit. in Perrson et al. 2010: 14). If the capacity to ask for and take appropriate quotas of money becomes a recognized indicator of the power and authority of a subject, the expectations formed in the corruption network effectively reinforce the bribe receiver's prestige and reputation. In conjunction with corruption revenue, their capacity to influence decision-making also increases in a self-perpetuating process.

For the same reason, upon taking his first bribe, a politician from Milan felt more satisfied by the recognition of power that the money meant than by the money itself: "I felt like an upstanding politician, from top to bottom. But not because I had more money in the bank" (Andreoli 1993: 58). The former Christian Democratic mayor of Reggio Calabria confirms, "For the way things are nowadays and with the mechanisms currently in place, the more money you take in politics the more they have to bring you" (Licandro and Varano 1993: 222). This statement is also valid in the opposite sense: the more bribes you take or are given, the higher up the power ladder you feel.

The fight for bribes thus becomes a decisive battlefield for political actors' success. The possibility of handling corruption money increases the resources power is founded on: the money invested in internal party competition or in electoral struggles allows opponents to be marginalized, affiliates to be bankrolled, and the electorate to be won over. "Having money and taking bribes is a good power," recognizes a political representative from Milan (*Panorama*, July 5, 1992: 41). Any new power equilibria—or disequilibria—are thus mirrored in the division of bribes. According to entrepreneur Vincenzo Lodigiani, when the leader of the Christian Democrats in Lombardy, the monopolist receiver of his bribes, disappeared, "a kind of fight of the colonels [...] who created serious difficulties to the company precisely because each of them was looking for an economic return from their institutional activities and didn't follow the directives arriving from the centre" (*L'Espresso*, November 29, 1992: 59). The fight for power is reflected—symbolically and in practice—in the fight for bribe-taking. Anybody managing to get paid, or paid more, proves to himself and others that he proportionally matters.

At the end of this path, when any activity by a public agent is naturally associated with the expectation of a bribe, any individual refusing to pay will not be considered upstanding because he lacks any real power.[14] By not accepting money, the path to promotion toward more significant political positions is blocked: because there will be less to share out to buy the goodwill of the decision-maker,

---

[14]   According to Licandro, "in the South, and definitely in Reggio Calabria, the choice is clear: either you become mayor and take money or you don't become mayor and you stay at home. You aren't a thief, but a robbery function. It is the electoral mechanism, the institutional political system, which is made up in a way that if you don't accept it you'll be sidelined" (Licandro and Varano 1993: 49). The same politicians who did not accept bribes, given the prevailing climate, were also forced to pretend they were corrupt due to the fear of appearing weak.

and also because they will be considered as figures of scant importance, and will consequently be marginalized. Precisely to compensate for this risk, a Calabrese politician had assumed the habit of personally delivering a share of the bribes collected at his party headquarters in Rome; according to a party colleague, by doing so, and despite the risks, he "wants to prove that he still holds power. [...] He wants to show that it is he who personally distributes them and not the party, and above all he wants to show that they came through him." Another politician from Reggio Calabria, feeling offended, initially refused an envelope: "I could understand his tragedy—the former mayor comments—*the strength of each person depends on the weight of the bribe*. With 10 million he felt like he was being treated in low regard" (Licandro and Varano 1993: 58–9, emphasis added).

Once the money from corruption is symbolically associated with power, the ostentation of wealth and opulence—common among kleptocrats in authoritarian states, but also among some political leaders of democratic countries—also becomes a kind of *selective publicity* which channels expectations of corruption by middlemen. Language reflects this perspective: discursive repertoires—metaphors and terms used to describe bribes and conduct—reproduce and enforce the cultural codes and expectations of audiences and partners in corrupt deals. In Latin America and Africa, for instance, "the idiom of corruption tends to be very sexualized and cast in terms of male virility. By using sexualized languages and metaphors to describe the phenomenon it is obvious that corruption is not necessarily considered to be bad but also a manifestation of strength and audacity. Especially men known to be corrupt are often in a certain way envied because of their wit, seductiveness, and virility" (Nujten and Anders 2007: 18).

Similarly, frequenting fashionable places and luxury bars and restaurants and the predilection for expensive houses, clothes, boats, and cars reassures corruptors that the bribe money will be welcomed and presumably also well reciprocated. Take the example of the political assistant of a minister who, lacking in any specific professional qualifications, paraded "a white Porsche, a house of three hundred squared metres in the Parioli district, another villa in the greenery of Villa Borghese." He admits to the *publicity* function of this luxurious ostentation: "I undoubtedly left the door open to the idea that I could be corruptible" (R, August 22, 1993: 12). A *sumptuous* private lifestyle becomes an index and expression of power, as well as wealth. But at this point, money is not pursued just for power, or power just for wealth. In a game of mirrors, money and power are reflected in one another, multiplying in the eyes of the observer.

Some Conclusive Remarks: Path Dependence in the Development of Corrupt Networks

In this chapter we examined different mechanisms that, through resultant multiple individual choices, generate positive feedback in practices of corruption, encouraging diffusion of the practice and tolerance of illegal activities. Naturally, a conflicting "virtuous" dynamic is generated when corruption is regarded by the public as a phenomenon destined to be eradicated or become marginal, and the amount of the bribe is not seen as a signal of power, but of dishonesty. These beliefs deter corrupt practices, increase the expected costs of finding a trusted middleman, and accentuate the perception of legal risks. In both cases, a step in one particular direction—as well as in the other one—can trigger further steps along the same path in a self-increasing mechanism.

Like other path-dependent phenomena, the development of corruption networks are characterized by four features (Pierson 2000: 263):

(i) Starting from the same initial conditions, we may arrive, ceteris paribus, at a wide set of different equilibria. Economic models often concentrate on two alternative scenarios, a high-corruption and a low-corruption equilibrium, but a large number of intermediate situations are potentially conceivable—and empirically observable.

(ii) Contingent or casual events—such as the (lack of) ability of a public prosecutor in a judicial inquiry or the appearance of a charismatic leader with a personal interest in corrupt dealings—may generate large and lasting effects on the robustness and size of corrupt networks, especially if they occur at some critical moment. Conversely, a "virtuous" process may start due to the rise of a new leadership unexpectedly committed to the values of integrity: "reforms sometimes occur simply because a charismatic and committed leader pushes them through. Strong leaders can inspire people to accept major reforms" (Rose-Ackerman 1999: 198).

(iii) Timing is crucial. *When* an event occurs may be decisive to the following path. Earlier events in a sequence often matter more than later actions, but events that are too premature may also fail for the same reason. For instance, in Italy an identical fact—the capture of leading Milanese socialist politicians personally involved in the management of systemic corruption—had virtually no effect in 1982 when one of the city's leading figures was arrested, but in 1992 when another political boss was denounced produced the collapse of the system with more than 3,000 trials.[15]

(iv) The process may finally halt in a single equilibrium that, once established, may be resistant to change, and the resilience of "institutionalized corruption" is directly related to its duration: "*all other things being equal, an institution will be more resilient, and any revision more incremental in nature, the longer the institution has been in place*" (Pierson 2004: 147). Significant variation in the amount of perceived corruption in countries

---

[15]   In the Public Prosecutor's Office in Milan in 1992, contingent conditions particularly favorable to the success of a corruption inquest were fulfilled by chance: the presence of a chief prosecutor independent of public pressure and the presence of a pool of very capable and tight-knit magistrates possessing complementary qualities (investigative intuition, experience, strong legal skills).

with similar institutional arrangements and cultural values, as reflected in the Transparency International Corruption Perception Index (see figure 1.1), is compatible with a similar stance. The missing convergence toward low-corruption equilibria, despite similar anticorruption policies and international pressure for the adoption of analogous regulations, may be explained by the status quo bias of resilient corrupt environments. *Inertia* can characterize outcomes of high-density, institutionalized corruption (Mahoney 2000: 511). Once created, informal "rules of the corruption game," with their enforcement mechanisms, live their own life, shaping individual beliefs and expectations, and promoting the formation of influential economic and political organizations—beneficiaries of the status quo—opposed to external pressure for change.

These considerations on the dynamics of a possible diffusion of the phenomenon of corruption have also fallen into anticorruption policies, as we will see better in the concluding chapter. Indeed, in this perspective no unambiguous connection between the content of reform measures and their effects exists. The same policy may succeed or fail depending on its context and the moment of its implementation. The effectiveness of anticorruption measures in fact depends on their capacity to "substitute" the informal rules of "institutionalized corruption," by modifying the expectations of the actors and dismantling the corresponding governance structures of corruption. The more the latter are consolidated over the passage of time, the more difficult it will be to enforce reform policies able to produce tangible and lasting results. Furthermore, niches of systematic corruption can also resist and consolidate in relatively transparent institutional environments. In these cases robust and persistent policies that considerably reduce the expected advantages of the corrupt and corrupting individuals' calculations are desirable, thus overthrowing the tangle of adaptive expectations in favor of honest strategies. By the same logic, "big" policy instruments are not always necessary to produce enduring effects. If carried out at the right time, for instance, when there is a "critical juncture" in the informal rules of corruption due to internal pressures or external factors (an economic or political crisis, etc.), "little" or even symbolic measures may produce large and long-lasting positive consequences as well.

Chapter 10
Conclusion:
Anticorruption Policy and the Disarticulation of Governance Structures in Corrupt Exchanges

The Hidden Order of Corruption and the Democratic Process: Concluding Remarks

The tendency for corruption is not etched in the genetic heritage or cultural roots of a society. Corruption, in a similar way to good governance, is the product of a multitude of individual and collective choices, supported and discouraged by the characteristics of an institutional system, social relationships and circles of recognition, and the structure of common values. The combination of these elements creates expectations, habits, beliefs, preferences, ways of thinking and of judging one's own and others'—actions that direct the evolution of corruption over time, slowly changing public opinion toward corruption and its diffusion throughout the state and civil society.

The illusion that democratic procedures and the rule of law may enhance control mechanisms and social antibodies sufficient to deter or minimize corruption has been frustrated in past decades. Radically divergent perceptions concerning diffusion may be observed, despite similarities in institutional and cultural contexts—for instance, among EU or OECD countries. Consolidated liberal democracies and developed economic systems coexist with the widespread presence of multiple forms of politico-administrative illegality; indeed, their conditions are akin and in some cases even worse than those of developing countries. Different empirical studies have demonstrated that corruption tends to increase with the complexity and the degree of discretion in regulations, the inefficiency of public administration, the length of time companies require to manage their relations with the state, and a lack of trust in the workings of democracy. On the other hand, it tends to decrease the higher the quality of the welfare state (and the quantity of public services provided), levels of economic freedom, observance of the rule of law, freedom of information, and degree of criminal punishment provided for (Treisman, 2000; Lambsdorff, 2007; Hopkin and Rodriguez-Pose, 2007).

The persistence and development of new forms of corruption are joined by the "environmental conditions" that still characterize many countries, democratic and non: a gloomy, complex legal system; a public administration with pockets of inefficiency and clientelism; a lack of trust in state institutions; electoral campaigns with inflated costs; mass media with low levels of professionalism and high levels of politicization; a welfare state unable to guarantee rights universally and impartially; and high levels of illegal activity in civil society, ranging from the black economy to tax evasion.

In our study, we have not lingered over the analysis of interactions between macro causes and macro effects, focusing our attention instead on some *mechanisms* that allow corrupt practices to take root and flourish at the level of specific organizational contexts. Indeed, the presence of general factors that make corruption more appetizing and less risky do not suffice to explain its spread within certain spheres of social interaction, particularly public structures. Like every other form of exchange, corruption also requires individual preferences and activities to be constrained by the emergence of appropriate institutions. In the corruption market in particular, mechanisms of governance have developed that guarantee that an alternative set of rules to legal ones, which are however no less binding, are widely observed. In order to gather information on opportunities for corruption and potential partners, invest resources and energy in reaching an agreement, and find a way to realize and enforce that agreement, some degree of adhesion to certain behavior patterns is necessary, whether these are internalized or externally imposed.

In the previous chapters, we looked at the informal rules governing networks of corrupt exchange and examined in detail the different factors that can lead to any form of "order" and predictability in the bribery system. We have singled out different categories depending on the predominant role that different *centers of power* (politico-administrative, economic, organized crime) and "coordinators" able to guarantee the protection of the uncertain rights of the corrupt and corruptors play, by the length and frequency of their involvement, and the type of resources available for the protagonists involved.

Self-fulfilling expectations and other coordination devices based on informal norms and their enforcement mechanisms, which accompany the diffusion of corruption, are difficult to disrupt. In the absence of counterweights, corruption feeds on itself and thus causes a spiral founded on the spontaneous marginalization or distancing of noncorrupt parties. For example, according to an Italian public employee, in his organizational structure there exists

> a reasonably accurate mechanism of selecting personnel. On the one hand there are the honest, on the other the "available". The ones who advance in their careers and hold the most important positions are exclusively from the latter category [...] . The honest are marginalised, threatened [...] . This is how it works: when you start to work here, they keep you under observation for a few months, and then one day a colleague arrives and makes you an offer. If you appear hesitant, he explains that everybody does it, that you need to raise a family, that you need to get a mortgage to buy a house. If you play along, there's something in it for you too. If you refuse, you're finished. When you walk down the corridors, you hear are a kind of beep-beep which follows you, which points you out as being in danger. (R, December 14, 2004)

These factors explain why widespread corruption within particular organizational structures reduces risks of being reported or discovered and increases the cost of the choice to remain honest. The mere expectation that corruption is commonplace drives a growing number of individuals to resort to it. Expertise in the best techniques to pass around bribes—while remaining unpunished—builds up as time passes and laws evolve, procedures and practices pander to interests favoring the impunity of leading administrators, while selection processes in political, administrative, or business careers reward unscrupulousness, the ability to muscle up the ladder thanks to political friends or support, and a lack of qualms in getting hold of money for personal use, or for a relative party or faction.

In this context, the moral barriers condemning corrupt activity also tend to weaken as corruption becomes increasingly diffused, thus facilitating the development of a so-called *culture of corruption*: "In this way corruption, which is initially a response to dissatisfaction towards public affairs, is decisive in causing further, deeper disaffection, which, in turn, paves the way for greater corruption" (Hirschman 1982: 135).

The development of widespread corruption systems can therefore be explained as an evolutionary process of increasingly sophisticated *regulatory* and *governance* mechanisms for corrupt transactions. For this reason—besides the obvious interest in underestimating their involvement in illegal practices—many individuals involved in investigations depict corruption using the imagery of a "system" with strict "laws," which are able to replicate and regulate the behavior of the different protagonists: "I ended up," states a public official convicted of corruption, "inside a mechanism which had its own life, and yet was engaging, and I didn't know how to escape it" (TAM: 94). Here, an official in a tax department, in which 29 employees out of 30 were arrested for taking bribes in exchange for fiddled tax assessments, explains the reasons for his involvement to the magistrate:

> You wouldn't be able to understand, because it belongs to a world where the choice between being honest and dishonest is a personal decision. It's your choice. In my case, my boss put the 250 thousand lira in my hand and after 15 days of work I perfectly understood the way things worked in the department. They would never have tolerated an honest person because everyone would have been in danger. (Davigo 2002: 138)

When the law, the regulatory system, the official mechanisms for controversy settlements and rights protection, the circulation of information, and other public assets that necessarily accompany any market system also become bargaining chips, the minimum conditions of certainty and predictability supporting economic and social development fail. Incentives encouraging entrepreneurs to invest in innovation become weaker, while in the political and economic markets a process of *adverse selection* gets underway. Neither the public administrators who are best able to satisfy collective demands, nor the entrepreneurs most efficient in satisfying consumer needs are compensated with success. Instead, a competitive advantage in political and economic markets rewards individuals who are the most unscrupulous and the most skillful in building privileged relationships with centers of power, the most generous lavishers of bribes or greedy takers of them, the most capable in finding their way around the labyrinth of departments and officialdom as well as the informal relationship network governing the trading of bribes (Vannucci and Cubeddu 2006).

In situations in which networks of widespread, "regulated" corruption are present, efforts in tackling them through regulation and procedural reforms aimed at increasing responsibility, transparency, and public sector competition run into further difficulties. When we take a look at the institutions present in a given society, we must look not only at the formal laws that are in place but also at the rules, practices, and codes of conduct that steer the decisions of the protagonists *in concrete, factual terms.* As long as there remains, in a public activity sector, a common expectation or conviction that a "connection," "friend," or "referent," which is to say a bribe to be paid, is necessary to obtain a contract, license, or concession, soften an inspection, or handle the laborious task of dealing with public administration with relative ease, then *this* rule of behavior becomes the true orientation model directing the decisions of all protagonists involved. In this way, those protagonists, politicians and entrepreneurs, slowly slide toward these tried and tested behavior models, as though finding themselves on a slippery slope. The Italian case shows how rapidly after the upheaval caused by the "Clean Hands" inquiry in 1992, the textures of past habits and corrupt practices can form and consolidate. Take the testimony of an entrepreneur:

> Sacrificing a lot and with a lot of effort on my part, I stayed out of it until 3 or 4 years ago, I no longer wanted anything to do with that hassle, I wanted to be able to look my children in the eye [...] . When "Clean Hands" occurred, everyone in Milan was afraid to entrust people with jobs, [...] When I started, I started ... I can't remember ... They didn't ask you for money, but they showed you: "this is what you worked", then they went on: "You know, because here ... the costs ...". So at a certain point I brought down 25 million lira. (PMI-MG, February 27, 2003: 11, 13)

A deep-rooted and increasing lack of confidence in the honesty of their own administrators seems to characterize almost all European Union countries. A Eurobarometer survey in 2009—see Table 10.1—showed that "more than 80% of respondents believe there is corruption within local, regional and national institutions in their country." Europeans are now more likely to agree there is corruption in each of these institutions than they were in Autumn 2007. The opinion that there is corruption in local institutions has increased from 75 percent to 81 percent, for regional institutions from 73 percent to 81 percent, and agreement that there is corruption in national governments has increased from 77 percent to 83 percent in the same period (Eurobarometer 2009, 13). Significantly, in 20 out of 27 countries more than 80 percent of respondents believe that there is corruption in the national institutions of their countries.

Table 10.1   Percentage of people who totally agree or tend to agree with each of the statements

	There is corruption in national institutions in our country (%)	There is corruption in local institutions in our country (%)	There is corruption in regions in our country (%)
EU 27	83	81	81
EU 15	81	79	79
Belgium	82	82	81
Bulgaria	94	91	91
Czech Republic	96	86	91
Denmark	35	30	31
Germany	80	79	81
Estonia	84	78	78
Ireland	87	83	82
Greece	98	96	97
Spain	91	89	90
France	83	79	80
Italy	89	89	86
Cyprus	91	93	93
Lithuania	94	91	88
Latvia	96	93	92
Luxembourg	55	57	55
Hungary	91	92	91
Malta	89	87	83
Netherlands	56	59	56
Austria	66	63	65
Poland	86	84	83
Portugal	91	89	88
Romania	87	89	87
Slovenia	96	89	90
Slovakia	91	86	88
Finland	68	57	58
Sweden	60	58	57
United Kingdom	76	75	74

Source: Eurobarometer 2009.

As long as this profound distrust continues, with corruption perceived as present at every level of government, the reform of formal laws and procedures runs the risk of simply causing a contingent adjustment to the decisions of the corrupted and corrupters, who continue to carve out spaces for their illegal activities after changes in regulations while at the same time adapting the regulatory mechanisms of corruption. The conditions—in terms of shared beliefs—facilitating the capillary spread of corruption only fail if these individuals stop considering corruption as an inexorable, but nevertheless profitable, practice in the face of the uncertainty of the law and market relations. However, it is difficult to imagine this "virtuous" process happening exclusively through *external* commitments and stimuli, such as the progressive spread of European regulations, or the signature of international conventions.[1] Designing such external constraints on corruption is, however, not easy.

Anticorruption at Stake: Revolutionary or Incremental Policy Change?

In general terms, anticorruption policies are more effective when they reduce the opportunities for and increase the moral costs of corruption. But any reform that influences macro-variables may have only a remote connection—in both spatial and temporal terms—with the factual conditions that influence the choices of a specific subset of actors to accept or offer a bribe, while the *script* that regulates their transactions remains substantially unaltered.[2]

In this perspective, there is no simple recipe to deal with antibribery measures, since corruption is a complex phenomenon, influenced by a multitude of interrelated variables that affect both the expected benefits and the socially recognized cultural values that allow for such calculations to take place in the first place. Moreover, there is a recognized difficulty in their implementation: "the history of anticorruption campaigns around the world is not propitious. At the national and local levels, in ministries and in agencies such as the police, even highly publicized efforts to reduce corruption have tended to lush, lapse, and, ultimately, disappoint" (Klitgaard et al. 2000: 11).[3] Anticorruption policies typically produce narrowly

---

[1]   The growing concern of international organizations surrounding the fight against corruption is expressed in the 2003 European Commission Communication on a comprehensive policy against corruption, in the 1997 OECD Convention on Combating Bribery of Foreign Public Officials, in the 1997 EU Convention on the fight against corruption involving officials of the European Communities or officials of Member States of the European Union, in the Council of Europe's 1998 Convention on Corruption, and in the 2003 UN Convention against Corruption.

[2]   According to the script approach, any crime can be identified and classified according to the routine steps followed by its actors, and this identification can be used to find crime prevention measures (Cornish 1994).

[3]   Other challenges frequently arise in the design of appropriate anticorruption strategies, such as *oversimplification*—i.e., the failure to target the incentives behind the individual involvement in corruption and the structure of opportunities shaped by the

concentrated costs—suffered by small cliques of corrupt agents—and broadly diffused benefits—gained by the public. As a consequence, an elite composed of corrupt politicians, bureaucrats, and influential entrepreneurs will be strongly adverse to such measures, while citizens will show scarce interest, or at best mild support: we are therefore in the realm of *entrepreneurial politics* (Wilson 1980), since the many, rather than the few, benefit from implementation. As shown by the Hong Kong and Singapore cases, under such conditions anticorruption policies may require the active contributions of political entrepreneurs able to recognize and exploit an opportunity to adopt and promote them. Nevertheless, such policies tend to be occasional and ephemeral, depending on the considerations of public opinion and media attention.

In recent decades, however, there has been a progressive enrichment of the toolbox of measures that can potentially be employed by policy makers and the business sector in their anticorruption activities. A variety of potential reforms and interventions has been formulated by both scholars and international organizations, mainly inspired by shared views and principles.[4] It is no matter of controversy— political or academic—that bribery could be curbed by reducing the monopoly rents and discretionary power in their allocation, enhancing competition in the private and public sectors, increasing the transparency and accountability of public actors, introducing controls on the final outcomes of public activities, strengthening moral barriers and societal control over the public, and so on. It is an open question, however, under which political and institutional conditions effective reforms will be realistically approved and implemented. Quite obviously, public actors that are somehow involved in corrupt networks or benefit from their operation have no interest in promoting or pursuing such reforms (Johnston 2005). In the absence of countervailing forces *external* to the corrupt environment—such as the entry of "honesty-promoting" competitors in the political arena, the pressure of public opinion, the enforcement applied by "clean" control agencies, and so on—a paradox may emerge: the more an anticorruption policy is needed, because corruption is endemic even at top levels, the less probable its formulation and implementation becomes by policy makers who are somehow implicated in illegal deals. Moreover, in this context even formally robust interventions—the institution of an anticorruption authority, for instance—can easily be reversed into yet another corruptible or useless public agency, not executing or financing its operations. Corruption within anticorruption agencies is a possibility, but —more subtle means

---

specific institutional context—and the *narrow focus* on the legal dimension and definitions of corruption, which hampers tackling other rent-seeking and corruption-related forms of influence of private interests on public decision-making. The *multiplicity of goals* pursued in political activity also makes it more difficult for public opinion to distinguish corruption from other private agendas that politicians may have; and for policy makers to emphasize the relevance of the fight against corruption, which is hardly distinguished from other issues (Søreide 2010).

[4]   Among the latter, see, for instance, OECD (1999), World Bank (2000); United Nations (2004), and Transparency international (2004, 2006, 2009b, 2010a).

can also be used to discredit the body: uncertainty and doubts surrounding the arrest of two deputy commissioners of Indonesia's powerful anti-graft body, who were the *driving force* behind its successes, can be interpreted in this perspective (*Wall Street Journal*, October 30, 2009).

Another difficulty should be also considered: "when a crisis produces strong support for a change, politicians must act quickly, often without sufficient planning or expert advice. In contrast, during quiet, stable periods when reform could be thoughtfully implemented, political support is lacking" (Rose-Ackerman 1999: 209). Even well-intentioned policy makers have to consider *how, when,* and *to what extent* an anticorruption campaign should be waged, since they have to consider a trade-off in the use of scarce public resources with alternative uses: bribery cannot be their only and foremost concern. The general approach applied may be problematic in itself. Not going into too much detail, in fact, at least two main perspectives in anticorruption policies may be recognized:

1. an incremental change or step-by-step approach
2. a revolutionary change or big-bang approach

According to the step-by-step approach, policy makers should aim to identify which critical points of the institutional matrix may be affected by reforms limited in their scope, but which could nevertheless induce further achievements, starting a spontaneous virtuous circle of positive feedback. As exemplified in the United Nations anticorruption toolkit,

> When anti-corruption strategies are first instituted, a long-term process begins, during which corrupt values and practices are gradually identified and eliminated. In most cases, a complex process of interrelated elements is involved: reforms to individual institutions take place in stages as problems are identified; countermeasures are developed and implemented; personnel are reoriented and retrained. Often, progress at one stage or in one area cannot be achieved until other elements of the strategy have come into effect. (United Nations 2004: 17–8)

There is an isomorphism here with the evolution of governance structures within corrupt networks, as examined in Chapter 2. Reversing the logic underlying those mechanisms, we could hypothesize that the adoption and implementation of valuable antibribery measures would require the mutual reinforcement of a set of interacting factors: (i) an exhibited strong commitment among top-level political and bureaucratic actors, who can influence the approval and application of new transparency-enhancing formal regulations, while signaling their long-term determination to foster such activities, (ii) coordination effects, which may render anticorruption inquiries and policies more effective in one area of public intervention or at one level of government, as long as others are activated in contiguous sectors or levels, through the circulation of information and expertise, (iii) learning effects, which over time positively affect the capacity of specialized anticorruption agencies, magistrates, and policy makers to formulate and implement their decisions, (iv) adaptive expectations, which enter into play when a sufficient amount of actors' beliefs are shaped by a new mutually self-sustaining prospect—or hope—that the fight against corruption will be durable and successful, and (v) high fixed costs, which imply a considerable initial investment of resources in the reorientation of values and the set-up of institutional devices to combat bribery, infringing previous corruption-prone practices and routines.

Once the diffusion of corruption is conceived as a path-dependent process, then some institutional "keys" could be available to reformers to change the direction of the path: even small (or even symbolic) interventions at the right time and in the right place may start an incremental change toward good and transparent governance, since "initial steps in a particular direction may encourage further movement along the same path. Over time, 'roads not chosen' may become increasingly distant, increasingly unreachable alternatives. Relatively modest perturbations at early stages may have a large influence on these processes" (Pierson 2004: 64). For example, a policy aimed at strengthening civil society and local community participation in anticorruption policies may represent a potential preliminary *spark* to set in motion the positive feedback interplay between actors' interests and beliefs. Recognizing the importance of "appropriate cultural resources" in the promotion and maintenance of integrity, anticorruption projects should adapt to the social values prevailing in each country (Newell 2011). The mutual recognition of the role of the public in the monitoring of government activities and in generalized awareness about the costs of bribery (World Bank 2000: 44) could, in turn, increase the perceived significance of transparency and anticorruption commitment for bureaucrats and policy makers, who would pay a price in terms of consent and career prospects in the case of the issue's removal from the agenda, or even worse in the case of involvement in a corruption scandal. The shaping of similar beliefs about one's own and others' evaluations of the effects of bribe-taking or offering would therefore generate a self-reinforcing model of behavior: when everybody in a society expects that corruption is a marginal, risky, socially blamed, low-profit activity, nobody has any incentive to take the first step along the long (and winding) road of corruption. Moreover, incremental anticorruption decision-making has the well-known quality of avoiding the potentially catastrophic consequences of wider and ambitious reforms, while favoring learning processes among policy makers and bureaucrats—a positive-feedback mechanism in itself, as we have seen—through a trial-and-error approach.

There are limits and potential drawbacks, however, in the application of a similar scheme to antibribery campaigns. First, the effects of these interventions—which are by definition quite circumscribed in their scope—are nevertheless more uncertain and possibly less effective the wider their expected range of application. As we have shown in this book, context-specific, situational aspects that allow for different models of corruption to emerge and flourish in particular organizational structures are decisive to understand the relative effectiveness or weakness of their internal governance mechanisms. Therefore, there is no optimal "entry-point"—in time and space—for the formulation of *general* and *all-encompassing* anticorruption measures. Their consequences in terms of feedback loops may vary in different public sectors or decision-making processes within the same country, depending on their interaction with protection and enforcement mechanisms of corrupt dealings. Second, there is a possibility that the initial "inputs" into transparency-enhancing policies are too weak, come too late, or are applied to the wrong regulatory change. In general terms, anticorruption policies face specific constraints, since they can hardly modify moral barriers, nor affect the self-regulating force of petty, structural, and systemic corruption. This is especially true when "a long distance" has been covered in the path toward large-scale corruption. The *inflexibility* property of similar processes states that "the farther into the process we are, the harder it becomes to shift from one path to another [...] . Sufficient movements down a particular path may eventually 'lock in' one solution" (Pierson 2004: 18).

Within loci and organizations in which corrupt actors respond to deep-rooted informal governance mechanisms, low-scale incremental anticorruption measures may be easily curbed or internalized within the already structured system of mutually enforcing beliefs. The effects of law and regulatory reforms risk being restricted to some change or internal adjustment in the roles of actors involved in corruption, for example, their influence and bargaining power in benefits and bribe sharing. Paradoxically, such interventions may even worsen the situation, increasing the abilities and skills of bribers and bribees in terms of safely managing their business, and strengthening the pessimistic expectations of the public over the possibility of an "exit" from this high-corruption equilibrium. Similar beliefs tend to thwart the implementation of policies that are typically aimed at modifying the official institutional framework, but rarely affect the informal regulatory mechanisms of corruption. As an example we may take the ephemeral success of the Clean Hands judicial inquiries into systemic bribery in Italy during the early 1990s, which for a certain period seemed to represent the catalyst of a transition toward a new low-corruption equilibrium. In the last decade new mechanisms of endemic corruption—characterized by the coexistence of many dense local networks of corrupt exchanges—seem to be operating again with the apathy of the public, as epitomized by the case of Prime Minister Silvio Berlusconi, who won elections in 2001 and 2008 despite being under investigation in several corruption cases (Bull and Newell 2003; Vannucci 2009; della Porta and Vannucci 2011a).

The "revolutionary change" approach states that under certain conditions a non-incremental intervention should be preferred, in order to produce some sort of "big-bang" within the entrenched routines and reciprocally sustained beliefs that fuel endemic, widespread corruption (Rothstein 2007). Considering a stable equilibrium of corruption as the norm—in which everyone expects everyone else to offer or accept bribes—its collapse and change could be quick and, to some extent, unexpected: "provided that corruption generates small but cumulative social costs and the population contains a small number of irreducibly honest individuals—there will come a critical time at which a stable equilibrium of corruption becomes suddenly unstable. This catastrophic event should be rightly called the 'honesty revolution'" (Bicchieri and Rovelli 1995: 222). Such an approach is coherent with a "multiple equilibria" (see Chapter 1) perspective: "'crackdowns (attempts to shift out from a corrupt equilibrium by means of short, drastic campaigns) may work where more gradual measures would not" (Kingston 2008: 100).[5] Since the expected advantages of corruption critically depend on how many other actors are involved, there are typically several "frequency dependent" equilibria, with lower or higher levels of corruption (Bardhan 1997: 1331). Moreover, if the multifaceted interaction between corruption, administrative inefficiency, adverse selection of economic and political elites, and democratic governance is not recognized, "anticorruption policies which focus narrowly on the corruption issue will miss the complexity of the relations and are therefore likely to fail. [...] This understanding tells us that it does not make much sense to propose narrowly designed anticorruption policies. On the contrary, both analysis and policy recommendations ought to be forged at a higher level, that is, in terms of general governance" (Picci 2011: 116).

Virtually all phases of the corrupt transaction involve costs and risks that are related to the expected presence of other corruptible actors: the time spent in the identification of a reliable partners, the possibility of being denounced during that search, the negotiation of a deal, the delivery of what was promised, the possibility of being caught due to whistle-blowers, and so on. Moreover, moral aversion toward illegal activities is also influenced by others' practices and opinions. One's evaluation of the generalized diffusion of corruption may favor a self-absolving attitude. Moreover, the judgments of one's circles of recognition assume a crucial role here: if ethically condemned by his peers, colleagues, relatives, and so on, the monetary utility of corruption will be accordingly depreciated in one's internalized consideration, and vice versa (Pizzorno 1992). Therefore, under the same institutional framework, very different levels of corruption may be observed, due to positive feedback effects toward wider participation in honest or corrupt practices: "people may have similar values, within and across societies, and similar institutional structures and yet, for accidental reasons, end up in different equilibria" (Elster 1989b: 39–40).

When corrupt practices are deeply embedded within the political and social system, reforms should therefore be wide-ranging and robust enough to modify the—possibly short-term—expected benefits and mutual expectations of all—or almost all—players in games of corruption. Social and political conditions encouraging reforms may however require a considerable amount of time to emerge, since "developments unfavourable to institutional reproduction must reach a critical threshold level that makes reform possible. The moment of

---

5   As Piga (2011) notices, "If there can be multiple equilibria between corruption and competence, expectations and systemic shocks can lead to big changes. A change of focus by the leaders in the country or in the profession toward efficient and honest procurement might represent one of these positive shifts."

institutional innovation will often play the starring role in the dramatic conclusion, but their appearance in the final chapter is often heavily dependent on preceding developments occurring over an extended period" (Pierson 2004: 164). In fact, long-term processes, invisibly underlying the operations of the corruption market, are often crucial to the success of antibribery reforms. These processes might operate by gradually diminishing the benefits associated with corruption—when, for instance, too many firms or too many citizens enter the circle in which everybody pays bribes to get access to a given amount of public benefits; or when the expected advantage that excluded, "honest" entrepreneurs, politicians, and citizens hope to obtain by pushing for institutional change increases. The hypothesis underlying this approach is that "countries can move from a high- to a low-corruption equilibrium. [...] The goal is to encourage developments that undermine the monopolies and organization of entrenched corruption while strengthening the forces that elsewhere sustain the low corruption alternative" (Johnston 1999: 16). A sort of *critical juncture* is required to reverse the path leading to increasing bribery, that is, a "jump" to another path where honesty and transparency are the reciprocally recognized moral standards. In other words, a revolutionary change approach could be preferable whenever the governance mechanisms that regulate corrupt exchanges offer all—or almost all—actors an alternative informal set of rules (i.e., an institutional framework) that shapes their beliefs and directs their choices. A specific approach is then required in the fight against systemic corruption, attacking the disease through stronger measures aimed at subverting corruption from the inside (Klitgaard 2006: 306). The goal is to weaken corrupt institutions, disrupting mechanisms of internal recruitment, trust circulation, and protection.

The idea that under such conditions a revolutionary change could be recommended to destabilize the self-fueling dynamics of corruption may be logically consistent, but it remains problematic. First, its deliberation and implementation would require a political and bureaucratic elite strongly committed to the values of transparency and alien to the ordinary practice of bribery. This is hardly likely to be the case if not accompanied by a similarly radical change in the overall institutional apparatus. The radical change in anticorruption regulation, in other words, may turn out to be the simple by-product of a drastic transition to a different political regime whose final outcome cannot be easily predicted, subverting initial expectations. For instance, the perception of generalized corruption was one of the factors that provoked the overthrow of the Iranian Shah Reza Pahlavi, but the Islamic revolution does not seem to have produced an improvement in public morality under the new theocratic political framework. According to Transparency International (2010b), at present Iran is perceived as one of the most corrupt countries in the world, 146th out of 178 countries considered.

There is a fundamental constraint, moreover, on any attempt to modify the expectations and internalized beliefs that structure the interactions among bribers and bribees through a large-scale reform of *formal* regulations and laws. Even when the change is *allegedly* revolutionary, its means are written norms and instructions that have to be read, interpreted, applied, and enforced. In each of these passages, there is space for a substantial undermining of their effects over the perceptions that shape individual behavior. In this perspective,

the overall failure of anti-corruption reforms is by and large the result of an implementation problem. In particular, there seems to be an absence of actors willing to enforce existing laws by reporting and punishing corrupt behaviour and, as such, acting as 'principals' [...] . Rather, the rewards and costs of corruption—and hence the existence of actors willing to enforce reform— should be expected to depend critically on how many others individuals in the same society are expected to be corrupt. (Perrson et al. 2010: 4)

For instance, individuals and firms will hardly be willing to engage in whistle-blowing against corruption "unless local levels of corruption are considered to be low" (Søreide 2008: 423). When actors operate in an environment characterized by high levels of opacity and uncertainty—as in the case of corrupt networks— they are heavily biased by the "mental maps" through which they filter new information (Denzau and North 1994). The development of these basic views of social reality is a path-dependent process in itself, with high start-up costs and learning effects (Pierson 2004: 39). Once established, the shared belief that "corruption is unavoidable" in a specific context may become the cognitive filter that dictates which kind of information is relevant, and which is filtered out. Hence the new "disconfirming" anticorruption regulation may simply be ignored or narrowed in its scope, nobody would be able or willing to enforce the formally rigorous anticorruption punishment scheme, letting the well-established norms of corruption continue to dictate *how to move* in that context.

Moreover, policies oriented by a "big-bang" approach are typically designed through general changes in macro-level institutional variables, such as regulations, the allocation of resources, the organization of control agencies, and so on. Such measures will produce dissimilar effects in the various *specific* arenas where decision-making takes place. The governance mechanisms of corruption may be more or less affected by reforms depending on the frequency of interaction between corruptors and corruptees, or the amount of resources at stake, that is, the characteristics of the established "models" that structure networks of corruption. For example, a new all-embracing regulation that destabilizes rampant petty corruption in a sector may be useless in another sector, where structural corruption prevails. As long as some "breeding grounds" of bribery persist after an attempted "revolutionary change," conditions are favorable for the beginning of another self-reinforcing process of corruption that will spread to other sectors and levels of power.

The same holds true, however, when considering the potentiality of a "virtuous circle" starting with a vigorous reform, even if limited in its scope. We may take as an example the successful Hong Kong anticorruption case, where "a remarkable initiative to root out corruption, particularly in the police department, became a vehicle for the modernization of service delivery and the empowerment of citizens in local government." The institution in 1974 of an independent commission against corruption—the initiative came directly from the governor, who played the role of the leading antibribery "political entrepreneur"—turned out to be the kingpin of "a bold new strategy" based on prevention and citizen participation. Some symbolic initiatives—like the extradition of a former chief superintendent who had escaped to England—signaled "that the rules of the game had changed" in the police force, and more generally in the public service (Klitgaard et al. 2000: 17, 21).[6]

Despite its legacy of widespread corruption, after attaining self-government in 1959, Singapore experimented with a similar transition toward an almost corruption-free civil service, through the implementation of some effective anticorruption laws and administrative measures, promoted by top political leadership and accompanied by the institution of an independent agency with investigative and prevention functions (Leak 1999).[7] In particular,

> civil servants' pay relative to the private sector increased substantially; public officials were routinely rotated to make it harder for corrupt officials to develop strong ties to certain clients; rewards were given to those who refused bribes and turned in the client; and importantly, rules and procedures were simplified and often published, permits and approvals were scrapped, and fees (including import duties) were lowered or removed. (Svensson 2005: 35)

What is missing here, however, is any link with a democratization process: in neither of these cases did the advancement in the quality or extension of

----

6   The success of this "quiet revolution" is quite evident: 38 percent of respondents in 1977 thought corruption was widespread in most government departments, only 7.8 percent in 1994 (de Speville 1999: 52). In 2010, Hong Kong, according to Transparency International (2010b), is perceived as one of the "cleanest" countries, ranked 13th out of 178.

7   According to Rothstein (2007: 23), Sweden in the eighteenth century also had high levels of corruption and clientelism, an equilibrium that was subverted by a "non incremental and dramatic" change toward a new model of bureaucracy, which came between 1855 and 1875, when "almost all major political, social and economic institutions were changed in a relatively short period of time [...] . A reasonable conclusion is that this would cause the agent to thoroughly reconsider 'how to play' and 'what to expect'." Similarly, in England the approval of a radical reform of political financing in 1883, the Corrupt and Illegal Practices Prevention Act, determined a successful transition from a regime of universalized bribery—where candidates corrupted electors, the executive and lobbies corrupted MPs, etc.—toward a much cleaner political environment, in which from 1950 to 1980 political expenditure per campaign was less than 5 percent (in constant prices) as compared with a century earlier (Pizzorno 1997; Pinto-Duschinsky 1981). Both cases, however, are temporally located in the eighteenth century, when the sphere of public decision-making and the loci of potential corruption were much less ample than nowadays. Presumably a "revolutionary change" required relatively simple reforms within such institutional frameworks to provoke a sudden change in beliefs and expectations as compared with the requirements of the complex apparatus of modern states.

democratic institutions accompany the start of successful reforms, which were instead fostered by autocratic leaderships. The ambiguous relationship between corruption and democracy is thus corroborated: democratic procedures are not a sufficient condition to deter corruption, nor are they a necessary condition to defeat it.

From Positive to Normative Analyses of "Organized Corruption"

In our research we did not assume any normative or prescriptive stance, limiting ourselves to a positive explanation of the multifaceted reality of "organized corruption." Some general hints for the design of anticorruption policies, coherent with our previous analysis, may however be suggested. To sum up briefly,

> (a) while the adoption of some wide-ranging principles (competition, accountability, regulatory simplification, the meritocratic recruitment of public servants, judicial strengthening, civil society oversight, etc.) is naturally recommended as a guideline for reform, anticorruption strategies should be adapted to the specificity of sectors, local characteristics, and phases of decision-making.[8] Public contracting procedures in municipalities, hospitals, armies, schools, or infrastructure projects, for instance, may differ significantly in their frequency, in the amounts of resources and actors involved, and so on. Zoning decisions, permit granting, tax collection and controls, appointments in the public service, law enforcement and policing, driving licenses, housing subsidies, and judicial procedures enlarge this incomplete list of potentially corrupt environments in central and local governments. Each of these decision-making processes may develop its specific governance structures and norms of systemic, structural, individual, or petty corruption. Each of them require specific tools to be effectively countervailed, and their main objective should be the disarticulation of each distinctive internal "ordering mechanisms."

Table 10.2 details some possible objectives and anticorruption policy instruments, calibrated to different models of bribery. Petty corruption, with its pervasive and low-profile arrangements, could be better contrasted by guaranteeing to the public certainty in their rights and the quality of public performances (through citizens' empowerment and oversight, silent-consent in procedural steps, etc.). Individual corruption may require an effort to dismantle communication, trust, and exchange relationships between bribers and bribees, introducing significant

---

[8]   As Johnston (2008: 206) observes, "Appropriate reforms require an understanding of the deeper, long-term forces shaping and sustaining corruption, their links to observable local characteristics and contrasts, and careful thought as to how corruption controls might function in a given context."

Table 10.2   Anticorruption policies and models of corruption: Some objectives and examples

	General objectives of anticorruption policy	**Examples of specific anticorruption measures**
Petty corruption	*To guarantee certainty of rights and quality of public performance to citizens in their interactions with public officials*	Citizens' empowerment and oversight over public decision-making Simplification of procedures, recognized standards for public performance, silent-consent to guarantee certainty of time in procedural steps, competition among offices In-depth random controls of the patrimonial condition of public officials Strengthening nongovernmental initiatives and movements in the fight against corruption, for instance, through phone helplines and websites for anonymous denunciations (cfr. http://ipaidabribe.com/)
Individual corruption	*To hamper communication channels and infringe the direct trust linkage between briber and bribee*	Strong asymmetry in penalties toward those who started the deal Heavier sanctions against brokerage activities and influence-trafficking
Structural corruption	*To dismantle reputational circuits in corruption networks, encouraging defection and shortening the time horizon in interactions between bribers and bribees*	Rotation in office for functionaries in more "vulnerable" sectors Protection of whistle-blowers Incentives for whistle-blowing, for instance, a percentage of resources seized or court award Impunity for those who denounce corrupt deals in which they were involved
Systemic corruption	*To reduce the resources available to protectors to enforce corrupt deals, injecting distrust into corruption networks*	Agent provocateurs and infiltrators in more "vulnerable" sectors Stronger controls and heavier sanctions against illegal political financing Stronger controls and heavier sanctions against companies' accounting frauds

asymmetries in penalties,[9] or heavily sanctioning intermediation and "influence trafficking." Structural corruption, with its informal norms and reputational circuits for enforcing illegal deals may be attacked by shortening the expected time-horizons of interaction among the actors involved and encouraging defection, for instance, through rotation in office for functionaries operating in more "sensitive" areas, or protecting—and promoting via incentives—"whistle-blowing." The pervasive networks of systemic corruption and their "third-party" enforcement mechanisms may instead be fought with a "surgical" intervention aimed to weaken guarantors, injecting distrust and alarm among corrupt agents, for instance, through the use of "agent provocateurs," or by introducing stricter controls on parties' and public contractors' financial activities. Moreover, in the long-term anticorruption policies should "alter the relative advantage—over the life cycle of an individual—of acquiring productive abilities, rather than simply cultivating improper connections": the policy adopted in a wider time-horizon should thereby produce a shift toward a low-corruption equilibrium characterized by efficient public procedures, discretion with accountability, rewards for qualification, appropriate benchmarking, and sharing of best practices (Piga 2011).

(b) The practice of corruption should be analytically subdivided into simpler phases, as a succession of different prearranged activities: the search for information on opportunities for bribery, the identification of reliable partners, the negotiation of an agreement (which may require meetings, signals, threats, etc.), implementation and its related activities (collecting and giving bribe-money, active participation in decision-making or influence trading, etc.), the control and enforcement of the result of the deal, the exploration of future opportunities for similar or related affairs, and so on. Each of these steps has its weak sides, with the involvement of several actors employing various resources.[10] Effective prevention and anticorruption policies may likewise require the application of dissimilar tools and measures to break this chain at its weakest points, which would otherwise lead to the successful conclusion and reproduction of corrupt

---

[9]   A similar scheme of sanctions should dismantle confidence between partners in corrupt deals: "sanctions for accepting bribes should be low and those for illicitly reciprocating bribes high; in turn, penalties for paying bribes should be severe, while those for accepting illicit reciprocity (contracts, permits, etc.) mild" (Lambsdorff 2007: 230).

[10]   This approach is coherent with a situational crime prevention perspective, which emphasizes the relevance of each crime's specificity and the procedural phases in any criminal act, in which the progressive involvement and management of criminal activities is conceived as a sequence of unitary actions in which actors are engaged. Some logical steps are outlined within the criminal activity, divided into different script scenes: preparation, enabling conditions, target selection, "doing," and the post-conditions or aftermath. See among others, Clarke and Felson (1994); Clarke (1997); and Clarke and Cornish (2000); see also Savona (2010) for an example of the infiltration of organized crime into public contracting.

dealings. One of the critical aspects, as we stressed in the previous analysis, is the demand for trust and protection within networks of bribers and bribees. (c) In general terms, as we have seen, *revolutionary change* approaches should be preferred when corruption is endemic.[11] A sudden transition, however, could also be the result of a "critical mass" being reached in the simultaneous application of a variety of *incremental* reforms in several interrelated decision-making contexts. Under this perspective, the two approaches outlined above are not incompatible. A mix of the two could be applied as long as anticorruption measures are calibrated to the specific features of illegal practices. Throughout repeated "multi-sector pulls" in several areas, a stable change in beliefs may be produced by a perceived change in the overall climate. Moreover, in a wider time horizon, temporary pauses in the reform process could be useful for at least two reasons: they may give stakeholders the opportunity to assimilate and implement previous measures, and they may favor learning among policy makers about which measures were most successful and could therefore also be applied in other contexts, pushing forward the anticorruption campaign and which were instead ineffective, requiring the reorientation of reforms. In this perspective, the informal institutions of systemic corruption could be destabilized by applying some sort of "punctuated equilibria" model, alternating longer periods of incremental anticorruption policy with drastic measures aimed at inducing a breakdown in previous arrangements (Steinmo and Thelen 1992: 15). The timing of reforms is also crucial: "half-hearted reforms, or reforms undertaken 'too early' (before cooperative equilibria are feasible) may not only fail to reduce the level of corruption, but may also sabotage future reform efforts" (Kingston 2008: 100). A history of unsuccessful policies may, in fact, generate mistrust or cynicism about the capability of the political class to reform itself, thereby undermining prospects of success.

(d) Anticorruption policies require advocacy coalitions and societal support to be more effective and politically sustainable. General interest groups, that is, lobbies promoting the "public goods" of integrity and transparency in the public sphere are, however, quite rare. Education on such values, as well as the organization and mobilization of groups promoting reforms and fostering them, could then become a necessary precondition for the success of antibribery campaigns. The strict regulation of political financing and competitive public procurement could, besides, reduce the amount of rents gathered by potential pro-corruption actors, weakening

---

[11]   As observed by Diamond (2007: 119), "Endemic corruption is not some flaw that can be corrected with a technical fix or a political push. It is the way that the system works, and it is deeply embedded in the norms and expectations of political and social life. Reducing it to less destructive levels—and keeping it there—requires revolutionary change in institutions."

them. Moreover, effective antibribery campaigns entail continuity, that is, an orientation toward long-term outcomes by their actors, supporters, and stakeholders, since a time-lag usually divides commitment to collective action and tangible results, if these are observable. Otherwise, the resulting disappointment, as Hirschman (1982: 123–5) explains, may generate an impulse toward further disengagement and corruption.

(e) A reform-induced change in the structure of the economic incentives/costs of corruption can be undermined by the lack of a corresponding adjustment in the structure of actors' shared beliefs, expectations, and values (i.e., moral costs). This process may not require any institutional fracture, as mentioned above. An alternative could be the adoption of anticorruption campaigns based on education and communication strategies, supporting a socialization of functionaries and the public to values of integrity and transparency, and therefore strengthening those social "circles of recognition" that sustain the respect of the law through peer pressure and social control (Pizzorno 1992).

No straightforward formula, no optimal set of norms, institutions, or policies, with well-defined timing and content, can be generally applied as a parameter for the evaluation of policies against bribery. Every society, organization, and decision-making process should find its own elusive amalgam of measures and tools, calibrated on a case-by-case basis to an array of contingent factors. Despite its intrinsic difficulties and potential failures, the fight against corruption encompasses a fundamental symbolic value in itself, especially in democratic countries. The spread of corruption within a democratic regime implies the corruption of virtually all basic liberal-democratic principles, and contaminates values of equality, transparency, justice, and the rule of law. The preservation of an anticorruption stance within the public sphere entails then a shared commitment toward the possibility of improving the quality of public life, and the persistence of some trust in the potential of a democratic system to reform itself. If not enough to defeat corruption, this may be sufficient to preserve the democratic power from the corrupting influence of its dark side.

Bibliography

Abadinsky, H. 1990. *Organized Crime*. Chicago: Nelson Hall.

Aidt, T.S. 2003. Economic Analysis of Corruption: A Survey. *Economic Journal*, 113(491), F632–F652.

Alam, M.S. 1990. Some Economic Costs of Corruption in LDCs. *Journal of Development Studies*, 27(1), 85–97.

Alatas, S.H. 1990. *Corruption: Its Nature, Causes, and Functions*. Aldershot: Averbury.

Allen, D.W. 1991. What Are Transaction Costs? *Research in Law and Economics*, 14(3), 1–18.

Allen, D.W. 1999. Transaction Costs. In *Encyclopedia of Law and Economics*. Vol. I, edited by B. Boudewijn and G. De Geest. Chelthenham: Edward Elgar, 893–925.

Allum, Percy. 1995. Le double visages de la Démocratie Chrétienne italienne. *Politix*, 30(1), 24–44.

Almond, G. and S. Verba. 1963. *The Civic Culture: Political Attitudes and Democracy in Five Nations*. Princeton: Princeton University Press.

Alou, M.T. 2006. Corruption in the Legal System. In *Everyday Corruption and the State*, edited by G. Blundo and J-P. Olivier de Sardam. Cape Town: David Philip, 137–76.

Anderson, A. 1995. *Organised Crime, Mafia, and Governments*. In *The Economics of Organised Crime*, edited by G. Fiorentini and S. Peltzman. Cambridge: Cambridge University Press, 33–53.

Andreoli, M. 1993. *Andavamo in Piazza Duomo*. Milano: Sperling & Kupfer.

Andvig, J.C. 1995. Corruption in the North Sea Oil Industry: Issues and Assessments. *Crime, Law, and Social Change*, 28(4), 289–313.

Andvig, J.C. 1996. *Corruption and Softening of Government: The International Dimension*. Paper to the International Conference on Corruption in Contemporary Politics. Salford: University of Salford, November.

Andvig, J.C., O. Fjeldstad, I. Amudsen, T. Sissener, and T. Soreide. 2000. *Research on Corruption: A Policy-Oriented Survey*. Chr. Michelsen Institute (CMI) and Norwegian Institute of International Affairs (NUPI).

Andvig, J.C. and K.O. Moene. 1990. How Corruption May Corrupt. *Journal of Economic Behaviour and Organization*. 13(1), 63–76.

Aoki, M. 2001. *Toward a Comparative Institutional Analysis*. Cambridge, Mass., and London: MIT Press.

Arlacchi, P. 1992. *Gli uomini del disonore*. Milano: Mondadori.

Arnone, M. and E. Iliopulos. 1995. *La corruzione costa*. Milano: Vita e pensiero.

Arthur, W.B. 1994. *Increasing Returns and Path Dependence in the Economy*. Ann Arbor: University of Michigan Press.

Axelrod, R. 1984. *The Evolution of Cooperation*. New York: Basic Books.

Bako Arifari, N. 2001. La corruption quotidienne au Benin. In *La corruption au quotidien en Afrique de l'Ouest*, edited by G. Blundo and J-P. Olivier de Sardam. Marseilles, Research report, EHESS-IUED-IRD, 51–95.

Bako Arifari, N.B. 2006. 'We don't eat the papers': Corruption in Transport, Customs, and the Civil Forces. In *La corruption au quotidien en Afrique de l'Ouest*, edited by G. Blundo and J-P. Olivier de Sardam. Marseilles: Research report, EHESS-IUED-IRD, 178–224.

Banfield, E.C. 1958. *The Moral Basis of Backward Society*. New York: Free Press.

Banfield, E.C., and J.Q. Wilson. 1967. *City Politics*. Cambridge: Cambridge University Press

Banfield, E.C. 1975. Corruption as a Feature of Governmental Organisation. *Journal of Law and Economics*, 18(3), 587–605.

Barbagallo, F. 1997. *Napoli fine novecento*. Torino: Einaudi.

Bardhan, P. 1997. Corruption and Development: A Review of the Issues. *Journal of Economic Literature*, 35(3), 1320–46.

Barzel, Y. 1989. *Economic Analysis of Property Rights*. Cambridge: Cambridge University Press.

Barzel, Y. 2002. *A Theory of the State: Economic Rights, Legal Rights, and the Scope of the State*. Cambridge: Cambridge University Press.

Baumol, W.J. 1990. Entrepreneurship: Productive, Unproductive, and Destructive. *Journal of Political Economy*, 98(5), 893–921.

Bayar, G. 2005. The role of intermediaries in corruption. In *Public Choice*, 122(3), 277–98.

Becchi, A. 2001. *Professionisti e mediatori*. Roma: Donzelli.

Beck, J.P. and M.W. Maher. 1986. A Comparison of Bribery and Bidding in Thin Markets. *Economic Letters*, 20(1), 1–5.

Becker, G.S. 1968. Crime and Punishment. An Economic Approach. *Journal of Political Economy*. 76(2), 169–217.

Becker, G.S. and G.J. Stigler. 1974. Law Enforcement, Malfeasance, and Compensation of Enforcers. *Journal of Legal Studies*, 3(1), 1–18.

Benni, S. 1990. *Baol. Una tranquilla notte di regime*. Milano: Feltrinelli.

Benson, B.L. 1988. Corruption in Law Enforcement: One Consequence of "Tragedy of Commons" Arising with Public Allocation Processes. *International Review of Law and Economics*, 8(1), 73–84.

Benson, B.L. 1990. *The Enterprise of Law: Justice without the State*. San Francisco: Pacific Research Institute for Public Policy.

Benson, B.L. and J. Baden. 1985. The Political Economy of Governmental Corruption: The Logic of Underground Government. *Journal of Legal Studies*, 14(2), 391–410.

Besley, T. and A. Prat. 2006. Handcuffs for the Grabbing Hand? Media Capture and Government Accountability. *American Economic Review*, 96(3), 720–36.

Bianchi, A.M. and A. Nerazzini. 2005. *La mafia è bianca*. Milano: Bur.

Bicchieri, C. and C. Rovelli. 1995. Evolution and Revolution: The Dynamics of Corruption. *Rationality and Society*, 7(2), 201–24.

Bjørnskov, C. and C. Paldam. 1995. Corruption Trends. In *The New Institutional Economics of Corruption*, edited by J. Graf Lambsdorff, M. Taube, and M. Schramm. London and New York: Routledge, 59–75.

Block, A. 1983. *East Side West Side: Organizing Crime in New York, 1930–1950*. New Brunswick: Transaction Publisher.

Blundo, G. 2006. An Ordered Corruption? The Social World of Public Procurement. In *Everyday Corruption and the State*, edited by G. Blundo and J-P. Olivier de Sardam. Cape Town: David Philip, 225–62.

Blundo, G. 2007. Hidden Acts, Open Talks. How Anthropology Can "Observe" and Describe Corruption. In *Corruption and the Secret of Law: A Legal Anthropological Perspective*, edited by M. Nuijten and G. Anders. Farnham: Ashgate, 27–52.

Blundo, G. and O.J.P. de Sardan. 2006. The Popular Semiology of Corruption. In *Everyday Corruption and the State*, edited by G. Blundo and J-P. Olivier de Sardam. Cape Town: David Philip, 110–35.

Bobbio N. 1980. La democrazia e il potere invisibile. *Rivista Italiana di Scienza Politica*, 10(2), 181–203.

Boeri T. and B. Severgnini. 2008. *The Italian Job: Match Rigging, Career Concerns, and Media Concentration in Serie A*. IZA DP No. 3745, October.

Bouissou, J.M. 1997. Gifts, Networks, and Clienteles: Corruption in Japan as a Redistributive System. In *Democracy and Corruption in Europe*, edited by D. della Porta and Y. Mény. London: Pinter, 132–47.

Bowden, M. 2001. *Killing Pablo*. New York: Atlantic Monthly Press.

Bray, J. 2005. The Use of Intermediaries and Other "Alternatives" to Bribery. In *The New Institutional Economics of Corruption*, edited by J. Graf Lambsdorff, M. Taube, and M. Schramm. London and New York: Routledge, 112–35.

Brief, A.H. 2005. The Wuhan Court Bribery Case. *China Rights Forum*, 1(2), 30–32.

Brunetti, A. and B. Weder. 2003. A Free Press Is Bad News for Corruption. *Journal of Public Economics*, 87(1–7), 1801–24.

Bryce, J. [1921]. *Modern Democracies*, Vol. II. London: Macmillan. [New edition. 2008 New York: Cosimo].

Bryce, J. 2008. *Modern Democracies*, Vol. II. New York: Cosimo.

Buchanan, J.M. [1975]. *The Limits of Liberty*. Indianapolis: Liberty Funds, 2000.

Buehn, A. and F. Schneider. 2007. Shadow Economies and Corruption All Over the World: Revised Estimates for 120 Countries. *Economics: The Open-Access, Open-Assessment E-Journal* [Online]. 1, 2007–9 (version 2). Available at http://dx.doi.org/10.5018/economics-ejournal.ja.2007-9, accessed January 31, 2011.

Bull, M. and J. Newell. 2003. *Political Corruption in Italy*. In *Corruption in Contemporary Politics*, edited by M. Bull and J. Newell. New York: Palgrave, 37–48.

Buscaglia, E. and J. van Dijk. 2005. *Controlling Organized Crimes and Corruption in the Public Sector*. ALACDE Annual Papers, Berkeley Program in Law and Economics. Available at http://escholarship.org/uc/item/7wf424p5, accessed January 31, 2011.

Cadot, O. 1987. Corruption as a Gamble. *Journal of Public Economics*, 33(2), 223–44.

Caiden, G.E. and N.J. Caiden. 1977. Administrative Corruption. *Public Administration Review*, 37(3), 301–8.

Carlucci, A. 1992. *Tangentomani*. Milano: Baldini & Castaldi.

Cartier-Bressons, J. 1997. La corruption dans les pays capitalistes tardifs. In *Pratiques et controle de la corruption*, edited by J. Cartier-Bresson. Paris: Montchrestien, 37–67.

Casas-Zamora, K. 2010. Dirty Money: How to Break the Link between Organized Crime and Politics. *Americas Quarterly* [Online]. Available at http://www.americasquarterly.org/casas-zamora, accessed November 12, 2010.

Casas-Zamora, K. (ed.) 2011 (forthcoming), *Dangerous Liaisons: Organized Crime and Political Finance in Latin America and Beyond*. Washington, D.C.: Brookings Institution Press.

Catanzaro, R. 1991. *Il delitto come impresa. Storia sociale della mafia*. Milano: Rizzoli.

Charap, J. and C. Harm. 1999. *Institutionalized Corruption and the Kleptocratic State*. Washington D.C: International Monetary Fund, WP/99/91.

Cheung, S.N.S. 1987. Economic Organization and Transaction Costs. In *The New Palgrave Dictionary of Economics*, Vol. 2. London: Palgrave Macmillan, 55–8.

Chu, Y.K. 2000. *The Triads as Business*. London: Routledge.

Ciconte, E. 1994. Ludovico Ligato. In *Cirillo, Ligato e Lima. Tre storie di mafia e politica*, edited by N. Tranfaglia. Bari-Roma: Laterza, 99–183.

Clarke, R.V. 1997. *Situational Crime Prevention*. Collompton: Willan Publishing.

Clarke, R.V. and M. Felson. 1994. *Routine Activity and Rational Choice*. Edison: Transaction Publisher.

Clarke, R.V. and R.V. Cornish. 2000. Rational Choice. In *Explaining Crimes and Criminals: Essays in Contemporary Criminological Theory*, edited by R. Paternoster and R. Bachman. Los Angeles: Roxbury Publishing Company.

Coleman, J.W. 1987. Toward an Integrated Theory of White Collar Crime. *American Journal of Sociology*, 93(2), 406–39.

Coleman, J.S. 1990. *Foundations of Social Theory*, Cambridge, Mass., and London: Belknap Press of Harvard University Press.

Cornish, D. 1994. Crime as Scripts. In *Proceedings of the International Seminar on Environmental Criminology and Crime Analysis*, edited by D. Zahm and P. Cromwell. Coral Gables: University of Miami, 30–45.

Cotta. M. 1996. La crisi del governo di partito all'italiana. In *Il gigante dai piedi di argilla*, edited by M. Cotta and P. Isernia. Bologna: Il Mulino, 11–52.

CSD. 2003. *Corruption, Contraband, and Organized Crime in Southeast Europe*. [Online: Centre for the Study of Democracy, Sofia]. Available at http://unpan1.un.org/intradoc/groups/public/documents/UNTC/UNPAN016997.pdf, accessed January 31, 2011.

CSD. 2009. *Crime without Punishment: Countering Corruption and Organized Crime in Bulgaria*. [Online: Centre for the Study of Democracy, Sofia]. Available at http://www.csd.bg/fileSrc.php?id=2650, accessed January 31, 2011.

CSD. 2011. *Examining the Links between Organized Crime and Corruption.* [Online: Centre for the Study of Democracy, Sofia; European Commission, Bruxelles.] Available at http://ec.europa.eu/home-affairs/doc_centre/crime/ docs/study_on_links_between_organised_crime_and_corruption_en.pdf, accessed March 31, 2011.

Dahl, R. 1961. *Who Governs? Democracy and Power in an American City.* New Haven: Yale University Press.

Dasgupta, P. 1988. *Trust as a Commodity.* In *Trust: Making and Breaking Cooperative Relations,* edited by D. Gambetta. Oxford: Oxford University Pres, 49–72.

Davigo, P. 2002. Obbedire ai potenti? *MicroMega,* 18(1), 135–78.

Davigo, P. and G. Mannozzi. 2007. *La corruzione in Italia.* Roma-Bari: Laterza.

de Speville, B.E.D. 1999. The Experience of Hong Kong, China, in Combating Corruption. In *Curbing Corruption,* edited by R. Stapenhurst and S.J. Kpundeh. Washington, D.C.: World Bank, 51–8.

della Porta, D. 1992. *Lo scambio occulto.* Bologna: Il Mulino.

della Porta, D. 2000. Social Capital, Beliefs in Government, and Political Corruption. In *Disaffected Democracies: What's Troubling the Trilateral Countries?* edited by S.J. Pharr and R.D. Putnam. Princeton: Princeton University Press, 202–29.

della Porta, D. 2006. *La politica locale.* 3rd edition. Bologna: Il Mulino.

della Porta, D. 2009. *I partiti politici.* 3rd edition. Bologna: Il Mulino.

della Porta, D. and A. Vannucci. 1994. *Corruzione politica e amministrazione pubblica.* Bologna: Il Mulino.

della Porta D. and A. Vannucci. 1999a. *Corrupt Exchanges.* New York: Aldine De Gruyter.

della Porta, D. and A. Vannucci. 1999b. *Un paese anormale. Come la classe politica ha perso l'occasione di mani pulite.* Bari-Roma: Laterza.

della Porta, D. and A. Vannucci. 2005a. The Governance Mechanisms of Corrupt Transactions. In *The New Institutional Economics of Corruption,* edited by J. Lambsdorff, M. Taube, and M. Schramm. London: Routledge, 152–80.

della Porta, D. and A. Vannucci. 2005b. The Moral (and Immoral) Costs of Corruption. In *Dimensionen politischer Korruption,* edited by U. von Alemann. Wiesbaden: Vs. Verlag, 109–34.

della Porta, D. and A. Vannucci. 2007. *Mani impunite.* Roma-Bari: Laterza.

della Porta, D. and A. Vannucci. 2011a (forthcoming). When Anticorruption Policy Fails: The Italian Case Eighteen Years after the "Mani Pulite" Investigations. In *Cultures of corruption in Europe,* edited by A. Giannakopoulos. Fahrnam: Ashgate.

della Porta, D. and A. Vannucci. 2011b (forthcoming). The Godfather's Party: Organized Crime and Political Financing in Italy. In *Dangerous Liaisons: Organized Crime and Political Finance in Latin America and Beyond,* edited by K. Casas-Zamora. Washington, D.C.: Brookings Institution Press.

Denzau, A.D. and D.C. North. 1994. Shared Mental Models and Ideologies. *Kyklos,* 47(1), 3–31.

Dey, H.K. 1989. The Genesis and Spread of Economic Corruption: A Microtheoretic Interpretation. *World Development*, 17(4), 503–11.

Diamond, L. 2007. A Quarter-Century of Promoting Democracy. *Journal of Democracy*, 18(4), 118–20.

Diamond, L.J. and L. Morlino (eds.). 2005. *Assessing the Quality of Democracy*. Baltimore: Johns Hopkins University Press.

Dimitrov, G. 2008. The Case of Bulgaria. In *The Balkans: Curbing Challenges*, edited by M Stoicheva. Sofia: European Studies Department, 53–62.

Dixit, A. 2004. *Lawlessness and Economics: Alternative Modes of Governance*. Princeton: Princeton University Press.

Doh, J.P., P. Rodriguez, K. Uhlenbruck, J. Collins, and E. Lorraine. 2003. Coping with Corruption in Foreign Markets. *Academy of Management Executive*, 17(3), 114–27.

Dreher, A. and F. Schneider. 2010. Corruption and the Shadow Economy: An Empirical Analysis. *Public Choice*, 144(1), 215–38.

Duverger, M. 1951. *Les parties politiques*. Paris, Colin.

Eggertsson, T. 1990. *Economic Behavior and Institutions*. Cambridge: Cambridge University Press.

Ellickson, R.C. 1991. *Order without Law: How Neighbors Settle Disputes*. Cambridge, Mass.: Harvard University Press.

Elliott, K.A. 1996. Corruption as an International Policy Problem: Overview and Recommendations. In *Corruption and the Global Economy*, edited by K.A. Elliott. Washington, D.C.: Institute for International Economics, 175–233.

Elster, J. 1982. *Explaining Technical Change*. Cambridge: Cambridge University Press.

Elster, J. 1989a. *Nuts and Bolts for the Social Sciences*. Cambridge: Cambridge University Press.

Elster, J. 1989b. *The Cement of Society*. Cambridge: Cambridge University Press.

Eurobarometer. 2009. *Attitudes of Europeans towards Corruption: Full report*. [Online: European Commission]. Available at: http://ec.europa.eu/public_ opinion/archives/ebs/ebs_325_en.pdf, Brussels, accessed August 8, 2010.

Faccio, M. 2006. Politically Connected Firms. *American Economic Review*, 96(1), 369–86.

Falcone, G. 1991. *Cose di Cosa Nostra* (with M. Padovani). Milano: Rizzoli.

Fipe. 1992. *Malati di tangente*. Rome: Federazione Italiana Pubblici Esercenti.

Fishman, R. and E. Miguel. 2008. *Economic Gangsters: Corruption, Violence, and the Poverty of Nations*. Princeton: Princeton University Press.

Freille, S.M., E. Haque, and R. Kneller. 2007. A Contribution to the Empirics of Press Freedom and Corruption. *European Journal of Political Economy*, 23(4), 838–62.

Gambetta, D. 1988. Anatomia della tangente. *Meridiana*, 4, 237–47.

Gambetta, D. 1992. *La mafia siciliana*. Torino: Einaudi.

Gambetta, D. 1993. *The Sicilian Mafia*. Cambridge, Mass.: Harvard University Press.

Gambetta, D. and Reuter, P. 1995. Conspiracy among the Many: The Mafia in Legitimate Industries. In *The Economics of Organised Crime,* edited by G. Fiorentini and S. Peltzman. Cambridge: Cambridge University Press, 116–36.

Giglioli, P. 1997. Processi di delegittimazione e cerimonie di degradazione. In *Rituali di degradazione. Anatomia del processo Cubani,* edited by P.P. Giglioli, S. Cavicchioli, and G. Fele. Bologna: Il Mulino, 15–74.

Goffman, E. 1974. *Frame Analysis.* New York: Harper and Row.

Golden, M. and E.C.C. Chang. 2001. Competitive Corruption: Factional Conflict and Political Malfeasance in Postwar Italian Christian Democracy. *World Politics,* 53(4), 588–622.

Golden, M. and L. Picci. 2005. Proposal for a New Measure of Corruption, Illustrated with Italian Data. *Economics & Politics,* 17(1), 37–75.

Gomez, P. and M. Travaglio. 2006. *Onorevoli Wanted.* Roma: Editori Riuniti.

Good D. 1988. Individuals, Interpersonal Relations, and Trust. In *Trust: Making and Breaking Cooperative Relations,* edited by D.Gambetta. Oxford: Oxford University Press, 31–48.

Granovetter, M. 1992. Economic Action and Social Structure: The Problem of Embeddedness. In *The Sociology of Economic Life,* edited by M. Granovetter and R. Swedberg. Boulder, Colo.: Westview Press, 53–81.

GRECO. 2009. *Evaluation Report on Italy.* [Online: Group of States Against Corruption, Strasbourg]. Available at http://www.coe.int/t/dghl/monitoring/greco/evaluations/round2/GrecoEval1-2(2008)2_Italy_EN.pdf, accessed November 12, 2010.

Grødeland, Å. 2006. Bulgaria, Czech Republic, Romania, and Slovenia: The Use of Contacts and Informal Networks in Public Procurement. In *Fighting Corruption and Promoting Integrity in Public Procurement.* Paris: OECD, 59–74.

Groenendijk, N. 1997. A Principal-Agent Model of Corruption. *Crime, Law, and Social Change,* 27(3–4), 207–29.

Grossman, M. 2005. *Political Corruption in America.* Santa Barbara: Abc-Clio.

Hasker, K. and C. Okten. 2008. Intermediaries and Corruption. *Journal of Economic Behavior & Organization,* 67(1), 103–15.

Hall, P.A. 2003. Aligning Ontology and Methodology in Comparative Research. In *Comparative Historical Analysis in the Social Sciences,* edited by J. Mahoney and D. Reuschmeyer. Cambridge: Cambridge University Press, 373–405.

Haller, D. and C. Shore. 2005. Introduction. Sharp Practice: Anthropology and the Study of Corruption. In *Corruption: Anthropological Perspectives,* edited by D. Haller and C. Shore. London: Pluto Press, 1–28.

Hayek, F.A. 1973. *Law, Legislation, and Liberty.* London: Routledge.

Heidenheimer, A. [1970]. Perspectives on the Perception of Corruption. In *Political Corruption: Concepts and Contexts,* edited by A. Heidenheimer and M. Johnston. New Brunswick: Transaction, 2002, 141–54.

Herrera, A.M., L. Lijane, and P. Rodriguez. 2007. *Bribery and the Nature of Corruption.* Working Paper, May. Available at https://www.msu.edu/~herrer20/documents/HLR_may07.pdf, accessed February 28, 2011.

Heywood, P. 1995. Sleaze in Spain. *Parliamentary Affairs*, 48(4), 726–37.

Heywood, P. 1997. From Dictatorship to Democracy: The Changing Forms of Corruption in Spain. In *Democracy and Corruption in Europe*, edited by D. della Porta and Y. Mény. London: Pinter, 65–84.

Hill, B.E. 2006. *The Japanese Mafia: Yakuza, Law, and the State*. Oxford: Oxford University Press.

Hill, D. 2009. To Fix or Not to Fix? How Corruptors Decide to Fix Football Matches. Global Crime, 10(3), 157–77.

Hirschman, A. 1982. *Shifting Involvements*. Princeton: Princeton University Press.

Hobbes, T. [1651]. *Leviathan*. Harmondsworth: Penguin Books, 1968.

Holzner, B. 1972. *Reality Construction in Society*. Cambridge, Mass.: Schenkman.

Hopkin, J. 1997. Political Parties, Political Corruption, and the Economic Theory of Democracy. *Crime, Law, and Social Change*, 27(3–4), 255–74.

Hopkin, J. and A. Rodriguez-Pose. 2007. "Grabbing Hand" or "Helping Hand"? Corruption and the Economic Role of the State. *Governance*, 20(2), 187–208.

Huntington, S.P. 1968. *Political Order in Changing Society*. New Haven: Yale University Press.

Husted, B. 1994. Honor among Thieves: A Transaction-Cost Interpretation of Corruption in the Third World. *Business Ethics Quarterly*, 4(1),17–27.

Husted, B. 1999. Wealth, Culture, and Corruption. *Journal of International Business Studies*, 30(2), 339–60.

Johnson, O.E.G. 1975. An Economic Analysis of Corrupt Government with Special Application to LDC's. *Kyklos*, 28(1), 47–61.

Johnston, M. 1994. *Comparing Corruption*. 16th World Congress of the International Political Science Association, Berlin, August.

Johnston, M. 1999. What Can Be Done about Entrenched Corruption? In *Curbing Corruption*, edited by R. Stapenhurst and S.J. Kpundeh. Washington, D.C.: World Bank, 14–8.

Johnston, M. 2005. *Syndromes of Corruption: Wealth, Power, and Democracy*. Cambridge: Cambridge University Press.

Johnston, M. 2008. Japan, Korea, the Philippines, China: Four Syndromes of Corruption. *Crime, Law, and Social Change*, 49(3), 205–23.

Kasper, W. and M. Streit. 1999. *Institutional Economics: Social Order and Public Policy*. Cheltenham: Edward Elgar.

Kawata, J. 2006. Mafia, Corrupted Violence and Incivism. In *Comparing Political Corruption and Clientelism*, edited by J. Kawata. Fahrnam: Ashgate, 133–56.

Kahanna, J. and M. Johnston. 2007. India's Middlemen: Connecting by Corrupting. *Crime, Law, and Social Change*, 48(3–5), 151–68.

Katz, R.S. and P. Mair. 1993. The Evolution of Party Organizations in Europe: Three Facets of Party Organizations. *American Review of Politics*, 14(4): 593–617.

Key, V.O. 1936. *The Technique of Political Graft in the United States*. Chicago: University of Chicago Press.

Kingston, C. 2008. Social Structure and Cultures of Corruption. *Journal of Economic Behavior & Organization*, 67(1), 90–102.

Kirchheimer, O. 1966. The Transformation of the Western European Party System. In *Political Parties and Political Development*, edited by J. La Palombara and M. Weiner. Princeton: Princeton University Press, 177–200.

Klitgaard, R. 1988. *Controlling Corruption*. Berkeley and Los Angeles: University of California Press.

Klitgaard, R. 2006. Introduction: Subverting Corruption. *Global Crime*, 7(3–4), 299–307.

Klitgaard, R., R. MacLea-Abroa, and H.L. Parris. 2000. *Corrupt Cities*. Washington, D.C.: World Bank.

Krueger, A. 1974. The Political Economy of the Rent-Seeking Society. *American Economic Review*, 64(3), 291–303.

Lambert-Mogiliansky, A. and K. Sonin. 2006. Collusive Market Sharing and Corruption in Procurement. *Journal of Economics & Management Strategy*, 15(4), 883–908.

Lambert-Mogiliansky, A., and G. Kosenok. 2009. Fine-Tailored for the Cartel: Favoritism in Procurement. *Review of Industrial Organization*, 35(1), 95–121.

La Porta, R., F. Lopez-de-Silanes, A. Shleifer, and R.W. Vishny. 1997. Trust in Large Organizations. *American Economic Review*, 87(2), 333–8.

La Porta, R., F. Lopez-de-Silanes, A. Shleifer, and R.W. Vishny. 1999. The Quality of Government. *Journal of Law, Economics, and Organization*, 15(1), 222–79.

Lambsdorff, J. 2002. Making Corrupt Deals: Contracting in the Shadow of the Law. *Journal of Economic Behavior & Organization*, 48(3), 221–41.

Lambsdorff, J. 2007. *Institutional Economics of Corruption and Reform*. Cambridge: Cambridge University Press.

Lambsdorff, J.G. 2011. Corrupt Intermediaries in International Business Transactions: Between Make, Buy and Reform. *European Journal of Law and Economics*, 1–18, January 4. Available at http://www.springerlink.com/content/2262424h211tq486/, accessed January 31 2011).

Leak, T.A. 1999. The Experience of Singapore in Combating Corruption. In *Curbing Corruption*, edited by R. Stapenhurst and S.J. Kpundeh. Washington, D.C.: World Bank, 59–66.

Ledeneva, A.V. 1998. *Russia's Economy of Favours: Blat, Networking and Informal Exchange*. Cambridge: Cambridge University Press.

Lee, K. and K. Hahn. 2002. Bid-Rigging in Auctions for Korean Public-Works Contracts and Potential Damage. *Review of Industrial Organization*, 21(1), 73–88.

Leff, N. 1964. Economic Development through Bureaucratic Corruption. *American Behavioural Scientist*, 8(3), 8–14.

Leonard, W.N. and M.G. Weber. 1978. *Automakers and Dealers: A Study of Criminogenic Market Forces*. In *White Collars Crime*, edited by G. Geis and R.F. Meier. New York: Free Press.

Levy, D. 2007. Price Adjustment under the Table: Evidence on Efficiency-Enhancing Corruption. *European Journal of Political Economy*, 23(2), 423–47.

Licandro, A. and A. Varano. 1993. *La città dolente. Confessioni di un sindaco corrotto*. Torino: Einaudi.

Liebowitz, S. J. and S.E. Margolis. 1994. Network Externality: An Uncommon Tragedy. Journal of Economic Perspectives, 8(2), 133–50.

Lien, D.D. 1986. A Note on Competitive Bribery Games. Economic Letters, 22(4), 337–431.

Lipsky, M. 1980. *Street Level Bureaucracy*. New York: Russel Sage.

Lui, F.T. 1985. An Equilibrium Queuing Model of Bribery. *Journal of Political Economy*, 93(4), 760–81.

Lundhal, M. 1997. Inside the Predatory State. *Nordic Journal of Political Economy*, 24(1), 31–50.

Magone, J.M. 1996. *Political Corruption and Sustainable Democracy in Small Countries: The Portuguese Case in Comparative European Perspective.* International Conference on Corruption in Contemporary Politics, University of Salford, November.

Mahoney, J. 2000. Path Dependence in Historical Sociology. Theory and Society, 29(4), 507–48.

Maltz, M.D. 1985. Toward Defining Organized Crime. In The Politics and Economics of Organized Crime, edited by H.E. Alexander and G.E. Caiden. Lexington: Lexington Books, 21–35.

Markovits, A.S. and M. Silverstein. 1988. Introduction: Power and Process in Liberal Democracies. In The Politics of Scandal, edited by A.S. Markovits and M. Silverstein. New York: Holmes & Meier, 1–13.

McKay, J. 2003. Political Corruption in Germany. In *Corruption in Contemporary Politics*, edited by M. Bull and J. Newell. London: Palgrave, 53–65.

McMillan, J., and C. Woodruff. 2000. *Private Order under Dysfunctional Public Order. Michigan Law Review,* 98 (8), 2421–58.

Médard, J.F. 1997. *France-Afrique: Within the Family*. In *Democracy and Corruption in Europe*, edited by D. della Porta and Y. Mény. London: Pinter, 22–35.

Mendras, M. 1997. Rule by Bureaucracy in Russia. In *Democracy and Corruption in Europe*, edited by D. della Porta and Y. Mény. London: Pinter, 118–30.

Mény, Y. 2000. France: The End of the Republic Ethic?. In *Corruption in the Developed World*, edited by R. Williams, J. Moran, and R. Flanary. Cheltenham: Edward Elgar, 202–17.

Merton, R.K. 1972. The Latent Functions of the Machine. In *Urban Bosses, Machines and Progressive Reformers*, edited by Bruce M. Stave. Lexington, Mass.: Heat.

Mete, V. 2009. Fuori dal comune. Lo scioglimento delle amministrazioni locali per infiltrazioni mafiose. Acireale: Bonanno.

Milgrom, P. and J. Roberts. 1990. Bargaining Costs, Influence Costs and the Organization of Economic Activity. In *Perspectives on Political Economy*, edited by J.E. Alt and K.A. Shepsle. Cambridge: Cambridge University Press, 57–89.

Moe, T.M. 1990. Political Institutions: The Neglected Side of the Story. *Journal of Law, Economics, and Organization*, 6(special issue), 213–53.

Montanaro, S. and S. Ruotolo. 1994. *Mister & Lady Poggiolini*. Napoli: Pironti.

Morlino, L. (ed.). 1991. *Costruire la democrazia. Gruppi e partiti in Italia.* Bologna: Il Mulino.

Murphy, K.M., A. Shleifer, and R.W. Vishny. 1993. Why Is Rent-Seeking So Costly to Growth? *American Economic Review Papers and Proceedings*, 83(2), 409–14.

Myrdal, G. 1968. *Asian Drama: An Enquiry into the Poverty of Nations*. New York: Twentieth Century.

Nascimbeni, E. and A. Pamparana. 1992. *Le mani pulite*. Milano: Mondadori.

Newell, J. 2011. Where Crime and Politics Meet: 'It's the culture, stupid!' In *Usual and Unusual Organising Criminals in Europe and Beyond*, Liber Amicorum Petrus van Duyne. Apeldoorn: Maklu, 151–72.

North, D.C. 1984. Government and the Cost of Exchange in History. *Journal of Economic History*, 46(2), 255–64.

North, D.C., 1990. *Institutions, Institutional Change, and Economic Performance*. Cambridge: Cambridge University Press.

North, D.C. 1994. Economic Performance through Time. *American Economic Review*, 84(3), 359–68.

Nye, J.S. 1967. Corruption and Political Development: A Cost-Benefit Analysis. *American Political Science Review*, 61(2), 417–27.

OCTF, New York State Organized Crime Task Force. 1990. *Corruption and Racketeering in the New York City Construction Industry*. New York: New York University Press.

OECD. 1999. *Public Sector Corruption: An International Survey of Prevention Measures*. Paris: OECD Publishing.

OECD. 2003. *Managing Conflict of Interest in the Public Service*. Paris: OECD Publications.

OECD. 2007. *Bribery in Public Procurement: Methods, Actors, and Counter-measures*. Paris: OECD Publications.

Oldenburg, P. 1987. Middlemen in Third-World Corruption: Implications of an Indian Case. *World Politics*, 39(4), 508–35.

Olimpieva, I. 2006. *Informal Intermediaries and Civic Organizations in State-Business Relationships in Russia*. St. Petersburg: CiSoNet Perpectives, ASP and WZB.

Olken, B. and P. Barron. 2007. *The Simple Economics of Extortion: Evidence from Trucking in Aceh*. Cambridge, Mass.: National Bureau of Economic Research, WP n.13145.

Olson, M. 1993. Dictatorship, Democracy, and Development. *American Political Science Review*, 87(3), 567–76.

Opp, K.-D. 1989. The Economics of Crime and the Sociology of Deviant Behaviour: A Theoretical Confrontation of Basic Propositions. *Kyklos,* 42(3), 405–30.

Paldam, M. 2001. Corruption and Religion: Adding to the Economic Model. *Kyklos*, 54(2–3), 383–413.

Pantaleone, M. 1984. *L'industria del potere*. Bologna: Cappelli.

Panther, S. 2000. Non-Legal Sanctions. In *Encyclopedia of Law and Economics*, Vol. I, edited by B. Bouckaert and G. de Geest. Cheltenham: Edward Elgar, 999–1028.

Paoli, L. 2003. *Mafia Brotherhoods*. Oxford: Oxford University Press.

Paoli, L. 2004. Organised Crime in Italy: Mafia and Illegal Markets—Exceptions and Normality. In *Organised Crime in Europe*, edited by C. Fijnaut and L. Paoli. Dordrecht: Springer, 263–302.

Pareto, V. 1916. *Trattato di sociologia generale*. Firenze: Barbera editore.

Pasquino, G. 1990. Partitocrazia. In *Dizionario di politica*, edited by N. Bobbio, N. Matteucci, and G. Pasquino. Torino: Utet, 774–7.

Pasuk, P. and S. Piriyarangsan. 1998. *Corruption and Democracy in Thailand*. Chiang Mai: Silkworm Books.

Pazienza, F. 1999. *Il disubbidiente*. Milano: Longanesi.

PCOC. 1985. *President's Commission on Organized Crime, Organized Crime and Labor-Management Racketeering in the United States*, Hearing VI, Chicago. Washington, D.C.: Government Printing Office.

Pérez-Diaz, V. 1996. *Espana puesta a prueba, 1976–1996*. Madrid: Alianza.

Persson, A., B. Rothstein, and J. Teorell. 2010. *The Failure of Anti-Corruption Policies: A Theoretical Mischaracterization of the Problem*, QoG Working Paper Series, 10, University of Gothenburg.

Picci, L. 2011. *Reputation-based Governance*. Stanford: Stanford University Press.

Pierson, P. 2000. Increasing Returns, Path Dependence, and the Study of Politics. *American Political Science Review*, 94(2), 251–67.

Pierson, P. 2004. *Politics in Time*. Princeton: Princeton University Press.

Piga, G. 2011 (forthcoming). A Fighting Chance against Corruption in Public Procurement? In *International Handbook on the Economics of Corruption*, Vol. II, edited by T. Soreide and S. Rose-Ackerman. Cheltenham: Edward Elgar.

Pinheiro, P.S. 1994. *Corruption in Brasil*. In *Corruption & Democracy*, edited by D.V. Trang. Budapest: Institute for Constitutional & Legislative Policy, 37–40.

Pinto-Duschinsky, M. 1981. *British Political Finance, 1830–1980*. Washington, D.C.: American Enterprise Institute.

Pizzorno, A. 1987. I mafiosi come classe media violenta. Polis, 1(1), 195–204.

Pizzorno, A. 1992. La corruzione nel sistema politico . In *Lo scambio occulto*, edited by D. della Porta. Bologna: Il Mulino, 13–74.

Pizzorno, A. 1993. Le radici della politica assoluta. Milano: Feltrinelli.

Pizzorno, A. 1997. Il contesto della corruzione, preface to A. Vannucci, *Il mercato della corruzione*. Milano: Società aperta, i–ix.

Pizzorno, A. 2007. Il velo della diversità. Milano: Feltrinelli.

Pujas, V. 1996. Political Scandals: The Illegal Financing of Political Parties in France, Spain, and Italy. International Conference on Corruption in Contemporary Politics: University of Salford, November.

Putnam, R.D. 1993. *Making Democracy Work: Civic Traditions in Modern Italy*. Princeton: Princeton University Press.

Putnam, R.D. 2001. Social Capital: Measurement and Consequences. *Isuma: Canadian Journal of Policy Research*, 2(1), 41–51.

Qizilbash, M. 1994. *Corruption, Temptation, and Guilt: Moral Character in Economic Theory*. University of Southampton: Discussion Papers in Economics and Econometrics, n. 9419.

Ramey, G. and J. Watson. 2002. Contractual Intermediaries. *Journal of Law, Economics, and Organization*, 18(2), 362–84.

Reuter P. 1983. *Disorganized Crime*. Cambridge, Mass., and London: MIT Press.

Reuter, P. 1987. *Racketeering in Legitimate Industries: A Study in the Economics of Intimidation*. Santa Monica: Rand Corporation.

Rhodes, M. 1997. Financing Party Politics in Italy: A Case of Systemic Corruption. *West European Politics*, 20(1), 54–80.

Robinson, M.S. 1985. Collusion and the Choice of Auction. *Rand Journal of Economics*, 16(1), 141–5.

Rodriguez, P., K. Uhlenbruck, and L. Eden. 2005. Government Corruption and the Entry Strategies of Multinationals. *Academy of Management Review*, 30(2), 383–96.

Rose Ackerman, S. 1975. The Economics of Corruption. *Journal of Public Economics*, 4(2), 187–203.

Rose Ackerman, S. 1978. *Corruption: A Study in Political Economy*. New York: Academic Press.

Rose Ackerman, S. 1999. *Corruption and Government*. Cambridge: Cambridge University Press.

Rothstein, B. 2007. *Anti-Corruption: A Big Bang Theory*. Gothenburg: QoG Working Paper Series, 3.

Sartori, G. 1970. Concept Misinformation in Comparative Politics. *American Political Science Review*, 14(4), 1033–53.

Savona, E.U. 2010. Infiltration by Italian Organised Crime (Mafia, N'drangheta, and Camorra) of the Public Construction Industry. In *Situational Prevention of Organized Crimes*, edited by K. Bullock, R.V. Clarke, and N. Tilley. Devon: Willan Publishing, 130–50.

Sberna, S. 2010. *Organized Crime and Political Capture of Local Government in Italy (1991–2009)*, unpublished dataset.

Sberna, S. 2011. *Electoral Competition and Criminal Violence in Italy (1983–2003)*. ECPR Joint Sessions, St. Gallen, April 12–7.

Schelling, T. 1960. The Strategy of Conflict. Cambridge, Mass.: Harvard University Press.

Schelling, T. 1984. *Choice and Consequence*. Cambridge, Mass.: Harvard University Press.

Schmitter, P. 2009. The Nature and Future of Comparative Politics. *European Political Science Review*, 1(1), 33–62.

Sciarrone, R. 1998. *Mafie vecchie, mafie nuove. Radicamento ed espansione*. Roma: Donzelli.

Scott, J.C. 1972. *Comparative Political Corruption*. Englewood Cliffs: Prentice Hall.

Seung-Hyun, L. and K.O. Kyeungrae. 2007. Corruption in Asia: Pervasiveness and Arbitrariness. *Asia Pacific Journal of Management*, 24(1), 97–114.

Shearman & Sterling. 2009. *FCPA Digest: Cases and Review Releases Relating to Bribes to Foreign Officials under the Foreign Corrupt Practices Act of 1977*. New York: Shearman & Sterling LLP. Available at http://www.shearman.com/files/upload/fcpa_digest.pdf, accessed December 31, 2010.

Shelley, L.I. 2001. Organized Crime and Corruption Are Alive and Well in Ukraine. [Online: The World Bank, Beyond Transition]. Available at http://www.worldbank.org/html/prddr/trans/janfeb99/pgs6-7.htm, accessed January 30, 2011.

Shleifer, A. and R.W Vishny.. 1993. Corruption. *Quarterly Journal of Economics*, 108(3), 599–617.

Shleifer, A. and R.W. Vishny. 1999. *The Grabbing Hand: Government Pathologies and Their Cures*. Cambridge, Mass.: Harvard University Press.

Smart, A. and C.L. Hsu. 2007. Corruption or Social Capital? Tact and the Performance of *Guanxi* in Market Socialist China. In *Corruption and the Secret of Law: A Legal Anthropological Perspective*, edited by M. Nuijten and G. Anders. Farnham: Ashgate, 167–89.

Stefes, C.H. 2007. Measuring, Conceptualizing, and Fighting Systemic Corruption: Evidence from Post-Soviet Countries. *Perspectives on Global Issues*, 2(1), 1–16.

Sutherland, E.H. 1983. *White Collar Crime*. New Haven: Yale University Press.

Sutherland, E.H. and D.R. Cressey. 1974. *Criminology*. 9th edition. Chicago: Lippincott.

Svensson, J. 2005. Eight Questions about Corruption. *Journal of Economic Perspectives*, 19(3), 19–42.

Søreide, T. 2008. Beaten by Bribery: Why Not Blow the Whistle? *Journal of Institutional and Theoretical Economics / Zeitschrift für die Gesamte Staatswissenschaft*, 164(3), 407–28.

Søreide, T. 2010. *Why Is Anti-Corruption So Difficult*. Scuola Superiore della Pubblica Amministrazione, Working Paper, n. 1, November. Available at http://integrita.sspa.it/wp-content/uploads/2010/12/pa_workpaper_1.pdf, accessed June 31, 2011.

Steinmo, S. and K. Thelen. 1992. Historical Institutionalism in Comparative Politics. In *Structuring Politics*, edited by S. Steinmo, K. Thelen, and F. Longstreth. Cambridge: Cambridge University Press, 1–32.

Taylor, M. 1987. *The Possibility of Cooperation*. Cambridge: Cambridge University Press.

Thachuk, K. 2005. Corruption and International Security. *SAIS Review*, 25(1), 143–52.

Thelen, K. 2003. How Institutions Evolve. In *Comparative Historical Analysis in the Social Science*, edited by J. Mahoney and D. Rueschemeyer. Cambridge: Cambridge University Press, 208–40.

Theobald, R. 1996. *Can Debt Be Used as a Weapon in the War against Corruption (The Uganda Plan)?* International Conference on Corruption in Contemporary Politics, University of Salford, November.

Tilly, C. 1985. War Making and State Making as Organized Crime. In *Bringing the State Back In*, edited by P.B. Evans, D. Rueschemeyer, and T. Skocpol. Cambridge: Cambridge University Press, 170–71.

Tirole, J. 1996. A Theory of Collective Reputation (with Applications to the Persistence of Corruption and to Firm Quality). *Review of Economic Studies*, 63(1), 1–22.

Transparency International. 2004. *Anti-Corruption Handbook: National Integrity System in Practice*. Berlin: Transparency International.

Transparency International. 2006. *Handbook for Curbing Corruption in Public Procurement*. Berlin: Transparency International.

Transparency International. 2008a. Organized Crime and Corruption. [Online: Transparency International, U4 Anti-Corruption Resource Centre]. Available at http://www.u4.no/helpdesk/helpdesk/query.cfm?id=171, accessed January 31, 2011.

Transparency International. 2008b. Bribe Payers Index. [Online: Transparency International]. Available at http://www.transparency.org/policy_research/surveys_indices/bpi/bpi_2008, accessed November 12, 2010.

Transparency International. 2009a. *Corruption Perception Index* [Online: Transparency International]. Available at http://www.transparency.org/policy_research/surveys_indices/cpi/2009/cpi_2009_table, accessed November 12, 2010.

Transparency International. 2009b. *Business Principles in Countering Bribery*. Berlin: Transparency International.

Transparency International. 2010a. *Preventing Corruption in Humanitarian Operations*. Berlin: Transparency International.

Transparency International. 2010b. *Corruption Perception Index* [Online: Transparency International]. Available at http://www.transparency.org/policy_research/surveys_indices/cpi/2010/results, accessed December 27, 2010.

Treisman, Daniel. 2000. The Causes of Corruption: A Cross-National Study. *Journal of Public Economics*, 76(3), 399–457.

Turone, S. 1992. *Politica ladra. Storia della corruzione in Italia 1861–1992*. Bari-Roma: Laterza.

Turvani, M. 1997. Illegal Markets and the New Institutional Economics . In *Transaction Cost Economics: Recent Developments*, edited by C. Ménard. Cheltenham: Edward Elgar, 127–47.

Ullmann-Margalit, E. 1977. *The Emergence of Norms*. Oxford: Oxford University Press

United Nations 2004. *The Global Programme against Corruption: UN Anti-Corruption Toolkit*. 3rd edition. Vienna: United Nations.

U.S. Court of Appeals. 1991. *Appellee v. Anthony Salerno, a/k/a "Fat Tony" et alii*, decided June 28. Available at http://ftp.resource.org/courts.gov/c/

F2/937/937.F2d.797.88-1547.88-1474.88-1477.88-1470.88-1464.html, accessed August 5, 2010.

U.S. District Court. 2008. *Criminal Complaint, United States of America v. R.B. Blagojevich and J. Harriss*, December 7.

UNODC. 2005. *Transnational Organized Crime in the West African Region.* [Online: United Nations Office on Drug and Crime, New York]. Available at http://www.unodc.org/pdf/transnational_crime_west-africa-05.pdf, accessed November 12, 2010.

U.S. Department of Justice 2009. *Price Fixing, Bid Rigging, and Market Allocation Schemes.* [Online: Antitrust Division, U.S. Dept. of Justice]. Available online at http://www.justice.gov/atr/public/guidelines/211578.pdf, accessed August 2, 2010.

Uslaner, E.M. 2005. Trust and Corruption. In *The New Institutional Economics of Corruption*, edited by J. Graf Lambsdorff, M. Taube, and M. Schramm. London and New York, Routledge: 76–91.

Van Duyne, P.C. 1997. Organized Crime, Corruption, and Power. *Crime, Law, and Social Change*, 26(3), 201–38.

Van Rijckeghem, C. and B. Weder. 1997. *Corruption and the Rate of Temptation: Do Low Wages in the Civil Service Cause Corruption?* International Monetary Fund Discussion Paper, n. 97/73.

Vannucci, A. 1997a. Il mercato della corruzione. Milano: Società aperta.

Vannucci, A. 1997b. Politicians and Godfathers: Mafia and Political Corruption in Italy. In *Democracy and Corruption in Europe*, edited by D. della Porta and Y. Meny. London and Washington, D.C.: Pinter: 50–64.

Vannucci, A. 2001. Istituzioni, costi di transazione e organizzazioni mafiose. *Polis*, 15(3), 363–84.

Vannucci, A. 2005. Invisibili contropartite. Corruzione e collusione nel sistema degli appalti. In *Appalti e responsabilità. Da tangentopoli agli attuali scenari*, edited by M.A. Cabidda. Milano: Franco Angeli, 75–108.

Vannucci, A. 2009. The Controversial Legacy of 'Mani Pulite': A Critical Analysis of Italian Corruption and Anti-Corruption Policies. *Bulletin of Italian politics*, 1(2), 233–64.

Vannucci A. and R. Cubeddu. 2006. *Lo spettro della competitività*. Soveria Mannelli: Rubbettino.

Varese, F. 2001. The Russian Mafia. Oxford: Oxford University Press.

Ware, A. 1996. Parties and Party Systems. Oxford: Oxford University Press.

Ware, G.T., and G.P. Noone. 2005. The Anatomy of Transnational Corruption. *International Affairs Review*, 14(2), 29–51.

Weber, M. [1922]. *Economy and Society*. Berkeley: University of California Press, 1978.

Williams P. 2001. Organizing Transnational Crime: Networks, Markets, and Hierarchies. In Combating Transnational Crime: Concepts, Activities, and Responses, edited by P. Williams and D. Vlassis. London: Frank Cass Publishers.

Williams, R. 1996. *Watergate to Whitewater: Corruption in American Politics*. International Conference on Corruption in Contemporary Politics, University of Salford, November.

Williams, R. 2003. Political Corruption in the United States. In *Corruption in Contemporary Politics*, edited by M. Bull and J. Newell. London: Palgrave, 66–78.

Williamson, O.E. 1989. Transaction Cost Economics. In *Handbook of Industrial Organization*, edited by R. Schalensee and R.D. Willig. Amsterdam: Elsevier Science Publishers, 136–82.

Williamson, O.E. 1997. Hierarchies, Markets, and Power in the Economy: An Economic Perspective. In *Transaction Cost Economics: Recent Developments*, edited by C. Medard. Cheltenham: Edward Elgar, 1–29.

Wilson, J.Q. 1980. *The Politics of Regulation*. New York: Basic Books.

Wolfinger, R.E. 1973. *The Politics of Progress*. Englewood Cliffs: Prentice Hall.

Woodhall, B. 1996. *Japan under Construction: Corruption, Politics, and Public Works*. Berkeley: University of California Press.

World Bank. 1997. *World Development Report 1997: The State in a Changing World*. Oxford: Oxford University Press.

World Bank. 2000. *Anticorruption in Transition: A Contribution to Policy Debate*. Washington, D.C.: World Bank.

Yates, D.A. 2001. France's Elf Scandals. In *Where Corruption Lives*, edited by G.E. Caiden, O.P. Dwivedi, and J. Jabbra. Bloomfield: Kumarian Press, 69–78.

Zampini, A. 1985. *Il faccendiere*. Torino Zeta.

Zampini, A. 1993. *Io corruttore*. Napoli: Tullio Pironti editore.

Zerilli, F.M. 2005. Corruption, Property Restitution, and Romanianness. In *Corruption: Anthropological Perspectives*, edited by D. Haller and C. Shore. London: Pluto Press, 83–102.

Archival Documents from Court Records, Parliamentary Investigations, Reports, and Other Sources

APN. Request of judicial action, April 7, 1993. Supplement to *la Repubblica*, April 15, 1993.

APRC. Tribunal of Palermo. Report of the President of the Appeal Court. January 15, 2005.

CAF. Referring to the federal attorney. Italian federation football game. Rome, June 22, 2006.

CCA. Police of Milan. Report concerning the judicial procedure n.9706/02 R.G.N.R./Mod. 21.

CD. Italian Chamber of Deputies and Senate. XI Legislature. Request of judicial action against members of the Parliament, doc. VI.

CD-2. Italian Chamber of Deputies. XVI Legislature. Request of judicial action against Alfonso Papa, doc. IV, in the judicial procedure n.39306/2007 RGNR,

n. 13075/2011 GIP, June 15, 2011, available online at http://www.camera.
it/_dati/leg16/lavori/documentiparlamentari/indiceetesti/004/018/pdfel.htm,
accessed June 21, 2011.

CDEM. Public Prosecutor at the Court of Milan. Request of judicial action,
October 8, 1993, in *Avvenimenti*, n. 42, November 3, 1993.

CP2. Parliamentary Commission of Investigation on the Masonic Lodge P2. Final
Report and alleged documents, doc. XXIII, n. 2.

CPAA. Anti-Mafia Parliamentary Commission. Final report, July 30, 2003.

CPAAC. Anti-Mafia Parliamentary Commission. Hearing of the repentant
Antonino Calderone, session 11, XI legislature.

CPAGM. Anti-Mafia Parliamentary Commission. Hearing of the repentant
Gaspare Mutolo, session 25, XI legislature.

CPALM. Anti-Mafia Parliamentary Commission. Hearing of the repentant
Leonardo Messina, session 15, XI legislature.

CPAM-IVX-II, Anti-Mafia Parliamentary Commission. Final report, doc XIII,
n.16, vol. II, January 19, 2006.

CPAPG. Anti-Mafia Parliamentary Commission. Hearing of the repentant Pasquale
Galasso, sessions 51 e 61, XI legislature.

CPASA. Anti-Mafia Parliamentary Commission. Hearing of the repentant
Salvatore Annacondia, session 56, XI legislature.

CPATB. Anti-Mafia Parliamentary Commission. Hearing of the repentant
Tommaso Buscetta, session 12, XI legislatura.

CPMF. Anti-Mafia Parliamentary Commission. Final report on Mafia and politics,
April 6, 1993. Supplement to *la Repubblica*, April 10, 1993.

DAP. Attorney's Office at the Court of Palermo. Request of judicial action against
G. Andreotti, March 27, 1993. Supplement to *Panorama*, April 11, 1993.

GFV. Revenue police of Verona. Elaboration from the "file Seg," seized to A.
Montagnana in the judicial procedure n. 1367/90.

I-1. Interview with a Judge. December 12, 2004.

MF. Tribunal of Milan. Report of evidence of the interrogation with L. Sciascia,
December 22, 1994 (in *Le mazzette della Fininvest*. Milano: Kaos edizioni,
1996).

PFD. Decree on the referral to the federal attorney on the Comm. Uff. n. 1/C,
Rome, July 14, 2006.

PM. *Mani Pulite*. Supplement to *Panorama*, October 1992.

PMI-DE. Attorney's Office at the Court of Milan. Questioning of E. Dardano.
Judicial procedure n. 9706/02 R.G.N.R.

PMI-LP. Attorney's Office at the Court of Milan. Questioning of P. Lamberti.
Judicial procedure n. 9706/02 R.G.N.R.

PMI-MA. Attorney's Office at the Court of Milan. Questioning of A. Martinelli.
Judicial procedure n. 9706/02 R.G.N.R.

PMI-MG. Attorney's Office at the Court of Milan. Questioning of G. Martinelli.
Judicial procedure n. 9706/02 R.G.N.R.

PP. *Memoria by* Public Prosecutor at the Court of Palermo in Judicial Procedure n. 3538/94 N.R. against Giulio Andreotti (published as *La vera storia d'Italia*, Napoli, Tullio Pironti, 1995).

PPLA. Attorney's Office at the Court of Palermo, District Anti-Mafia Office. Report on Penetration of Cosa Nostra in the entrepreneurial environment and public procurement. Edited by the judge Sergio Lari. December 12, 2002.

PPTO. Attorney's Office at the Court of Turin. Procura della Repubblica presso il Tribunale di Palermo, Warrant of remand in custody against Tolentino Angelo + 49. Judicial procedure n. 3779/03 R.G.N.R./Dda, n. 1855/04 R.G./Gip.

PR. Attorney's Office at the Court of Rome. Request to remand. Judicial procedure n. 10726/88A e 6302/88°. February 20, 1991.

PRBA1. Attorney's Office at the Court of Bari. Warrant of remand in custody against G.S. e S.D.M.

PRIM. Public Prosecutor at the Court of Milan, PP C in JP n.990/83 against Rodi Luciano + 29.

PRNAP. Attorney's Office at the Court of Neaples. Public statement on the warrant of remand in custody against Romeo Alfredo + 19. December 17, 2009.

PROM. Public Prosecutor at the Court of Milan, Public Prosecutor's Charge in Judicial Procedure n. 2537/88A, and Judicial Procedure n. 2620/88A, 12/2/1991.

PRREMI98a. Attorney's Office at the Court of Milan. Warrant of remand in custody. Judicial procedure n. 10155/97 R.G.N.R./Mod. 21, n. 2110/98 R.G./Gip. March 20, 2000.

QGT. Tribunal of Turin. Sentence against Zampini Adriano + 19. March 15, 1986 (in *Questione Giustizia*, n. 2, 1987: 356–97).

TAM. Tribunale di Milano, sentence n.1891/91, 15/5/1991.

TBSA. Attorney's Office at the Court of Bari. Warrant of remand in custody against A. Silvestri and L. Pepe, April 19, 2004. Judicial procedure n. 491/03 R.G.N.R.

TI-2001. Transparency International. *Global Corruption Report 2001.*

TI-2003. Transparency International. *Global Corruption Report 2003.*

TI-2004. Transparency International. *Global Corruption Report 2004.* London: Pluto Press.

TI-2005. Transparency International. *Global Corruption Report 2005: Corruption in Construction and Post-Conflict Reconstruction.* London: Pluto Press.

TI-2006. Transparency International. *Global Corruption Report 2006: Corruption in the Health Sector.* Cambridge: Cambridge University Press.

TI-2007. Transparency International. *Global Corruption Report 2007: Corruption in the Judicial Systems.* Cambridge: Cambridge University Press.

TI-2008. Transparency International. *Global Corruption Report 2008: Corruption in the Water Sector.* Cambridge: Cambridge University Press.

TI-2009. Transparency International. *Global Corruption Report 2009: Corruption in the Private Sector.* Cambridge: Cambridge University Press.

TMAR. Tribunal of Milan. Sentence n. 4522, Novembre 10, 2005. Judicial procedure n. 9706/02 R.G.N.R.

TMBMP. Tribunal of Milan. Sentence against B. Primarosa + 6. Judicial procedure n. 4688/03.

TMENI. Tribunal of Milan. Sentence Eni-Sai. December 6, 1994.

TMIIF. Tribunal of Milan. Questioning of I. Fanesi. Judicial procedure n. 5788/94 R.G.N.R., n. 2258/94 R.G./Gip.

TMIMB. Tribunal of Milan. Questioning of M. Brughiera. Judicial procedure n. 5788/94 R.G.N.R., n. 2258/94 R.G./Gip.

TMISL. Tribunal of Milan. Questioning of S. Larini. Judicial procedure n. 6380/91, R.G.N.R., n. 671/92 R.G./Gip.

TMLB. Tribunal of Milan. Questioning of L. Bisignani. Judicial procedure n. 8655/92, R.G.N.R., n. 671/92 R.G./Gip.

TMPAM. Tribunal of Milan. Sentence n. 4521. Judicial procedure n.9706/02 R.G.N.R. Novembre 10, 2005.

TNM. *Tangentopoli. Le carte che scottano.* Supplement to *Panorama*, February1993.

TPAA. Tribunal of Palermo. Sentence in the trial against Andreotti Giulio, Appeal Court, May 2, 2003

TPAN. Tribunal of Palermo. Sentence in the trial against Andreotti Giulio, October 23, 1999.

TPAS. Tribunal of Palermo. Judicial procedure against De Eccher + 31. Statement of the repentant A. Siino. May 25–June 11, 1998. Radio Radicale archive, tapes n. 177797–177798, 179827. Transcripted by M. Centofante. Available online at www.antimafiaduemila.it., accessed June 21, 2006.

TPAZ. Tribunal of Palermo. Sentence against Abdel Azizi Afifi+91. Judicial procedure n. 2234/86 R.G.U.I.

TPBA. Tribunal of Palermo. Abstract from the Ordinance against A. Buscemi + 9, October 2, 1997. Judicial procedure n. 937/96 R.G.T., n. 5902/95 R.G.N.C.

TPBU. Tribunal of Palermo. Sentence n. 2537. July 2, 2002.

TPCG. Tribunal of Palermo. Public prosecutor's Nino Di Matteo final speech in the trial against G. Crini + 9. October 2, 2001.

TPGB. Tribunal of Palermo. Testimony of the repentant G. Brusca in the trial against S. Castello + 5. December 12, 2005.

TPGO. Tribunal of Palermo. Sentence n. 454 against F.P. Gorgone. Judicial procedure n. 844/96 R.G.T., n. 5347 R.G.N.C. April 27, 1999.

TPMA. Tribunal of Palermo. Exhibit seized on October 10, 1997 to G. Maniscalco in the judicial procedure n. 1687/96 R.G.N.R./Dda.

TPMP. Note of the Public Prosecutor in the Judicial Procedure n. 3538/94 R.G.N.R. against Andreotti Giulio (in *La vera storia d'Italia*. Napoli: Tullio Pironti, 1995).

TPSC. Tribunal of Palermo. Sentence against S. Schimmenti + 6. Judicial procedure n. 1199/02, R.G.T., n. 2962/98 + 1669/2002 R.G.N.R., n. 856/04 R.S. February 23, 2003.

TRBA1. Tribunal of Bari. Warrant of remand in custody. Judicial procedure n. 10388/01-21 and 5598/03 R:G:/Gip.

TRBA1. Tribunal of Bari. Warrant of remand in custody. Judicial procedure n. 10388/01-21; procedimento penale n. 5598/03 R.G./Gip.

TRBA2. Tribunal of Bari. Warrant of remand in custody. Judicial procedure n. 491/03 R.G.N.R.

TRCAS. Tribunal of Caserta. Warrant of remand in custody, proc. n.1243/08 R.G.N.R., January 26, 2009.

TRCOS. Tribunal of Reggio Calabria. Excerpts from ordinance "Onorata Società", gennaio, I–V. Available at www.repubblica.it/2008/01/sezioni/cronaca/arresti-ndrangheta/indice-intercettazioni/indice-intercettazioni.html, accessed: August 12, 2010.

TRFIR. Tribunal of Florence. Warrant of remand in custody, proc.n.1460/09 R.G.I.P., February 8, 2010.

TRIB. Tribunal of Bari. Sentence n. 861. November 29, 1985.

TRMBL. Tribunal of Milan. Sentence against Bussi + 4. February 19, 2004.

TRMI03. Tribunale of Milan. Sentence against Abbiati et al., 2003.

TRNOC. Tribunal of Neaples. Ordinance against N. Cosentino, November 7, 2009, n. 36856/01 R.G.N.R., n.74678/02 R.G.GIP.

TRP. Tribunal of Palermo, SC n. 411/90/R.G., January 17, 1992.

VICM. Attorney's Office at the Court of Milan. Interrogation of G. Mura in the judicial procedure n. 5805/85.

VPI. Attorney's Office at the Court of Pisa. Interrogations in the judicial procedure n. 2853/88 R.G./Pm. March 1987–April 1989.

Index

Advances in Criminology

Full series list

Integrating a Victim Perspective within
Criminal Justice
International Debates
Edited by Adam Crawford and Jo Goodey

Blood in the Bank
Social and Legal Aspects of Death at Work
Gary Slapper

Engendering Resistance: Agency and
Power in Women's Prisons
Mary Bosworth

Governable Places
Readings on Governmentality and Crime
Control
Edited by Russell Smandych